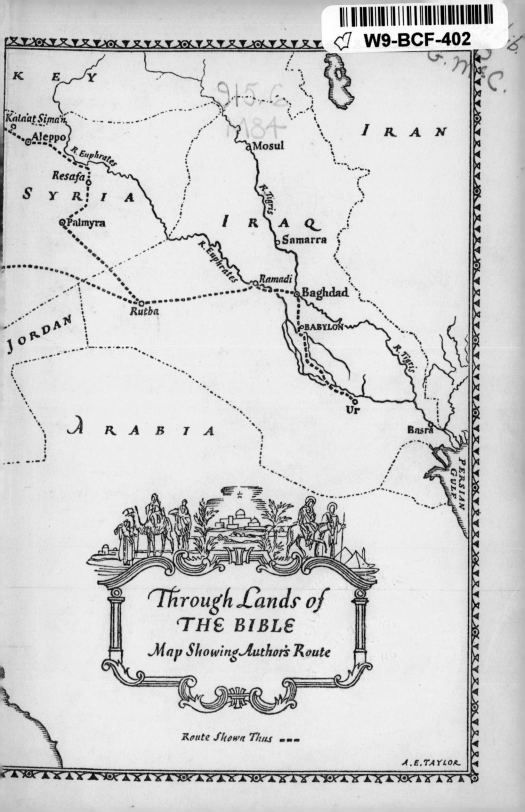

KEY

Kalaat Sima'n
Aleppo
R. Euphrates
Resafa
SYRIA
Palmyra

Mosul

IRAN

R. Tigris

IRAQ
Samarra

R. Euphrates
Ramadi
Baghdad

JORDAN
Rutba
BABYLON
R. Tigris

ARABIA
Ur
Basra

PERSIAN GULF

Through Lands of
THE BIBLE

Map Showing Author's Route

Route Shown Thus ▪▪▪

A.E.TAYLOR

THROUGH LANDS OF
THE BIBLE

Books by H. V. Morton

IN THE STEPS OF THE MASTER

IN THE STEPS OF ST. PAUL

IN SEARCH OF ENGLAND

IN SEARCH OF SCOTLAND

IN SEARCH OF IRELAND

IN SEARCH OF WALES

IN SCOTLAND AGAIN

THE CALL OF ENGLAND

BLUE DAYS AT SEA

OUR FELLOW MEN

THE COPTIC MONASTERY OF DÊR ES SURIÂN, WADI NATRÛN

THROUGH LANDS
OF THE BIBLE

by

H. V. Morton

Twenty-five Illustrations
and
Two Endpaper Maps

Dodd, Mead & Company

New York - 1938

INTRODUCTION

W<small>HILE</small> I was travelling in the Holy Land, gathering material for my last two books, the desire grew on me to make a Christian pilgrimage from the Euphrates to the Nile, and into Sinai, and to tell the story of the Christian life of the Near East. This book is the result of my journey.

The Near East is scattered with the remains of splendid churches which indicate that in centuries gone by this land was sainted, and in the Moslem countries of to-day exist communities of native Christians who have held true to their faith through centuries of persecution. No better example of these could be found than the Copts of Egypt.

H. V. M.

London

Jan. '41

CONTENTS

desert road to Cairo, and see the ruins of the city of St. Mena. In the Wadi Natrûn I visit four Coptic monasteries where Christian monks have lived since the Fourth Century.

ILLUSTRATIONS

From photographs taken by H. V. and Mary Morton

From drawings by A. E. Taylor

ix

THROUGH LANDS OF
THE BIBLE

CHAPTER I

Describes a journey to the Church of St. Simeon Stylites in Syria and to the ruined pilgrimage city of St. Sergius. I stay at Palmyra on my way to Babylon.

§ I

WHILE it was still dark the little cargo-boat came into the Gulf of Iskanderûn and cast anchor, waiting for day to break.

I was awakened by the sudden silence as a Londoner is sometimes awakened in the country. For a moment I wondered what had happened, and then I realized that the engines had stopped, the iron doors had ceased to bang, the steel-shod giants no longer stamped the deck, and even the hideous stammer of the donkey-engine was stilled at last. Against these noises I had built such a splendid resistance that now, when they no longer existed, my defences crumbled and silence strode over them like an invader and tapped me on the shoulder.

But there was one sound so low that I had to listen for it: the lovely ripple of water running along the side of the ship, touching the iron plates with a gentle playfulness and then stealing away into the darkness. I lay half awake, enjoying this sound. Then suddenly and inappropriately a cock crew, surely one of the strangest of all sounds to hear at sea. I knew this bird by sight. He lived among the angular Syrian cattle in the forward hatch, and as I heard him, I became entirely awake: putting my feet down on the cabin floor, I found myself as thrilled as if I were eighteen again and about to set foot for the first time in a foreign land. We were at Alexandretta.

It was difficult to believe that only ten days had gone by since that cold January morning in England when I had set out for Babylon. The train, the boat, the waiting in a foreign port, an-

I

other boat, the hastily encountered people, the sudden glimpses into other lives, the half-made friendships, and the slow progress up the Syrian coast in this little coastal steamer, had built such a barrier between myself and the start of my journey that I could well have believed the ten days were ten months. And now the moment had arrived of which I had almost lost sight: the moment when I would step ashore in Syria and motor across mountain and desert to Palmyra, to Baghdad, to Babylon.

I went on deck into a bitterly cold wind. There was a mountain blacker than the night rising out of the land, with a few sleepy lights clustered at its base, but elsewhere was the sea, dark and empty. A few stars were still burning and a pale light was growing in the east. I could smell snow. It was lying all round on the yet invisible mountains. The cold north wind came down from the Taurus. The Greeks, I thought, must have worn warm woollen underclothes. It is strange to think of them muffled to the eyes and probably suffering from colds in the head; but these Hellenistic cities, Antioch, Tarsus, and the rest, must have been bitterly cold in January.

Slowly, uneasily, the light grew in the east, until it became almost warm and spread fanwise into the sky, touching the sea with a glint of yellow: and then, as the sun came up behind Alexandretta, I saw all the mountains of Syria lifting white heads into a windless morning, for with the coming of the sun the wind dropped and the sky was blue.

2

The Gulf of Iskanderûn has a grand and beautiful name. All over the Arabic-speaking world Iskander is the name of Alexander the Great. He left his name in these waters, as he did in places as far away as Kandahar, when he came down over the Taurus and fought the Battle of Issus, which gave him the keys of the East.

less follows the line of the old Roman road from Antioch to Berœa, which was the Greek name for Aleppo before Islam conquered this portion of the Christian world.

Well metalled, wide and straight, the road ran eastwards between fields where the first wheat was already tracing green lines on the brown earth. Then leaving the fertile valley of the Orontes, it invaded a rocky wilderness inhabited only by herds of goats. Sometimes we met French police, rifles slung on their backs, riding fine Arab horses; and now and then we passed gangs of half-clad Arabs breaking stones to mend the road.

If you walked a little way among the rocks beside the road, you would find traces of older European roads: a Roman road, or perhaps a Crusading road. But you would have to look closely for them. The big, well-quarried stones were carted off centuries ago, and you will probably find them in the wall of a mosque in the nearest village. All attempts to bring Western civilization to this hard, lion-coloured country have failed, and the roads which once led to Hellenistic, Roman, and Crusading towns and castles have long since fallen into ruin.

4

As we made our way across this bleak landscape, I found myself thinking of the lost cities of North Syria. There are about a hundred of them scattered about this bare land, and little is known about them. They were Christian cities which existed and flourished from the Peace of the Church in the Fourth Century until they were swept away by the Arab Conquest in the Seventh. Many were pilgrimage cities grouped round the shrine of a Christian saint, and they were spiritually and architecturally children of the great Church of Antioch. It is surprising to realize that in the first centuries of Christianity hosts of pilgrims from Britain to the boundaries of Persia were travelling from shrine to shrine. Such spiritual migrations

were no doubt possible because Roman Christendom knew no
frontiers, and the splendid military roads offered the pilgrims
easy and safe access to the most distant portions of the Empire.
It is a little difficult, perhaps, to understand how thousands of
men and women could suddenly leave home, sometimes for
years, to go on pilgrimage, or how they fared financially; but
it is clear that an organization as efficient and as well known as
the tourist organizations which now move large numbers of
people from here to there, existed in those distant times to provide for the needs of the Christian traveller.

If you ask anyone to draw a picture of a pilgrim, he will
without hesitation draw a little man in a wide hat with a cockle
shell in it, and he will give him a long staff: the typical mediæval
pilgrim. We have forgotten that pilgrimage has an infinitely
longer history. Its first period began in the Byzantine Age,
when St. Helena discovered the Holy Cross and the site of
Calvary, and this period lasted until the Crusades. It was a time
when Greeks and Romans went on pilgrimage, when great ladies set out to see the hermits of the Egyptian desert, and gave
up their houses in Rome to go and live at Bethlehem. Then the
second period, which is the period most people think of, is the
post-Crusade period of the Middle Ages.

There is still a lot to be known about the first period of Christian pilgrimage. Many a holy man is now forgotten whose
name was once revered all over the Christian world. Every devout Christian in the Fifth Century would, for instance, have
known of the shrine I was on my way to see, Kala'ât Sim'ân,
the place where St. Simeon Stylites spent his life sitting on top
of a pillar. Pilgrims came to him from Gaul and Brittany, from
Italy and from Spain. They came travelling easily along the
great Roman post-roads and they arrived at last, not in this
Islamic land of mosques, but in a Christian Syria as full of saints
as a field of poppies.

Simeon Stylites was the first of the pillar hermits. He was

born in a village called Sisan, or Sis, on the borders of Cilicia, in the year 338 A.D., in the reign of the Emperor Theodosius. His parents were well-to-do Christians. At the age of sixteen Simeon began to show that indifference for his own physical comfort which marked him out for the spiritual life: he spent the whole of one summer buried to his neck in the garden. If this actually means that his hands were buried and unable to wave away flies, I really cannot understand how any human being could have endured this torture.

He then entered a monastery near Antioch and, like all the more noted ascetics, soon found that the ordinary monastic rules, though strict enough for others, imposed no hardship on his ardent nature. He believed that only by the complete humiliation of his body could his soul set itself free and fit itself to contemplate God. He invited the dislike of his fellow-monks by devising all kinds of self-torture, including a girdle sewn with sharp goads and pricks which tore his skin. He devised what was probably the forerunner of the tilting choir-stall: a piece of wood so balanced that if he fell asleep during his nightly prayers, it would fling him to the ground.

After nine years, the monks succeeded in expelling him. Simeon then went to another monastery nearer Aleppo, where he asked to be walled up in a cell for the whole period of Lent. The monks agreed, and the cell was sealed by Bassus of Edessa, a periodeutes or assistant bishop, who happened to be in the monastery at the time. Six loaves and a jug of water were walled up in the cell, but when the door was opened after Lent Simeon was found on his knees in a state of exhaustion, and neither bread nor water had been touched. Simeon's feats of fasting, which are well vouched for by contemporary authorities, appear to us almost incredible. He seems frequently to have gone without food until he was at the point of death.

His next move was to a hillside not far from the monastery. He sat with a heavy iron collar round his neck, chained to a pillar six feet high, rarely moving and never descending. As time went on he increased the height of his pillar bit by bit, until it was sixty feet high. An iron rail on the top prevented the saint from falling, and his disciples, with the aid of a ladder, provided him with the bare necessaries of life. Throughout the bitter frosts of thirty Syrian winters and the intolerable heat of thirty summers, Simeon sat there in devout contemplation. At one time he had a little shelter of boughs to save him from the burning sun, but disdaining this as a sinful luxury, he threw it down one day and never used it again.

The news of the holy man who sat on a pillar naturally spread through cities and villages, and even across the deserts. Simeon's visions, and the miracles of healing which he performed, drew thousands of pilgrims, both Christian and pagan, from all parts of the country. An account of his life and of the influence which he exerted would be incredible were they not described by trustworthy contemporary historians, such as Theodoret, Bishop of Cyrrhus, who knew him personally.

Many were the letters on contemporary Church problems which Simeon wrote or dictated from his pillar, even addressing his communications to the Emperor Theodosius and, after him, to the Emperor Leo. When the saint became gravely ill with an ulcerated foot, Theodosius wrote him a letter begging him to descend from the pillar to receive the attention of the royal physician. This letter was delivered by three bishops, who added their entreaties to the supplication of the Emperor. But Simeon, while he was grateful for their sympathy and advice, would have nothing to do with the doctor, neither would he consent to descend to earth. He sent the messengers back to the Emperor with a rather sharp letter on a current matter of government. It is recorded that during the following Lent Simeon remained without food, and at the end of the fast found his foot to have been healed.

His nights and early mornings were spent in meditation,

prayer, and prostrations, for the early Eastern Christians prostrated themselves as the Moslems do to-day. One admiring observer has recorded that he counted while the saint performed
one thousand, two hundred and forty-four consecutive prostrations during his devotions. In the afternoons Simeon held
court and issued verdicts on the theological, legal, and domestic
problems which large crowds brought to the foot of the pillar.
Among the spectators were crowds of wondering Bedouin,
among whom, it is said, the saint made many converts, for the
birth of Mohammed was then more than a century distant.
From remote deserts they brought their grazing disputes for
him to settle.

Some writers say that Simeon's approaching death at the age
of seventy-two attracted enormous crowds to the pillar, all
anxious to hear his last words and to receive his blessing; others
say that his death was kept secret in case his corpse should be
stolen. His body, probably embalmed, was carried in magnificent procession to Antioch in the autumn of the year 459
A.D., to be interred in the church built by Constantine. The Emperor Leo was anxious to remove the remains to Constantinople,
but refrained from doing so in answer to the prayers of the
people of Antioch, who had just suffered two frightful earthquakes and hoped that the body of Simeon would avert another
one.

About fifty years after Simeon's death, when the Eastern
Empire was at war with the Persians, it was requested that the
head of the saint should be sent to Philippicus, Commander-in-
Chief, for the protection of the armies in the East. It was at this
time that the church historian, Evagrius, saw it. He noted that
the head was in a remarkable state of preservation, that several
teeth were missing, having been extracted by devout visitors,
and that near the head lay the collar which Simeon had worn
during his life, "for not even in death," commented Evagrius,
"has Simeon been deserted by the loving iron."

An interesting sidelight on the time in which St. Simeon lived is that pilgrims from France brought news to him of the austerities which were then being practised in Paris by Ste. Geneviève; and the saint looked down from his pillar and requested them to take back his greetings and ask her to pray for him.

We bumped slowly over a villainous road, frequently making détours to avoid the sharp stones and boulders in our way. Turning a corner, we saw the ruins of Kala'ât Sim'ân not far off, outlined against the sky. It was now afternoon: the sun was warm, the sky was blue, and as we ascended the track towards the ruins a stillness which the church had never known in its life-time enfolded it now in death.

I climbed the hill, unprepared for the lovely sight that awaited me. Burning and glowing in the sun as if flood-lit in day-time, for that is the effect of the warm, brown stone of Syria, I saw the skeleton of Kala'ât Sim'ân, silent and roofless. The hillside fell away into desolate brown distances. The only sign that these ravaged slopes had ever known mankind was a mass of masonry on a lower hill, the remains of the inns and guest-houses used by pilgrims in the Byzantine Age. Remote and blue to the north-west I saw the mountains which I had left that morning, with the snow-capped peak of Casius rising sharply above them all.

The Church of St. Simeon is entered from the west by a majestic triple archway, which is almost undamaged. I looked into the church beyond, which was piled with fallen pillars and big, honey-coloured blocks of stone. Walking inside, I climbed over these stones, astonished by the size of the church and by its design. Before the church was built there was nothing on the hill but Simeon's pillar, and the problem of erecting a church round it cannot have been a simple one. The architects solved it brilliantly by leaving the pillar in a wide space open to the sky, and this was made the centre of the church, which was built in the form of a Greek cross.

This central space is an octagon formed of eight superb double arches which admit to the four arms of the church, so that no matter from which door you entered, north, south, east, or west, you were faced by a central shrine open to the sky, a blaze of golden light in the day and a blue bowl of starlight at night. If you can imagine the four arms of the cross roofed, and light pouring down into the central octagon, it is not difficult to realize that the Church of St. Simeon Stylites must have been in its time one of the most impressive churches in the world.

The architecture of this remarkable building is neither Roman nor Byzantine. The style is massive, yet never heavy; decorative without being too ornate. It is a style peculiar to Syria. When the church was built, and Evagrius visited it in 560 A.D., Antioch was still a great and stately city; and though it has vanished to-day, we can catch a reflection of its architectural splendour in this church and in many another stately ruin of North Syria.

One of the unexpected features of the church is the stone platform on which St. Simeon's pillar was erected, which is still in position in the centre of the octagon. It lies surrounded by a chaos of lesser stones in which—who knows?—might be discovered the complete pillar, broken as it fell. I wonder why the French archæologists, who are so good at putting things together, have not attempted to salvage the pillar of Stylites, or why the Société Tourisme, which exists somewhere in Syria, has not insisted on this; for no one will dispute the strange fact that if these stones were perpendicular, instead of horizontal, the place would once again be famous. Pilgrims would flock to it as once they did in the days of Evagrius, and the authorities would be obliged to make a decent road.

I can well imagine how eerie the church must have been in the time of which Evagrius writes, for he clearly believed that it was haunted; in fact, he is sure that he saw the ghost. It took the form of a moving light in a gallery round the octagon, and he saw it one day while he was standing there with a crowd of rustics, some of whom were dancing round the pillar. There was a more impressive ghost, which he did not see. It was the head of St. Simeon, bearded as in life, which would flit here and there about the church. As I sat in the ruins I thought how ironic it is that a man who asked of life only one sixty-foot pillar should have been given so many pillars after his death. And may it not be possible that the bearded head of Stylites flitted about the church from time to time in the hope of finding someone with whom it might lodge a complaint?

The ruins were deserted save for a barefoot Arab boy in charge of a herd of velvet-eared kids, black, white, and tan-coloured. They swarmed over the ruins, devouring each blade of green in their path with that eager voraciousness which has deforested classical and Biblical lands. Now and then two of them would pair off and, lowering their pretty heads on which no horns yet sprouted, would tilt at one another with a lift of forefeet. The kids, the boy, and the ruins made me think of those sad pictures that Piranesi loved to draw; I say sad because so many civilizations have ended in just such a scene as this: broken arches, voracious goats, and picturesque but destructive little Arab boys.

While I looked at Kala'ât Sim'ân, which is certainly one of the grandest Christian ruins of its period in the world, I thought it almost unbelievable that such a place, with its attached monasteries, its elaborate guest-houses, in fact a whole town devoted to pilgrims, could have grown up round the memory of a man who had spent his life on a pillar. I am sure that we have no right to criticize either St. Simeon or his age, because it is only with difficulty that we can even try to understand the mental attitude of the Fourth Century world. It was a world in revolt against materialism. After centuries of persecution the Christian Church had emerged into the light of day, and, in the sudden release from oppression, Christians expressed their faith in a number of eccentric ways. An age that thought more of the other world than of this did not, of course, think them eccentric, and probably for every man who scoffed at St. Simeon on his pillar, a hundred gazed up at him, and beyond him to the heavens. He was merely expressing in his own uncomfortable way the ascetic movement which was sweeping over the East, and which drove a proportion of the population of Egypt into the desert to live in hair-shirts and on bread and water.

His fame and his example were so powerful that Syria became a land of pillar hermits. They perched like owls on every favourable vantage point, and some even took up their abode in the branches of ancient trees. It is recorded that in the reign of Constantine II, a great storm in Syria caused havoc among them, blowing the holy men from their perches and even uprooting their pillars.

From Syria this peculiar cult spread into Asia Minor, Palestine, and Mesopotamia, but there is only one recorded example of a pillar hermit in the West; the monk Wulflaïcus of Carignan, in the Ardennes, who, according to Gregory of Tours, mounted a pillar from which his bishop ordered him to descend. In the East isolated Stylites were still to be seen in the Sixteenth Century, and one, the last, is said to have lived in Georgia as late as the first half of the Nineteenth Century. It occurs to one naturally that such men were expressing a belief voiced first, maybe, in India and echoed in all Oriental faiths, and even in the philosophy of Greece, that the body and the soul are always at war, and only by the defeat of the body can the soul achieve freedom. Therefore the hermits strove not to control the passions by rule and will as the monks did, but utterly to stamp them out. And the extraordinary fact about the movement is that the hermits and anchorites were not churchmen but laymen who, in the sudden revolt against materialism which seems to have swept over the East in the Third and Fourth Centuries, gave up everything to go out into the desert and train their souls.

Strangely enough this physical hardship seems to have been extremely healthy. Most of the hermits lived to a good old age. There was one pillar hermit who sat on his perch until he was over a hundred years of age. Daniel of Constantinople, who was the most famous of all the Stylites after St. Simeon, sat on his pillar for thirty years and died at the hale old age of eighty. In the winter he was frequently covered with snow and ice and frozen hard by the bitter winds that sweep down from the Black Sea, in which condition he once so touched the compassion of the Emperor Leo that men were sent up to build a little hut over him. But the frozen old saint on top of the pillar refused to have anything to do with such a frivolous pandering to the flesh, and they were obliged to descend. So it would seem that the wicked body took its revenge on those who were trying to slay it by making up its mind to live as long as possible.

My driver came up to say that we must be moving because after dark the Aleppo road swarmed with thieves. I said goodbye to Kala'ât Sim'ân and we were soon speeding across a lonely countryside. The sun, sinking behind us, flushed the sky with a fan of flamingo pink that turned to red and died away in long streamers of dark blue. The queer villages, so characteristic of the Aleppo plain, like rows of eggs in their trays, lay sometimes near the road, sometimes on the edge of the sky. Darkness fell and the stars shone. A hare with enormously powerful hind-legs, like the hares on the old coins of Messana, ran for a time in the whiteness of our lamps. Then suddenly we saw the lights of Aleppo lying on the plain.

5

I was introduced that night to a young Bey of Aleppo. This may suggest a picturesque person with a gold scimitar across his knees, but times change and this Bey was a diffident young man in a flannel suit and a pair of brown suède shoes. His interests were rich and youthful. He knew Paris and he hoped one day to fly to London to see the Motor Show.

I happened to mention to him that I was finding it difficult to procure a Syrian driver who would face the desert road to Palmyra. One man said he did not know the way and was afraid of getting lost, another said the road was too bad, and a third, though willing, had become extortionate.

"I will motor you there. I have nothing to do," said the Bey.

I reminded him that I wanted to start at four o'clock in the morning.

"That is nothing," he replied. "I will call for you at four o'clock."

Palmyra is a little under two hundred miles from Aleppo as the crow flies, but I wanted to go north first to Resafa and then south to Palmyra, and this journey was nearer three hundred miles. It is perhaps a reflection on the West that if a stranger offered to motor one to Carlisle on the spur of the moment, it would not be unnatural to expect to see the famous gold-brick in the course of the journey. But in the East sudden surprising streaks of generosity are encountered, from that of the poor Bedouin who will give you his last sheep, though he has never seen you before, to that of the Bey's sudden impetuous and entirely sincere offer. I was only too glad to accept, and went to bed to snatch a few hours' sleep, feeling that in Aleppo at least the mantle of the Caliph is not yet quite thread-bare.

Shortly after four o'clock on the following morning the Bey arrived in a small but powerful car. He was dressed in a leather jacket lined with fur, Bedford cord breeches, and polo boots. Sitting beside him was a man in a tarbush and a long overcoat, who grasped a twelve-bore gun and wore across his chest a bandolier stuffed with cartridges.

I crouched in the small space behind, and we went off through the cold, sleeping town along a road that eventually lay across country which was already half desert. Had there been anyone to wonder about us, we must have presented an interesting problem. The car was of the kind whose dashing, cream-and-crimson body is seen rolling down the Champs Elysées, generally driven by a fashionable woman. We offered a choice of many possibilities to the inventive and even more perhaps to the apprehensive, with the Bey at the wheel, wearing an air of Hollywood in one of its out-of-door moments, the retainer, with the gun poked out of one window, and myself like a pallid captive at the back.

The Bey at the wheel quite lost his air of weary detachment and became superbly alert and competent. The car was fitted with those balloon tyres and reinforced springs which have killed the camel caravan traffic. When we came to any serious inequality in the road—though for sixty miles it was excellent —the car just poured over it with an almost imperceptible shudder.

As dawn was breaking we left this good road at a little group of huts and sheds called Meskéné, and plunged into a region of low, ravaged-looking hills where the road became the wheelmarks of previous travellers. I shall never forget Meskéné, because it was here that the retainer turned to me and, pointing, said, "El-Frât."

Looking to the left, I saw an ice-green river winding through the desert. It was the Euphrates. How modest and unlike my conception of the Euphrates was this slow stream just beginning its long journey across Mesopotamia into Babylonia! In the course of centuries it has changed its bed. The famous ford at Thrapsacus, where Xenophon crossed with the Ten Thousand and where Alexander forded the river, is only a few miles from Meskéné, but it is now high and dry, about eight miles from the river-bank. Around us lay the ruins of cities which once drew their life from the Euphrates and from the commercial routes of the ancient world. These remains, lying dead in what was once green country, proclaim themselves as mounds in the sand and as ruins seen on low hills against the sky.

The country gradually changed. Slight foot-hills on either side advanced and retreated, sometimes opening into wide, level plains or into broken, steppe-like country bare of all vegetation. The only living creatures were enormous flocks of sheep moving slowly westward in charge of their shepherds.

As a desert driver the Bey was at his best. He was quick-minded, resolute, and daring: almost too daring at times, but he always managed to pull up before an obstacle. While we were crossing a hard, level plain he performed a spectacular act which I had never before seen. He suddenly ordered his man to load the gun, and accelerating his car, he aimed the gun through the window, firing both barrels at a flock of desert pigeons. It was a feat which reminded me of Buffalo Bill's famous bottle-shooting act from the back of a galloping horse.

He then settled down to two and a half hours' hard, nerve-racking desert motoring, speeding across the flat plains, crawling across sandy declivities, threading his way between sudden outcrops of stone, sometimes finding his path barred by a six-foot drop which forced him to go back and find a way round.

At last we saw the dead city lying ahead of us. A wall surrounded it, formed of massive blocks of stone and above the wall we could see the masonry of buildings in the town. This was Resafa. From a distance the city looked as though it might be inhabited, then, as we drew nearer, we saw breaches in the wall; and as we came to the superb northern gate of the city, we saw that débris and sand lay piled almost to the lintels of the gateway.

What made the place so eerie was that, even when we got out of the car and approached the gates, no Arabs emerged to gaze in curiosity or to offer themselves as guides. The place seemed to have been forsaken even by those natural inheritors of ruins. The retainer saw a jackal and went off with the gun, but I saw only this impressive Byzantine town lying in the desert, silent as the grave. We walked towards the gate that in its time had known all the restless sounds of life. What a superb gate it is. Under a stately colonnade of Roman arches, upheld on columns with Byzantine capitals, are three rectangular gates, the big central one for wheeled traffic, the two flanking entrances for foot passengers and horsemen. At first I thought that the walls, the gate, and those ruins which we could see beyond the gate, were all of marble, for the white stone shone and glittered in the sun. It was, however, white gypsum, and the Bey told me that it had been quarried about fourteen miles away.

When I passed under the gate I saw a whole town lying dead within its massive walls. Everything softer than this marble-like stone had vanished, leaving upright only the great buildings and the churches standing in empty spaces. The Bedouin had grubbed about in the ruins until the line of the streets had become lost beneath thousands of pits like shell-craters. Apparently cart-loads of Byzantine and early Arab pottery have been discovered there and sold to dealers in Aleppo. The Bey said that he knew an old Arab who had made thousands of francs in that way. On top of the pits lay beautiful fragments of iridescent pottery, which the Bedouin had rejected as not worth selling, and I could have filled a sack with them in half an hour.

As I climbed into ruined halls, to pause astonished by the beauty of the carved stone, which greatly resembles the work at Kala'ât Sim'ân, I recalled what little there is to remember about this town. It is mentioned in *Isaiah*, chapter xxxvii, verse 12, when Sennacherib, in an insulting message to Hezekiah, boasts that he has captured it with other towns. This reference is duplicated in II *Kings*, chapter xix, verse 12. The name is spelt Roseph in the Vulgate and Rezeph in the Revised Version. There is then a long gap in its history until it emerges in the

A GATEWAY, RESAFA

Fourth Century A.D. as the great pilgrimage town of St. Sergius, the saint who is generally coupled with St. Bacchus. These saints were Roman officers and friends, who died for their faith early in the Fourth Century; one date given is 305 A.D., the year of Diocletian's abdication.

Bacchus is believed to have received martyrdom on the Euphrates, and Sergius three days later at Resafa. For some reason the fame of St. Sergius soon eclipsed that of Bacchus, and a pilgrimage town began to grow up at Resafa, where the remains of Sergius were buried. Pilgrims came from all parts of the world to visit the holy relics, and it is obvious from the magnificent remains visible to-day that the town of Sergiopolis, as it came for a time to be called, was one of the great shrines of the Fourth Century and remained so until the Arab conquest.

Like St. George, St. Sergius was a great warrior saint who was seen in shining armour, fighting in the Christian ranks. He linked Resafa with heaven and surrounded it with protection. The Emperor Justinian, who strengthened the frontiers of his empire by building forts and supporting the shrines of protective saints, sent to the shrine of St. Sergius, in the name of the Empress and himself, a beautiful cross of gold encrusted with precious stones. He also gave great sums for the building of a wall round the town and for the enrichment of the churches: thus Resafa is the same date—about 530 A.D.—as the Monastery of Mount Sinai.

Planted right in the path of the Persian attacks on the Byzantine Empire, the town must have led an anxious life, and many a time it beat off armies with the aid of the warrior saint. Some indication of the fame of St. Sergius is the strange fact that one of his greatest devotees was Chosroes II, King of Persia, the famous pagan ruler of the time. During a crisis in his affairs, Chosroes appealed for help to St. Sergius and vowed to the martyr a golden cross should his wish be granted. Not only did he fulfil his promise, but he sent back to Resafa the gold cross of Justinian, which had been looted during a Persian raid in the time of Chosroes I. On a second occasion the Persian King appealed to St. Sergius, this time that one of his wives might have a son. This desire was also granted. In order to show his gratitude, the Persian sent to the priests of Resafa many precious gifts, including rich vessels to be used in the services of the church and bearing his name. From the hazy accounts of these remarkable acts in the pages of Evagrius, it would seem that a promising convert was lost in Chosroes II.

Such stories help us to realize what a mighty power these pilgrim sanctuaries were in the Fifth and Sixth Centuries. There was hardly a thing that could not be asked of the saint: victory in war, children, riches, health. And heathen monarchs testified that the saint's generosity extended even to those who were not of the Christian faith. Swiftly the cult of St. Sergius spread all over the East, and in the Sixth Century he was regarded in that part of the world as the most important martyr after the Apostles. His fame spread to France, where Gregory of Tours recorded that he had heard how a king of the East had gone into battle with a relic of the saint strapped to his arm. He had only to raise his arm and instantly the tide of battle turned in his favour. There are two recorded fire miracles. Once when a fire raged in Bordeaux, the house of a Syrian was found to have escaped the flames, and it was then discovered that it contained a relic of St. Sergius. On another occasion, when a Jew was to be burned at the stake, a horseman in shining armour, who was instantly recognized as St. Sergius, appeared in the flames and rode round and round the victim, protecting him until the people, struck with fear and pity, dragged the Jew from the pyre.

As you look at Resafa in its thirsty desert, it is easy to forget that once it stood on one of the world's main roads, with populous towns and cities all around. It was on the great caravan road, with Palmyra to the south and Dura-Europos to the southeast. Hardly a day can have passed that did not see streams of traffic converging on its walls. The pilgrims and other travellers who found their prayers answered at the saint's tomb would rapidly have spread the fame of St. Sergius as far as Rome and the Bosphorus to the west, and Persia to the east. So it is not difficult to understand why St. Sergius, again united with his friend St. Bacchus, crossed the Mediterranean and received the reverence of the Western Church. In Rome and Chartres churches were dedicated to them. The traveller in Istanbul to-day, when he enters Justinians' church of St. Sergius and St. Bacchus, is often heard to wonder who St. Bacchus was.

The ruins of Resafa have never been properly explored, and I believe that they may hold many a secret for us. I entered a roofless hall whose richly decorated arches were lifted against the open sky. Débris lay almost to the top of the walls. This was the site of the martyrdom of St. Sergius. Some distance away, towards the south-east of the city, stands the noble ruin of the great church of St. Sergius, the splendid nave and aisles almost complete, but, like every building in Resafa, high with fallen masonry. The saint was buried before the high altar, in a crypt which was reached by a double stairway. This part of the church is a chaos of fallen stones on which grass and weeds are growing, and it is only just possible to see the design of this shrine, and impossible to penetrate into the choked entrances of the vault. Here again, as at Kala'ât Sim'ân, I felt that this superbly decorative Syrian architecture recompenses us for the disappearance of Antioch. If a man should wish to know what Antioch looked like in the Sixth Century, I think a visit to Baalbec, to Kala'ât Sim'ân, and Resafa would give him a fairly good idea.

We examined the massive walls which surround Resafa almost without a break. It is possible to follow the sentry-walk for hundreds of yards at a stretch, and to enter the guard-houses where Byzantine garrisons kept watch over the desert. Ruins stand up here and there all over the city area, and there are four immense, vaulted underground rain-water cisterns, each one as high, I should think, as the aisles of Westminster Abbey.

While we were looking at them, a number of Bedouin stole up and sat watching us, rifles across their knees. The Bey soon established good relations, and looks of villainy were soon replaced by childlike smiles and laughter as they accepted our cigarettes. They were a wild-looking lot, evidently descendants of those tribes who gave travellers to Palmyra such a bad time as recently as fifty years ago. Nearly all descriptions of a visit to Palmyra in the days of horses and camels mention the danger of being captured by bands of horsemen flourishing spears and flintlock guns.

One of the most pathetic sights in the modern desert is the expression of a Bedouin's eyes as he looks into a car and sees so much easy plunder rolling off into the distance. I have seen my cat look like that when someone has walked past with fish on a plate.

The Bey said it would take six hours to reach Palmyra. Before the war, travellers had to take tents, a dragoman, a retinue of servants, an escort of Turkish soldiers, a consular permit, which was only granted when the tribes were quiet, and it took five days to get there.

We sped on across the desert, sometimes crawling over rocky country, sometimes travelling at eighty kilometres an hour for three or four minutes at a time. There was no road except marks made by previous cars. Suddenly we met three motor-lorries staggering along, driven by Arabs, tarpaulins strapped over their loads. I wondered what kind of cargo they could be carrying.

"Truffles!" explained the Bey. "They grow in the desert after rain, and the Bedouin find them. The cars go round the desert now and then to collect them."

That this hungry country could have any connection with a restaurant struck me as fantastic. I have often thought, watching a gourmet in a fashionable restaurant pouting at the menu, how little we know of the fantastic organization that exists in the world for the filling of the discriminating diner, and how no head-waiter, dealing with a petulant feeder, will ever admit that absence of lobster may be due to a hundred mile an hour gale. There is in fact a suggestion in restaurants that such riches fall out of heaven; that if a certain rare food is not visible, it can be called into being by a slight gesture on the part of the *maître d'hôtel*. Truffles in the middle of the Syrian desert! Imagine the astonishment of the consumer of these truffles if behind the waiter there walked in procession the brown Bedouin women who had picked them, their children, who had helped, the sheik who had haggled with the wholesaler, the Arab drivers, with their faces bound from chin to eyes in *keffiehs*, and all the various Greeks, Jews, and Armenians who had taken a rake-off before the truffles came anywhere near the chef.

"Who are these people?" he would cry in alarm.

"Sir, you ordered truffles. They found them for you. . . ."

We sped on across the desolate landscape, and I understood why Palmyra should have remained lost in the desert for so long. Although Arabs had often told stories of the wonderful lost city of the sands, whose pillars were more numerous than the desires of men, no one had paid any attention until some English merchants of Aleppo went there in 1678. They were the first Europeans to see Palmyra after the Arab Conquest. They returned there in 1691, accompanied by Dr. William Halifax, who wrote an account of the city in the Proceedings of a learned society. But the men who really reintroduced Palmyra to the world were two Englishmen, Robert Wood and James Dawkins, who visited the ruins in 1751 and wrote a massive volume full of wonderful engravings entitled *A Journey to Palmyra, otherwise Tedmor in the Desart.* Wood's book was translated into a score of European languages and helped, no doubt, to give the warrior queen of Palmyra, Zenobia, until then quietly interred in the pages of Trebellius Pollio, the romantic vogue which she enjoyed in the early Nineteenth Century.

Strangest of all visitors to Palmyra was Lady Hester Stanhope, the first woman who penetrated its mysteries. She had heard about Palmyra from travellers in Syria and had bought Wood's book, which her Arab associates naturally thought was a plan of buried treasure. In the confusion of this lady's mind there existed some idea that she was destined to rival Zenobia and to restore the ruined city to its ancient splendour. On March 20, 1813, she set out from her stronghold in the Syrian hills, dressed as an Arab sheik and surrounded by her Arab bodyguard. Bedouin chiefs, who had been well paid to ensure her safety, pranced beside her, grasping lances tufted with ostrich feathers. Forty baggage-camels padded behind the cavalcade.

Among the curious things which her vanity prompted was the queenly imposition of a tax of a thousand piastres on all European visitors to the ruins. The sheiks were naturally charmed with this idea. But it was imposed in the hope that it would deter other travellers from venturing to Palmyra.

Late in the afternoon the Bey removed one hand from the wheel and pointed ahead: he said, giving the Arabic name: "Tadmor!"

Looking into the distance, I saw a conical hill with a castle on its crest. At the foot of this hill, in all directions and the colour of the bright, sunlit sand, were columns standing and prostrate, like the bones of some mighty skeleton lying in the desert.

6

An Arab boy came riding on a white donkey up the main street of Palmyra, which was designed long ago for great processions and mighty caravans from Parthia. He was singing one of those long wailing songs which the Arabs sing with closed eyes and their heads flung back, and every now and then the donkey's hoofs hit a stone which made a sharp little sound in the hot silence of the afternoon.

There was no living thing but this singing Arab and his donkey going up the great street, along a path striped by the black shadows of the standing columns. Everywhere rose the remains of Palmyra, a great arch, temples, broken pavements: a ghostly city lying in a golden desert. Sometimes when you are travelling in the desert, even in these days of motor transport, you come across the skeleton of a camel lying on the sand. Palmyra is like that: a long Hellenistic back-bone, which is the main Street of Columns, and ribs leading off to right and left; a ruin picked clean by Time and bleached by the sunlight of centuries to the colour of pale honey.

It is a perfect example of the romantic ruin which the Nineteenth Century adored. So secure in itself and so tolerant of the unhappy past, this age could contemplate Palmyra, and indeed all ruins, with a calm detachment. The drums of columns and the scattered capitals seemed to invite visitors to sit down and moralize upon the crash of civilizations. But the traveller of a less certain period cannot drive away the thought that if Belgravia suffered a severe aerial bombardment and were set out in hard sunlight on the sand, it would bear a startling resemblance to Palmyra, especially if some of Barclay's larger banks were included.

I wandered all afternoon among the remains of this city, for the Bey had gone onward to Damascus, where he had business, and could not be persuaded to stay even for an hour. I thought the triumphal arch which links the Street of Columns to the gigantic brown temple of Baal one of the finest and richest pieces of Syrian architecture I had ever seen. It is about two centuries earlier than the pilgrimage churches of Syria, but you can see in its decoration the designs which the Christian architects adopted and introduced into the richly chased arches of their church doors and windows. They carved stone as if it were soft wood.

Palmyra is a strange ruin. It is not haunted by saints or warriors, but by merchants. Its history is one of trade. There is a legend that it began as "Tadmor in the wilderness," which the Bible says was one of the cities built by Solomon, and the Arabs call it Tadmor to this day. If it is the Tadmor of Solomon, he founded it for the protection of his caravans at a strategical point where two great trade routes met on their way to the sea; one from the Persian Gulf and the other from the land of the Queen of Sheba. There is nothing now left of Solomon's city. The ruins are of a later city, which rose to its greatest power in 270 A.D., and declined with the ambitions of its queen, Zenobia.

She had a great vogue in the Nineteenth Century. If a modern biographer revived her memory, she might have another lease of life, for even Gibbon said complimentary things about her. She was a woman of great force of character, who ruled this strange plutocracy of Palmyra during a time when it seems rather to have lost its head. The population was half Arab, perhaps part Jew, and part Persian. It was a strange, half-breed city of fabulously rich merchants who had piled up fortunes on the eastern caravan trade. A constant river of gold flowed through the main colonnade of Palmyra. Men lived in this desert city who owned ships in Italian waters; others were wealthy merchants controlling the Indian silk trade; and their financial ventures were as various and as involved as such transactions tend

ground tombs and tower tombs. The underground tombs were mostly hidden beneath the sand, but sometimes a camel fell in if the roof was weak; and, as he put it, this "was very interesting." The man said that there were hundreds of tombs still to be discovered—hundreds; and he kissed the tips of his fingers and made a gesture of abundance.

He unlocked a door and I walked down to a dark chamber full of warm air. The sides of the tomb were cut into shelves for the reception of bodies, and they reminded me of the wine cellars to be found in the basements of Victorian houses. I struck a match and saw that some of these niches still contained bones. The light from the open door fell on a startling sight. It was my first Palmyrene. He was carved life-size in white limestone, reclining gracefully on the lid of his sarcophagus. He was the owner of the tomb and the founder of the family who were buried there.

He was middle-aged, clean-shaven, and had staring eyes. His face, in fact his whole body, might have been modelled by a backward first-term student in any school of sculpture. He was reclining on rich cushions and rugs as if at a banquet. He wore a brimless cap rather like a tarbush, surrounded by a wreath; a long tunic, probably of silk, fell in folds over his body, and his legs were encased in thin trousers of the same material, gathered at the ankle. He wore buskins of soft leather richly embroidered or tooled. Instead of being some stray Persian, this was a typical wealthy Palmyrene of the Roman period. We entered other tombs, and many of them contained similar reclining figures, some with wine-cups in their hands. The women were shown reclining or sitting upright, covered with jewellery and wearing a Roman dress, often with a head-veil. The sculptors were good at jewellery. Each stone, each setting, the details of earrings and bangles, were carved with meticulous care, as if these women were determined to carry the ghosts of their jewellery with them into the next world. The impression I had was of a crowd of Orientals, some of whom imitated the Romans and some who did not; people devoted to couches and cushions, wine-cups, silks and jewels. They were far from unpleasing people. Behind the conventional stiffness of the sculptor's work I seemed to detect the quickness and intelligence of the living men and women.

This mixed race loved to spend its money with Greek architects, and prided itself on colonnades and buildings which no doubt they boasted were bigger and finer, and more expensive, than those of Antioch. But when it came to the intimacy of death, a touch of appealing sincerity seems to have caused them to employ their own native artists to perpetrate these hideous staring tomb portraits. It was strange to leave the splendid Hellenistic ruins of Palmyra, which might have belonged to Greeks, and to descend into the darkness of the tombs, where you discover this odd-looking race of semi-Persians, reclining in silk trousers on couches. Immense wealth had lifted them to terms of equality with the fashionable world which they loved to imitate in public, but death brought them down to realities; they never pretended to be Greeks in the tomb.

The tower tombs were extraordinary places: storey above storey, reached by a stone staircase, and each floor devoted to the dead. It was in one of these towers that an Arab attached himself to me, a young man in a *keffieh*, a blue serge jacket, a *gallabîa*, and a pair of new brown shoes. I have no idea where he came from, for the place had seemed empty when I went in. He told me that he was cook to a French officer's family, for Palmyra is now a French air station.

Looking at him, I thought he resembled a thinner, more Arab version of the wide-eyed men in the tombs, perhaps his remote ancestors. He had a disconcerting fixity of expression and, I was to discover, of mind also. I wondered whether this restless desire to see the world was the old caravan feeling coming out. How much did cooks get in England? he asked suddenly. I said, probably a fairly good cook received about a pound a week. He stood up and cried with terrible earnestness:

"I will come to England with you! I will come this night! All I get here is . . ." and he named a sum in Syrian money equivalent to five shillings a week. "In England I shall be rich," he cried. "Sir, I beg of you—take me back to England with you!"

I am told on good authority that cooks are difficult to find, but for the rest of that day my problem was how to lose one. He followed me everywhere, begging to be engaged and promising gigantic and indigestible meals. After dark that evening I heard a tap on the hotel window, and looking up, I saw his white figure standing outside, his face pressed to the glass, making mysterious noddings and mouthings. I went outside. He had been running hard. Evidently he had cooked and served his dinner and the French family were probably lying about in a state of comatose repletion, and would not miss him.

"When do you go to England?" he whispered quickly.

"Not for a long time," I said as gently as I could, for his anxiety was pathetic. "I go to Baghdad to-morrow." I regretted this instantly, fearing that he might try and attach himself to me. But he sighed hopelessly, then brightened.

"Then—you write to me and I shall come," he said, pressing into my hand a bit of paper which contained his name and address. He turned and ran off into the darkness.

Suddenly the air, already chilled at sunset, had a touch of ice in it. The winter which I had seen spread over the Taurus was blowing down upon the Syrian Desert. I piled every coat and available cloth on the bed. Glancing through the window, I saw Palmyra lying in the white light of the stars. It was silent and still. Columns rose over the ruins like marching ghosts. I

thought of the men and women reclining beneath the ground
at their last banquets, and it seemed to me that this city shared
to the full the pathos of all those silent places which have known
the hopes and the desires of mankind.

CHAPTER II

I cross the desert to Baghdad, and on the way encounter a strange fragment of England in the wilderness. In Baghdad I meet the Chaldean Christians. I visit the holy city of Kadhimain, sacred to the Moslem Shias, and am taken at night to see the Shia flagellants pass through the streets of Baghdad.

I

STANDING outside the window in the early morning was a long, experienced-looking motor-coach. It was touched everywhere with brown dust. The words "Nairn Transport Co." were written on its side. It was a heavier, longer version of those coaches which roll so swiftly through the English countryside. It had made a special stop at Palmyra to take up passengers, for its normal route is straight from Damascus to Baghdad.

I went into the hotel lounge. A few cold passengers were drinking Turkish coffee, and looking rather like mail-coach travellers in a print by Alken. Instead, however, of the buxom wenches of those prints, a sleepy Arab boy in a striped *gallabîa* slip-slopped round with trays of native bread and plates of crushed honeycomb the colour of dark sherry. The stove filled the room with a blinding injection of wood smoke.

A broad-shouldered man over six feet in height sat filling in official forms at the manager's table. He wore a pair of old flannel trousers and a leather golf-jacket. When he looked up I saw that he was one of those large men who seem to have a schoolboy hiding somewhere inside him. He asked for my passport, and I gathered that he was the driver of the Baghdad coach, and everybody called him Long Jack.

While we were having a cup of coffee together, he told me that he had been born in Wellington, New Zealand, and had come to Syria as a boy of eleven. The Nairn brothers, Jerry and Norman, were also New Zealanders. They had served in Palestine during the war and then started their desert transport company. They gave him a job as driver—and how many times he'd driven the coach to Baghdad and back to Damascus, he really couldn't say! A Syrian came in and whispered to him.

"My mate," he explained. "We have two drivers in each desert car. One sleeps while the other drives, and so we keep it up all night."

He stood up and called out, "All aboard!"; and we trooped out into the morning sunlight.

There was a mighty roar of the seventy-five horse power engine as the coach turned gently and rolled away through the ruins of Palmyra. It was not quite eight o'clock. We should be in Baghdad on the following morning.

2

The distance between Damascus and Baghdad is five hundred and twenty-seven miles, and the Nairn coaches accomplish the journey in twenty-four hours, with only two official stops: one, at Rutba Fort, half-way, and the other at Ramadi, the Irak passport station. Before cars crossed the desert, the journey was possible only by camel caravan and these sometimes took two months. I do not know whether the two New Zealanders who have originated this extraordinary adventure in transport will make a fortune, but no one can deny that they have made history.

Long Jack had given me some printed information about the Nairn venture, which I read with interest after I had become accustomed to the car. It was the most remarkably sprung car in which I have ever travelled, for the enormous coach, weighing twelve tons, had an almost miraculous capacity for taking a series of holes in the road at thirty miles an hour. I became tired of looking ahead at some bad piece of track, waiting for us to feel the bump, for these disturbances were never communicated.

I was sitting in the front seat immediately behind Long Jack, who was driving. He sat in a high seat rather like that of a steam tractor, grasping a steering-wheel twice the size of an ordinary one. The only sign that we were crossing rough country was the rhythmic undulation of his large body; over really bad ground he actually bobbed up and down.

Enormous electric fans were placed above the driver's seat, facing the passengers, and it was possible for each passenger to pull down blinds to exclude the sunlight, a reminder of the heat in which such journeys are made later in the year. The seats were of tubular steel, extravagantly padded and specially sprung, and were fitted with a device enabling you to tilt them backwards until you lie almost flat. This was designed for extra comfort during night travel.

I turned with interest to my literature, where I learned that the pioneer car journey across this desert took place in April 1923, when two Buicks and two Dodges did the journey in four days, and, I gathered, had a rough time. In the autumn of the same year the first service was started with Cadillac cars. The route had to be altered during the Druse rebellion, when one of the cars was attacked and a driver killed; but the Company was determined to run the mail service regularly, and never allowed it to lapse. It has always been necessary to pay safety money to the Bedouin tribes, who for centuries have regarded travellers in the desert as their rightful prey. Sheik Ali Basan, a Bedouin living in Damascus, at first provided the safe conduct and received as his reward a third of the mail contract, but during a reorganization he was given shares in the company, a delightful modern touch.

In 1927 a new type of car, the result of four years' experience, was made specially for desert travel. It was built in the United

States and shipped to Syria. Since then the history of the Company has been that of mechanical improvements, of extra comfort for travellers, and cheaper fares.

Long Jack turned now and then, speaking above the roar of his engine, but conversation was not easy in the noise. He told me that the car travelled a mile on five gallons of petrol and that ? it consumed one hundred and ten gallons between Damascus and Baghdad.

"Why don't you use British cars?" I shouted.

"Because when the idea was put up to British manufacturers, they made so many difficulties that we had to go to America," he bellowed back.

The desert which lay to the sky on each side was not sand, but a gravelly plain, reddish in parts. It is firm in dry weather, but becomes glutinous after rain. Ranges of low brown hills relieved the monotony of the flat surface, and there were occasional outcrops of volcanic looking rock. Long wadis, or watercourses, cut the plain, generally in a north-easterly direction towards the Euphrates; but they are bone dry except immediately after a storm. The road, like that from Resafa, was merely the wheel-marks of previous cars. When the plain became hard these tracks disappeared and Long Jack seemed to drive instinctively, but I noticed that sooner or later he always picked up the trail again on soft ground.

In the distance we saw herds of four or five hundred camels grazing on thorn bushes, all facing the same way. Whenever we saw camels or sheep we knew that a water-hole or a well was somewhere about. How few and far between these were, we could judge by the miles of lifeless desolation. It was at a place called Helba Wells that we saw our first sign of desert life. Men and women of the Ruwàlla tribe were watering their sheep and camels. Two concrete well-heads, made by the French military authorities, rose out of the stony earth, and round these were grouped Bedouin girls drawing up water. There were about two hundred camels and several hundred sheep, and the picture they made in that desert place might have come straight from the Old Testament.

Long Jack stopped the car and told us that we could have five minutes there. Walking with him to the wells, I found that he was a voluble speaker of Bedouin Arabic. He had the gift of making the Bedouin laugh, and soon these tall, brown people were all rocking with merriment like a lot of children. The Ruwàlla, who are frequently mentioned by Doughty in *Arabia Deserta*, are among the best camel-breeders in the Syrian Desert. Some of the women, I thought, had typical Mongolian faces, with high cheek-bones. They were impeded in their actions by long garments which looked far too big for them—some had tied cords round their waists and bunched their robes so that they exposed bright yellow heelless boots. All the time we were talking to the men, the women continued to work, and showed only by an occasional smile that they had heard the jokes that were flying around.

The wells were extraordinarily deep. The women sank a leather bucket at the end of a rope that seemed to descend into a bottomless pit. When the bucket was full, three girls would take the rope, and running back for at least forty yards over the desert, would draw the dripping bucket to the well-head. A man tipped the water into a trough, where a girl crouched, filling goat-skins, and another girl would load these on the back of a donkey.

When the goat-skins had been filled, Long Jack said that they would take away the buckets and ropes and, departing with their flocks and herds, would leave the well without any apparatus for the drawing of water. The custom that each Bedouin shall bring his own bucket and tackle, means, of course, that it would be possible for a traveller to die of thirst on the parapet of a well if no-one were there with a bucket and rope.

There came to my mind the words of the Woman of Samaria when she saw Jesus sitting beside the well at Sychar. He asked her for water, obviously because she had brought with her the necessary bucket and rope. But before she lowered the bucket, Jesus spoke metaphorically of the "water of life," which she did not understand, thinking that He referred to the well-water. I thought that her words to Jesus are the first that would spring to the lips of any Bedouin girl if she came on a man sitting beside the wells of Helba without a rope and a bucket, yet promising apparently to draw water. "Sir, thou hast nothing to draw with, and the well is deep."

Towards noon heat haze trembled over the wide plain. Our eyes, seeking for variety, seized eagerly on any rock or low hill, or even the ragged line of a wadi, just as on the high seas one looks with pleasure at a passing ship. At some point, where I believe there was a post or some barbed wire, we passed into Irak. There was no customs-house or passport office—that happens nearer Baghdad—nothing but the plain rising and falling, scattered with stones and gravel like the dry bed of an enormous lake.

We crossed a plateau swarming with gazelle. These beautiful, swift creatures, alarmed by the desert car, always galloped in herds straight across our path. It seemed as though they were hypnotized by the line of our advance and had to cross it, or perhaps we had caught them away from their natural haunts and they instinctively made for them. Sometimes we saw them far away, visible only as a moving line of dust on a dust-coloured plain, or against the sky-line as a gliding black line which became invisible as they disappeared from the horizon. Only once were we fortunate enough to see them fairly close, straight ahead of us, galloping at about fifty miles an hour, their white scuts shining through the dust of their gallop.

Men in town clothes and women in fur coats and Paris shoes walk on the desert sand, perhaps have something to eat, and vanish again into the air. The Arab accepts it all without wonder, having obviously heard of the magic carpet in his cradle. It was strange to find these people, some air travellers, some from desert cars, drawn together in the darkness in an atmosphere so strongly English that even the Iraqis, though on their native soil, appeared guest-like and faintly apprehensive.

Leading from this room was a little dining-room with tables set for dinner, all neat and clean and—English. There is a wonderful English way of setting a table which we don't notice at home because we see it so often. The cloth droops almost to the ground, decently covering the table's legs, and it generally has ironed creases in it. The knives and forks are set with precision, not with Gallic inconsequence or Latin fire, and the cruet is given a place of honour beside a bottle of sauce. Tumblers, the right size for half a pint of ale, stand to the right-hand, and inside each one is popped a little bishop's mitre—a folded table-napkin. No other nation sets a table like that, and when I saw all those tables looking so English, reminding me of country hotels in Hampshire and Yorkshire and Devonshire, of little restaurants run by tall, grey-haired gentlewomen in select seaside places, a feeling of love for this dear country of ours filled my heart, and I determined to pour Lea and Perrins Sauce over everything that night, out of sheer love for England.

Pinned to an announcement board in this fantastic room, next to an apology for the high price of bottled beer, was a notice which brought me back to reality.

NOTICE

Passengers are warned when leaving the fort always to keep the fort in sight. Cases have occurred of passengers becoming lost (through losing their bearings) when out for a stroll, owing to darkness falling suddenly and the fort not being in sight. The result of this causes danger to the passengers and trouble to the police.

By Order.
Administrative Commandant.

My eye lingered lovingly over "when out for a stroll," which brought memories of Eastbourne into Mesopotamia. No-one but an Englishman could have talked about having "a stroll" at Rutba.

While I was wondering from whom all these blessings flowed, my curiosity was answered by the appearance of a short, stout man in a grey flannel suit, who passed rapidly through the dining-room, talking like a machine-gun in sudden rapping bursts of fluent Arabic. Every waiter addressed by him seemed to have been given an electric shock. Some fled into the kitchen, some attempted to hide, and several stumbled over chairs and upset the salt in a passion of obedience. He smoked a cigarette all the time, rapping out his orders between puffs of smoke and with a glance of pale blue eyes which had the fixed expression of expecting the worst; a look which men acquire from long contact with foreign troops. I put him down as an old soldier, and from the quick way he moved and the way he held himself, as a boxer or an athlete. And in none of these things was I far wide of the mark.

He was George Bryant, commandant of the rest-house. As I sat down to dinner, we attempted to talk, but this was difficult because he was interrupted every two seconds by one of his waiters. He would spring lightly to his feet and disappear with a terrifying gleam of frosty blue eyes, to return a minute later with the air of having quelled a rebellion. During his first absence I gazed incredulously at the card which was propped against the cruet.

Dinner.

Tomato Soup
Fried Fish
Tarter Sauce
Roast Beef
Horse-Radish Sauce
Roast Potatoes
Cauliflower
Yorkshire Pudding
Raisin Pudding, Lemon Syrup
Fruit.   Coffee

I invite you to look at the map which is at the beginning of this book, and, having found Rutba, to believe that this very night a meal of such superb Englishness is probably being eaten in that hut behind the fortress wall. In an age of half-belief, it is inspiring to meet that mood of stern faith which will recognize in no part of the earth a place that cannot be made a little like home; that must, in fact, be made like home before it can be called good. And although we may laugh at people who go about the world taking England wherever they may be, what finer thing is there to take about the world? For one brief hour, as we sat at the parting of the ways in this desert, some of us to travel towards the Mediterranean, others towards the Indian Ocean, we sat in peace, sharing the solid comfort of a tradition built up in generations of English families.

When George Bryant returned, I looked at him with renewed interest. No; he had no woman to help him. He had trained the cooks and the waiters himself. Where did he come from? Born at Bath, played rugger for Bristol, entered the Palestine police force, stationed at Nazareth, left the force, and had been in the desert ever since. So much I got out of him in a quick-fire way between his jumpings-up and his sittings-down.

"Enjoy your dinner? Not too bad, is it?" And a frosty smile

came into his eyes for a second. "Difficult? It's not too easy. You've got to keep them up to the scratch. That's the secret. You can't let one detail escape you. Excuse me a minute . . ." He came back. "Do you like the fish?"

"I was going to ask how you get fish in the middle of the desert."

"Comes from Baghdad. Tigris. Get it when the desert mail goes East. It's a bit coarse, naturally, but it's not too bad, is it?"

It was not, because the poor Tigris fish, entering into the spirit of the thing, had consented to look and taste very like the "fried fish with sauce tartare" of more familiar places.

Long Jack came in to say the coach was ready, and I was given a pillow and two blankets. I walked across the dark courtyard with George Bryant, through the gate into the desert, enormously wide and silent under the stars. The car stood throbbing, and two beams of white light shone into the emptiness that was our way.

"Cheerio!" said George Bryant. "Look in again on your way back."

And he strode swiftly past the sentry into the fort.

There was no moon that night and a blue wash of starlight lay over the desert, in which stones almost achieved shadows. Our headlights sprang forward and became lost in the immensity of the space ahead. I was conscious of things moving in the light and escaping from it, for now the desert seemed to be livelier than by day. Sand-grouse rose in front of us and flashed off; a flock of desert pigeon flew in and out of our light, and all around us the desert moved with strange hopping creatures, propelled, it seemed, by springs: these were jerboas, little kangaroo-like desert rats. You had to watch carefully to see them, for they were the same colour as the earth and moved with the speed of birds, hopping in every possible direction.

I tilted my seat back, wrapped myself in blankets, and enjoyed those disconnected periods of unconsciousness which are usually accompanied by vivid and unlikely dreams. I was in London at one moment and at the next I would awaken to see Long Jack's broad back undulating in front of me, and the stars snapping overhead. Or I was in my room in Hampshire, sitting at my table in that inexplicable state of happiness which comes sometimes in dreams; and then, awakening with a sense of bereavement, I would see Long Jack lying crumpled in the spare seat, his huge body sagging as if he had been shot, and the Syrian driver at the wheel, the smoke of an Iraqi cigarette streaming back.

So the night wore on; first crouched on the left side, then on the right; asleep for ten minutes, awake for half an hour; and always the pale wash of starlight all round; the rising and falling headlights; the roar of the engine.

I was suddenly wide awake. The coach had stopped on a sandy road with buildings on each side. It was still dark, and looking at my watch I saw that it was only 2.30. Long Jack was standing outside talking to a policeman, holding in his hand the passports of passengers. We were at Ramadi, the Iraqi passport station, about ninety miles from Baghdad. I got out, and walking a few paces along the road, became conscious of something new and pleasant in the air. It was the sound of wind in acacia trees; and I remembered that I had seen no real trees for many days.

Near the customs shed was a small building with a front garden. It was the Babylon Hotel, and there were lights in the windows. I entered a lounge where little brown waiters in white jackets, who might have been the waiters of Rutba Fort, were bustling about serving the sleepy passengers with pots of tea and trays of English biscuits. We had been offered tea and English biscuits at Rutba, and here they were again! This could not have happened in Syria. I drank four cups of strong tea, and smoked a cigarette. The hotel lounge was interesting. The walls were hung with Persian rugs so that the place looked like a carpet shop, and a picture of young King Ghazi of Iraq hung on the wall. But the waiters spoke English, and, from the way they served the tea, you could tell that whatever they knew of waiting was derived from English sources.

When I gave the waiter a ten-shilling note, he returned my change in the first Iraqi money I had handled. Since 1931 Iraq has had a currency of its own, based on the pound sterling. One *dinar*—which surely holds some vague memory of *Chu Chin Chow*—is worth an English pound, and this is divided into a thousand *fils*. Silver coins are of twenty, fifty, or a hundred *fils*; nickel coins of irregular shape, rather like our new three-penny pieces, are of four and ten *fils*; and copper coins are of one and two *fils*, but my tastes are evidently so expensive that I never discovered what I could buy with them, except the fleeting gratitude of small boys.

An insistent note from the klaxon sent us running to the coach. We crossed a wooden bridge. I saw the movement of swift water. This is the point where the Euphrates, after winding through Mesopotamia as if it were going to Baghdad, suddenly makes up its mind to turn south and leave Baghdad to its companion, the Tigris.

Awakening from a sound sleep, I found that we were running through flat country, over a rough road of beaten brown earth, and ahead of us a cluster of mud-coloured buildings, minarets and a few cupolas was spread out on a land as low, as wide, and as conscious of the sky, as Holland. And the sun was up.

4

The irreproachable edition of Lane's *Arabian Nights*, which could be found in all Victorian libraries, probably explains why Baghdad is a magic name to most people. To me, it was one of those towers of romance which experience had not yet demolished, and I approached it with some apprehension, already aware that it was going to be—well, different.

As the car approached Baghdad through the sunrise of that morning, I took with me a certain proportion of juvenile dreams, and I told myself that the line of buildings, with a golden gleam of a distant mosque, was indeed the city of the Caliphs.

We crossed the river by a wooden pontoon bridge whose sections lift gently under heavy traffic. The Tigris at Baghdad is about twenty yards wider than the Thames at London Bridge: on the west bank, white-balconied houses stand amid the green fringes of date-palms; on the east bank modern Baghdad clusters, with its one main street and its incredible chaos of lesser streets and lanes. Blue skies, warm sunlight, a long, wide main street (called, I saw with a pang, Al Rashid Street) lined with little shops and animated by the movement of two-horse open carriages—these were my first memories of Baghdad.

I entered a hotel in this street which is named after General Maude. The servant who answered the bell called me "sahib"; and in the breakfast-room the waiter, who gave me the best cooked bacon and eggs I have ever eaten, also called me "sahib." It was the first time that anyone had seriously referred to me in this Kiplingesque manner; and it made me think that there is a point in travel when the West fades out and the East tunes in; when the Mediterranean is a far-off, alien sea and the Indian Ocean is real and near. This point is Iraq. India is only round the corner.

I remembered that men I knew who had served as administrators in Iraq had also been Indian civil servants, and suddenly many things were made clear: the bacon and eggs, the tea and *petit buerre* biscuits at Ramadi; and goodness knows what else.

Pleased with this deduction, I went out to see Baghdad.

5

For three centuries before the war, Iraq shared in the living death of the Ottoman Empire. The war released it from its torpor, and, after ten years of British mandated rule, it is now an independent Arab state ruled by Feisal's son, King Ghazi.

Baghdad, which may possess carefully concealed charms visible only to the resident and the native, is, to the visitor, a large, mud-coloured city on the banks of a mud-coloured river. With the slightest wind, powdered mud as fine as talc-powder flies through its streets. In true Babylonian tradition, the native building material is mud brick and, like the towers and temples of Biblical times, the chief architectural decoration is the glazed tile, which in modern Baghdad is sparingly applied to the cupolas of a few mosques.

The terrible poverty and inertia of the old Turkish rule are still written on the face of Baghdad. It will take more than ten years of Western influence to wipe out the memory and tradition of three hundred years of mental and material corruption. It is true that a new spirit is fighting the old ways; there are hospitals, public services, an excellent police force, schools, and a stirring feeling of national pride which may mean that the old tree, having been pruned and trained in the way it should grow, is putting out new wood. The long main street, with its ramshackle booths and shops, is still mainly Turkish in appearance, although an occasional ladies' hair-dresser, or an up-to-date chemist's shop, seem to herald the dawn of a new day.

This main street is filled with activity. From morning until night earnest little 'arabîyât drawn by two horses ply up and down. There are so many of these questing victorias, and their fares are so cheap, that there is no need to walk anywhere. In the absence of finer shades of social distinction the people in the street may be divided, like a hymn-book, into ancient and modern. The modern wear European clothes with the national head-dress, a forage cap of blue cloth rather like that worn by members of the Church Lads' Brigade; and the ancient wear anything from the green turban and robes of religious aristocracy to the squalid sacks which cover the limbs of the Khurdish porters.

In the capital of a land which resembles nothing so much as a billiard table, the presence of mountains is curiously proclaimed by fierce, ragged men who by their bearing would be recognized anywhere as highlanders. They are nomads from the mountains of Kurdistan or from the high country round Mosul. Then there are Persians, Arabs, Jews, Afghans, Indians, and negroes; a curious mixture that rides, walks, or lies in the dust of Baghdad's main street.

The reason why nothing now survives of the cultured city of the Abbasid Caliphate is to be found in history. Baghdad has been plundered and destroyed, rebuilt and flooded, time and again, so that little remains to-day to remind the visitor of "the golden prime of good Hārūn al-Rashīd."

The bazaars are a confusing warren of twisting alleys crammed with life, with cheap Japanese cotton prints, with copper work of infinite variety, and with trivial silver and gold work; they are dark, save for dusty stabs of sunlight that fall from rents in the cloth covering overhead. I looked in vain for ancient khans such as I have seen in Cairo, Damascus, Jerusalem, and Aleppo, for Baghdad is a city with a great but invisible past, and there are no architectural relics worth speaking about.

The Museum is Baghdad's greatest attraction. Here are to be seen the astonishing objects found at Ur, and much else besides. It is strange, perhaps, that while everybody knows something about the Tut-ankh-Amûn discoveries, which did not really increase the world's knowledge, the finds at Ur, which removed the dawn of history from Egypt to Babylonia and set it back another thousand years, seem to have made little impression, except on those people who happen to be interested in such matters.

It was in Baghdad's main street that I came on the only really surprising shop in the city. It is called Mackenzie's Book Shop. Although it might pass without comment in Oxford or Cambridge, it stands out from the oriental booths on each side. It is packed from floor to ceiling with new and second-hand English books, and is, of course, a relic of the British Mandate. It is, however, more significant now that the Mandate has been surrendered than ever it was when the British patronized it; for the customers are chiefly modern young Iraqis. You will always find a group of young men wandering about there, dipping into the latest books, and it will occur to you that Mackenzie of Baghdad is proof that though England and France have made little cultural impression on Palestine, Trans-Jordan, or Syria, this is not so in Iraq.

Ten years of British rule have taught Iraq to speak our language and to read our books. And from the size of Mackenzie's shop and, still more, from the kind of books that fill it, you can confidently assume that Baghdad's literary appetite is critical and intelligent.

In the afternoon I hired a taxi and told the man to drive for a couple of hours anywhere outside Baghdad.

We bumped along a road of beaten mud with cultivated land on each side. Every passing horseman covered us in brown dust, and our wheels made a sand storm for the unfortunate people behind. The cultivation soon began to thin out, and I had some idea of the difference between the country to-day and in ancient times.

The modern habit of giving the name Mesopotamia to the lower reaches of the Tigris and the Euphrates probably originated during the war, when the Press and the Army always referred to these parts as Mespot. But the Mesopotamia of the ancient world was the country north of Baghdad—the wide, grassy plains between the two rivers—and the country south of Baghdad was known as Babylonia.

When you look at this land to-day, stretching brown and barren to the sky, a land green only on its river-banks and in irrigated areas, it is difficult to believe that such a desert could ever have been the home of great civilizations. But when Abraham lived at Ur, and when the Children of Israel were carried captive to Babylon, they saw a different country. If we can imagine the wheat-prairies of Canada varied by groves of date-palms and intersected in every direction by canals, we have some idea of the appearance of ancient Babylonia.

Agriculture has always been impossible in this land unless the flood-waters carried down by the two rivers in the spring are retained and used to water the land during the dry season. The Chaldeans, the Babylonians, and the Assyrians were irrigation experts who harnessed the Tigris and the Euphrates, and by a complicated system of control distributed the water as it was required. The system was taken over by the Persians and by the Arabs of the Caliphate, but when the Arab Government weakened it fell into disrepair, until, with the Mongol invasions of the Thirteenth Century, the magnificent series of waterways with their intricate dams and dykes fell into utter ruin, and a legacy from the world's first civilizations was lost.

At the present moment engineers are tackling the problem of irrigation, but it is not an easy one. The river-beds have been ruined by centuries of neglect. Water has been tapped to serve individual needs in a way which makes it impossible for the rivers to scour their beds properly, and canal-cutting, which has gone on without plan, has diverted the flow of water and helped to cause floods. Thus the restoration of Babylonia to its former prosperity presents not one problem, but hundreds, and not the least important is the problem of population. Neverthe-

less, even a glance at the immense dry plains suggests that if
Iraq, like ancient Babylonia, could once again become pro-
ductive, she might influence the wheat markets of the world.

6

Back in Baghdad, I found myself forbidden, like any Seven-
teenth-Century "Christian Dog," to enter the Shia mosques.
It was the first week in Muharram, the opening month of the
Moslem year, a time when Shias flagellate themselves, cut their
heads with knives, and achieve a condition of religious ecstasy
which culminates in the passion play commemorating the death
of Mohammed's grandson.

I stood outside the mosques and watched the lowering crowds
of men passing in and out, each mosque like a hive about to
swarm. An intense crowd devoid of humour is a terrible spectacle, especially when you are detached from the object of its ob-
session. These purposeful fanatics, urged, it seemed, by some
power or instinct beyond themselves, were terrifying in their
single-mindedness. They were men not humbled by grief, but
made savage and revengeful. Looking at them, I realized how
quickly a human sacrifice must have cleared the air in pagan
times; for these Shias, whether they were aware of it or not,
wanted blood.

I must explain that Islam is not an undivided faith. It is split
by a schism twelve centuries old into two great sects, the Sunnis
and the Shias. The majority of Moslems are Sunnis ("those of
the faith") or traditionists; a minority, centred in Persia and
India, are Shias, or "dissenters," a rigid fanatical sect with its
own religious hierarchy, its own mosques, its own festivals,
and its own interpretation of the Koran. It is possible to travel
in Palestine, Syria, Egypt, and Asia Minor and never to realize
that the Shias exist, but as soon as you enter Iraq you become
conscious that you have crossed a theological frontier: you are

in the holy land of the Shia. And the schism came about in this way.

When the Prophet died in 632 A.D., he left no son to succeed him, neither did he appoint a successor. There were signs that Islam would fall to pieces unless a strong hand took immediate and undivided control, and the choice fell on Mohammed's bosom friend, Abu Bekr. This election passed over a man who might have succeeded by right of blood. He was Ali, Mohammed's cousin and son-in-law. Two more caliphs were, however, chosen by election before Ali eventually succeeded to the headship of Islam; but he was a gentle and unlucky person, the last man in the world to hold together wild desert tribes, and after a reign of only five years he fell to the stroke of a poisoned sword at Kufa, in Iraq.

He left two sons, Hasan and Husein, who succeeded to a divided empire. Hasan abdicated and died at Medina in 669 A.D., some say slain by his wife; his brother Husein, marching to establish his claim to the caliphate, was surrounded by his enemies and mercilessly slaughtered at Karbala, in Iraq. So ended the tragedy of the house of Ali.

The Shias have always held that the succession should have proceeded immediately through Ali, Hasan, and Husein. Their theory is that these men were sacred by virtue of their blood. They claim also that the three first caliphs, Abu Bekr, Omar, and Othman, were usurpers, as were all the caliphs after them. Omar in particular they detest, and I have heard that Sunnis named Omar often prudently change their names to the most popular of the Shia names, Ali, when venturing into Persia. A horrible pious exercise in Persia is the repetition of this curse: "O God, curse Omar, then Abu Bekr and Omar, then Othman and Omar, then Omar—then Omar!"

So it is clear that as the Shias regard with horror and loathing three pillars of the Sunni faith, and all the caliphs after them, the rift is as complete as it could be. But the Shias have also built up a whole school of mystical theology which further separates them from the Sunni. The emotional abandon with which these people worship their dead prophets seems far removed from the stern self-control of the rest of Islam.

Iraq is the holy land of the Shia because Ali and Husein are buried there. The four holy cities of Iraq, Najaf, Karbala, Kadhimain, and Samarra, are sacred to the Shia world, and it is said that about two hundred thousand Shia pilgrims go there every year, most of them from Persia, India, and Afghanistan. Each holy city has a large cemetery attached to it, for it is the desire of every Shia to be buried in ground as near as possible to the holy Ali or the equally holy Husein. Coffins strapped to a Ford car or a pack-animal are the commonest of sights on all roads that lead to these four cities. While the Sunni turns to Mecca and Medina, the Shia turns to the holy cities of Iraq.

The great festival of the Shia year falls on the first ten days of Muharram, when the faithful celebrate with all manner of morbid austerity the death of Husein at Karbala. Their grief for Husein is so deep that he might have died last week instead of twelve centuries ago. Every detail of his death is dwelt on with sorrow and love, until one feels that these people are mourning, not a man, but a god. And the story of his death moves indeed with the inevitability of great tragedy.

Husein and his family, with a small force of about seventy followers, camped at Karbala, not far from the Euphrates. They suffered terribly from thirst, as they were cut off from the river, but no one would give them a drink of water. Husein knew that he was fated to die. On the night of the tenth day his sister, who had been lying awake in her tent listening to the sound of Husein's servant burnishing his master's sword for the coming combat, slipped weeping to his bedside.

"Sister," said Husein, "put your trust in God and know that man is born to die, and that the heavens shall not remain; everything shall pass away but the presence of God, who created all things by his power, and they shall return to him alone. My father was better than I, and my mother was better than I, and my brother was better than I; and they, and we, and all Moslems, have an example in the 'Apostle of God.' "

He called his followers and asked them to leave him to his fate and depart to their homes. But they said: "God forbid that we should ever see the day wherein we survive you." So he commanded them to cord the tents together as a barrier against the enemy cavalry, and to dig a trench behind them filled with brushwood that could be set on fire, in order to protect them from the rear. And on the following morning he prepared for battle, first washing and anointing himself with perfumes. When some of his men asked why he was doing this, he replied cheerfully: "Alas, there is nothing between us and the black-eyed girls of Paradise but that these troopers come down upon us and slay us." Mounting his camel, he first read the Koran, and then rode into battle.

He was wounded on the head and retired to his tent to rest a moment. While he sat holding his young son in his arms, the child was killed by a flying arrow. He rushed into the fight again, and, becoming thirsty, found his way to the Euphrates; but as he was stooping to drink an arrow struck him in the mouth. He charged the enemy again and again until, finally overcome by numbers, he fell transfixed by a spear. A troop of horsemen was ridden backwards and forwards over his dead body. His head was carried to the stern ruler of Basra and flung on the ground. As the governor turned it over with his staff, a voice was heard saying: "Gently! It is the Prophet's grandson. By God! I have seen these very lips kissed by the blessed mouth of Mohammed."

7

I was anxious to go to the holy city of Kadhimain, which is four miles from Baghdad. The gold cupolas and the four gold minarets of the Shia mosque are a landmark visible everywhere in that flat country.

I was told on no account to linger near the gate or to attempt to take a photograph, but as the Shias whom I had seen in Baghdad looked surly but not dangerous, I put this warning down to the nervousness of my adviser. Still, I thought it would be sensible to take someone who had been there before. My companion was a Syrian Christian who was visiting Baghdad; he said that years ago he had entered the mosque at Kadhimain in disguise.

"I would not do it again for all the money in the world," he said. "Had I been detected, they would have killed me!"

As we drove out to Kadhimain, he told me that dead bodies are brought from immense distances in order that they may lie in the sanctity of Iraqi soil, some from distant parts of India and others from the remote highlands of Afghanistan.

"It is not cheap to be buried in the holy cities," he explained. "A good grave at Najaf would cost about forty English pounds; but in less popular places, like Samarra, you can buy a grave for about seven shillings. It all depends how near the grave is to the mosque. In the old days, which I remember well, bodies were brought from India by boat to Basra, and then carried by caravan to Najaf or Karbala. But bubonic plague broke out and the Turks stopped such things."

I asked him why Kadhimain was sacred to the Shia.

"They are strange people," he replied. "For instance, it is their belief that the almost divine power of Mohammed was carried on through a number of men called Imāms, or Mahdīs, but the last of these, the twelfth, disappeared long ago. They believe that someday a Mahdī will come back to earth and take all the Shias up to heaven. The mosque at Kadhimain contains the tombs of two important Mahdīs, the seventh, Musa-bin-Tafar, and the ninth, Mohammed-bin-'Ali."

As we drew near Kadhimain the golden domes and minarets

grew larger, until the building achieved a meretricious splendour; but I did not think it beautiful.

"It is real gold," said the Syrian. "Real!"

"Tell me honestly, would the Shias kill an unbeliever who entered their mosque?" I asked.

"There is no doubt," he said; "that is why it is forbidden. They have killed unbelievers for much less. I have heard that they killed an American who took a photograph of their mosque in Teheran. They poured boiling water on his body!"

He looked at me out of the corner of his eye.

"You understand we must be quick?" he asked. "Just one look and then we go. At this moment the Shias are more fanatical than ever. They go without food, and their bodies are sore from much beating and cutting."

"Do they still do this at Kadhimain?"

"Not only at Kadhimain. At Baghdad. Everywhere. This very night they will be beating themselves in Baghdad, and every night until the tenth day of Muharram."

"Where can I see this?" I asked him.

"It would not be advisable," he replied with a solemn shake of his head; and at this moment the car in which we were driving pulled up in front of the main gate of the mosque.

We stepped into an atmosphere of hostility that would have penetrated a tank. Only a nice-minded English tourist accustomed to the kindly ways of Tunbridge Wells or Harrogate might have remained unconscious of the dull, blistering animosity. The glances cast at my European clothes were like a blight. Whatever I did, or wherever I moved, those same resentful eyes followed. I began to feel personally responsible for the death of Husein, which I noticed was commemorated by immense black funeral cloths fixed to the outside wall of the mosque.

The great gateway, towering to a height of about fifty feet, is covered with glazed tiles of pink and turquoise-blue arabesque, and across each of the seven gateways hangs a chain that falls from the centre and is caught up in two graceful loops on either side.

Framed in these gates we saw a wide open space, beautifully paved: porticoes, ablution tanks, and the sanctuary itself, with its tall doors and archways covered with tiles of pink and turquoise-blue flowers. Men were constantly passing in and out of the mosque, touching, as they did so, the chains at the door; for this, I believe, is good for the soul. Most of the pilgrims were rough, unkempt men, some of whom count it a privilege to walk from Afghanistan or India to make a journey which in Shia eyes takes precedence of the Haj to Mecca. I was fascinated by the hot, vindictive eyes and the dazed, fanatical faces, like those of men awakening from some confused dream. These people seemed to live on hate. I said so to the Syrian.

"It is the time of their sorrow," he whispered back.

That I had not exaggerated the feeling of the crowd was proved by the appearance of a policeman with a rifle, who politely invited us inside the station, saying that from the roof we could have a much better view. We followed him up a rickety stair to a roof of mud and palm wood. Telling us where it was safe to stand, he left us, and we trod like Agag until we reached the parapet, where we gazed down over the two golden mustard-pots and the four golden candlesticks of Kadhimain.

Having looked long enough on the evidence of a wound that is as fresh to-day as it was when Ali died at Kufa over one thousand three hundred years ago, we passed through shabby, dark bazaars, meeting everywhere the glance of curious eyes, and returned to the calmer atmosphere of Baghdad.

I was talking about the Shias to an Englishman staying in the hotel, a man who knew Iraq well. He told me that on the tenth of Muharram, the ancient passion play, which is acted all over India and Persia, takes place in Iraq. The death of Husein is reproduced by actors who apparently leave nothing to the imagination. The climax of the drama is reached when the body of Husein is paraded beneath a blood-spattered sheet.

In *A Second Journey through Persia*, James Morier gives a description of the play as it was performed at Teheran at the beginning of the last century. He says that the most extraordinary part of the performance was the appearance of the headless martyrs lying in a row on the sand. The actors who played these parts buried themselves until only the head was above ground, while others put their heads underground, leaving their bodies visible. They were arranged so that it looked as though the heads of the buried actors belonged to the apparently decapitated bodies. Members of a profession which is notoriously self-sacrificing will, however, be interested to know that the actors cast for these parts were men fulfilling a penance, and some of them entered so fully into the spirit of it that they sometimes died during the performance.

The crowd became so worked up when Morier saw the play, that the soldiers who slew Husein were stoned from the stage, and he says that so difficult was it to get actors to play these dangerous parts that Russian prisoners were forced to enact them.

I went to sleep that night wondering how I could see the flagellants.

8

I rose early in the morning, and from the flat roof of the hotel watched the sunlight falling over Baghdad. The brown river was running swiftly; a man in a small, beaked boat, piled with a cargo of thornwood, was coming down with the current; the first passengers were crossing the Maude Bridge, whose line of mooring-buoys was tilted against the forceful waters; and four miles away, over the line of palm trees, the morning light touched the gold of Kadhimain.

In the hall downstairs, an eager little brown boy was waiting to guide me to the Chaldean Church.

"Are you a Christian?" I asked him, as we set off down Al-Rashīd Street.

"Yes, sahib," he said, "and my father and mother, too, and all our relations."

We entered a network of streets, some of them too narrow even for a laden camel, and, passing beneath a gateway, he led me to the steps of a fairly large building. Although it was not yet 7 o'clock, the gaunt church was half full of men, women, and children. A priest was saying Mass before an altar raised on steps above the main level of the church. Two little acolytes, whose movements revealed bare, knobbly knees below white robes and sent my thoughts flying back to Ireland, hovered with book and thurible.

The church was cracked with the heat of Baghdad summers. The blades of electric fans, so large that they looked like aeroplane propellers, hung overhead among the candelabra. Like all Christian churches in the East, the building had collected within its walls a varied and puzzling assembly, not one member of which was distinguished in appearance from his Moslem fellow-townsman in the streets outside. There were Iraqis in European suits, men wearing the Bedouin keffieh, numbers of rough porters—whom I should have put down as Khurds if I had seen them anywhere else—women of all ages, who wore black or purple veils over their heads, and a whole school of boys with satchels on their backs.

The Mass bore a resemblance to the Roman Catholic Mass, though not a word of Latin was spoken. The language was Chaldean, an Aramaic language, dead except for the Chaldean liturgy. It is possibly a survivor of the ancient language of Babylonia, the tongue in which Chaldean astrologers answered Nebuchadnezzar, as described in chapter two of the Book of Daniel. How strange it was to hear those guttural accents, born of a dead world, which may once have been spoken on the smoking summits of the ziggurats of Baal, and uttered now in the mystery of the Christian Mass.

There was a beautiful moment when the "kiss of peace," which has long since been discontinued in its literal form in the West, was given by the priest to the two acolytes. With hands fresh from the chalice, he touched the hands of the boys, who came running down the altar steps to touch the hands that were everywhere stretched out towards them. I was at the end of a pew, and one of the boys cupped my hand between his palms and passed on quickly. My neighbour, a big, rough man clothed mostly in rags, a man whom I should have avoided in any dark lane, turned to me with his hands ready to accept the "kiss," then noticing that I was a foreigner, he did not know what to do, and faltered, dropping his arms. I offered my hands to him with the "kiss of peace" still fresh on them; and the man, with a smile of gratitude which was a beautiful thing to see on that hard face, touched my hands with his and passed the blessing along the line.

I sat there while the candles were put out, with the knowledge that this Chaldean Church, in which I had not understood one word of the service, was yet the only place in Iraq where I was at home, at ease and off my guard. It was Christian, and it belonged to the civilization which had created the world I knew. Nothing was really strange to me in this place, or alien or unfriendly. I may not have known the language of the sacrifice, but I knew the sacrifice. I may not have known the names of the Eastern saints whose pictures hung on the walls, but I knew of other saints like them.

Seeing me sitting there, the priest came down and hesitantly spoke to me in English. I was a stranger in Baghdad? Would I care to go with him to the patriarchate behind the church and drink a cup of coffee? I followed him gladly, nearer to him in spirit and in friendship than I could ever be with a Moslem, no matter how long or how well I might know him.

We entered a long, simply furnished room, whose only decoration was a picture of the Chaldean Patriarch in his crown and vestments. A huge pectoral cross was almost lost among the white hairs of his beard. The priest went out and returned with another, a dark, bearded man, who spoke excellent English.

"I know England," he said, "I have not long been back from your country."

"What part do you know?" I asked.

"Farnham, in Surrey," he replied. "I have been there at a monastery of Benedictine monks."

It was strange to sit in this room in Baghdad, talking about Farnham with two swarthy priests whose faces were like those of Assyrian kings. Did he ever hear anyone in Farnham speak of Cobbett? No, he replied gravely. Was he a bishop? No, I said, with equal gravity, Cobbett was not a bishop.

Then we talked of Baghdad and the Chaldean Church, and the unhappy Nestorian Church, of which it was once a part. The Nestorian Church is now called, most confusingly, the Assyrian Church. The Chaldean Church broke away from the Nestorians in the Sixteenth Century, and became united with the Church of Rome. For three centuries, with the exception of lapses now and then, their church had been in communion with Rome.

We spoke with sorrow of the terrible misfortunes of the Nestorian (Assyrian) Church and of the splendour of its early days, when its missionaries carried the Christian Faith into China.

"It is like an army," he said, "worn out and scattered after many great battles."

We talked of the Chaldean Patriarch, whose splendid title is "Patriarch of Babylon."

Promising to revisit them, I said good-bye, but they insisted on leading me through the tangle of lanes: three men in black, with melon-shaped turbans of black satin on their heads; and the faces beneath, the long, straight noses, the pallid sallowness, and the ebony-black beards, reminded me of the copper head of an Assyrian king in the museum at Baghdad. Although this king lived two centuries before Christ and dressed his beard in a thousand little separate scented curls, his face has come down unchanged through twenty-one centuries to the Chaldean priests of Baghdad.

9

I was fortunate enough to meet many members of the Chaldean Church, who kindly invited me to their homes. They showed me the flat roofs on which they sleep in summer, and the cool cellars—*serdabs*—some fitted with punkas, in which they live, lizard-like, during the heat of August.

To all these people I confided my desire to see the Shia flagellants, and at last one man said that he had a friend from whose house we might see them pass at night from one mosque to another. He promised to call for me at eight o'clock that evening, and take me there.

It was dark when we set out, but crowds filled the main street, for Baghdad has contracted the Western habit of aimless night sauntering, the result, probably, of electricity and of a new clerkly class unwearied by physical labour. The small cinema was offering a drama of European life and, as I watched the kind of people who were going to the cheaper seats, some of whom had probably seen no more of the world than the country round Baghdad, I wondered what they would make of it, and if it would do them much harm. Perhaps the bad influence of the cinema at home is exaggerated, because it seems to me that the great virtue of the film is the ease with which it is forgotten by intelligent people. But in the East, and before an adult audience most of whom have never learnt to read, the film is accepted, not as a narcotic or a fairy-tale for grown-ups, but as a literal interpretation of life in Europe; hence its power for good or evil, a power which is not always realized by those responsible for showing films to Eastern audiences.

It was easy, too, to feel ashamed of this poor Western return for *The Thousand and One Nights*. That we should send these shoddy dreams to Baghdad is one of Time's bitter ironies; yet the cheaper attractions of our civilization are so infectious that the young men of Baghdad obviously prefer the film to Hārūn al-Rashīd.

Leaving the main street, we walked through narrow lanes in which our steps were hushed. Some alleys were like the Shambles in York. The houses leaned together, thrusting forward their top storys until only a knife-cut of sky lay overhead; and the lanes meandered so confusingly that they might have been designed by a flock of crazy sheep. After dark something of the mystery of old Baghdad returns to haunt the sleeping alleys of the old city. For the first time I felt that it would be possible to see the Caliph passing on some night adventure, or, glancing up, to see the dwarf, so dear to Eastern story, peeping from behind a lattice.

The men encountered in these lanes were not the capped and collared *effendis* of the main street: they were silent men who passed with a bat-like scrape of heelless slippers, giving a sidelong glance, as they went by, from the shelter of their headcoverings. Sometimes a long, yearning wail of Turkish gramophone music would sound from beyond a blank wall, and I went on with knowledge of life packed away there, of people sitting together as if in ambush.

My guide halted before one of the blank walls and knocked on a door. We heard the sound of feet descending a flight of stairs, and a voice on the other side asked who it was. At once the door was opened, to reveal not the eunuch which the street suggested, or the merchant in turban and silk caftan, but a young man in a black coat, a pair of striped trousers, and black patent-leather shoes.

Speaking good English, he led the way up a flight of stone

stairs to a room leading off a galleried courtyard. Two divans, upholstered in Persian fabrics and fitted with white antimacassars, faced each other under the unshaded electric bulbs. A few Chinese pictures hung on the walls, and a number of knick-knacks were dotted about on bamboo tables. The most spectacular was a stuffed cobra strangling a mongoose; it stood on a side-table, very realistic and horrible, providing that touch of India which I was beginning to look for everywhere in Baghdad.

A smiling, dark girl of about eighteen, wearing a poppy-red dress, rose from the divan where she had been sitting in an attitude of formal expectancy, and shyly shook hands. She was our hostess. Although she had not left school for long, she was too timid to exercise her knowledge of English; but now and then she would contribute the words "yes" or "no" to the conversation, which we greeted with polite applause until she cast down her eyes and turned as red as her dress.

A servant brought in a tray of tea, English biscuits, oranges and sweet limes.

We sat talking of the Shias whom they, as Christians, deplored as dangerous and fanatical persons, and they told me of the physical mortification endured by the sect every year during Muharram. The body-beaters, which we should see passing down the street that night, were the commonest of the flagellants. Every night for ten nights they would march from one mosque to another, beating themselves. There were others who scourged themselves on the back with chains. The most savage mortification was the head-cutting which takes place on the morning of the tenth day of Muharram.

My host had seen this at Najaf and also in Baghdad. He told me that all kinds of people took part in it, but the Turcomans were the most violent performers, sometimes slashing too hard and killing themselves. There were several men in the Government office in which he worked who occasionally got a day's leave to join the head-cutting procession.

I asked my host to tell me how the head-cutting is done. He said that a band of men, who for days have been dwelling on the gory emotionalism they are about to enjoy, would gather at the mosque.

"In Karbala or Najaf," he said, "you can see these men for days whispering to the swords which they carry about in their arms, polishing and sharpening them."

Arriving at the mosque, they form a circle and revolve round a leader, working themselves into a state of emotional excitement by uttering the names of Ali, Hasan, and Husein, until, suddenly, the leader gives a great cry and brings down his sword on his head. As soon as the others see the blood they go mad. With cries and shouts of "Husein!," "Ali!," "Hasan!," they cut their heads until their white robes are stained everywhere with blood.

They then go off together in twos and parade the town, cutting and slashing until the blood falls in the gutter and spurts on the walls of the houses. Spectators, hearing the cries and the sound of the swords on skulls, and seeing the streaming blood, begin to cry and give the mourning wail, and sometimes people who have nothing to do with the orgy lose all control, and pulling out penknives or scissors begin to stab at their arms and wrists until the blood flows.

While he was describing this, we heard, far off, a dull, rhythmic sound.

"They are coming!" said my host. "We must go up."

He led the way up a flight of stairs to a little bedroom overlooking the street. Someone switched on the light, but he turned it off at once, asking if I minded sitting in the dark. It was better, he said, not to attract attention to ourselves. As the room protruded for a yard or so into the lane, sitting in the window was rather like being in a box at a theatre. I could have touched with a cane the head of anyone passing below. The buildings rose dark and mysterious, and the lane twisted away out of sight, merging itself into another as dark, as narrow, probably as serpentine. The only light came from a booth let into the opposite wall, where an old man sat cross-legged among a chaotic assembly of cigarettes and tobacco. I was aware of something pleasantly adventurous and exciting in sitting concealed in the dark, watching the shrouded figures in the lane below, the customers suddenly appearing in the glow of the booth and going off again into the darkness. At intervals, growing gradually nearer, came a queer sound, as if a thousand nurses, taking their time from the matron, were delivering in rhythmic chastisement a thousand resounding smacks on the posteriors of a thousand children. But as it came nearer, we heard the fierce, grief-stricken background of this sound—the sound of men groaning, crying, and shouting. Their noise then became horrible. There came into view, swaying down the lane, the strangest procession I have ever seen. Boys and young men came first, holding banners which, with true Eastern inconsequence, slanted this way and that. Behind them were men bearing on their shoulders the poles of palanquins on which rested boat-shaped clusters of lights. The dark lane now blazed with the moving orange glow of paraffin flares. Behind these lights, eight abreast, came rank after rank of men naked to the waist, the sweat of their austerities clammy on their faces and shining on their brown bodies. They were like a regiment of half-naked soldiers marching as captives to their doom. Each company was preceded by a leader, and above each company one of the strange, barbaric boats swayed in the smoke and yellow light. The companies halted every few yards and the leaders faced them, crying out: "Husein!" A deep, agonized wail immediately rose from hundreds of voices. "Hasan!" Another wail. Then in a rhythmic Arabic chant the whole company would shout:

"Welcome, O Husein,
When you enter Karbala."

At the beat of each word the men lifted their arms in unison and brought them smack against their naked chests. Some chests were bleeding, a revolting sight; others were swollen with weals which would soon become wounds; and as they beat themselves, their eyes gazed fixedly ahead from faces pale and terrible in the torchlight, like the faces of martyrs on their way to the stake.

Their soldierly bearing, the perfect rhythm of their arms, the timed responses, their implicit obedience to their leaders, were a contrast to the disorder of the dipping banners and swaying boats. These breast-beaters were like men transfigured in some sorrowful dream, and in their fanatical eyes was something of the anguish of Husein, parched and wounded on the plain of Karbala.

As I looked at these hundreds of faces, men old and young, men with hairy chests of bulls, men smooth and slender, men with beards, and others with the clean-shaven faces of boys, I wondered why human beings behave like this for the good of their souls, and from what dark jungle of antiquity had such spectacles their beginning.

Surely this beating of the body, and the cutting with knives, was the sight that Elisha saw on Carmel, when the priests of Baal "cried aloud, and cut themselves after their manner with knives and lancets, till the blood gushed out upon them." A writer of one of the books of the Old Testament might have called this strange, savage sorrow for the death of Husein one of the last sins of Babylon. As I looked at the faces and wounded bodies, and the sailing tabernacles of light, I felt that I was watching something which had happened long ago in this country, when the altars of Baal and Ashtoreth were smoking on the ziggurats.

About a thousand men passed by, and the sight of their red-dened torsos and the sound of their chant became monotonous, for each group was in every way like its predecessor. Now and again an added vigour was given to the breast-beating when women standing in the street or gazing from behind latticed windows would set up the twittering funeral cry, and at the sound men would beat themselves with renewed frenzy.

The last group disappeared down the lane, and I felt that never in my life should I forget the "lil-hala, lil-hala," of their wailing chant which had sung itself into my brain. I rose to go. My host switched on the light and said that it would not be wise to venture into the streets until the Shias had reached their mosque. These kind people produced more tea, more biscuits and sweet limes; and with the clock nearly at midnight, I went through the now silent lanes back to my bed.

CHAPTER III

I go to Babylon and see the ruins of Nebuchadnezzar's city. I make a journey to Ur of the Chaldees and walk the streets of the city in which Abraham was born. I cross the desert again and pass south through Syria and Palestine into Egypt.

I

AMONG the most incongruous acts of my life is the journey I made in a taxi-cab to Babylon. The Baghdad driver is unaware of any conflict in association between his cab and Babylon, and he often pulls up at the curb and suggests that you might like to take a taxi there at a specially cut price.

The ruins are sixty miles south of Baghdad, and the journey takes three to four hours. The road begins well enough, but soon becomes rough and uneven. I knew we were drawing near when we crossed a single railway track running over the sand, and I saw a notice-board bearing, in English and Arabic, the words: "Babylon. Halt."

I have read books which have described the humiliations visited by Time upon what was once the mightiest city in the world, but this notice-board translated them into the idiom of our own civilization. That "the glory of kingdoms, the beauty of the Chaldee's excellency" should be known as a "halt," a place which even local trains pass with a derisive whistle, seemed to me as bitter as anything prophesied by Isaiah.

As we went on, I saw on every side sandy mounds lying in the sunlight of mid-day: some were large enough to be called hills, others were low ridges, and still more were only uneasy risings and fallings of the earth. But for miles around, wherever this astonishing ruin lay, the earth was blasted and unhappy with the memory of Babylon. So this was the city whose Hanging Gardens were among the Seven Wonders of the World.

72

Four-horsed chariots could pass each other on its walls; on one altar alone a thousand talents' worth of incense was burned every year. I looked at it in astonishment, remembering the words of a man who had tried to dissuade me from going to Babylon: "There is nothing to see," he had told me. "You will be sorry if you go."

But even before I left the car, I thought I had never seen anything more impressive and more terrible. As for there being "nothing to see," I doubt whether there is any place in the world in which the imagination can see more.

I climbed a sandy hill in which are embedded the impressive remains discovered by German archæologists from 1899 to 1917. At first it is difficult to understand them, for you see acre upon acre of brown mud brick walls, broken vaulting, and the lower storys and cellars of buildings lying in such confusion that only a trained architect could sort them out with any certainty. Palace and hovel, wall and roadway, are equally humbled in this post mortem. But one section of the ruins still stands in unmistakable splendour: the great Ishtar Gate of Babylon built by Nebuchadnezzar. Its towers rise to a height of forty feet, and its mud bricks bear the impression in high relief of a hundred and fifty-two animals, almost life size, alternate rows of bulls and dragons, once brilliantly enamelled, but now bared to the mud from which they were moulded.

What a fortunate discovery this was! Nothing looks drearier than mud bricks all the same shape, dull in colour, crumbling and already returning to the dust whence they came. Even uncarved stone has a quality and a beauty which are absent from mud. And as I looked at these acres covered with Babylonian bricks, I wondered if the buildings in this land were really as beautiful as we have been told they were. But the survival of the bulls and the dragons on the Ishtar Gate leave no doubt. The bulls stride forward with the grace and spirit of young horses, clipped like French poodles. Their hair from head to tail along the back, round the jaw, under the belly, down the chest, and curving round the haunches, was arranged in fringes of tight little curls, in which jewels or beads may have been tied. What superb animals they are; not massive and heavy like the Egyptian Apis, nor fantastic and half-human like the Assyrian bull, but proud, vigorous, young creatures, striding forward into the morning and capable of taking a five-barred gate. I think the bulls of the Ishtar Gate are the finest surviving examples of Babylonian art.

Their companions, the dragons or "sirrush," are equally well done, but they are not so appealing because they represent no known animal. They may have been put there to frighten Medes and Persians. The "sirrush" is really a compromise between a serpent, a lynx, and an eagle: the head, body, and tail are those of a scaly snake, the forelegs are those of a lynx, and the hind legs, which end in talons, might be those of any large bird of prey.

The "sirrush" is pictured on many other Babylonian works of art. Professor Koldewey, who discovered the Ishtar Gate, thinks it possible that the priests kept some strange reptilian creature in the darkness of a temple and exhibited it as a living "sirrush." If this is so, it lends colour to the story of Daniel and the Dragon, which appears in many forms but is not printed in the *Book of Daniel*. The story is that Daniel refused to worship a dragon in Babylon and offered to slay the creature single-handed. He was therefore placed in the animal's den, presumably in the belief that he would never emerge from it; but he took with him a potent pill, composed chiefly of hair and bitumen, which he persuaded the dragon to swallow. The poor "sirrush" then died; some accounts say that it blew up.

From the top of the mound you look down over the basements and the brick vaulting of Nebuchadnezzar's Palace. And how hard it is to realize that those incoherent masses of building material near by are all that remain of the Hanging Gardens, or

THE ISHTAR GATE, BABYLON

that the mark like the shadow of a broad road losing itself round Babylon is the line of the mighty walls which once astonished all who saw them.

The flat country stretches to the sky, featureless, bare, and arid, except to the west, where the Euphrates flows in a narrow belt of palm trees. You see no river, but you see this line of foliage running for miles, like a green snake on the sand. Even the "waters of Babylon" have deserted the city, for in ancient times the river ran along the west side of the Kasr, bringing with it the happy sound of water and trees and flowers. As if obeying a command that no touch of life should remain anywhere near Babylon, the Euphrates has carved a new channel for itself and has departed, taking all life with it.

While I stood on the summit of the ruins, an Arab approached and told me that he had worked there with Professor Koldewey. His name was Umran Hamed, "the guide of Babylon." He was a good fellow, and he had absorbed a quantity of accurate information from the German archæologists, which he was tireless in imparting. We walked about the ruins and he pointed out many things which I should have missed without him.

He showed me the vestiges of three wells in the foundations of the Hanging Gardens, and a chamber which he said was a "refrigerator." As he had just confused the word partridge with cartridge, I wondered whether he had got this right.

"Yes; where food was kept cold in snow," he said earnestly.

"Have you ever seen a refrigerator?"

"No, sir," he replied, "but I have heard the Germans talking."

So if Umran overheard correctly, perhaps the lower stages of the Hanging Gardens were stored with cold foods, iced sherbets, and other cool things for the Median princess for whose pleasure Nebuchadnezzar made these gardens. It is believed that in this flat land she became homesick for her native mountains, just as the Jews must have done, and to please her the

King ordered the construction of an artificial mountain terraced with gardens. The word "hanging" is not a good description of these gardens. The Greek word is *kremastos*, which
was used in ancient Greek for a man hanged and is used in modern Greek for a suspension bridge.

It is certain that the Hanging Gardens were as solidly anchored to the earth as a pyramid. Like everything else in Babylonia, they were built of mud brick and constructed like a pyramid, or ziggurat, rather like the Mappin Terraces at the Zoo.
Water was pumped up from the wells in the foundations to irri-
gate the gardens. Each series of terraces was planted with trees
and flowers, and artificial water-courses may have run musi-
cally here and there. In this lovely botanical garden the princess
wandered—longing, perhaps, for a piece of real rock. One
hopes that Nebuchadnezzar's manly attempt to compensate a
lady for a change of scenery was a success. No man, certainly,
could have done more; but history, and even the lives of humble men, suggest that such gigantic gestures are not always the
most acceptable. Perhaps beneath the troubled bones of Babylon there lies a tablet which records how the maid of the mountains received this proof of the King's affection, when, after
many months of labour and laborious rock-gardening, Nebuchadnezzar led her forth.

"Do you call that a garden? Why, it isn't even a hill!"

I asked Umran what he thought the Hanging Gardens were
like. He smiled rapturously and replied:

"Like the gardens of Paradise."

He led me to a convulsion in the earth such as you see behind
a scaffolding in the City of London when a large building has
been pulled down. It was the site of the great ziggurat of Babylon, the temple tower called E-temen-an-ki, which archæologists say was the traditional Tower of Babel. It was evidently
a ziggurat of typical Babylonian form, rising by a series of
stages sufficiently high above the dusty plain to give astrono-

mers an uninterrupted view of the sky. On the topmost stage was a temple, which Herodotus said contained only a table and a couch which was occupied at night by a single woman chosen by the deity out of all the women in the land. It has been proved by inscriptions that this temple and its high tower go back to the first age of Babylon, and that it was reconstructed from time to time by various kings.

We came to a series of broken arches which once supported the banqueting-hall of Nebuchadnezzar. This was the hall where, according to the *Book of Daniel*, Belshazzar saw the writing on the wall.

And as we wandered over the lonely mounds, silent except for the hum of the wild bee and the hornet, I thought how literally Isaiah's prophecy of the fall of Babylon had been fulfilled. It is, indeed, overthrown as God overthrew Sodom and Gomorrah.

"It shall never be inhabited, neither shall it be dwelt in from generation to generation: neither shall the Arabian pitch tent there; neither shall the shepherds make their fold there. But wild beasts of the desert shall lie there; and their houses shall be full of doleful creatures: and owls shall dwell there, and satyrs shall dance there. And the wild beasts of the islands shall cry in their desolate houses, and dragons in their pleasant palaces. . . ."

The "broad walls" of Babylon have been "utterly broken," as Jeremiah prophesied; her gates have been "burned with fire"; the city has indeed become "an astonishment" and "an hissing without an inhabitant." The words of Jeremiah have become literally true; the city is in "heaps." What word better describes this awful desolation: "And Babylon shall become heaps."

Isaiah prophesied that among the haunters of the ruins would be the *kippôd*, a Hebrew word which has puzzled translators of the Bible. In the Authorized Version it is translated as "bittern"; in the Revised Version it has been altered to "porcupine." I drew an admirable porcupine in my note-book and asked Umran if he had seen anything like it in the ruins.

His face lit up with recognition at once.

"Ah, yes," he said, "it is the *kunfudh*. It is shy and comes in the night."

I saw no porcupines, jackals, serpents, owls, or any of the prophet's fauna, but I saw a creature that was not mentioned—a hare. He was the only living creature we disturbed all the time we were walking about the ruins. We put him up not far from Nebuchadnezzar's banqueting-hall.

"Look," cried Umran, " *'Arnabeh!*"

And a big hare sprang up and went off across the centre of the city.

When we returned to the Ishtar Gate, Umran pointed out the site of the "den" in which Daniel is said to have survived his ordeal with the lions. It is probable that lions were kept in the moat round the Ishtar Gate, and when Professor Koldewey began his excavations, he discovered thousands of coloured tiles at this place. When put together, these tiles formed lions, some with white bodies and yellow manes, and others with yellow bodies and red manes. He thought that about a hundred and twenty lions must have guarded the main gate of Babylon.

Among the most interesting things to be seen in Babylon are bricks still stuck together with asphalt instead of mortar, exactly as Herodotus described them. He was in Babylon about a century after its fall, when it was still the greatest city in the world, although some of the buildings had been torn down. Possibly the punishment it had received from Xerxes gave the builders plenty to do, so that Herodotus may often have watched the asphalt gangs at work with their trolleys of boiling pitch.

The method of building was to lay a thin film of hot asphalt between each row of bricks; and bricks cemented in this way are so firm that they have to be broken apart with a pick-axe. Every now and then a layer of reeds would be inserted, and you can see their clear impression in the asphalt, in places where the reeds have rotted away. Supplies of asphalt were available, says Herodotus, at Hit, about seventy miles west-north-west of Baghdad, a town which even to-day smells horribly of sulphurated hydrogen, and has two asphalt wells, one hot and the other cold, within thirty feet of one another. Asphalt is, of course, found all over the Persian oilfields, and also round about Mosul.

In ancient times writers from the West were invariably surprised and interested by the bricks and asphalt, which they regarded as a Babylonian characteristic, as indeed it was. The Tower of Babel was constructed of mud brick and asphalt, a word translated in the Bible as "slime." What better account of a Babylonian building operation could we have than the verse in *Genesis* which describes the building of the ziggurat of Babel:

"And they said, Go to, let us make brick, and burn them thoroughly. And they had brick for stone, and slime had they for mortar."

The Ark received a coat of asphalt outside and inside; and this is still given by the natives of Irak to the boats and barges which sail on the Tigris and the Euphrates to-day.

2

It is more interesting to the Bible student that the excavated ruins in Babylon are nearly all of the time of the Jewish Captivity. If you see an inscribed brick still in position in the walls of Babylon—and there are still many such—you may be almost sure that it bears the name of Nebuchadnezzar.

I suppose everyone who has visited Babylon says to himself the opening words of that exquisite psalm:

By the rivers of Babylon,
There we sat down, yea, we wept,

When we remembered Zion.
We hanged our harps
Upon the willows in the midst thereof.

No misfortune in history has produced a greater literature than the Exile, and never has the emotion of home-sickness been so surely and beautifully expressed. I had brought a Bible with me, and I turned here and there to the pages of Isaiah, Jeremiah, and that hero of the captivity, Ezekiel, who between them have preserved, as nowhere else is preserved, the atmosphere of a doomed city of the early world. What burning, living words they are! The story is bitter with the salt of tears and burning with a fire of anger and contempt. As long as the words of these men live, the dust of the Egyptian chariot-wheels is suspended in the air, the Assyrian archers stand with bent bows, and Babylonian rams are lifted against the walls. They do not write calmly, like Greek historians, but wildly, like men shouting from a street corner, and there is a rise and fall of their voices which at times drops to tears and at others lifts itself into a scream. There are many beautiful and heart-rending incidents in ancient literature, but never, I think, have men handed to another age such an impression of frenzied emotion, such hope, and such blistering hatred.

The modern world had already been born when the prophets were hailing the downfall of the great oriental empires— Nahum shouting the death of Assyria, Isaiah prematurely killing Egypt, and Ezekiel exulting over the death of Babylon. Greek ships and Greek soldiers were serving with the Egyptian army as it marched into Syria under the Pharaoh Necho. The poet Alcæus had a brother named Antimenidas, who took service under Nebuchadnezzar; he was present at the destruction of Jerusalem in 586 B.C., and probably saw the second batch of Jewish exiles carried off to Babylon. When Babylon fell in 539 B.C., and the Exile was over, there were men alive who were destined to fight at the battle of Marathon.

The Jews were not taken into Babylon all at once, but in three groups, over a period of sixteen years, and the longest term of captivity was about sixty years. Therefore it is possible that Daniel may have entered Babylon as a young boy, have lived there throughout the Exile, and, as an old man, have seen his people receive permission to return to Jerusalem. The Jews were not the only people taken into captivity in this age, for it was the custom at that time to deport whole populations and give the land to other settlers; but they are the only exiles who retained their racial and religious identity.

There was good reason why Nebuchadnezzar should have deported them. Long before his time it had been the policy of the Egyptians to interpose a barrier of rebellious and unfriendly states between themselves and Assyria, and, when Assyria fell, against its successor Babylon.

Before he became king, Nebuchadnezzar was obliged to march an army south to purge Syria of Egyptian influence, and had his father not died as he was nearing Egypt, it is probable that he would have marched on into the Delta. As it was, Nebuchadnezzar hastily concluded an armistice with Egypt by which he retained sovereignty of the Syrian states, and, taking with him a squadron of light cavalry, returned swiftly to Babylon to make sure of his inheritance.

Hardly was his back turned than Egyptian agents continued their propaganda among the tribute people of Syria, who were ready, like all debtors, to think the worst of the creditor. Judah, a small state torn by faction and rebellion, was all too willing to intrigue. The Jews were divided into two parties: the nationalist pro-Egyptian, anti-priest party, which talked of casting off the Babylonian yoke, and the priestly party, which viewed the impending disasters as the just vengeance of God for the sins of His chosen people. God had made Assyria the scourge of His wrath when the Ten Tribes of Israel had been taken away into

Assyria a hundred and thirty years previously. He would again place the whip in the hands of Babylon and chastise Judah in the same way. That was the message of the prophets.

As we read the prophets, we must admit that the list of Jewish sins is a hair-raising catalogue of transgression. The Jews had lapsed into all manner of vice and paganism. Incense was burned to Baal every morning on the house-tops, and Jehovah's Temple was the scene of secret rites which may have been borrowed from Egypt. The priests of Moloch lit their fires in the Vale of Hinnom, and false gods were set up everywhere. Through the chaos of the times the prophets strode, proclaiming the coming vengeance; and in the palace the King, his Court officials, and his officers whispered with Egyptian envoys.

Nebuchadnezzar's intelligence department was well chosen, for the great King seems to have heard of plots in good time to take action. There is ample evidence that he was a man of a kindly, patient nature: Judah would never have received the same consideration from the fierce Assyrians. Nebuchadnezzar's warnings had no effect, however, on the factions in Jerusalem, and in 597 B.C. he set out with an army to call Judah to order. It was the approach of this army, with its Chaldean and Babylonian infantry, its notoriously fierce Scythian and Median cavalry, and its strangely armoured Greek mercenaries, that inspired the prophet Habakkuk to one of those utterances which, though splendid as prose, must have been intensely nerve-wracking to an already overwrought population:

"They are terrible and dreadful," he cried, "their judgment and their dignity shall proceed from themselves. Their horses also are swifter than the leopards, and are more fierce than the evening wolves: and their horsemen shall spread themselves, and their horsemen shall come from afar: they shall fly as the eagle that hasteth to eat. They shall come all for violence: their faces shall sup up as the east wind, and they shall gather the captivity as the sand."

But when the Babylonian armies came before Jerusalem the Jewish King, Jehoiakim, lay dead within the walls, and his eighteen year old son reigned instead. Realizing the futility of opposing Nebuchadnezzar, the young King and his mother, accompanied by the high officials and officers of state, the ministers and the eunuchs, came out and prostrated themselves before the King, who dealt with them not at all in the manner of an oriental despot. Men had been blinded, made dumb, and crucified for lesser crimes than the Jewish sedition. But Nebuchadnezzar contented himself by sending the royal family, the Court officials, the leading army officers, and all the best artisans into exile in Babylon. Among this first group of exiles was the prophet Ezekiel. After appointing the twenty-one year old Zedekiah to be king—Judah's last king—Nebuchadnezzar marched his armies home.

Jerusalem was not destroyed and the bulk of her population was undisturbed; and so it might have remained had the Jews not stubbornly resumed their intrigues with Egypt. Young Zedekiah, a weak, amiable noble, who in less dangerous times might have made an ideal monarch, lacked the firmness necessary to stand out against the violently nationalist court faction. Jeremiah could see the futility of further revolt, and did everything in his power to save his countrymen from rushing on disaster.

"Serve the king of Babylon and live," he cried, "wherefore should this city be laid waste?"

Hissed, shunned, and imprisoned as a pacifist and pro-Babylonian, he still continued his warnings. There were some who said that the Exile would be a short affair and that the exiles would soon be home again. In order to stamp out this belief and to prepare Judah for her ordeal, Jeremiah wrote to the exiles, telling them to settle down in Babylon:

"Build ye houses and dwell in them; and plant gardens and eat the fruit of them; take ye wives and beget sons, and give your daughters to husbands, that they may be increased there, and not diminished. And seek the peace of the city whither I have caused you to be carried away captives. . . ."

He turned to his own people in Jerusalem and prophesied the new woes that would fall upon them for their sins. His words were unheeded, and Nebuchadnezzar, seeing that the Jews despised his former clemency, determined no longer to deal gently with them.

It was 586 B.C., eleven years after the first captives had been taken to Babylon. Zedekiah had allowed Jerusalem to become a centre for the plotting of the discontented neighbouring states, Tyre and Sidon, Moab and Ammon. A revolt was planned, probably under the general direction of Egypt, from which at the last moment Edom, Moab, and the Philistines retired. But Judah, Tyre, and Ammon held firm.

When Nebuchadnezzar came south, he was faced by three enemies, with, of course, the shadow of the real enemy, Egypt, always in the background. Ezekiel, who was in Babylon and had heard the story from the Babylonian side, gives us a glimpse of the great King halting by the Orontes and wondering which of his enemies to attack first. He used divination by arrows, and sought an augury by gazing into the liver of an animal. Then remaining behind with a reserve force, he launched two armies, one against Tyre and the other against Jerusalem. Rock inscriptions cut by the army sent against Tyre are still to be seen below the gorge at Nahr-el-Kalb, near Beyrout.

After a siege of eighteen months, the Babylonian battering-rams made a breach in the mighty wall of Jerusalem, and the city, which had been defended with gallantry, though with frenzied discord, was entered by the armies. This time Nebuchadnezzar showed small mercy. He levelled the walls, destroyed the Temple, laid waste the city, put out the eyes of Zedekiah, slew his sons, and sent the King with all the nobles in chains to Babylon. This was the second group of exiles.

A population still remained under a Governor, Gedaliah, and among them was the prophet Jeremiah, who had been singled out by Nebuchadnezzar for special treatment. Had the King heard, one wonders, those impassioned pleadings, so well known to us, in which Jeremiah begged his countrymen to respect the power of their masters? Surely we can have no doubt about it. And, having read them, Nebuchadnezzar recognized in the prophet one who, from entirely unworldly motives, was an unexpected ally. Therefore the King himself gave orders that Jeremiah was to be offered the choice of going to Babylon or of remaining in the ruined city. "All the land is before thee, whither it seemeth good and convenient for thee to go, thither go," he was told. And Jeremiah elected to stay in Judah. He saw with despair how even the Jews left behind continued to plot and rebel until, having murdered the Governor and allied themselves with the Moabites, the Babylonians again descended on them and made a third deportation. From far off in Babylon a warning cry came from Ezekiel condemning the rebels pitilessly, for the full time of retribution was not yet. But the rebels answered that they would fight on and continue to burn incense to the Queen of Heaven. In the last moments of the expiring state, Jeremiah retired into Egypt.

But what happened to the Jews during their exile in Babylon? How did they employ themselves? Were they all weeping on the river banks, or was there another side to the picture? That a brighter side existed is proved by the reluctance shown by the Jews to return and rebuild Zion when the captivity was over. They were not poor slaves as their ancestors had been in Egypt. No one compelled them to make bricks, although they were in the greatest brick-making country on earth. We can be sure that had they been oppressed, we should have been told about it by the prophets. That there was hardship, and that the various groups of exiles received different treatment, some good and some bad, goes without saying. The prophet known as the second Isaiah, who detested Babylon, mentions that the Babylonians showed no mercy and that upon the aged the yoke was heavy, which suggests that perhaps some were forced, regardless of age, to labour on the canals and dykes, or to engage in the hard work that is always going on in an artificially irrigated country. On the other hand, there is no hint of oppression in Ezekiel's description of the land of exile as "a land of traffick," "a city of merchants," "a fruitful field" into which a colony was transplanted like a willow beside many waters. For Jeremiah, who was a realist, would not have written from Jerusalem to tell the exiles to settle down, plant gardens, and eat the fruit thereof unless this comfortable life had been possible.

The immense city of Babylon, with its fertile country, its hordes of officials, its bankers, its markets, its quays, and its countless industries, offered the quick-witted Jews thousands of opportunities for getting on in the world. It was no doubt in Babylon that the Jew first went into business.

Was the wealthy and old-established firm of Egibi, which for generations handled the financial business of the Babylonian court, a Hebrew firm, one wonders? Hundreds of clay tablets recording their banking and mercantile transactions have been found in the ruins of Babylon, and are now in the British Museum. It has been pointed out that Egibi is Babylonian for Jacob, and it has been suggested that the founder of the firm may have been a member of one of the lost Ten Tribes who, having found his way to Babylon from Assyria, set up in business and prospered. Many of the tablets record the lending of money at 20 per cent. interest, so that Egibi and Company had obviously cast over any old-fashioned Hebrew prejudice against usury. It is interesting, too, that although the name of the firm remained Egibi (Jacob and Company), all the members of the family had taken Babylonian names such as Itti-Marduk-balâtu and Marduk-nasir-aplu, which incorporate the name of the local diety in an encouraging and disarming manner, much in the same way, perhaps, as many a Jew has been known to consider Mackintosh a better trade name than Cohen.

The house of Egibi was evidently an organization that managed estates, sold land and house-property, dealt in slaves and palm-groves, and was ready to lend anything from onions to shekels of silver. Even if the firm observed a chilling attitude to their brethren from Judah, which as members of Israel they may well have done, there can be little doubt that their success must have fired the exiles with ambition and have opened up new and glorious horizons.

But for the presence of a small group of religious men whose splendid vision and high faith in the future shone bright in exile, the Jews might have been lost among their conquerors. First among the teachers was Ezekiel, whose house at Tel-Abib, "the Cornhill," was the meeting-place of those who were building a new Judah. Ezekiel, while he welcomed the Exile as his nation's second chance, lived in the future, with a complete programme for the new state in his mind; a theocratic state with the Temple of the Lord, and not the King's palace, as its centre and core. Ezekiel is interesting also because, as he went from house to house preaching, prophesying, and laying down the rough draft of the New Jerusalem, he not only for the first time developed the conception of the Good Shepherd who tenderly cares for his fold, but for the first time in the history of religion exhibited a care of souls which almost reminds one of St. Paul.

"As a shepherd seeketh out his flock in the day that he is among his sheep that are scattered, so will I seek out my sheep, and will deliver them out of all places where they have been scattered in the cloudy and dark day. . . . I will feed my flock, and I will cause them to lie down, saith the Lord God."

With these words of Ezekiel, written in Babylon, we seem to have entered the New Testament. Another great prophet, perhaps the greatest of all, was the unknown writer of chapters xl–lv of *Isaiah*—a prophet called the Second Isaiah—whose whole heart was set upon a return to Jerusalem.

In the literary atmosphere of the great city, where scribes were numerous and accounts of even the most casual daily transactions were committed to clay tablets, stored, and docketed in vast libraries, it is natural that those who believed in the future of Judaism should have written and edited the history of their nation. Many of the books of the Old Testament, as we have them in the Bible to-day, date from this period. Thus the literary work of the Exile kept alive the religious and national spirit, and helped the God-fearing among the captives to possess their souls in humility and patience and to bring up their children in righteousness. In this way was Judaism born, preserved, and eventually sent forth into the world. The history of the Children of Israel had ended: the history of the Jews had begun.

At the end of their sixty years' nominal captivity, the Jews were to witness an event which is often misinterpreted and is always known misleadingly as the "Fall of Babylon." After Nebuchadnezzar's death the crown passed swiftly from head to head, coming at last to Nabonid or Nabonidus, who was literally a devout antiquary. He spent his time digging up ruined temples and inquiring into ancient cults. There is something pathetic in the thought of this monarch attempting to bring the past of his country to light, while all the time the future was rising to overwhelm him. He made the fatal mistake of introducing into Babylon another band of exiles, the gods of Babylonia. He gathered them from all parts and centralized worship in Babylon. They were expensive guests, and funds had to be diverted from the normal ecclesiastical endowments for their upkeep. Thus the priests of Babylon were angry, and the people from whom the exiled gods had been wrenched considered themselves unrepresented in heaven. So the reign of

Nabonid holds a warning to all antiquaries and archæologists who may feel inclined to introduce their harmless passions into public life. This King eventually locked himself up with his studies in a palace at Teima, and may even have abdicated in favour of his son, Belshazzar, whose hands, it seems, held the government of Babylon.

The great power now rising in the world, Persia, was hailed by Babylonians and Jews alike as their deliverer from archæological monarchy. Cyrus the king was only too ready to act the part, and he marched on Babylon. It will probably never be known how Babylon fell. The *Book of Daniel*, which describes the last night in Babylon and the writing on the wall, is now generally admitted to have been written two centuries after to encourage the Maccabees against the Seleucids, and to have had more religious significance than historical accuracy. It is not counted among the prophetical books in the Hebrew scriptures, neither do its facts agree with those in the genuine literature of the Exile.

What is clear from history is that when Babylon fell, all the horrible details of its fall, as prophesied by the Second Isaiah and Jeremiah, were unrealized. The capture of Babylon by Cyrus was as calm as Mussolini's march on Rome. Thus the "Fall of Babylon," which sometimes creates in the mind a vision of burning houses, falling ramparts, and dead bodies, was merely a peaceful change of dynasty.

The prophets had sung of children dashed to pieces before their parents' eyes, of houses sacked, of men cut down like animals in a shambles, of fountains dried up in the heat of the conflagration. Even the most lovely of the exilic psalms, which begins "By the rivers of Babylon," concludes with the horrible words:

"Happy shall he be that taketh and dasheth thy little ones against the stones."

But the sack of Babylon, so eagerly anticipated by the Jewish prophets, never took place. Instead, the Persian armies entered the city in the year 539 B.C. without striking a blow and with orders to respect property and to do nothing likely to offend the populace. "Babylon is fallen and destroyed, howl for her!" Jeremiah had shrieked before the event, but there was nothing to howl about, because Babylon seemed delighted with her fall. The nations were indeed astonished, as the prophets had said, but not by the fall of Babylon, but because Babylon, with the finest defences and the greatest city walls in the world, had fallen without striking a blow.

Entering the city a fortnight after his army, Cyrus presented that sight rare in history, the conqueror turned philanthropist. Instead of knocking down the walls, he rebuilt them, and made necessary improvements and restorations to temples and public buildings. He sent the exiled gods back to their empty shrines and told the Jews, to their surprise and consternation, that they were free to go home. A close reading of the Second Isaiah, and of the books of *Haggai* and *Nehemiah*, combined with the irrefutable evidence of the great strength of Babylonian Jewry in Hellenistic and later times, proves that only a small number of exiles were willing to uproot themselves from Babylon in order to rebuild the National Home.

"Now that they were free to go, they discovered that they were well off in Babylon," wrote Maspero in *The Passing of the Empires*. "They would have to give up their houses, their fields, their business, their habits of indifference to politics, and brave the dangers of a caravan journey of three or four months' duration, finally encamping in the midst of ruins in an impoverished country, surrounded by hostile and jealous neighbours—such a prospect was not likely to find favour with many, and indeed it was only the priests, the Levites, and the more ardent of the lower classes who welcomed the idea of a return with a touching fervour."

It was therefore a pathetically small contingent that set out with Sheshbazzar two years after the end of the Exile, and something like twenty years was to pass before the Temple was again built on Zion. Meanwhile the Babylonian Jews increased in numbers, in power, and in wealth. Though they had declined to go home, they yet regarded the Temple in Jerusalem as their spiritual home, and never failed to contribute to its upkeep. At the head of the Jewish community in Babylon there lived a shadowy king of the Jews, a prince of the house of David, whose title was "Prince of the Captivity"—the Resch-Glutha. This potentate kept his own bodyguard, his ministers, his court officials, and appeared in public clothed in gold tissue and accompanied by the officers of his guard. He was famous for his hospitality and the splendour of his entertainments. When Babylon died, Seleucia inherited her fame, and from Seleucia it passed to Baghdad. Here in the time of the Caliphs the Prince of the Captivity still held his court, and he, in whom we see the last reflection of Solomon's glory, was still reigning over Babylonian Jewry in the Twelfth Century A.D.

I left Babylon, its lonely, silent mounds, its cavernous ruins, and its dusty, chocolate bricks, with the thought that though the prophets may not have seen the expected desolation of this city, still their words came true; for time is always on the side of prophets.

At Hillah, in a feathery gloom of palm-gardens on the banks of the Euphrates, I saw life passing on its leisurely way as it has done in the Land of the Two Rivers since the beginning of history. It was pleasant and cool in those green groves. The hot, white world outside was held at bay by a stockade of hairy palm-trunks, and overhead the fan-like branches met and mingled, and through the quietness and the shadows the Euphrates flowed south towards the Persian Gulf.

Men and women moved lazily in the shadows, always down to the life-giving river, always taking up water in great pots and petrol tins. That is the story of this country: men taking up water from the river and putting it on the land. Not far away a sound like muted bagpipes told me that a *djird* was working. Beneath a vast mulberry tree an ox was slowly moving, lifting from a canal a dripping leather bag of water that tipped itself wastefully into the irrigation channel and then descended, by means of machinery as effective yet as clumsy as a loom, to continue this slow, laborious work. I am sure the *djird* has not changed since the days of Nebuchadnezzar. It has the look of an old and wheezy inhabitant on whom progress and the march of events have had no effect whatsoever. Indeed, you might imagine that the *djirds*, answering one another in different tones from grove to grove all along the Euphrates, are the voices of this ancient land.

Here, too, I saw a strange coracle called a *gufa*, which I believe Noah would have rejected as primitive and old-fashioned. It is a round basket capable of holding about twenty people— some *gufas* are big enough to carry sheep and horses—and made water-tight with a coat of bitumen. I promised myself that I would go to the British Museum and look for *gufas* in the Assyrian and Babylonian rooms, for I am sure that these boats must have existed on the Euphrates since prehistoric times. The *gufachi* paddles his black bowl with skill along the banks, prodding his way with an oar; and he is always jumping out to tow it, then leaping in again to resume his voyage.

While I watched the *gufa*, three women in black came softly through the green shadows with jars on their shoulders. Before they filled them, they lifted their veils, thinking that no man was near, and stood talking for a moment "by the rivers of Babylon." When I hear that psalm, I shall always remember the little group standing on the edge of the Euphrates, three women in deep black, the blue sky above palm fronds, and the running water.

I should like to have remained longer at Hillah, for in his

book, *By Nile and Tigris*, the late Sir Ernest Wallis Budge says that "the Jews of Hillah are undoubtedly the descendants of those who migrated thither from that part of Babylon which was inhabited till the tenth century of our era, and for many generations past they have occupied themselves with the trade in antiquities." There is a savage irony, which would, I am sure, have recommended itself to Jeremiah, in the thought of buying a bit of Babylon from a descendant of the exiles.

3

At 8.30 every morning King Ghazi, the late King Feisal's son, drives to his office from his modest palace on the west bank of the Tigris. He goes across the Maude Bridge and along Al-Rashīd Street. The traffic is stopped. Cars, carriages, country carts, horses, and an occasional camel draw in to the side of the road and wait for the King to go past.

He comes preceded by two policemen on motor-cycles, and, if you are quick, you can see, as his car passes, a slight figure sitting back dressed in khaki and wearing sun-glasses. It is a modest enough procession, and in an Eastern city a good object lesson in punctuality; and as I watched the King go by, my mind turned back to Feisal, wondering what he would have said could he have foreseen this in the days when he and Lawrence talked revolt in the desert among the palm-trees of Wadi Safra.

One morning, as soon as the King had passed, I took another taxi to Babylon. I walked over the mounds and explored the ruins of the Temple of Marduk, the ziggurat of Babylon.

When the Germans were digging, they discovered two puzzling underground rooms behind the sanctuary. Professor Koldewey believed them to be the dormitories in which those seeking the Oracle, or hoping for a dream-cure, spent the night. It was there, he said, that Alexander's generals kept an all night vigil while their leader lay dying of fever.

Of all the events that have happened in Babylon, there is not one, I think, which touches the imagination more than the death of young Alexander, a man not yet thirty-three, who had created a new world in twelve years. Contemporary records of his career were written by his generals, his admiral, his doctor, his road surveyors, and the pilot of his fleet, but these have all perished; and though the later histories on which we rely paint him merely as a soldier, something outside literature has preserved the rare splendour of his spirit. Any Arab in the desert can tell you a story of Iskander Dhu 'l Quarnâin, Alexander two-horned; in the mountains of Persia, in India, and, of course, in his own Macedonia, the peasants still speak of him, and, though their tales may have grown more marvellous with the years, they perpetuate the memory of one who became a legend even in his own short life-time.

There is something pitiful and beautiful about Alexander which no writer can ever explain. The secret lies, perhaps, in what he called his *pothos*, a longing, a yearning, for absent things, a state of mind which one of his latest commentators has described as "this human and heart-felt longing, this meek and submissive yielding and yearning tenderness," that "grew to become the motive force of the conqueror of the world." Every history of Christianity should begin three centuries before the birth of Christ, with the story of the young man who, having levelled the barriers between East and West, loosed upon the world the flood of Greek speech and culture which launched the Hellenistic Age. Those who see the hand of God in all things may find no accident in this. It seems as if the world that grew out of Alexander's conquests was being prepared for Christianity with slow care and thoroughness, as a garden is prepared for seed. St. Paul, a product of this Greek world, travelled to Europe speaking the Word of God in Hellenistic cities. When the Gospels came, they were written in the *koine*, the ordinary everyday Greek language which became the Esperanto of the Hellenistic world after Alexander's time. The story of Jesus was told to the people of the First Century in the language of the Hellenistic market-place. No Christian can therefore visit Babylon without the feeling that one who was the unconscious forerunner of Christianity met his untimely death there among the mounds of black dust and yellow sand.

The bare facts of Alexander's death are well known, but there is much that we should like to know. "In the spring of 323 before Christ the whole order of things from the Adriatic to the Panjab rested upon a single will, a single brain nurtured in Hellenic thought," wrote E. R. Bevan in *The House of Seleucus*. "Then the hand of God, as if trying some fantastic experiment, plucked this man away."

It was the beginning of June, and Babylon was full of Alexander's armies waiting the order to march. He had built a naval harbour big enough to float a thousand men-of-war, many of which had been built on the spot; others had been carried overland from Tyre and put together at Thrapsacus, on the Euphrates. The oldest ships were those which had made the historic voyage down the Indus, across the Indian Ocean, and up the Persian Gulf. Mariners and shell-fishers of the Phœnician coast had made the fleet ready for sea.

On the eve of departure the Emperor developed fever, probably caught in the swamps south of Babylon, which he had visited in order to plan a new irrigation scheme. Though his fever was severe, he insisted on performing the daily sacrifices, but had to be carried to the altar on a couch. He spent the second day of his illness in bed discussing with his admiral the forthcoming fleet operation, which he ordered to take place in four days' time. In the evening he was rowed across the Euphrates to a pleasant house among gardens, where the air was cooler than in the city. For six days he lay there in a fever, performing the daily sacrifices and reluctantly postponing the fleet's departure from day to day.

As his temperature rose, he became more impatient of delay, and would not rest until he had been carried back to the palace in the city, where he could be near general headquarters. Now it became obvious to those around him that he might die. The generals who waited in the hushed ante-rooms, and the officers who thronged the outer halls and courtyards, found when they were admitted to the sick room that Alexander could no longer speak to them. The rumour spread among the armies, as it had done once before, when he had leapt alone into a fort in India, that he was dead; and his Macedonian soldiers came clamouring to the palace in such numbers that the bodyguard fell back and was forced to let them in.

Then one of the most tragic scenes in history was enacted round the couch of the dying Emperor. The rough old warriors of his campaigns, the Macedonian spearmen and the old cavalry veterans who had conquered Asia, filed in their last parade past his couch. Gallantly Alexander tried to speak to them, but was unable to do so. He greeted each one by slightly moving his head and signing with his eyes.

That night seven of his marshals kept vigil in the temple at Babylon, seeking a message from the Oracle. Should they bring the Emperor to the temple to be cured by the god? And in the night they were told to let things be. On the evening of the next day, the eleventh day of his illness, Alexander died; and it is said that a silence fell upon Babylon for four days and nights.

It is easy to understand how those who had lived in the shadow of his genius, and even those who were conscious only of his success, felt at the time that the world could not possibly continue without him. He had gathered all earthly power into his hands in such an incredibly short time, and if his pretensions to divinity may have been a joke to those who knew him well, even these cannot have doubted that he was the greatest man in the world. One might say that he died just as the curtain had lifted on the second act of his life, and at this distance one feels more than the usual sadness for a life cut short before its time: one feels also the disappointment of an audience denied a great spectacle. Reading his short life, we are like people in a theatre turned away in the middle of a play because of some grave calamity, to go home saddened, but wondering all the time what the last act would have been like. The conquered Orient lay behind him; Carthage and the West before him. Rome? Who can say? "Had Alexander lived" is one of the most fascinating speculations in history.

It was not long before men began to whisper that Alexander had been poisoned, but this has never been proved. Arrian mentions a story that poison, "a drug" he calls it, was taken to Babylon in a mule's hoof. Plutarch says that the poison was the icy water of Nonacris, which could be held only in the hoof of an ass. This was the water of the Styx, a thread of melted snow-water which pours down from the head of Mount Chelmos, in Arcadia, a water so cold and poisonous, declared the ancients, that it would rot any vessel but an animal's hoof: and some even specified the type of animal, such as a Scythian female ass! That Alexander was poisoned by the Styx is unlikely, and the story was, no doubt, the usual poison rumour that normally attaches itself to a royal death-bed in the East. When Leake discovered the Styx a century ago, he found the water wholesome to drink, but though no one in the neighbourhood had ever heard of the Styx, there was an inherited belief that the water could not be held in any ordinary vessel.

There is a strange mystery about Alexander's funeral and the quarrel for the possession of his body, all the stranger because out of that quarrel the new world shaped itself. We can see a reflection of his power and authority in the violent ambitions that clashed now he was dead; for the men who fought to share the world he had conquered, like gamblers dividing a spoil, were once his obedient servants. The sovereignty which he wore with such grace and ease, even finding it insufficient for his ambition, was almost too much for the crowd of lesser men who struggled for a share, their only claim the fact that they had been good enough to work for him.

It is probable that Alexander's body was mummified like that of an Egyptian pharaoh, though no writer has left an account of this. Diodorus merely says that the coffin was filled with aromatic herbs which gave out a pleasant scent. Strangely enough, evidence of mummification comes, not from classical, but from Eastern, sources. Historians like Mas'ûdî, though writing long after the event, had ancient authorities at their disposal, and although a great deal of their narratives are inaccurate, there is in parts a solid basis of fact. It is interesting that Mas'ûdî should say that, at the order of Alexander's mother, the body was first dipped in tar and then taken out of a gold coffin and put in one of marble less likely to rouse the cupidity of tomb robbers. There is confusion of facts here, for the change of coffins belongs to a later episode, but the reference to the tar may well be a memory of the mummification of Alexander. An Ethiopic manuscript says that, after having been washed with aloes, the body of Alexander had "honey of bees" poured over it. This again looks like a reference to mummification.

But whether the body was embalmed or not, it is certain that a long time elapsed, nearly two years, before it set out towards its resting-place. Artists, jewellers, goldsmiths, and engineers were engaged to make a splendid funeral car, and the result of their labours must have been a remarkable construction. It was a huge golden temple on wheels, whose roof was upheld by rows of Ionic columns. From the roof hung bells which gave out a solemn tolling with the motion of the car. The shrine inside, which held the huge golden coffin, was decorated with four paintings: one of Alexander with a baton in his hand, surrounded by his marshals; a second of elephants advancing in battle order; a third of cavalry manœuvring; and the fourth, a seascape of warships going into action. The car was crowned with a golden wreath of immense size, which produced rays of dazzling brilliance when seen in sunlight from a distance. The weight of the carriage must have been immense, and in order to fit it for the rough desert roads, shock-absorbers were devised. Four poles were attached to the car, and to each pole were attached four yokes, and to each yoke four mules, making a train of sixty-four mules. The animals wore golden crowns, little gold bells hung from their head-harness, and their collars were encrusted with precious stones.

Such was the fantastic shrine in which the scarred body—for Alexander's body was covered with battle wounds—was carried across the desert from the Euphrates to the Nile; and we can imagine how the imagination of the rude, superstitious tribes was touched as they saw it pass on its way to a sound of bells, with a fence of spears round it and men marching. The story of the intrigues that led to this departure will never be known. Which six feet of earth should receive the man who had owned most of the civilized world? It was a political problem. Obviously he should have been buried with the Macedonian kings at Ægæ; but once, at the beginning of his Eastern triumphs, urged perhaps by that "longing for absent things," he had made a long, romantic journey across the Libyan sands to consult the famous Oracle of Ammon at Siwa. The god greeted him as a divine pharaoh, and the young King seized eagerly on such proof that he was more than man, and in days to come would wear the ram's horns of Ammon on his head, the symbol of his divine "father." Then to Siwa, some said, he should go at last, to lie in the sanctity of his "father's" dwelling-place. Ptolemy, who had seized Egypt as his share of the spoil, urged it passionately, for he wanted Alexander's body in Egypt, a talisman of great strength and power. Seeking a convenient time, Ptolemy arranged for the body to leave Babylon, presumably for Macedonia, but with a powerful escort he met it in Syria and took it, not to Siwa, but to the ancient capital of Egypt, Memphis. It was moved, either by him or by his son, to Alexandria, where it remained in a crystal coffin until the beginning of the Christian era.

I asked one of the local Arabs if stories were still told about Alexander in his village. He replied that there were many, and pointing to a high ridge of reddish earth about half a mile east of the ruins, said that there was the place where King Alexander's body was burned on a great fire.

I walked over to this mound, and on the way met another Arab who told me the same story, adding that the whole mound was full of signs of burning. As I approached it, I saw that it was about fifty feet high; its sides were steep in parts and it had the appearance of a huge earthwork, or fortification. On top of it was an Arab boy, who again told me it was the place where Alexander was burned; so I felt justified in assuming that it was a well-known legend in Babylon. And grubbing about in the piles of soft earth and mud brick, I found that the whole mound is blackened as if with fire.

I wonder if this was the remains of the colossal funeral pyre which Alexander erected for his friend Hephæstion. It sometimes happens that while the memory of an event is preserved by word of mouth from generation to generation, names are forgotten or famous names are substituted for the right ones. Months afterwards, when reading Professor Koldewey's book on the excavations, I came across this passage:

"Indications of a great conflagration are to be found in blocks of mud brick smelted together by a fierce fire, and bearing clear imprints of palm and other wood. In many places the prints show the sharp edges of good carpenter's work. All this is remarkable, and we should like to find the explanation of it.

"This may perhaps be found in the report given by Diodorus (XVII. 115) of the funeral pyre Alexander the Great caused to

THE ROAD TO UR

be erected to solemnize the funeral ceremonies of Hephæstion.
. . . The magnificent pyre, which is said to have cost 12,000
talents, when seen from the Acropolis must have stood out in a
most impressive manner against the eastern horizon."

4

Ur of the Chaldees, the town of Abraham, lies a hundred and
thirty miles south of Baghdad, and a hundred and twenty miles
from Basra, on the Persian Gulf. To most people the name probably suggests a place lost in the silence of a dead land, remote
and difficult to visit and I was surprised to find that the modern
traveller is able to journey to Abraham's town in a sleeping-car!

One of the results of European influence in the Middle East
is that such places as Ur, Gath, and Ascalon, previously found
only in the pages of the Old Testament, now have a place in the
railway time-table. With the same sense of incongruity which
came to me when I took a taxi to Babylon, I bought a ticket to
Ur of the Chaldees. The train leaves Baghdad at night and arrives at Ur in the early hours of the morning.

Baghdad station offered the odd spectacle of Biblical-looking
sheiks, their families and attendants, packing into third-class
carriages with supplies of food, while people from another age
and another world gazed curiously at them from first-class windows. And I observed how the grave and fatalistic Orientals,
their composure gone, rushed and shouted excitedly up and
down the platform, bidding one another passionate and affecting farewells, even though they might be going only a few miles
down the line. There is something about departure by train
which destroys the last shred of self-possession in the Eastern
peasant: perhaps it is the horrible thought that the train will depart at the advertised time.

The sleeping compartment was comfortable and adequate,
and the wash-basin stated that it was a pattern used on the In-

dian railways. During the day the carriage was an ordinary first-class compartment, but in the evening it was invaded by one of the polite officials of the Iraqi Railways, armed with sheets, pillows, and blankets. How can officials be trained to such a pitch of politeness? I can only say that the care and attention bestowed by these men on their charges may, perhaps, be equalled, but certainly not exceeded, by those remarkable women whose duty it is to nurse royal infants. Every time the train stopped, my khaki nurse came running along the lines either to lock the carriage door or to stand outside and guard me from the terrors of the Babylonian night. At first I thought he was making sure that no one would kidnap me; but as the stations at which we stopped began to show a uniform desolation, I concluded that he was only making sure that I did not escape. Like so many others in Irak, he credited me with an insatiable hunger for tea and biscuits, which he promised to bring at some unearthly hour in the morning.

So I lay trying to sleep, watching the night sky powdered from horizon to horizon with stars. In such flat country the pattern of the sky at night is a compensation for the featureless landscape by day. It is easy to understand why the Chaldeans were among the world's first astronomers. The sky is a superb spectacle every night, and the absence of mountains, or even hills, means that the mind of the star-gazer is never drawn back to earth, but is encouraged to wander in terrifying speculation among the constellations. In ancient times the summit of every ziggurat must have held its little group of men looking up into the violet immensity of the sky, alone with the mystery of the Universe like sailors on the sea.

That the Wise Men from the East were Chaldean astronomers is more than a pleasing fancy. Kepler discovered that the conjunction of Jupiter and Saturn in the constellation Pisces, normally seen once only in eight hundred years, occurred no fewer than three times just before the birth of Christ. In no place would it have been more eagerly noted than in the ancient home of astronomy. "We have seen His Star in the East," said the Magi, "and have come to worship Him." How many artists have pictured them setting out from these level plains on the way to Bethlehem, with the Star burning above them.

As the train pounded to the south, I lay reading Sir Leonard Woolley's book, *Ur of the Chaldees*. This book describes what will probably go down in history as one of the most valuable and interesting archæological discoveries of our time. The excavators found evidence of the Flood. They found the tombs of highly civilized people who lived centuries before the Pyramids were built. Then, advancing in time, Sir Leonard uncovered the city in which Abraham may have lived. He entered the ruins of houses which Abraham may have known. Seven years' work with a spade at Ur has undone half a century's destructive criticism with the pen.

With the earth rolled back from this ancient city, we now think of Abraham as the citizen of a cultured, highly civilized community; he left it to become a sheep farmer and to wander about the world, as deliberately as a man to-day might leave London for Australia or New Zealand.

"Now the Lord said unto Abram, Get thee out of thy country, and from thy kindred, and from thy father's house unto a land that I will show thee: and I will make of thee a great nation. . . ."

Thus Abraham left the busy quay-sides and markets of this earlier, smaller Babylon, and set out across the world, not by birth a nomad, but a townsman in search of his destiny: the first colonist in history.

The train stopped just before sunrise at Ur Junction. This is merely a buffet for locomotives which, having drunk there, go onward to the Persian Gulf.

No sooner had I stepped down on the track than I became

aware of something familiar. I had often seen the Junction before. It was the lonely station of the silent films, where the hero
arrives in circumstances which never vary. First, a towering lo-
comotive with its chain of shining Pullman coaches would
charge the spectator at full speed, swerving at the moment of
impact to draw gently to a halt. Then the hero would descend,
casting glances of dismay at a landscape in whose complete
desolation the tracks converge towards the horizon. As if to
accentuate his abandonment, full attention was given to the
train's departure. There were pictures of the passengers, of
helpful negro attendants, of wheels gathering speed, and eventually the hero would be left alone, standing in a dazed condition on the permanent way.

Every detail of this scene was reproduced at Ur in the half-
light of that morning. There was nothing but the station and the
railway lines drawn north and south. The air was piercing and
cold, and the silence was intense. The very fact that I had arrived in comfort in a train now seemed to make Ur more desolate and remote than I could have imagined.

Unlike my predecessors in this situation, I was not met by a
girl swinging a sun-bonnet or by an ancient man driving a
buggy, or even by the crowd of rusticated persons who always
come to the rescue of the man in a film. There was nothing at
Ur but dawn breaking over the flat land. As the light grew
stronger, it served only to reveal a wider wilderness. But when
the sun rose, it shone on a remarkable feature of the landscape.
About two miles away a mound of reddish earth rose like a
pyramid with a crushed apex. It was an enormous structure, and
it was unmistakably the famous Ziggurat of Ur. I had seen many
a photograph of it and had read about it in many a book; and
there it was in the lonely early morning, only a short walk away
across the desert.

As I drew near to it across a dry, salty marsh, I could see in
the sharp sunlight that it was not a mound of earth, neither was

it shapeless: it was a great structure of mud brick, and the ramps which led to its summit were clearly defined, even from this distance.

I had not realized that the Ziggurat of Ur would be so impressive, or that so much of it remained. All these temple towers of Babylonia and Chaldea were of the same design: a series of vast, almost square platforms rising one above the other, each platform smaller than the one below. Every nursery makes ziggurats with those bricks that fit one inside another! The shrine of the god was on the topmost platform, and huge inclined ramps led up to it from the ground level.

It may seem odd to say that my first feeling, as I looked at the Ziggurat of Ur, was one of genuine pleasure. I am never at home in perfectly flat country, and I instantly appreciated the intention of the long-dead architects of Ur, which was to break the monotony of the plain by building an artificial mountain. The theory is that the ancient conquerors of these plains in remote ages were mountaineers who, either from homesickness or from religious conservatism, or perhaps both, wished to worship their gods on the high places, as they always had done. In Chaldea they had to make the high places with their own hands, and the account of the building of the Tower of Babel is the record of such an event.

Impressive as the Ziggurat of Ur is, even in decay, it must have been an amazing sight when the platforms rose above the plain in bands of vivid colour: the lower stages in black, the upper in red, and the shrine in blue with a roof of gilded metal. And when the priests in coloured robes ascended and descended the ramps, or escorted the statue of the deity down to some great festival, well may the scene have inspired, as Sir Leonard Woolley suggests it may have done, the dream of Jacob's Ladder, with its train of angels going up and down.

I climbed the Ziggurat by the very ramp, uncovered during the excavations, which the worshippers used twenty-three centuries before Christ. It was a strange feeling to explore a structure that was old when Abraham lived; a temple whose vast ground space had last seen the light of day centuries before the Pyramids were built. I noticed the regular rows of slits, like loop-holes in a fortress wall, which puzzled the excavators until they realized their object. These slits go straight through the outer casing of burnt brick and bitumen into the solid, unbaked mud core of the structure. They were put there to drain moisture from the building and were accepted by the archæologists until it occurred to them that there would be nothing to drain! The bricks and the mud core would have lost all moisture soon after the erection of the building, and provision had been made to lead off the occasional torrential rains. What then was the object of this elaborate drainage system? The answer was provided by an inscription made by the last king of Babylon, Nabonidus, whose antiquarian exploits I have already mentioned. He found the Ziggurat of Ur in ruins and restored it, taking care to mention in his inscription that he had cleared it of "fallen branches." Then at once it became clear that the platforms had been planted with trees, and the drainage holes carried off the water which irrigated the terraces.

When I reached the top of the Ziggurat, which is about fifty feet above the plain, I looked round at a view I shall never forget. Immediately below, clustered at the foot of the ruined temple, lay Ur, one of the earliest cities known to us. There were thousands of small, roofless houses of mud brick, intersected everywhere by streets and lanes. The morning sun, slanting across the dead city, threw buildings and streets into relief in sharp lines of white and black. I could follow the main streets through a network of intersecting lanes until they ended in huge mounds of sand, which marked the limits of the excavation. And this was the city, built on the ruins of still older cities, in which Abraham lived twenty centuries before Christ.

As far as the eye could see, a brown plain stretched to the sky-line. In one place only was it relieved from complete desolation by a thin band like a green tape curving across the landscape. This was the Euphrates, flowing towards the Persian Gulf beneath its tunnel of date palms.

As I looked from the Ziggurat of Ur I found it easy to imagine what this country was like thousands of years ago. The sea was much nearer, for the silt brought down by the Two Rivers has been piling up and forming the alluvial plain century by century, and the sea is now a hundred and twenty miles away. Babylonia is merely a deposit of river silt gently tilted towards the south. Baghdad, two hundred and thirty miles to the north, is a hundred and five feet above sea level, Ur of the Chaldees is only fifteen, and Basra, a hundred and twenty miles to the south, is eight feet above the sea. In Abraham's time seagoing ships sailed to the docks of Ur; and in addition to the sea, the Euphrates, or an important tributary stream, washed the western walls. Instead of this brown desert, the surroundings of Ur must have been a mass of luxuriant vegetation. Palm-groves and fields of growing corn would have stretched for many a mile round the city, intersected by fresh-water canals running here and there, reflecting the blue of the sky. Instead of scorching desert winds, there would have been a fresh breeze from the sea; instead of the enveloping stillness, there would have been the sound of a busy city and the movement everywhere of ships sailing down the river to the sea, or gliding softly on the blue canals. And from the centre of the one story houses lying crowded within the walls rose the Ziggurat of Ur in coloured bands, visible for miles over the flat land, the sun striking on the golden roof of its shrine, sending a heliograph to the cornfields of the north and the blue sea lying to the south. In this brilliant and cultivated city lived Terah, the father of Abraham, and from this city Abraham set forth on his wanderings.

I climbed down from the Ziggurat and entered the town of

Abraham. If a square mile of Baghdad streets were stripped of roofs and left for a year or two, it would look much like Ur, except that numbers of Abraham's friends probably lived in better houses than many I could point out in Baghdad. The lanes are narrow, some of them barely wide enough to allow a laden donkey to pass, but some of the houses had fourteen rooms, built round a central courtyard. One might picture life in ancient Ur as almost perfect but for a revolting custom. Attached to many houses are what Sir Leonard Woolley calls "private chapels," in which members of the family were buried in huge clay coffins rather like old-fashioned hip baths. In more humble abodes the dead were buried beneath the floor. "It was the custom," says Sir Leonard, "that the dead man continued to inhabit the house in which he had lived and his heirs dwelt on in the rooms above his grave: the custom, barbarous as it may seem at first sight, accords with that feeling of family continuity which is so strong, for example, in the ancient Hebrews." That may be so, but it is difficult to understand why Ur was not wiped out by plague, and in spite of the lagoons, the canals, the river, and all the other pleasant features of Ur, I think that Abraham was fortunate to get away into the desert.

While I was sitting in a house where Abraham and Sarah may have sat, I heard an eerie sound. It was a human whisper. Ur is not, perhaps, the place in which one would choose to hear someone whispering on the other side of a wall. Tiptoeing to the door, I glanced into the lane, where I saw two men standing with rifles slung across their backs. They were the guardians of the ruins.

I often wonder what these men really talk about among themselves, for superstition runs in their blood and, in spite of their rifles and bandoliers, I think they must often feel unprotected as they prowl the ruins. I asked them to show me the place where Sir Leonard Woolley had discovered signs of the Flood, and I am glad that I did so, for I should never have found it by myself. They led the way out of the lanes of the dead city to a series of low mounds near by, where they pointed into an enormous pit. They warned me to go gently because the sides are not too safe, and I descended into a cavity whose walls record the passage of over five thousand years.

It was interesting to look up at these walls and see the history of the men who have lived on that spot lying in strata like layers in a rich cake. Potsherds protruded from the layers in great numbers; so did bones and other less identifiable odds and ends. The sides of this excavation are in parts an almost solid jumble of jug handles, necks of jars and pots, and rims of plates and basins; and all of them beautifully preserved. Then with dramatic suddenness all such light-hearted evidence of human carelessness and muddle stops, and there succeed eight feet of solid, unstratified water-laid clay. Those eight feet were deposited by the Flood about six thousand years ago. Below them the evidence of Man begins again—the men who lived before the Flood. Sir Leonard Woolley's description of this discovery is interesting:

"The shafts went deeper," he says, "and suddenly the character of the soil changed. Instead of the stratified pottery and rubbish we were in perfectly clean clay, uniform throughout, the texture of which showed that it had been laid there by water. The workmen declared that we had come to the bottom of everything, to the river silt of which the original delta was formed, and at first, looking at the sides of the shaft, I was disposed to agree with them, but then I saw that we were too high up. It was difficult to believe that the island on which the first settlement was built stood up so much above what must have been the level of the marsh, and after working out the measurements I sent the men back to work to deepen the hole. The clean clay continued without change—the sole object found in it was a fragment of fossilized bone which must have been brought down with the clay from the upper reaches of the river

—until it had attained a thickness of a little over eight feet. Then, as suddenly as it had begun, it stopped, and we were once more in layers of rubbish full of stone implements, flint cores from which the implements had been flaked off, and pottery."

They had worked right through the time of the Flood to the men who had lived before it.

"So much for the facts," writes Sir Leonard. "What then is to be built up on them? The discovery that there was a real deluge to which the Sumerian and the Hebrew stories of the Flood alike go back does not of course prove any single detail in either of those stories. This deluge was not universal but a local disaster confined to the lower valley of the Tigris and Euphrates, affecting an area perhaps 400 miles long and 100 miles across; but for the occupants of the valley that was the whole world!"

It would be impressive to see, as the excavators did, the line of human habitation before the Flood, but the drift sand and the always crumbling top and sides of the deep pit have now concealed it from view. Nothing, however, could be plainer than the Flood deposit. It is like a great silence suddenly followed by a shout of human voices, the resumption of life again after "the waters had dried up from off the earth."

I saw the site of the royal cemetery at Ur in which the excavators found the tombs of King A-bar-gi and Queen Shub-ad, and the skeletons of eighty attendants, mostly women of the court. These tombs were made, and the bodies buried in them, a thousand years before Abraham was born, and it is from this cemetery that most of the exquisite jewellery was found which is now in the Baghdad Museum.

Sir Leonard Woolley's description of these tombs is a brilliant piece of reconstruction. The bones and the objects found with them, the remains of waggons and oxen, were discovered crushed so flat that a solid wooden wheel was merely a grey-white circle of decay in the soil, yet he has managed to build up a vivid picture of the tomb as it was five thousand years ago, when the royal persons were buried there: the soldiers dead at the gate with their copper spears, the harpist dead beside his harp, the grooms dead at the head of the oxen, the drivers dead in the waggons, the circle of court ladies dead in their gala dresses, and the Queen Shub-ad herself, dead on a wooden bier, in a fantastic head-dress of golden rings and beech leaves, her body covered with amulets and beads and a gold cup near her hand.

None of the bodies showed any signs of violence, and neither had these people died in agony. In fact, one piece of evidence suggests that all these people ran, perhaps willingly, to their fate as to a court ceremony. It was noticed by the excavators that all the women save one had worn a circlet round the head, either of gold or of silver. As the body without a head-band was removed, an object was found at waist-level which turned out to be the missing circlet. The lady had evidently arrived late, perhaps carrying the head-band in the pocket of her gown or in a bag at her waist, meaning to put it on in the tomb; but this she forgot to do. So she lay for five thousand years until her forgetfulness was discovered.

It has been suggested by Sir Leonard Woolley that these people may have been drugged before death came to them. It would seem that they went of their own free will to a ceremony which they believed would be a rapid transition from one world to another.

5

On the way back to the Ziggurat I fell in with a group of people, several men, three or four women, and some children, all modern Iraqis. The leader of the party introduced himself as the post-master of Ur, and told me that he was entertaining some friends, railway officials, their wives and families. They were going to have a picnic in the ruins and would I care to join them? I replied I would gladly do so, and we mounted a sand-hill near the temple of the Moon Goddess and sat on the ground.

It was going to be a feast of *bunni*. I did not know what *bunni* was, but asked no questions, knowing that the *bunni* would soon reveal itself. Two young Arabs came up the hill carrying a wooden box in which lay six monstrous fish, very thick in the body and covered with large iridescent scales the size of a finger nail. They had come out of the Euphrates, from a village called Nasariya, about ten miles away. Any one of these fish would have been a meal for us, but all six were split open with a knife and prepared for cooking.

While this was going on the Arabs lit a fire and added to it pieces of hard, dark wood which they had brought with them, for in this treeless country no wood can ever be picked up. I asked what kind of wood this was, and they told me that it came from India. It was part of an old railway sleeper.

The split *bunni* were pegged upright in a circle on the sand with their scales away from the flames, and allowed to grill. Now and then a *bunni* fell into the ashes, to be swiftly rescued by a lean, dark hand. Soon the first fish was ready. The post-master produced a lemon, a bag of curry powder, a packet of salt, and a bottle of Lea and Perrins Sauce. These were dashed with rough artistry on the *bunni*, which was then placed on the ground in the centre of the circle, and we were soon detaching portions of it with our fingers.

If you can imagine an oily cod-fish tasting of smoke and wood ashes, you have a rough idea of roast *bunni*. It is white, flaky, and extremely rich. The greediest cat on earth would slink away defeated from a fraction of a full grown *bunni*. But at our feast *bunni* succeeded *bunni* with oriental lavishness. Into some we just dipped our fingers as if in a finger bowl and let the Arab lads take it away to devour over the embers.

When I made a remark about the size of the fish, my friends smiled and said that another fish found in the Euphrates, called a *bizz*, was often seven feet long and weighed as much as a hundred pounds.

I spent the remainder of the day with these kindly folk. We made an excursion to Nasariya, where I saw the Euphrates, broad and strong, flowing through a white town among palm trees. The river was covered with primitive boats, and on its banks walked veiled women with water-pots, and small, black-haired, milk-chocolate babies. Through the streets of the town roamed sombre Shias, enjoying their mournful festival.

It was odd to think that my friends, the railway officials, were of the same race, or even of the same century, as the unchanged peasants in this town. In their blue-serge suits, they were almost as foreign as I was. In all these countries which have been administered by European mandates, a clerkly administrative class with European ideas has been created, and I sometimes wonder whether this class will succeed in educating its peasantry, or whether some day the intelligentsia will go under and the people relapse into their natural chaos.

The night train came in, and, saying farewell to my friends of Ur, I was soon on my way back to Baghdad.

6

Early one morning I took the Nairn coach across the desert to Damascus. I slept nearly all the way, awakening at intervals to see the desert lying in long, peaceful brown distances. In such moments I thought that I was making a journey which no traveller of the last century, or even before the war, would have believed possible. I was going overland to Egypt, and had every hope of being there in three days. So I should have journeyed from the Euphrates to the Nile in a little over sixty hours.

Before the war there was no way of crossing this desert except by camel, and the railway between Palestine and Egypt had not been built. I cannot imagine how many weeks this now simple and comfortable journey would have taken even twenty years ago.

We stopped at Rutba as the sun was setting. George Bryant was presiding over his incredible fragment of England. I drank tea, ate biscuits, and had another wonderful English dinner: then off again into the night, roaring on in the white track of the head-lights. As a lovely day was breaking, we stopped in the hills east of Damascus and made a little fire of twigs. We were soon drinking strong black tea. The desert car, covered with brown dust, stood there on its gigantic balloon tyres, every bit as romantic as the Deadwood Coach. All motorists will agree that this conquest of the desert by two enterprising New Zealanders is a remarkable and romantic achievement, and my admiration goes out to them and to the drivers, who steer their swift juggernauts by day and night across what a British Tommy once eloquently described as "miles and miles and miles of damn-all."

To drive from Damascus into Palestine is a wonderful experience. The road descends gradually towards the Lake of Galilee, and there comes a moment when you see its blue water far beneath, through a dip in the hills to the left of the road. The sun and the air become warmer as you dip down to the lake-side, and if the day is fine, as this one was, you may encounter the heat of June in January.

The Lake lay in calm sunlight. Fishermen from Tiberias were at work with their nets round the Jordan inlet to the north of the Lake, and in the little wood of eucalyptus trees at Tabgha the black and white kingfishers were flashing and diving over the water. The only thing that had changed since I was there last is the preservation of the Fourth Century mosaics in the

"Church of the Loaves and Fishes." An Arab no longer sweeps away the sand from these beautiful relics of one of the earliest basilicas in Palestine. They have been roofed over, thanks to the energy of a Scotsman, Major A. A. Gordon of the Bridge of Allan.

It was hard to leave the lake-side and take the road to Haifa, which leads upward into the hills through Nazareth to the coast. At Haifa I heard much of the hatred of Arab for Jew and of the Jew's determination to make Palestine his own land. A Jew came to see me and cried vehemently:

"What has my race done to deserve the world's hate? Where can we go, if not to our own land?"

A Christian Arab came to see me and he said:

"Do you English people think that God intended atheists to come back to the Promised Land? I could take you to the Jewish colonies round about in which men openly scoff at God. Why should we sit down and see our country bought up by Jewish communists?"

To all of which I had nothing to reply. I was heartily glad to get away from the blistering hatred of a country which should be the Holy Land. There had been an explosion on the line and I was advised to take a boat that was on the point of leaving for Alexandria. Although this made my journey a little longer, what did it matter? We steamed southward past the low green Plain of Sharon, past Jaffa, past Gaza, and we were soon in the open sea.

I stepped ashore at Alexandria.

CHAPTER IV

I go to Cairo, meet the descendants of the Ancient Egyptians, visit their churches and a nunnery, hear of strange saints, and attend a Coptic wedding. At Mataria, where the Holy Family are said to have lived during the Flight into Egypt, is a tree, a legend, and an obelisk.

§ I

I TOOK the morning train from Alexandria to Cairo. As it sped south on its three-hour journey, I sat at the window of a white Pullman car and looked out on Egypt.

I saw a flat and low-lying land, stretching to the sky, emerald-coloured with crops of maize and sugar-cane, chocolate-coloured where the plough had turned it: a land steeped in sunshine. There were dense groves of date palms, and banana plantations where the yellow fruit lay among leaves huge and tattered like the ears of green elephants.

Embankments rising twenty feet or so above the fields carried the varied traffic of the Delta: a slow-moving string of camels, arching their necks towards some neighbouring market, or donkeys trit-trotting in the dust, bearing upon their backs, with an air of blithe servitude, a more than full-sized human being. Sometimes brown girls passed by in single file with water-jars on their heads, followed by a herd of goats in charge of a child, both girls and goats moving in a foot-high black powder which is the Eleventh Plague of Egypt—dust.

In the fields stood the *fellah*, who has probably changed less with the centuries than any character in Egypt. He stood bent above his hoe, the same kind of hoe which is to be seen in museums, labelled 3000 B.C., or he walked behind a plough drawn

by two black oxen or by an ox and a camel, a plough like those
to be seen on the tomb paintings of the Old Empire.

All the way from Alexandria to Cairo I saw young men and
old men, burned almost black by the sun's rays, sitting beside
the irrigation canals, ceaselessly turning the handle of an object
like a slender wooden barrel, which sucked up water from the
canal and directed it to a higher level.

These poor brown men are pumping life blood into Egypt.
Day after day, year after year, century after century, they have
been at their monotonous task, moving water from here to
there; and if they ceased to do so the land of Egypt would dry
up and become a desert. The student of ancient things looks
at these water turners with amazement, for the thing they are
turning all over the Nile Delta to-day is the water-screw which
the mathematician Archimedes invented over two hundred
years before Christ.

The train passed village after village, many of them set with
exquisite picturesqueness among groves of date palms, or beside
blue canals where high-masted *giyasât* lay at anchor with reefed
sails, like butterflies with folded wings.

The houses in these villages were small brown boxes of two
and three storys, built of mud. Unshaped palm trunks formed
roofs and ceilings, and protruded from the walls. On the flat
roofs were built elaborate pigeon houses, round which thousands of blue and white birds fluttered.

Brown children, turkeys, chickens, donkeys, camels, and
water-buffaloes crowded the narrow, dusty space between the
houses, while the women, quite aged at twenty-five and old at
thirty, sat at their house doors, or beneath acacia and eucalyptus
trees, pounding maize for bread or baking flat cakes in outdoor
ovens.

Even during a short railway journey in Egypt you can understand the two main factors in the life of the people: the sun and
the Nile. The Nile makes life possible in the narrow strip of

green which is Egypt, and the sun pulls up the crops as if by a magnet.

From the beginnings of civilization Egyptian agriculture has always depended on the annual flooding of the Nile, and on the covering of fresh mud which the river brought down from the Abyssinian highlands and spread over the valley. This mud raises the level of the land four inches a century, and the general level of the Nile valley is to-day seven feet higher than it was in the time of Cleopatra, and from twenty to thirty feet higher than it was when the Pyramids were built.

Every year Nature carefully spreads a new carpet of mud on which the Egyptians grow crops, which in ancient times was chiefly wheat. It was not until a century ago that cotton was introduced into Egypt, and with it came a great change in the system of irrigation. Nile water is now stored in dams during flood time and released as it is required, so that in addition to the annual inundation there is a controlled irrigation which has made it possible to grow two and three crops a year instead of one. And that is why, as you travel in Egypt, it often seems that the seasons are all mixed up in the space of a few acres. Here a field is brown from the plough, there it is green with growing crops, and next to it is a field ripe for harvest.

The peaceful countryside gave place to the outskirts of Cairo, where only the eternal sunlight redeemed from squalor an incredible assortment of shacks and houses. Palm trees and the minarets of mosques stood up above the low flat roof-line, and kites hung in mid-air watching the earth.

2

When I jump out of bed and push forward the green slatted shutters, the sun leaps in, yellow and strong. The dim room becomes full of blinding light. In the hotel garden palm trees are standing in a windless morning, outlined against a blue sky. A gardener below on the paths of reddish sand is directing a water-hose towards a bank of purple bougainvillæa, and kites fly whistling from roof to roof.

The plaintive whistle of the kite is one of the characteristic sounds of early morning in Cairo. These big brown birds, which sometimes measure five feet from wing-tip to wing-tip, have for centuries scavenged the streets of Cairo. No one would kill a kite in Egypt. To do so would bring bad luck, and there is also a belief that if a kite haunts a certain balcony or window, it is a sign of death. Like the ibis and the cat in Ancient Egypt, the kite is privileged and protected.

I stand on my balcony every morning to watch these birds. They have no fear of human beings, and many a time I have seen them swoop among a group of street cleaners and, without pausing in their flight, rise grasping in their claws some fragment of offal. They love to perch on high places such as the tops of flag-poles, where they look rather like eagles as they keep watch on the streets below.

Some people say that a kite will never attack a living animal, but friends in Cairo assure me that they have seen these birds rising in the air with rats and snakes in their claws. One friend tells me that a kite went off with a kitten from his balcony; another told me a story of an out-door lunch party ruined by the arrival of a kite, which flew off with the fish course!

These birds, now so rare in England, were once common to all our cities. Visitors to London four centuries ago mention their whistling, and the way they swooped down on the street garbage. There is an old English proverb which says "a carrion kite will never make a good hawk," which is equivalent to that eloquent maxim: "You can't make a silk purse out of a sow's ear," a belief seldom heard in these democratic days, when you have only to open the purse to see a hair or two.

As I stood on my balcony one morning, a kite illustrated a line of Shakespeare for me. There is a portion of Shepheard's

Hotel garden which is railed off as a drying ground for table napkins and cloths. Some of these had fallen from the line. The kite dived and, with his beautiful unchecked motion, which one never tires of watching, went up into the air grasping a napkin in his claws.

"When the kite builds, look to lesser linen," says Autolycus in *The Winter's Tale*—a puzzling warning until you see a kite fly off with a linen cloth to pack between the sticks of his nest.

Having breakfasted, how good it is to find the sun warm on the hotel terrace. Open carriages are clip-clopping through the streets. School-boys, European in appearance save for the little red flowerpots of felt on their heads, walk sedately to school with books under their arms.

The streets of modern Cairo are wide and spacious, and the romantic Cairo which appealed so strongly to our grandfathers is rapidly vanishing. It still exists in a warren of narrow streets always crammed with traffic, winding lanes crowded with little shops, and in the bazaars, with their alluring reek of musk and attar of roses, of incense and coffee, where you can spend a whole day in pleasant conversation over a possible purchase and leave without buying anything.

Embedded in the acres of tiny booths are a series of magnificent buildings constructed of immense blocks of honey-coloured stone, much of it stripped centuries ago from the Pyramids. These are the mosques of Cairo, whose minarets rise high above the roofs of the surrounding buildings. The most spectacular is the Mosque of Mohammed Ali, perched high on the rock of the Citadel, its slender Turkish minarets rising above everything in Cairo, poised above the city like a dream of the Bosphorus.

West of the city runs the Nile, the life-giver, the very mother of Egypt as the sun is the father, calm and blue in the heat of afternoon. House-boats and Nile steamers are anchored to the shore. Flotillas of *giyasât*, their slim masts towering to the sky, their white sails reefed, lie together in mid-stream. Some of them have come slowly down the river loaded with cargoes of sugar-cane, grain, rice, and cotton.

The crowds are as varied as the city. There is the modern Cairene in a European suit, with a tarbush on his head. You see him sitting at the pavement cafés, eagerly reading the latest political sensation in the newspaper, for Egyptian politics proceed from crisis to crisis, while he drinks a little cup of Turkish coffee and slowly lifts first one foot, then the other, towards the bootblack crouching at his feet.

Women of the rich classes, who only a few years ago used to drive about the streets attended by slaves, now drive their own cars and attend dance teas at Shepheard's Hotel. But in the poorer streets of Cairo the women still go veiled. You can see them coming in from the country or the suburbs, seated, five or six together, on a two-wheeled cart drawn by a donkey. Sometimes the cart is stopped before the mediæval gate, the Bâb-el-Mitwalli, in order that a woman may get down and attach to the massive structure some fragment of rag, or a tooth. The whole gate is covered with such relics. They are tied there in order to gain the sympathy of a spirit which is believed to live behind the gate.

Only a short walk from regions which have not changed spiritually since the time of the Caliphs is another part of Cairo, where motor cars, saxophones, the radio, the film, and other superficialities of modern life, are assessed at more than their true value.

3

I had not come to Egypt to see the familiar land of the Pharaohs, but the almost unknown Egypt of St. Mark.

Egypt has been a Moslem country for so long, that many people are surprised to learn she was once one of the cornerstones of Christianity. Even those who know this are sometimes unaware that Christianity has never died out in Egypt, and that nearly a million Egyptians, who regard themselves as the true descendants of the ancient Egyptians, still owe spiritual allegiance to an Egyptian Pope, the 113th successor of St. Mark.

The present head of the Egyptian Church is Yuannes (John) XIX, who is now eighty years old. His splendid title is: "The Most Holy Pope and Patriarch of the Great City of Alexandria and of all the Land of Egypt, of Jerusalem the Holy City, of Nubia, Abyssinia and Pentapolis, and of all the Preaching of St. Mark."

St. Mark the Evangelist is said to have been the founder of the Egyptian Church and to have been martyred and buried in Alexandria, where his relics were venerated until the Moslem Conquest. His first converts were Greeks, and Greek was the language of the Church. Second only in authority to Rome, and at one period her superior in intellect, the Patriarchate of Alexandria was one of the pillars of the Universal Church until the Fifth Century. Such names as St. Clement of Alexandria, St. Athanasius, Origen, and St. Anthony, the founder of Monasticism, indicate the contribution made by Egypt to Christianity during the first great period of her Church.

In order to understand how this intellectual equal of Rome crashed down in schism and heresy, it is necessary to know that Egypt was ruled from Constantinople by a Greek minority. This was nothing new in itself. For centuries Egypt had endured foreign masters, but so long as the Egyptians worshipped Amûn-Rē and the old gods, they were a race apart and lived in a different world from that of Alexandria, always the centre of Greek influence in Egypt. When the whole country became Christian, however, and millions of men and women up and down the Nile deserted the ancient temples and went to church, they found themselves in the spiritual world of their masters; and the result was the demand for a national church. Intense racial and other differences boiled up and took the form of a theological definition known as Monophysism, which concerns the nature of our Lord. The Monophysites declared that Christ was not Man, but only God, and that His earthly life was therefore only an apparition. This heresy was condemned by the Council of Chalcedon in 451 A.D., and from that moment the national church of Egypt separated itself from the rest of Christendom and went its own way in heresy.

The great bulk of the native-born population of Egypt either believed in Monophysism, or was ready to believe because this heresy had been condemned by the Byzantine Emperor. When the Monophysite Patriarch of Alexandria was deposed as a heretic, it had the same effect on Fifth Century Egypt as the exile of Zaghlul Pasha had on nationalist Egypt in the Twentieth. The whole country went up in riot and bloodshed, a situation which lasted on and off for nearly two centuries, as patriarchs representing the Egyptian or the Greek creeds succeeded each other on the throne. The riotous monks who broke into Alexandria and supported this or that patriarch or bishop, burning and slaying and then rushing back to the desert, were mostly ignorant *fellahin*, and the lover of parallels may see in them a faithful forecast of the ridiculous student demonstrators of modern Egyptian politics.

Nevertheless, out of this deplorable situation emerged the Egyptian National Monophysite Church, which was content to break away from the rest of Christendom in order to follow this heresy. It was natural, feeling as they did, that the Egyptians should wish no longer to use Greek in their churches, and the liturgy and the Gospels were therefore translated into Egyptian. It is to this that we owe the extraordinary fact—one of the greatest romances in the history of languages—that the Egyptian Church to-day still celebrates the Korbân, or Mass, in the language of the Pharaohs, or the debased form of it that was spoken in the Fifth Century.

Upon this divided Christian country the Arabs swooped in

the Seventh Century, rightly scenting an easy prey. The Byzantine garrisons were soon driven out and Moslem invaders
quietly occupied the country, receiving no opposition from
the Egyptians, who may even, as it has been suggested, have
welcomed this change of masters. At first the Arabs turned
almost with affection to their Christian subjects. They gave a
name to them which has remained ever since: they called them
Copts, which simply means Egyptians. It is an Arabic contrac-
tion of the Greek *Ægyptus*, and if we spelt it *gypt*, or *gupt*, we
should approach nearer to the Arabic pronunciation of the
word. The Copts were as useful to the Arabs as the Christian
Greeks were to the Turks when Constantinople was captured.
And the Arabs had the good sense to let the Christians run the
country for them, build their mosques, add up their books, and
make their jewellery. But it was not long before religious persecution crept into the relationship.

Copts were tortured and persecuted in every possible way.
With extraordinary resilience they would recover during a lull
in the storm, only to be flattened out by the next gale. Enormous numbers of them turned Moslem, but always a proportion
was ready to suffer and die for the Faith. "The wonder is rather
that any Copts at all kept faith during these hideous centuries,"
wrote Adrian Fortescue, the Catholic historian. "When the last
day comes, weightier than their theological errors will count
the glorious wounds they bore for Him under the blood-stained
banner of Islam."

Until recently the Coptic Patriarch had to be chosen from
the simple monks of the desert monasteries, a good rule in days
when the monasteries were seats of learning. For many centuries, unfortunately, it has resulted in the elevation to the
Chair of St. Mark of an ignorant and generally reluctant recluse.
In 1928 the rule was cancelled, and bishops have now become
eligible for the position of Patriarch. The head of the Coptic
Church must be over fifty, must never have been married, and

A COPTIC CHOIR

must abstain from meat and fish. He ordains the bishops, of whom there are seventeen, and consecrates the holy chrism, or sacred oil. The bishops are celibate, but the priests, who are drawn from the artisan class and are often uneducated, must be married before their ordination. The language of ancient Egypt, which is the liturgical language, is now dead, and few of the priests understand it. About thirty per cent. of the Coptic vocabulary consists of Greek words which crept into the Egyptian language at the time when the native Christians embalmed it, so to speak, in their liturgy fourteen centuries ago. There are two reasons why this ancient language died. After the Arabs had conquered Egypt, Arabic naturally became the spoken language of the country; also, the Church Coptic was the Alexandrian dialect, the Boheiric, which was not spoken by the country at large. Upper Egypt spoke the Sahidic, which differs from the official Church Coptic about as much as Cockney English differs from broad Glasgow. Therefore the last vestige of the old language of the Pharaohs died gradually as a spoken tongue, and it is difficult to say how much of the Boheiric Coptic spoken nowadays in the churches would be understood by a Fifth Century Egyptian of Alexandria.

It is strange that so little has been written in English about the Copts and their religious observances. Separated from the rest of Christendom for fourteen centuries and hidden away in their own misfortunes since the Arab Conquest, their one object has been to preserve and hand down intact their ancient religious life and customs. This causes them to be archæologically the most interesting of all the Eastern churches. They observe to this day customs once common to the Universal Church, which now have died out everywhere except in Egypt. In many of these customs can be heard the beautiful voice of Primitive Christianity. If it should be said that these Christians are ignorant, and that some of them have no very clear or elevated idea of the faith they profess, we should remember that they can boast as many martyrs as any community of their size in history.

Their virtues and their faults spring alike from the fact that for many centuries their whole energy has been spent in an effort to survive.

4

I went to Old Cairo one morning to see the Coptic churches. I had been told that I should never be able to find them by myself, but I thought I would try.

The taxi travelled four miles to the south and left me not far from the Nile, in a vague, dusty district of mounds, tombs, tanneries, and pottery kilns. It had the look of having been terribly kicked about by history. A stark aqueduct marched across the stricken ground. Ghoulish men squatted in black sand-pits, grubbing for the grave-cloths and vestments of early Christians, which now have a market value. These bright embroideries emerge badly crumpled after many centuries in the earth, but their colours are still beautiful. European collectors and museums eagerly buy bits of shirts, shoes, copes and so forth, and mount them between sheets of glass. The Victoria and Albert Museum has a wonderful collection.

I thought Old Cairo infinitely preferable to the Cairo of the big banks, the cinema, and the cabaret. It is dirty, ruined, poverty-stricken, but it is not pretending to be anything else: it is an honest piece of ground which the feet of history have trampled before moving elsewhere. And no one, fortunately, has tidied it up.

The busy quaysides were lovely to look at in that sharp morning light: the quick movement of the crowds expending terrific vitality in argument, the slender masts of *giyasât* lying against the sky, the singing men unloading corn, the lines of black female figures moving veiled along the river-side, with water-pots on their shoulders, and the half-naked children running to the water's edge—all this was beautiful to see. A brown man naked to the waist rose in the bows of a wooden boat and hauled at a rope, his body frozen for a second in that hieratic pose which the artists of ancient Egypt have carved on a hundred tombs. As I stood on the banks of the Nile, I could see three dark triangles to the west, away over the flat land, one slightly larger than the others, rising against the blueness of the sky like three brown cones: the Pyramids of Gizeh.

Turning from the quaysides, I came to a sight which is astonishing even in a land famous for ruins: the remains of the Roman fortress of Babylon. Buildings have been erected on the top, clustering and hiding most of it; and within its walls lies Old Cairo, a mass of tortuous lanes. One gateway of the fortress is almost perfect. It lies between high, rounded bastions, far down in the earth, and the present bed of the Nile, which in Roman times was below the level of the gate, is now above it. I think nothing more vividly illustrates the great age of a building than to look down into a pit and see far beneath the earth a dead roadway on which the feet of men walked many hundreds of years ago. The old fortress of Babylon, with its five courses of stone and three of brick, stands like a piece of Europe in Africa, and even in its decay it seems to cry the word "Rome" with a loud voice. Inside Babylon are the hidden Christian churches of Old Cairo, whose candles have shone through the darkest hours of Coptic history.

I descended some steps which led down towards a furtive little nail-studded postern which would not be out of place in one of the dungeons of the Tower of London. It opens protestingly with a wooden key about two feet long, called a *dabba*. The old woman who opens it sighs and groans with dramatic exaggeration as she pushes back the gate on its rusty hinges, shrewdly eyeing the visitor as she asks alms, not for the love of Allah, but for the sake of Jesus Christ and His Blessed Mother, Sitt Mariam. Such is one's introduction to the home of Christianity in Cairo.

I passed from the fierce sunlight of the quaysides into a network of shadowy lanes where houses nod together in an uncanny silence. The lanes were of beaten mud, the air was stale, and the only people I met were old men and women groping their way along the walls or peering out with pale eyes from dark cellars. The lanes are too narrow for wheeled traffic, and the busy jostling throng was absent which in the East fills the narrowest lanes with life; and I went on between the tumble-down old houses into a strange, deathly silence.

This, I could see, was a Christian ghetto. It had all the signs: poverty, silence, and, although the Copts have not been persecuted for many a long year, fear. The terror of past centuries lives still in these furtive lanes, where the houses nod together, not sleepily or from old age, but as if huddled together in fright. But where were the Coptic churches that I had come to see?

I had been told that the churches of Old Cairo are unique in Christendom in having no exterior architecture. This, by the way, is not correct, for the churches of Verria, in Macedonia, are even better hidden than these Coptic churches proved to be. And as I went on, looking for some sign of a church, I was reminded of a similar experience in Verria, when I once searched everywhere for the numerous churches which the Christians had built inside houses, or behind courtyards, in order to hide them from the eyes of the Turk. And the Copt in the Eighth and Ninth Centuries did exactly the same thing. He made his church look like anything but a church, so that the Moslem should pass it by.

At last, tired and defeated, I approached an old woman who was crouching in the dust of a courtyard. When I spoke to her, she got up and flapped away like an old crow. A small boy, who might have been her great-grandson, came out, and leading me back the way I had come, suddenly pointed to a flight of steps descending below the modern street level. I was sure I had passed the place before and had not noticed it.

"Abu Sarga," said the child.

So this was the famous church of St. Sergius and St. Bacchus, though the name of St. Bacchus is considered too pagan to be perpetuated, and the church is always called simply St. Sergius, or Abu Sarga, by the Copts.

I went down the steps towards what now I saw was obviously the door of a church. I entered a large, dark building smelling of stale incense and of something else which I can only call old age. It was oblong, of basilican shape, and the nave was divided into two aisles by twelve columns, eleven of grey marble and one of red granite. There were five columns on each side, and two at the west end, with a screen between them which shut off the nave and formed the wall of the narthex, or outer portico, where in early times converts not yet baptized were instructed and admonished. The sanctuary at the east end of the church was invisible, for it was concealed by a high screen of inlaid wood with a curtained opening in it. It was not covered with ikons like a Greek screen, and I could see above the screen the top of a domed canopy which evidently stood over the hidden altar. I ventured to draw this curtain aside in order to see the sanctuary. The altar stood by itself, under the painted wooden canopy whose top I had seen above the screen. This canopy rested on four small Saracenic columns, one at each end of the altar. Behind the altar was a wonderful rounded apse with a tribune decorated with alternate perpendicular stripes of light and dark marble, and in the centre of the tribune was a marble throne for the bishop or patriarch. The marble seats curved round the apse in seven tiers, with this throne in the centre.

While I was making some notes, I turned to see a rather angry-looking priest watching me. He was short, stout and dark, a soft black beard ringed his face, and he wore a black gown buttoned to the neck and a low round black turban on his head. From his expression I gathered that I had offended him by looking into the sanctuary, and I hastened to apologize; his anger was not with me, however, but with himself for being absent when I arrived. We got on well together, and I discovered that he spoke English, which he had taught himself.

He asked me to remove my shoes before he took me into the sanctuary. I did this, for when the Copt enters the sanctuary of his church he always obeys the words which the Lord spake to Moses from the Burning Bush: "Put off thy shoes from off thy feet, for the place whereon thou standest is holy ground."

In our stockinged feet, we passed through the opening in the screen into the holy of holies. I asked him the word for "altar" and he said "madbah," which is derived from an Arabic word which means to slaughter, or sacrifice. He told me that the altar in all Coptic churches must stand alone in an open space. It must never be fixed to a wall, as in many of our Western churches. It is necessary in the Coptic Mass for the celebrant to move right round the altar and cense it. Lifting the cloth, he showed me that the altar was made of stone; on the top was a ridge cut in the stone to take a wooden tray on which the chalice and paten stand during the Mass. I asked if any Coptic altars were made of wood. He shook his finger violently, and said no, such a thing was against the rules of his Church, but the vessels must always stand on a wooden tray. This is a reversal of Western practice. In the Latin Church the Eucharistic vessels must always rest on stone, and the stone slab is the only part of the altar which is consecrated.

I noticed a little cavity in the altar, which I thought might at one time have been a reliquary. He told me that on Good Friday a cross is always buried in this cavity on a bed of rose leaves, and taken out on Easter morning.

He allowed me to examine the painted wooden box which was standing on the altar. This is also a feature of all Coptic churches and is not used for the reservation of the Sacrament, a practice which was discontinued in the Coptic Church centuries ago: it is for the reception of the chalice during Mass. There is a semi-circular opening in the top of the box with which the rim of the chalice is level when it is standing inside, and it is placed inside the box during the consecration.

Seeing that I was interested, the priest went into a sacristry and came back with the vessels used in the Mass. These were a silver chalice, a round paten, a dome, and a spoon. The dome was two hoops of silver crossed at right angles. It is placed over the bread on the paten, and on top of it is cast a veil or corporal. The spoon is used for giving the sacrament, for it is the custom to place the eucharistic bread in the wine and to give each communicant both kinds together.

There was also a round fan which is used during Mass to wave away flies from the sacred elements. I believe the only survival of the fan to be seen in the ritual of the West is when the Pope enters St. Peter's in state, with men walking on each side of the papal litter holding magnificent fans of peacocks' feathers, mounted on handles about six feet in length. I asked him if fans were used in all the Coptic churches, and he said they were.

The eucharistic bread of the Coptic Church must always be freshly baked on church premises on the morning of the Mass, and it is generally made by the sacristan of the church. Every church has its own little bake-house where the bread, made from the finest flour, is carefully prepared on Sunday morning and stamped with a device of crosses. This is called the Korbân, a word the Copts also apply to the Mass itself. It is leavened bread, and each cake is about three inches in diameter and one inch in thickness. The priest was sorry he could not show one to me.

When we left the sanctuary and had put on our shoes, he took great trouble to explain the church. All Coptic churches have three altars in a line at the east end. In Abu Sarga they are hidden, like the high altar, by a continuation of the haikal screen.

The reason for the three altars is interesting. One Mass only may be celebrated on a Coptic altar in one day, for the altar, like the celebrant and the communicant, must come "fasting." If it is necessary to celebrate more than one Mass, the high altar is first used and then one of the two side altars; otherwise the side altars are used only on the day of the saint to which they are dedicated.

While we were passing down the nave, I pointed out the one pillar of red granite among the eleven marble pillars and asked if there was any significance in this. He replied that the pillars represented the twelve apostles, and that the odd pillar stood for Judas, who betrayed his Lord, and was therefore different from the others.

In the narthex we came to a space in the floor which was boarded over. He lifted a plank and exposed an enormous baptismal font, like a small swimming-bath. Coptic baptism is by total immersion, and in the early days, when the Church gained adult converts, they entered this tank of water together, but now the tanks are rarely used. I noticed that the pillars of the nave had once been painted with figures of saints, but on only two columns is it still possible to see a trace of painting. The priest told me that these figures represented Abu Sarga and his brother. I did not know that St. Sergius had a brother, and I wondered if the companion figure might not have been St. Bacchus. Having been to Resafa, I was naturally interested to hear if the priest had any stories about St. Sergius, but all he could say was that the saint was a gallant Roman soldier who was martyred long ago "at the village of Resafa."

The priest then led the way to the crypt of Abu Sarga, in which, says Coptic tradition, the Holy Family rested during the Flight into Egypt. This legend has given the church such fame that it is perhaps the only one of Old Cairo's churches where a European traveller may occasionally be seen.

Two flights of steps lead down from opposite sides of the

attitude during prayer is, I think, very beautiful. They stand upright, their feet together and their hands held outwards, the palms upward, the elbows close to the body. This is the attitude of prayer seen on the earliest Christian monuments, notably in the catacombs of Rome.

I went one day to a strange church called Al Mu'allakah, the "Hanging Church," which is built between two of the bastions of the fortress of Babylon. Although the date of all these churches is purely conjectural, there seems little doubt that this church was built in the Fourth Century, and a smaller one, which is attached to it, in the Third, or even the Second, Century. The church is full of intricate inlay work and carved screens, so that the general effect is a curious compromise between a church and a mosque.

The ancient Egyptians were experts in all kinds of delicate inlay work, as we can see in any museum and as the treasures from the tomb of Tut-ankh-Amûn prove, and it seems that their descendants have inherited this gift. Coptic inlay work is generally a geometric pattern carried out in wood and mother-of-pearl. A remarkable screen in this church is made of cedar-wood, inlaid with thin plates of ivory set in a complex pattern. When illuminated from the back, the whole screen glows with a beautiful rose colour as the light shines through the ivory.

But I was more interested in the poorer, shabbier churches of Old Cairo. Whenever I went to them, I now was preceded by a crowd of people eager to show me the way and determined that I should miss nothing. As I followed them through the narrow lanes between the gaunt, shuttered houses, the strangeness of Old Cairo grew on me, always so quiet that the mild excitement of my arrival and the sound of voices would draw faces to the grilles overhead. Sometimes a door would be opened wide enough to reveal an eye. Then I would suddenly find myself alone in a lane. The crowd had melted away through a narrow door, and I knew that we had come to a church.

There is the church of Sitt Burbârah, or St. Barbara, a huge, dark place where the stiff figures of saints gaze down from the screens. St. Barbara, the patron saint of gunsmiths, artillery- men and, strangely enough, architects, was a Greek of Heliop- olis who was martyred in the year 235, and I wondered how much these Egyptians knew about her life. When I asked them, a scene of the utmost confusion took place. First one man started to tell me, then another interrupted, three or four joined in, and very soon violent arguments were going on in various parts of the church. Eventually someone produced an old man who was, I think, the sacristan. He was suspicious and confused, but, given time, and with repeated interruptions from the crowd, managed to tell an accurate story of the saint's life, although I was surprised that he did not know that St. Barbara had been born within a few miles of the place in which he was standing.

She was a great lady, the "daughter of a Roman general," he said, and her father, loving her very much and disliking the thought that some man would wish to marry her, locked her in a high tower where she was allowed to see no one. But she had heard of Christianity, and a missionary was taken in to her disguised as a doctor, with the result that she was converted to the true Faith. Her father decided to build for her a beautiful *hammam*—a bathroom—and one day, when it was being built, she went to see it and gave orders that three windows, instead of two, should be placed in the walls. Her father was angry when he learned that she had altered his plans, and came in a towering rage to ask for an explanation. St. Barbara told him that the light of the soul came through three windows, one called the Son, a second called the Father, and a third called the Holy Ghost. The father, horrified to discover that his daughter had joined the new Faith, denounced her to the authorities and she was beheaded. On the day of her martyrdom a sudden storm broke when the father was returning from the execution, and he was killed by lightning; and that is the reason why St. Barbara is the patron saint of soldiers and gunsmiths, who deal in sudden death.

A saint popular all over Egypt is commemorated by the fine old church of Abu Sefain, "Father of the Two Swords." Here is a building that simply drips antiquity, although it is probably not so venerable as either Abu Sarga or Al Mu'allakah. It is, however, dustier and less frequented, and the screens lean together with their ikons as if tired of the weight of years. All kinds of dark, mysterious passages and side chapels lie around in almost pitch darkness, and the very wood reeks of incense.

My friends uncovered a leathern bolster which is said to contain the arm-bone of Abu Sefain. Above the relic hangs an ikon showing the saint riding on a black horse, carrying the two swords with which he is always painted and bearing the body of a dead man across the crupper of his saddle. An angel is appearing from the clouds, and a bishop in the foreground is appealing to the saint. This is the story as they told it to me.

Abu Sefain's Greek name was St. Mercurius, and he was a Christian officer in the army of the Emperor Decius. When the army was fighting the Persians, an angel appeared to the saint and gave him a new sword, commanding him to make the sign of the Cross on all war material. This he did, and the Persians were vanquished. But the Emperor, seeing the Cross, ordered Mercurius to sacrifice to idols. He refused to do so, proclaiming his faith in Jesus Christ, and was tortured and put to death at Cæsarea in Asia Minor. The Egyptian Patriarch Athanasius journeyed to Asia Minor and returned with the saint's arm.

Here they reverently patted the leathern bolster in confirmation.

The bishop in the picture was St. Basil. One day when he was praying before an ikon of St. Mercurius, he begged the saint to avenge the Christians who were being murdered by the wicked Governor of Alexandria. The saint faded from the picture and reappeared, and as he did so St. Basil saw that the sword had turned red, and knew that the Governor had been slain.

Although the Copts have eccentric ideas of chronology and mix up people and events with cheerful inconsequence, the story agrees surprisingly well with known facts. All the historical persons in this story could have done the things attributed to them. The "Governor of Alexandria" was the Emperor Julian the Apostate. Athanasius lived long enough after Abu Sefain's death to collect the relic, and Julian died while St. Basil was alive.

6

I asked one of my Coptic friends if it were possible to see a Coptic nunnery. We were walking through the streets of Old Cairo at the time and, rather to my surprise, he said that we might see one at that moment. He stopped and pushed open an unpromising-looking gate in a high wall, and we entered an untidy yard from which a flight of steps led to several Arab houses. An old woman was grinding corn at the bottom of the steps and another was crouched in the dust, picking over a mass of wilted-looking lettuce leaves.

Other women, some of them young girls, were sitting cross-legged on the balcony of one of the houses, and numerous infants playing about the stairs took to flight as soon as they saw us. A Coptic nunnery is more like an almshouse than our idea of a convent. The inmates are women whose husbands have died or who have no means of supporting themselves. They receive permission from the Patriarch to enter a nunnery, where their life seems singularly free from spiritual strain. They take no veil and make no vows, and are allowed to visit their friends. Some even leave the convent and marry.

A tall, dark woman in a black Arab dress descended the steps and nervously inquired who we were. She was the Mother Superior.

She led the way to the houses where the nuns live. There are about eighteen in the nunnery at present. She opened the door of a room which is kept for the reception of guests. A divan ran round the walls, piled with pillows for the guest to lean on. The walls were decorated with ikons of various saints. I noticed St. Paul the anchorite, with a beard that touched his knees.

The infants began to play again, and down in the narrow lane outside the quiet, furtive life of Old Cairo went on its way. I told her how interested I was in the traditions of the Coptic Church, and so the ice was broken; for these people are pathetically grateful if a fellow Christian visits them and asks to see their churches.

"We pray in the morning," said the Mother Superior in reply to a question of mine, "and then we busy ourselves with our household work. Once a week the priest comes for the Korbân."

A young nun entered with the little cups of coffee which form a preliminary to everything in the East. Each time I sipped my coffee I bowed and offered salaams to the Mother Superior; every time she sipped her cup she bent towards me and gravely uttered a compliment. I felt that we were getting along so well that I ventured to offer her a cigarette. She said that she never smoked as a rule, but that on this occasion she would break the rule.

I gathered that the chief duty of the nuns was to guard the shrine of Mari Girgis, which is the Arabic name for St. George. When the coffee was finished we went to see his shrine.

We entered a remarkable hall which might have come from a Norman castle in England. Stone walls towered to the shadows of the roof, and the stones were so massive that, had they been in Syria, they would almost certainly have been of the crusading period.

The hall was bare and empty save at one end, where an apse, or alcove, was railed off. This was the shrine of Mari Girgis. Tapers of unbleached wax were burning before an ikon which showed St. George in the act of destroying a terrifying dragon.

This picture reposed on the wall in a nest of rags of every size, shape, and colour. They were scraps from the clothing of people who had suffered from some illness; many of them, said the Mother Superior, had been tied there by Moslems.

One of the interesting things in Egypt is the reverence which many Moslems show for the magic powers of Christian saints, especially St. George. Most of the Christian festivals in the country are attended by Christians and Moslems, and one cannot help feeling that these pious Moslems are those whose ancestors apostasized centuries ago and, so to speak, have Christianity and a reverence for Christian saints in their blood.

The strangest object in the shrine, which I nearly overlooked in the darkness, was a heavy iron halter. This was attached to a long chain which was firmly bolted into a stone below the ikon.

The Mother Superior explained that mad people were brought here to be chained for a night, sometimes for days, until St. George lifted the madness from them. This, she said, often happened, and the mad were cured. At first they raged and foamed at the mouth and fought to get loose, and in this effort they exhausted themselves, eventually falling into a deep sleep. And while they slept St. George came in a dream and healed them.

This is a wonderful example of a living belief in the Æsculapian dream-cures that were once practised in pagan temples all over the world. The generals who kept vigil in the temple at Babylon just before Alexander's death were there to ask the god whether their general should be moved into the sacred precincts, probably to submit his fever to a dream-cure. And in all parts of Egypt to-day, wherever there is a church of Mari

Girgis, the faith in the efficacy of a dream-cure is as strong as it was in ancient times.

As I bade her farewell, the Mother Superior said that if I would come back some Sunday, she was sure that she would be able to show me a patient waiting to be cured by St. George.

7

In the Coptic Museum in Old Cairo early Christian relics are preserved amid lovely surroundings, thanks to the enthusiasm of Morcos Simaika Pasha, a gifted member of the Coptic community. Here may be seen the most interesting and varied collection of Coptic objects in the world.

What must astonish anyone who knows Ireland is the resemblance between Coptic antiquities and those of the Celtic Church. Though so far apart, the two countries must have been in close touch on religious matters during the first Christian centuries. Ireland's pre-eminence in classical studies during the dark ages, and the number of Greek and Latin scholars which she sent to educate Europe from the time of Charlemagne onwards, have often been cited as a remarkable and inexplicable fact of history. But I do not know why it should be so. The Irish monks were great travellers, and it is highly probable that they drew their Hellenistic culture straight from the theological schools of Alexandria. I would suggest that Egypt may be the answer to what so many writers have called the mystery of Ireland's intellectual brilliance at a time when the lamps of learning had been extinguished in the fall of the Roman Empire.

It is known that many Irishmen travelled to Egypt in the first six centuries of the Christian era, and that Egyptian monks visited Ireland. Seven Coptic monks are said to be buried in Ireland, at Disert Ulidh, and Professor O'Leary mentions in his recent book, *The Saints of Egypt*, that the Bibliothèque Nationale in Paris possesses an Irish guide book for the use of pilgrims to the Holy Land of Scetis, which was in the Egyptian desert.

But the association between the two countries was based on much deeper matters than the visits of occasional travellers or the interchange of scholars. It is believed that the Irish continued to observe the Egyptian monastic rule after the rest of Europe had adopted that of St. Benedict. The Egyptian rule first came to Europe when St. Athanasius visited Rome in 340 A.D. It was a system of individualistic asceticism as opposed to the asceticism in community which was a later Western development. Hermits lived alone in caves and rocks, and would build not one large church, but a number of diminutive churches scattered over a small area. The "Seven Churches" of Glendalough, in County Wicklow, are a perfect example of a primitive Egyptian monastery of the time of the Desert Fathers.

The wagon-vaulted Celtic churches of Ireland have frequently been termed unique and an Irish invention. But they are not. The wagon-vault is a characteristic of the Coptic Church, and was in use in Egypt from the earliest times. It is certain that Egypt is the home of the wagon-vaulted basilica, and that this type of roof should be unknown in the West except in Ireland would seem to indicate another significant link between the Celtic and the Egyptian churches.

No one can look at the illuminated gospels in the Coptic Museum without thinking of the Book of Kells. There is also a close resemblance between the beautifully ornate gospel-cases, of which every Coptic church has one example, and the *cumhdachs* so famous in Ireland. Another curious resemblance is the bells still used in the Coptic Mass. These little hand-bells are very like the bells known to every visitor to an Irish Museum as "St. Patrick's bells." I noticed a metal gospel-case in the Coptic Museum, decorated with spirals and richly jewelled, which might be placed side by side with the famous bell-shrine of St. Patrick. The carvings in wood and stone, showing men and beasts within circles, also bear a strong family resemblance to the sculptured stone crosses of Ireland.

When anyone tries to explain Ireland's classical brilliance during the dark ages, it is usually said that scholars fled there from Gaul and from the ancient seats of learning during the barbarian wars. And it is true that in biographies of the time the phrase that so and so, "forsaking his own country, sojourned in Ireland for the love of God and learning," becomes monotonously repetitive. I suggest that long before this, possibly in the Third and Fourth Centuries, Irishmen had studied in the schools of Alexandria and had taken back to their own country the riches of learning which could be found in that city.

There is a curious incident in the life of St. Patrick which did not seem to me to have any special significance until I became interested in the possible link between the Egyptian and the Celtic churches. When St. Patrick was travelling in the hills, I forget in what part of Ireland, he entered a cave and saw there an altar on which stood four glass chalices. The point of this story is that these chalices belonged to Christians who had worshipped in Ireland long before the time of St. Patrick. Chalices were obviously made of metal at the time of this discovery, otherwise glass chalices would not have struck St. Patrick as curious antiquities.

Now it is surely significant that glass chalices were commonly in use throughout Christendom during the first two centuries. It is believed that St. Urban prescribed the use of metal instead of glass in 226 A.D., over two hundred years before St. Patrick entered the cave. The Egyptian Church used chalices of glass in the First Century and uses them to this day, generally from reasons of poverty; but that they are still in use proves that Egypt has never known any rule or prejudice against chalices of glass.

It is possible, therefore, that when St. Patrick was walking the holy hills of Ireland so long ago, he stumbled by chance upon the oratory of some ancient Irish hermits who had learned their Christianity in Egypt. And I would also suggest that the lives and habits of the Desert Fathers of Egypt can be paralleled nowhere so well as in the story of the Celtic hermits. St. Kevin, who founded the settlement at Glendalough, in County Wicklow, was rather like St. Anthony. I remember hearing the story, when I was there, of the temptations of St. Kevin. He was pursued by an ardent maiden named Kathleen, who, says one version of the story, penetrated to his fastness in the Wicklow Hills, just as visions of women tempted St. Anthony among the hills near the Red Sea. The poet Moore causes St. Kevin to push the vision of beauty into the lake, which is probably exactly what St. Anthony would have done in a similar situation. It is known that after St. Athanasius visited Rome in 340 A.D., his *Life of St. Anthony*, translated into Latin, had a wide circulation in the West, where it stimulated the contemplative ideal. Who knows but that St. Kevin was in the habit of reading the temptations of St. Anthony in his Wicklow cave, and that the story of the beautiful maiden is a twisted memory of this book?

Perhaps scholars will some day work on this hidden chapter of Christian history and establish beyond doubt the connection between the Celtic Church and the Church that was probably its parent, the Church of St. Mark in Egypt. "The great difficulty in understanding the evolution of Celtic art lies in the fact that although the Celts never seem to have invented any new ideas, they professed an extraordinary aptitude for picking up ideas from the different people with whom war and commerce brought them into contact," writes A. J. Romilly in *Celtic Art in Pagan and Christian Times*. "And once the Celt had borrowed an idea from his neighbour, he was able to give it such a strong Celtic tinge that it soon became something so dif-

ferent from what it was originally as to be almost unrecognizable."

Still, I think it is possible to recognize the origins of Celtic
art in the relics which are to be seen beside the Nile.

While I was in the Coptic museum one day, the kindly
founder, Morcos Simaika Pasha, came out leaning on his stick
and walked round with me, lovingly caressing the brands which
he has torn literally from the burning.

"By the way," he said, "you are so interested in my church
that you might like to come to a ceremony to-night. It is a wedding. Be at the Church of El Adra, the Blessed Virgin, in the
Mouski, at seven-thirty. . . ."

8

It was dark when I set out to find the church in the Mouski.
The Moslem driver did not know where it was and we were
soon lost in narrow, crowded lanes, where the horse nosed his
way over the shoulders of the crowd to an accompaniment of
maniac cries and much whip-cracking. The Cairo cab-drivers
use their whips, I am glad to say, not so much on their steeds as
on their compatriots.

Once we had to stop, for the lane was so narrow, while a
man moved from our path a bright rampart of the superb vegetables which the black soil of Egypt produces in profusion:
majestic cauliflowers which would win a prize anywhere at
home, leeks as thick as one's wrist, fat purple aubergines, and
lizard-green cucumbers. Anyone unfamiliar with the East
might have expected murder at any moment, as green-grocer
and driver flung themselves into an ecstasy of vituperation.
Their faces became distorted with rage. They waved their
arms, their indignant palms lay upward in the lamplight, their

fingers outstretched, and at the precise moment when Englishmen would have knocked each other down and gangsters
would probably have produced their "rods," the contest in
abuse concluded and, with a smile which indicated that he had
enjoyed it all very much, the green-grocer politely removed his
cauliflowers. And we went on.

I enjoyed the feeling of gliding peacefully through dark
canyons full of life. Each lighted booth was a vivid picture
framed by darkness: in some, cross-legged men sat at coffee or
commerce; in others, Syrians or Armenians sat like spiders in
their webs, in shops loaded with Persian rugs; and sometimes,
when we came to a standstill and the faces seemed to close in on
me, I would see three or four black, veiled ghosts gazing into
the carriage, their dark eyes ringed with *kohl*, placid and ex-
pressionless. We came to a corner where several streets met. A
minaret, rising from the deeper darkness below, lay against the
sky, washed in a green light of its own, and the driver, pointing
down a lane with his whip, told me that even he could not venture there: it was filled from side to side with cars, taxi-cabs,
and *'arabîyât*.

The wedding guests were dodging round the fenders of the
cars, making for the end of the lane, where a large crowd had
gathered before the church door. They were waiting for the
bride. Facing each other in two lines stood a choir of young
men stretching from door to street. They wore white gowns
like night-shirts, with stoles crossed on the left shoulder. On
each head was a stiff little cap of white with a silver cross on
the top; in each hand was a lighted candle. One man held cymbals, another held a triangle. As they stood in the darkness, the
candle-light moving over their dark, clean-shaven faces, I
thought that I might be looking at priests of Isis.

There was some commotion as a car ploughed its way among
the spectators, and from it stepped a girl like a dark, full-blown
peony. She wore an evening dress of cream-coloured lace. Her

raven-black hair shone from recent treatment. Her plump, good-looking face was flushed beneath the rouge that sits so feverishly on dark skins. Four bridesmaids, likewise in evening dress, took their places beside her, whereupon the choir, suddenly breaking into a harsh chant punctuated by a clash of cymbals, led the way into the church.

In the confusion of the arrival, I was conscious only that we had entered a hot, crowded place in which lights from pendulous candelabra blazed everywhere. Presently a young usher took me away from my modest seat at the back, and, to my confusion and embarrassment, gave me a seat among the officiating clergy. There was, however, nothing to be done about it.

The bride and bridegroom sat a few yards from me on red and gilt chairs placed before the haikal screen. The bridegroom sat at the bride's left hand, wearing an expression of self-consciousness which is probably an international one at such a moment in a man's life. Candles burned all round them, so that they sat in a pool of golden light. The bridegroom wore evening dress, over which was draped a richly decorated cope. He wore a tarbush on his head, and gazed uneasily through horn-rimmed glasses beyond the fence of candles.

Here, I thought, we have a typical Coptic mixture of past and present, of East and West. The choir were singing an anthem in the tongue of the Pharaohs, the bridegroom wore a head-dress which suggested Mohammedanism, with a cope that might have been worn by St. Athanasius, and the evening dress of modern civilization, with a pair of glasses that at once suggested America. The bridesmaids, on the other hand, were as near Paris as they could be. And it was upon this fantasy in origins that the saints and fathers of the Egyptian Church gazed from their aged ikons through an ascending mist of incense.

Among the dignitaries with whom I sat were the Bishop of Tanta, the Bishop of Jerusalem, and the acting Bishop of Khartum. They wore black soutanes with silver pectoral crosses, and on their heads were the tight black turbans of the Coptic priesthood. The ceremony was a long and interesting one. The bishops rose one after the other to say prayers or to deliver long and powerful exhortations. A member of the laity read from the Scriptures in Arabic with considerable dramatic force; and I thought how strange it was to see a man in a tarbush reading lessons in a church. Between every prayer, and at the conclusion of the lessons, the choir, led by a young man who quietly beat time with one finger, plunged into long, harsh anthems. The sound of the triangle and the rhythmic beat of cymbals, which accompanied all the quicker anthems, lent an air of paganism to the scene. There were two choirmen in particular who might have come straight from a painting in any tomb of ancient Egypt. They had the same lips, noses, and almond eyes, and their hands, I noticed, were extraordinarily slender and well-shaped.

The bride was fanned throughout the ceremony by one of her maids. This bridesmaid was dark and slender, her face neat, round, and slightly negroid, with pouting lips, a type seen on the walls of certain 18th Dynasty Theban tombs. The dancers in the tomb of Nacht are the type I am trying to describe, and so are the women in the festive fresco in the British Museum, the one which depicts the full-face figures and the two naked girl tumblers. As this girl stood moving the ostrich feathers and gazing beyond the candle-light with dark, deer-like eyes, I thought that Charmian probably looked like that when she fanned her mistress in Alexandria.

To a solemn chanting, the bride and bridegroom were anointed with oil, and then came the culminating moment of the ceremony. Two golden crowns were produced and, as the bishop took them in his hands, he uttered the following prayer in Arabic:

"O God, the Holy One, who crownest Thy saints with unfading Crowns and hast joined heavenly things and earthly things in unity, now also, O our Master, bless these Crowns which we have prepared for Thy servants; may they be to them a Crown of glory and honour. Amen. A Crown of blessing and salvation. Amen. A Crown of joy and gladness. Amen. A Crown of delight and pleasure. Amen. A Crown of virtue and righteousness. Amen. A Crown of wisdom and understanding. Amen. A Crown of strength and confirmation. Amen. Grant to Thy servants who shall wear them the Angel of Peace, and the bonds of love, save them from all shameful thoughts and base desires, and deliver them from all evil assaults and all temptations of the devil. Let Thy mercy be upon them, hear the voice of their prayer, let Thy fear fall upon their hearts, watch over their lives, that they may be without want until old age. Gladden them with the sight of sons and daughters and bring up those that shall be born to them as useful members of Thy one only Holy Catholic Apostolic Church; and let them be established in the Orthodox faith to the end. Watch over them in the way of truth, according to the will of God."

Here he paused a moment and placed one crown over the tarbush of the groom and one on the dark hair of the bride, saying, as he did so:

"With glory and honour thou hast crowned them, O Lord; the Father blesses, the Son crowns, and the Spirit comes down upon them and perfects them. Worthy, worthy, worthy, place, O Lord, upon thy servants a Crown of grace that shall not be overcome. Amen. A Crown of high and abundant glory. Amen. A Crown of good and invincible faith. Amen. And bless all their actions, for Thou art the giver of all good things, O Christ our God."

Two rings were brought tied together by a red ribbon. The bishop untied them and placed one on the finger of the groom and the other on that of the bride. He then pronounced a benediction and, drawing their heads close together, touched them with his hand-cross. A beautiful and ancient ceremony was over.

All the wedding guests now approached to congratulate the enthroned couple as they sat together in the yellow light like Pharaoh and his queen. The ostrich fan moved all the time over the bride's head and the bridesmaids, in modern taffeta dance-frocks of mauve and yellow, rustled and whispered behind the throne, making large eyes at the court.

As we left the church we were each given a little present. It was hard and knobbly, and when I unwrapped mine in the hotel, I found a small gilt casket, velvet-lined, full of sugared almonds and silvered sweets.

9

It occurred to me that I had seen a faithful version of a marriage in primitive Christian times. Like all ceremonies of the Coptic Church, it had come down singularly unchanged from the Græco-Roman world, unvaried by the emendations, the omissions, and the alterations which Western churches have introduced into the ceremony.

All pagan and primitive Christian weddings were in two parts: the Betrothal and the Wedding. I had seen only the Wedding, or the second part, for the Betrothal had taken place weeks, perhaps months, before. This is a solemn business, as the attending priest reminds the contracting parties. The parents of the bride and bridegroom settle the bride's dowry, draw up a marriage contract, and choose the date of the wedding. This corresponds with ancient custom in Greece and Rome. The pagan and the early Christian bridegrooms all gave the bride an engagement ring at this stage of the proceedings. We have inherited our "ring finger" from the Romans, who wore an engagement ring on the fourth finger of the left hand because, as Gellius said, it is connected to the heart by a nerve. The solemn character of this contract, and a memory of its religious solemnity in Christian times, is still preserved in Coptic custom by the fact that it should be the priest, and not the bridegroom, who hands the bride her engagement ring.

The marriage at night is an obvious survival of a custom which goes back into a remote past, for no marriages were celebrated by daylight in the ancient world. Again, the crowning of bride and bridegroom is another pagan custom adopted by the Primitive Church, although only the Eastern Church still observes it: the wedding veil, which is Roman, was always more symbolically important in the West. As in ancient times, the Coptic Church regards the crowns as symbols of virtue and purity and, as in the earliest times, they are the property of the Church and are solemnly returned when a stated interval after the wedding has elapsed.

It is still the custom, though not among modern members of Coptic communities in the cities, to take the bride from her own home to that of her husband by torchlight, attended by musicians, and a noisy crowd in which walks a man carrying a lighted candle in a bunch of flowers. This is an extraordinarily interesting survival of the pagan "marriage pomp" that was sometimes condemned by the early Christian Fathers because it tended to become riotous. In the lighted candle we can see, no doubt, the nuptial torch of the Roman wedding, which was lit by the bride's mother before the procession set forth on its way. St. Gregory of Nazienzus wrote a charming little letter in the Fourth Century, in which he excused himself from the gaiety of a wedding on the plea that a gouty old gentleman would be out of place among dancers, though in his heart he would be with them in their amusements. Therefore some of these routs, although high-spirited, were among the functions to which saints were sometimes invited, and it is indeed pleasant to think of the Early Fathers of the Church smiling benevolently on such celebrations.

The casket of sugared almonds was clearly a token from the ancient world, for it was the custom of Roman bridegrooms to cast nuts among the crowd as the procession passed through the streets, while in ancient Greece sweetmeats were thrown over the bride as she entered her new home. Therefore sugared almonds are a happy blend of Greek and Roman custom.

I remembered that the last time I had seen this true *confetti* was in strangely different surroundings. It was at the wedding of Umberto, Crown Prince of Italy, to Princess Mafalda of Belgium, in the Quirinal Palace at Rome. As guests left the palace, sugared almonds were flung in such enormous quantities that stairs were strewn with them in every direction. It is obvious that our *confetti* and rice are a variation of this old custom, though real *confetti* is, as the name tells us, a sweetmeat.

All the venerable customs embalmed in the Coptic wedding have come from Hellenistic Alexandria in an unbroken chain of observance. But older than any of them is the scene at the bridegroom's door after the church ceremony, when the bride must not only witness the sacrifice of a calf but must step over its blood into her new home. That is neither Greek nor Roman; Christian nor Moslem: it something that has come down to the Copts of to-day from their ancestors of ancient Egypt.

10

The story of the Flight into Egypt has naturally inspired a mass of Coptic legend, most of it based on piety rather than on history. One only of the four Evangelists, St. Matthew, mentions the Flight into Egypt, and his words are the only record we possess of this event.

It is true that there are other accounts as full of detail as the account of St. Matthew is brief and reserved, but these are to be found in the apocryphal gospels which are compositions of a later time and have little historical value.

This incident in the life of Christ has always captured the imagination of artists. Some of the most beautiful pictures in Christian Art show the Holy Family travelling under cover of night, or passing in starlight beneath the shadow of the Pyramids. Those monuments were already ancient, and the bodies buried in them had long since been robbed, when Jesus, Mary, and Joseph journeyed into the land of Egypt.

"Behold, the Angel of the Lord appeareth to Joseph in a dream, saying, Arise, and take the young child and his mother, and flee into Egypt, and be thou there until I bring thee word: for Herod will seek the young child to destroy him.

"When he arose, he took the young child and his mother by night, and departed into Egypt: and was there until the death of Herod: that it might be fulfilled which was spoken of the Lord by the prophet, saying, Out of Egypt have I called my son. . . .

"But when Herod was dead, behold, an angel of the Lord appeareth in a dream to Joseph in Egypt, saying, Arise, and take the young child and his mother, and go into the Land of Israel: for they are dead which sought the young child's life. . . .

"But when he heard that Archelaus did reign in Judæa in the room of his father Herod, he was afraid to go thither: notwithstanding, being warned of God in a dream, he turned aside into the parts of Galilee: and he came and dwelt in a city called Nazareth: that it might be fulfilled which was spoken by the prophets, He shall be called a Nazarene."

Thus St. Matthew tells us that Jesus was taken out of Palestine in infancy and that he remained in Egypt until Herod's son, Archelaus, succeeded to the throne of Judæa. On the return journey, St. Joseph "turned aside into the parts of Galilee" because he was afraid to venture into the territory of Archelaus. St. Matthew does not mention the reason for this fear, but it was probably on account of the rebellion which broke out after Herod's death and was quelled by Archelaus only after three thousand Jews, among them many Passover pilgrims, had been slaughtered. This is almost certain to have been the reason why the Holy Family turned aside from Judæa. It may have been St. Joseph's intention to attend the Passover in Jerusalem, but, hearing of the massacre, he "turned aside into the parts of Galilee."

The Egypt which the Holy Family entered stands in the clear light of history. Twenty-seven years previously Antony and Cleopatra had been defeated at the naval battle of Actium, and with Cleopatra's death ended for ever the Greek dynasty which had begun with Alexander's general, Ptolemy. Rome then stepped in and added Egypt to the Empire of Augustus Cæsar. The Prefect of Egypt at the time of the Flight was Turrianus, about whom nothing is known except that, after the death of Augustus, he was the first to swear allegiance to Tiberius, the Cæsar of the Crucifixion.

The country which sheltered the Holy Family was a very different country from the land which Joseph and Moses had known. The Pharaohs, their glories over, lay in painted tombs, and the grandeur that once had been Egypt was merely a record written on a temple gate. In the reign of Augustus, Egypt had a Greek head and an Egyptian body. The head, Alexandria, was the New York and Paris of the age, a brilliant city, wealthy and famous all over the world for its intellectual achievements and its mechanical inventions. Its Library was the greatest university of its time, and its temples, public buildings, and baths were known the world over for their splendour.

But the Nile, flowing south, left all this modern brilliance behind and entered the ancient country which was still the land of the Pharaohs. Upper Egypt had nothing in common with the foreign city of Alexandria: it belonged to a different world. The native temples lifted their painted pylons above the still waters, and the shaven priests still offered sacrifices to the old gods of the land. The great cities from which the Pharaohs had once ridden in a splendour of nodding plumes, driving their gilded chariots of acacia wood, were now slowly dying of old age. Greek and Roman tourists sailed up the Nile to see the curiosities of that strange, unlikely country, gazing in awe on the face of the Sphinx, writing their names on the knees of the Colossi at Thebes, and coming, perhaps, to some small, lost temple in the palm groves where a few poor priests still fed the sacred crocodiles from force of habit, and mumbled prayers whose meaning they had forgotten. This was the old, dying country of the Flight into Egypt.

No wonder that artists have always seized with eagerness on this incident in the life of Jesus. What a significant picture it makes: the Infant Christ journeying through a land where the Egyptian, the Greek, and the Roman civilizations, the three great empires of antiquity, were living side by side in the last years of paganism. There is a picture—I cannot remember where I have seen it—which shows the Blessed Virgin with the Child in her arms, drawing aside from a great crowd which comes shouting down a street beside a mighty temple. And in the centre of the crowd, lifted high on the shoulders of the priests, is the image of an Egyptian god. Clouds of incense blow about him, priestesses strew flowers in his path; and Jesus and His Mother move to the side of the road to let this idol go past. Who can say that a meeting such as this did not, in fact, take place?

When we ask ourselves where the Holy Family stayed in Egypt, we are faced by a perplexing choice of locality. Devout monks, writing centuries after, have claimed all kinds of improbable places, some far up the Nile, as the resting-place of the Infant Christ. The oldest and the most likely tradition is that the Holy Family stayed at a place now called Mataria, which was near ancient Heliopolis.

I went to Mataria one morning. It is an easy drive of six miles from Cairo, and beside a dusty road on the outskirts of Heliopolis I found the little garden which contains the Virgin's Tree. This is a noble Egyptian sycamore, which bears a pink fruit rather like a fig, called *jamaiz*. Its gnarled arms sprawl about the garden and are held up by posts and stumps, so that it looks like a colossal invalid on crutches. Although it was not planted until after 1672, it is not difficult to understand why the peasants believe that it is the same tree beneath whose shade the Infant Jesus was laid to rest. Except, perhaps, for the great yew in Selborne churchyard, I cannot remember a tree which so impresses one with its age. But even the Selborne tree, which is infinitely older than this sycamore, has not the same kind of bearded and gnarled antiquity. A yew tree always carries its age with a certain heavy sprightliness, whereas the sycamore of Mataria wears all the wrinkles possible to a tree in extreme old age. Every branch within reaching distance is covered with rags tied by Christians and Moslems, for it is believed that the tree has potent magical properties.

A little bare-legged girl in a yellow dress was running about the garden. She said her name was Fatima, and she stood watching me with a shy finger on her lip. Her father came along, and I asked him why rags were tied to the tree. He replied: "If a lady have no child, she come and tie a rag and speak the name of Allah and go away." That is evidently the simple Moslem version.

The Copts believe that the Holy Family rested in the garden, and that as the feet of Jesus touched the earth two springs of sweet water sprang up. These springs still exist in the garden, and I was told that they are not brackish, like the other Nile-filtered water of the locality, but clear and good to drink. The garden was renowned in the Middle Ages as the Garden of Herbs, and is mentioned by many a mediæval pilgrim and traveller. Sir John Maundeville has a lot to say about it in his travels.

It was noted for the balsam trees, which, it was claimed, grew nowhere else in Egypt. Sir John described them as "small trees that are no higher than the girdle of a man's breeches and resemble the wood of the wild vine." When he visited the garden in 1322, he was told by the Saracens that the trees had to be tended by Christians, otherwise they would decline to render the balm.

The balm formed the most important ingredient in the elaborate myron, or chrism, the holy oil of the Coptic Church. In the Western Church, consecrated oil is a mixture of balm and oil, and was compared by St. Gregory the Great to the gifts of the Holy Spirit. The Church of Egypt has apparently always considered its extremely complicated myron to be the same "sweet spices" and "ointments" which Mary Magdalene and Mary, the mother of James, and Salome, took to our Lord's Sepulchre. Every drug used in the preparation of this chrism was defined by rigid prescription and the oil had to be boiled many times. Balsam from Mataria was mixed with herbs and spices, which included lilies and cassia, and the mixture had to steep for a day in fresh water. Next morning eight pounds of pure olive oil, which must never have touched a goat-skin or other leather receptacle, was poured over the herbs and allowed to boil all day on a fire fed with olive wood or old ikons. While the mixture was boiling, the whole of the Psalms were recited. On the following day Persian rose-petals were added, with white sandal-wood and other aromatic herbs, and the mixture was again boiled. On the third and fourth days white storax, saffron, aloes, and more red roses were added, and the oil was boiled as before, each boiling, of course, diminishing the liquid. On the fifth day amber and storax were added over a fire fed with oak charcoal, after which the chrism was cooled, strained through a linen cloth, and was ready for consecration.

This chrism was used in the Coptic Church at least as early as the Fourth Century, but the balsam trees of Mataria died out at some unknown period in the Seventeenth Century, so that balm used in the chrism is now replaced by balm from other sources. Morcos Simaika Pasha tells me that the chrism is now consecrated only twice in a century, and it is marked still, as it always has been, by a ceremony of great religious solemnity.

What is so interesting about the balsam trees of Mataria is that they were originally planted by Cleopatra, from cuttings taken from the famous balsam grove at Jericho. These groves were among the rich gifts which Antony gave her in the days of his success, and they were of great commercial value. Josephus tells us that Cleopatra once visited these groves and took back with her to Egypt a number of balsam cuttings, which she planted at Heliopolis or Mataria. When the Holy Family entered Egypt, the gardens had been in existence for about thirty years. Is it not possible, perhaps probable, that Cleopatra took Jewish gardeners from Palestine to tend these trees, which were such a rarity in Egypt? These men would have belonged to the Jewish community, which, it is almost certain, had existed near Heliopolis for centuries. It would be natural for St. Joseph, faced suddenly with the problem of flight, to turn to such a community of his fellow-countrymen. So far as I know, these curious circumstances have never been linked together, and they may perhaps explain why the garden should have been visited by the Holy Family, and have become a sacred site to the Christians of Egypt.

French Jesuits have built a little church next to the Garden of Herbs. It is called the Church of the Holy Family, and over the porch blaze in the hot sunlight the words: *Sanctæ Familiæ in Ægypto Exuli.* Among the frescoes which decorate this church is one which shows the Holy Family entering Heliopolis. This illustrates an ancient Coptic legend which says that as the Holy Child entered Heliopolis, the noise of a rushing of a mighty wind was heard, the earth trembled, and idols crashed from their pedestals.

THE OBELISK, HELIOPOLIS

I walked over to the site of Heliopolis. Nothing now remains but one lonely obelisk of red granite rising from a field of sugarcane. It is the last of many that once stood in front of the Temple of the Sun, a temple in which Moses may have been educated.

There is a fence round the obelisk, and when you look down you see in the soil below the pedestal of the ancient stone. That was the level on which men were walking in Egypt many centuries ago, and perhaps under this accumulated earth, which the Nile has spread over the fields century after century, may some day be found remains of the once mighty city of On, or Heliopolis, the City of the Sun.

Long ago the lonely obelisk saw the departure of its companions. In 13–12 B.C., eight years before the Holy Family entered Egypt, Augustus removed two of them to Alexandria. One of the obelisks, now blackened by the smoke of London, stands on the Thames Embankment; the other is in Central Park, New York. If, as tradition says, the Holy Family went to Heliopolis, well may the obelisk still standing there have cast its shadow on them as they went by; if they entered Egypt at Alexandria, they may have passed the twin stones which London and New York know as "Cleopatra's Needle." How gladly would we sacrifice the history written on such stones for a glimpse of that unrecorded moment in the year 4 B.C., when a Mother and her Child may have passed in and out of their shadows.

CHAPTER V

In which I go to see the gold of Tut-ankh-Amûn, visit the Cairo Zoo, fall ill, and am sent to the Pyramids. I journey to the Faiyûm, see the Canal of Joseph, live by a lonely lake-side, and return to Cairo to attend a Coptic Christening.

I

In 1923, which seems so long ago, I went to Egypt on behalf of a London newspaper to describe the opening of the mummy-chamber of the tomb of Tut-ankh-Amûn. It was an experience I shall never forget, for I was privileged to enter the tomb while the treasures were standing with the dust of three thousand years upon them.

Those wonderful objects, to which a floor of the Cairo Museum is devoted, are now among the best-known antiquities in the world. Visitors go to the Museum as soon as they arrive in Cairo, and return saying that it was worth while having come to Egypt to see them.

But I had my doubts. I was almost afraid to go there. Fifteen years ago I used to sit day after day in the sunlight outside the tomb, watching the treasures carried out to meet the sun after thirty centuries of darkness.

How could they be wonderful to me now, in the glass cases of a museum, with people peering at them and making inept remarks; with custodians sauntering about, gazing at their watches, hoping it is nearly closing time?

However, I went to the Museum one morning, and climbing a short flight of stairs, I came to the great floor which the Museum has devoted to the treasure; and my first impression was of gold.

Gold shining, gold gleaming, gold almost rose-red and dull,

gold in solid masses, gold hammered paper-thin; everywhere, as far as I could see right down to the end of the sunlit corridor, gleamed the metal for whose sake men have betrayed and enslaved their fellows since the world began.

As I looked in amazement—for the first impression of this treasure is something almost impossible to convey to anyone who has not seen it—the uncompromising words of St. Paul came into my mind:

"We brought nothing into this world, and it is certain we can carry nothing out. . . ."

When I saw the inside of the tomb fifteen years ago, very little had been touched. The treasures lay in confusion, some on top of others, just as they had been piled up three thousand years ago. And my most vivid memory is of two life-size, black-faced statues of the dead man which stood guarding the unbroken wall, as if saying: "Stop; go no farther!"

Those two figures, now in glass cases, are the first objects to be seen in the Museum. They still guard the treasure as they guarded it in the tomb for three thousand years, standing with left foot advanced, a wand in the left hand and a gold mace in the right. As I looked at them, I remembered all kinds of little things: the feel of the shallow limestone steps leading down into the tomb, the hot, stuffy air, and the indescribable smell of age.

Although beauty and majesty were there, the drama had gone from the two statues now that they were in the Museum; and how impressive they once were, in the dark of the tomb, among the tumbled vases and the chariot wheels, defying men to desecrate the body of the king.

They have been cleaned and brightened. When I saw them first, the gold was tarnished and stained with streaks of red like dried blood, the result of standing in the hot air of that limestone vault while Athens rose, while Rome rose, while London rose, while Constantinople rose—a long time to stand on one spot.

And I remembered, too, that someone three thousand years ago had cast linen shawls round them, and this linen had turned dark brown, after so many centuries in the tomb, and hung like cobwebs from their arms, the lightest touch sending it to dust. They wear no shawls now. They stride boldly forward, gazing, as the Sphinx gazes—as all Egyptian statues gaze—firmly, almost defiantly, into the eye of Eternity.

I moved from case to case, thrilled by what I saw in them. Even photographs in colour can give but a poor idea of the beauty and the delicacy of these objects. The skill of the artists, goldsmiths, silversmiths, and the workers in wood, ivory, and alabaster, who lived in Egypt three thousand years ago, has never been surpassed.

I saw a little loaf of bread which someone baked three thousand years ago to feed the Ka, or double, of the king; and it is still lying in the little form of palm fibres in which it went into the oven.

There are wreaths and bouquets of flowers which look like brown paper and are as brittle as sealing-wax. The mourners picked these one morning three thousand years ago in the gardens of Thebes, and carried them into the valley of death to cast on the king's coffin when at last the moment should come to leave him to the silence of centuries.

Scientists have examined these leaves and flowers. Some fell into dust when touched, but it was possible to find others strong enough to stand for a few hours in warm water. Some are cornflowers—which no longer grow in Egypt—some are olive leaves, some the petals of the blue water-lily, some are leaves of wild celery, and some the berries of the woody-nightshade, or bittersweet. These were the flowers cast on the coffin of Tut-ankh-Amûn so long ago; and they tell us that he was buried either in mid-March or in April.

There is a fascinating room reserved only for those objects

which were found on, or about, the king's mummy. The finest thing is the portrait of Tut-ankh-Amûn as he was at the time of his death, a wistful boy of eighteen. This mask was found in position over the head of the mummy. The face is of burnished gold and the striped headdress is of alternate bars of dark-blue glass and gold. Upon the forehead are the two emblems of his Kingdom, the vulture and the cobra of Upper and Lower Egypt, both of solid gold.

This is without doubt one of the great portraits of antiquity. I have been told by a man who has seen the uncovered face of the mummy that the mask is a superb portrait of the king. There is something ineffably sad and lonely about the face, as if the boy knew that he was fated to die before his time. He gazes at us across thirty centuries, a human being, and not a happy one, his eyes charged with the touching pathos of young manhood.

When they found Tut-ankh-Amûn each finger and toe was carefully cased in a separate little sheath of gold. They took these from him, and you can see them, curious little finger and toe stalls, lying together in a glass case. I cannot tell you why they look so pathetic. Surely enough has been taken from him. I wish they could have left him with ten gold fingers and ten gold toes.

2

Were it possible to bring to life the mummy of an ancient Egyptian, one of the things which would surprise him about modern Egypt would be the absence of wild animals.

Centuries ago, as the pictures on the tombs and sculptures in the temples prove, Egypt was a country in which the hippopotamus, the crocodile, and the lion were frequently hunted. To-day these animals have deserted Egypt, although they are still found in the Sudan. This is probably because a greater area of land is now under cultivation, and also because the Nile in flood no longer creates new marshes every year in which wild animals can make their lairs.

The cat, which in Egypt kills snakes as well as rats and mice, occupies a curiously privileged position. No Egyptian would dream of killing a cat. He might refuse to pull a drowning cat out of water, for a Moslem cannot interfere with the decrees of Allah, but he would never throw it in. In the atmosphere of almost superstitious awe which surrounds cats, there is no doubt a relic of the cat worship of ancient Egypt.

The cobra, which in ancient times was the symbol of royalty, is still found in town and country all over the Nile Valley. Although it is frequently killed—I have seen a policeman shoot one with his revolver—I have heard that in certain villages a cobra that takes up its abode in the cellar of a mud house is sometimes venerated as "the guardian of the hearth," and is fed on eggs and chickens. The peasant attributes extraordinary intelligence to the cobra. A country police officer, whom I met outside Cairo, told me a story which I do not believe—although I am sure he did—which illustrates the *fellah's* attitude to this snake.

He said that in a village in Upper Egypt, where he was once stationed, two cobras hatched a family of young snakes in the cellar of a mud house. One day the children of the house discovered the little cobras lying in the sun and began to tease them with sticks. The female cobra appeared and coiled herself round the body of the youngest child, and the cries of the infant brought out the man and his wife.

The parents were terrified, but to have made one move against the cobra might have caused the death of the child. Suddenly the woman cried out:

"Perhaps if *our* children stop tormenting *her* children, she will go away!" The father ran over to his children and gave them a sound thrashing, whereupon the cobra quietly uncurled herself and went away. This story surely suggests that a reverence for the royal snake has come down from ancient times.

One morning I decided to visit the Cairo Zoo.

A taxi took me in about fifteen minutes to a beautiful garden on the west bank of the Nile. It is entered through a charming and impressive gateway decorated with animals in relief, the work of a modern Egyptian sculptor.

In the blinding sunlight, and among fifty-six acres of tropical vegetation, the animals are kept in open pens which reminded me of Regent's Park. The gardens were once the private property of an opulent pasha who, it is said, built the unnecessary suspension bridge over an artificial lake in answer to his wife, who once asked him what a suspension bridge looked like. It is fortunate that she never asked questions about the Arc de Triomphe or the Empire State Building.

What impressed me about Cairo's Zoo was that the animals were of a size, cheerfulness, and condition unknown to us in Europe. I have always considered a hippopotamus one of Nature's more sombre jokes, and I have often felt sorry for this lumbering creature with his vast jaw, his swollen body, and his small legs. And as we know him, he is a sorrowful sight. In his native Africa, however, he is cheerful and full of surprising vitality. The hippo in the Cairo Zoo is a royal beast, mighty of muscle, with a wicked and roving little eye, and a pinkness under his skin.

Giraffes in Europe are poor, puny things compared with the huge animals in Cairo, whose hides are like spotted velour. The ostriches in the Cairo Zoo are so much at home there that ostrich eggs are sold in the ticket-office! They cost £2 each.

The one tragedy of the Cairo Zoo is the polar bear. Although a sympathetic authority has arranged a perpetual cold shower in its cage, this poor creature suffers agonies from the heat and should not be in Africa at all. It is a mangy and pitiable object, pointing the moral which would, I suppose, defeat the first object of all zoological societies, that wild animals should not be shown out of their natural climates. I wish the miserable polar bear of Cairo could be exchanged for some unhappy hippo from Europe.

The visitors to the Cairo Zoo interested me. I saw schools of Egyptian boys, aged about ten, dressed in European clothes with the exception of the little red tarbush on each small head. These children were just as excited about an elephant ride as little boys are in Regent's Park.

Numerous country sheiks and peasant farmers were wandering round the Zoo, men who had obviously come up to Cairo from the country. They would not dream of going to look at the mummies in the Museum, but were thrilled to see the crocodiles, the hippopotami, and the lions. When they came to some unfamiliar animal they would often smile with pleasure, and, as I watched them, I thought that people who love and understand animals often regard them with affectionate amusement.

The English are always doing this. The first books which our children read are animal fantasies like those by Beatrix Potter, in which the humour of the animal characterization is always delightful because it is based on observation and understanding. I am sure that Mickey Mouse would have been popular in ancient Egypt, for the people who built the Pyramids are the only people of antiquity who saw the humour of animals and attributed human characteristics to them.

Some of the most amusing tomb paintings of ancient Egypt are animal caricatures, one of which shows lions starting back in terror as a stately domestic cat walks across the road. Another shows a lion playing chess with a gazelle. Another shows a jackal paying a visit to a sick hippopotamus, and a fourth shows a leopard paying a flute to a flock of geese.

Even if the tomb paintings of birds and animals were not so full of life and so obviously the result of loving observation, we should know that the ancient Egyptians were fond of animals simply on the evidence of these few charming little caricatures, the work of some far-off Beatrix Potter.

As I watched the modern Egyptians in the Cairo Zoo, it seemed to me that they were touching hands across long centuries with the people who once lived on the banks of the Nile.

3

One evening as the sun was setting and the shadows were already cold, I stood on a portion of Cairo's mediæval wall with a professor who is the greatest authority on Islamic architecture in the world. With the kindness and thoroughness which are characteristic of him, he was giving me the benefit of his scholarship, and I was horrified to discover that I was paying little attention to him. As I went away through the darkened streets in an *'arabîa*, I felt intensely melancholy. I looked at the vivid native crowds with nausea, and wondered if I could catch a boat home to-morrow. It seemed to me terrible to be so far away in this land of sharp, cruel sunlight; and I began to think of the softness of rain falling at home and the friendliness of the clouds and shadows.

Something in my appearance made me take my temperature, which was nearly 103. I thought this alarming, and going down to the terrace, I drank a long, iced drink which made me feel terrible. I soon sank into that painful coma known to so many visitors to Egypt. Gyppy tummy is a fierce combination of internal chill and gastric influenza. Residents in Egypt seem to think nothing of it, but I considered it one of the darkest moments of my life. Panic-stricken at the thought of the golden days that were going by while I lay unable to move, I worried and fretted, listening to the clip-clop of *'arabîyât* outside, the bicycle bells, the whistle of the kites, and the sound of the boy selling paraffin, whose high chant at eight o'clock every morning became an event of my day.

A motherly Greek chambermaid would tell me, as the days went by, that I was better than yesterday, and the huge, black

Berberine floor-boys, who entered from time to time with a bowl of soup, would grin all over their faces and enjoy my illness to the full.

When at last I got up, I could hardly walk, and the doctor suggested that I should go away from the dust and the noise of Cairo and stay out near the Pyramids. This pleased me, for, like all people who are not used to being ill, I have an animal's hatred of the place in which I have been in pain; so I looked forward with joy to the clear air of Gizeh.

The road ends on the edge of the desert, where the Pyramids are lifted on a high sandy plateau. There are a few shops, a stall where you can hire a camel by the hour, and a huge hotel, one of the finest in Egypt, whose swimming-pool and open dance-floor are literally in the shadow of the Great Pyramid of Kheops.

In the course of a fairly varied life I have slept in many strange and interesting places, and I shall always think of my room at Gizeh as one of the most remarkable. Lying in bed, I could see the Great Pyramid only about two minutes' walk away. Its colossal triangle exactly filled the space of my balcony.

At first it inspired me with awe, especially by moonlight. Then becoming used to it, I would wish that it could move away a bit and give me a better view of the desert; and finally the sweat and blood of the unknown thousands who had slaved to build it, and the whistle of the lashes that drove them to their labour, began to haunt me; for the Pyramids are surely the monument of a vanity both cruel and futile. And even so they did not do their job properly—which was to guard the body of the Pharaoh in death—because they were broken into and robbed thousands of years ago.

For the first few mornings I was not allowed to go out. I would get up and lie on the balcony until the sun became too hot, watching the curious daily routine of the Pyramids.

The first thing that happens every morning is the arrival of police at seven a.m. Some march up to the Pyramids, others ride on smart little Arab horses; and they patrol the area until sunset, to see that nobody is robbed or pestered. There is little danger of robbery.

Then the guides assemble and with them the little pestering boys and the men who draw some incredible fake antique from their shabby robes with an air of tremendous secrecy; and they all go up the road and wait for the visitors.

From various points on the sandhills men appear leading camels and donkeys. They converge on the corral near the tram terminus. And they, too, wait for the visitors. From eight o'clock onwards the visitors arrive. There are earnest Germans in sun glasses and pith helmets, French, and Egyptians; the English and the Americans, to the annoyance of the camel and donkey men, sometimes insist on walking up the hill.

One morning an air of excitement was noticeable below the balcony. A great day had evidently dawned. More camels, more donkeys, more sand-carts than usual, emerged from the dunes to wait near the tram terminus and at last a string of powerful cars arrived from Cairo from which stepped about a hundred tourists, dressed as if for the exploration of Central Africa.

Some wore jodhpur breeches and open-necked shirts, others wore field boots and breeches, with pith helmets and spine pads, and others were even more strangely clothed.

While the camels bubbled and groaned with hatred, and the donkey and sand-cart men screamed and waved their arms in the ordinary way of business, the weird cavalcade mounted and slowly wound its way up the hill. A liner was passing through the Suez Canal.

Her passengers had seized the chance of rushing to Cairo and the Pyramids, and returning to the ship at nightfall.

It is clear that the traditions of Nineteenth Century travel die hard. All these people were convinced that a visit to the Pyramids and the Sphinx involved moments of hardship, if not of physical danger. And as I watched them going up the hill, I could tell how the ship's courtships were progressing from the way the young men tried to urge their cynical beasts within protective distance of the young women. More often than not they were forced to cry from the humiliating distance of ten yards:

"I say, Miss Robinson, are you all right?"

And the ship's funny man turned round on his camel and shouted to some member of the rearguard:—

"Come on, Steve!"

4

It was exasperating to be within sight of the Pyramids, and within five minutes' walk of the Sphinx, yet unable to go out and see them.

One morning the doctor said that I could go out, but he added, "Don't attempt to go inside the Pyramid, or you may get a chill. It isn't worth it, is it?" I agreed that it wasn't worth it; but no sooner had I walked to the platform of sand on which the Pyramids are built, than I forgot all about the doctor and of course I did as you and anyone else would have done—I went inside.

When I actually stood beneath the Pyramid of Kheops, it looked even larger and more improbable than any work of man's hands that I had ever seen.

When it was built, the Pyramid was sheeted from top to bottom in the finest white limestone, smoothed after the blocks had been placed in position, so that the immense structure looked as if made of one solid slab of polished stone. That was how the ancient world saw it, and the reason why the Pyramid is now a series of steep stone steps, narrowing to the summit, is because the Arabs stripped off the casing and used the stone to build Cairo.

The entrance is about forty feet from the ground, on the north side, and was made centuries ago by treasure-hunting Arabs. When you walk round the Pyramid, you notice that several attempts have been made to break a way in; but this is the only successful one, because the Arabs drove their tunnel immediately below the original entrance, and joined their passage with the main corridor up which the mummy of the Pharaoh had been dragged to the burial chamber.

This entrance is a big black hole in the hill of stone. I climbed up to it over slabs of limestone, where one of the Arab guardians took charge of me.

I walked upright for a few paces and then had to bend double and crawl for about twenty yards. I was surprised to find that the Pyramid is lit by electricity. When an Arab turned a switch, a row of naked electric lights shone in the darkness. After twenty yards the robbers' tunnel joins the main corridor which rises steeply into the Pyramid, a narrow stone tube about thirty feet in height, looking like a shaft of a moving staircase in a tube station.

The electric lights illuminate limestone walls whose masonry is so perfect that it is difficult to find the joints in the stones. Steps and a handrail have been fixed to one side. There was a steep climb for another fifty yards, when once again I had to crawl on hands and knees through a stone tunnel not more than three and a half feet high. This led to a really astonishing sight— the room in the heart of the Pyramid where Kheops was buried.

It was one of the most sinister apartments I had ever entered, a really horrible place, and I could well believe that it might be haunted. The air was stale and hot, and the reek of bats was so strong that I kept glancing up, expecting to see them hanging on the corners of the walls.

Although this room is a hundred and forty feet above the level of the sunlit sandhills outside, it gives the impression of being in the depths of the earth. The Arab who had followed me suddenly switched off the light and said with a horrid laugh: "Dark—*very* dark!"

It was indeed the darkness of the grave, and joined to the darkness was the silence of death. I have never known what claustrophobia is, but I have often felt frightened in coal mines. As I thought of the way up to this place, I was conscious of a faint feeling of panic.

The only object in the burial-chamber is a massive granite coffin without lid or inscription. The Arab went over and tapped it with his hand. It gave out a metallic, bell-like sound. This was the sarcophagus in which the Pharaoh Kheops was buried seven thousand years ago.

One of the remarkable things about the Pyramid is that it was built round this coffin; when the structure had reached the height of the mummy-chamber the coffin was brought in, and the top portion of the Pyramid was built over it.

Herodotus tells us that one hundred thousand men worked for three months every year, and that it took ten years to prepare the site and twenty years to build the Pyramid. During this time the king must have visited the site to see how it was getting on. He must have stood in this chamber when it was still open to the sun, with his coffin standing in the corner. He may have struck it with his hand to hear the sweet, bell-like note. He may have come again when the room was closed, dark, and ready. Then one day he came for the last time, with a gold mask on his face, to the straining of ropes and the chanting of priests.

In spite of all the ingenuity of the architects, those narrow tunnels blocked with granite slabs after the funeral, and the single stone swinging on a pivot known only to the priests, robbers entered the tomb within two hundred years or so of Kheops' death.

We shall never know who levered the lid from the great stone coffin and stripped the Pharaoh of his gold, strewing his bones about the floor. But we know that centuries after his tomb had been desecrated, men continued to smite the Great Pyramid, unable to believe that it did not still contain riches. Persians, Romans, and Arabs attacked it with battering-rams; they tunnelled and they mined. When gunpowder was invented, they even tried to blow it up. Now and then some would enter its dark passages and creep along them with beating hearts. Instead of piles of gold, they came to an empty coffin and the twittering of bats.

5

I decided to visit the Faiyûm, which lies some forty miles from the Pyramids, across the Libyan Desert. It is a depression about a hundred and forty feet deep, and roughly forty miles long by thirty broad, separated from the Nile by a range of low hills. There is, however, an opening in the hills through which a branch of the river used to flow in ancient times, forming an enormous natural lake which rose and fell with the Nile.

It was a brilliant hot morning when I set off by car for the Faiyûm. Leaving the Pyramids on the left, there was soon nothing within sight but a featureless expanse of burning sand. Forty miles of desert are just enough to show you what a desert is like, but not enough to fill your heart with despair and weariness. The sandy track lost itself on the horizon. The sandhills shouldered each other mile after mile, here smooth as brown velvet, there rippled with the wind as if the tide had just gone out. And the sun beat down angrily upon this dead land until the eyes grew weary and sore with looking at the burning flatness; until any object—a bird, the white bones of a camel, the chassis of a burnt-out Ford car—was a welcome relief from the monotonous sterility.

One feature of the desert is beautiful: the dry, clear air, blowing over thousands of miles of clean sand, stirring up the bloodstream and cheering the heart.

The track led downhill towards a scene that looked to me like a child's impression of the Garden of Eden. The desert ended suddenly against a wall of date-palms. Where the palm fronds sprayed upwards against the sky, I saw bunches of dates lying in heavy clusters, like a swarm of bees and the colour of Spanish mahogany.

Instead of barren sand, the road now lay along a high embankment of black earth—the rich, pregnant black earth of Egypt; and on either side flowed sluggish canals of fresh water, the veins that carry the life blood of this land.

The richness of this oasis was proverbial in the days of the Pharaohs. The earth can produce almost anything: oranges, bananas, mandarins, dates, sugar-cane, rice, maize, and olives.

How hard the *fellah* works! With what unremitting toil must he slave at this black land, giving his life in return for its fruitfulness. He stands knee-deep in water, his thin garment drenched with the drip of the *shaduf;* he stands in the clinging mud of the fields, the soles of his bare feet making him an easy victim to the terrible germ that lives in the soil of Egypt; he stands bowed above his Virgilian plough; he strides like Pharaoh's soldiers on a temple wall, slashing at the man-high maize stalks; covered like a Jack-in-the-Green, he staggers beneath a load of *bersim*.

Every day, year in and year out, century after century, it is the same. He is the *fellah*, the man whose sweat built the Pyramids and the temples, the man whose sense of fatality is perhaps the most colossal of Egypt's monuments.

As I passed his pretty villages, built in groves of date-palms beside shallow canals, the wood smoke was rising from the ovens where his women were baking the tough bread which is his staple food. I saw the little mud houses where he goes home to sleep for a few hours before the sun, like a trumpet in the morning, calls him out to strive again with water and with mud. There is little inside his house except small children playing in the dust.

I travelled through the villages to the edge of Lake Karoun, where a small, two-story hotel, kept by a young German, stands within a few yards of the water's edge. The hotel was empty because it was the middle of the week. At week-ends it is filled with sportsmen from Cairo who come to shoot the duck, snipe, and teal which haunt the lake-side in thousands.

I thought that this lake was the most beautiful thing I had seen in Egypt. It is a sheet of blue water lying in the sunlight, with the tawny desert on its western shores; a desert in which lie forgotten cities of the Greek age and old temples falling into dust. In the hush of this remote place, the blend of blue water and desert hills, I was reminded of the Lake of Galilee.

An Arab servant took my bag to a little bedroom overlooking the lake. The bed was covered with a mosquito net and the room smelt cleanly of camphor.

"I have just opened the hotel," said young Mr. Schumacher, the proprietor, "for I keep it shut until the shooting season begins. What a business it is, opening a hotel that has been shut for an Egyptian summer! The lizards, the snakes, the birds, and the frogs come and live here; and also wild bees!"

I knew that I was going to like Lake Karoun.

The Pharaohs took a great interest in this lake and fitted it with lock-gates and an intricate system of water-control, so that its level remained constant and the water could be used as required for irrigation. Among the ancient dwellers on the lake-side were some who worshipped a deity to whom the crocodile was sacred. The priests kept a crocodile, which they regarded as the embodiment of Sebek, the crocodile god, in a sacred lake in the temple at Shedet. Rings of gold and crystal hung in its ears, and its paws were decorated with jewelled bracelets.

In Greek times the waterworks had fallen into disuse, and the level of the lake having fallen, large areas of marshland were formed which the kings of the Ptolemaic dynasty drained in order to reclaim land for Greek and Macedonian ex-soldiers. What was once a famous lake then became a hot, low-lying, but amazingly fertile agricultural area dotted with Greek cities. And to-day the Faiyûm—an Arabic version of the Coptic word for "lake"—is noted for the richness of its soil and for the large farms and estates owned by rich Egyptians. The Faiyûm endeared itself to the Greeks because it was the only place in Egypt where good crops of olives could be grown, and it remains to-day the only olive-producing area in the country. The lake has now shrunk to a fraction of its former size, and occupies the deepest portion of the depression. Its waters are as salt as the Mediterranean because evaporation under great heat leaves mineral salts in solution, as they are left in the bitter waters of the Dead Sea.

Both Herodotus and Strabo mention this district, and reading their accounts, it is interesting to see how little the tourist route in Egypt has altered since Greek and Roman times. Starting by boat from Alexandria, tourists made the Nile trip just as modern travellers do, visiting the same places to see the same things. But where we see a ruin, or nothing at all, they were fortunate in finding temples where priests still performed their ancient rites. From Heliopolis they made an excursion to the Temple of the Sun to smile, no doubt, as they heard of the nightly ceremony enacted to make sure that the sun would rise in the morning. From Gizeh, they visited the Pyramids and the Sphinx, which were then as dead and as plundered as they are to-day.

In modern times the Faiyûm has dropped out of its place among the sights of Egypt. In Greek days, however, all tourists went there, for the old crocodile-god was by this time experiencing a god's final humiliation, which is to attract, not worshippers, but tourists.

It was the fashion to go there and feed him with fried fish and honey-cakes, which were sold by the priests. And as his jewelled paws broke the surface of the sacred lake, we can imagine with what Western irreverence the tourists may have greeted him. It was not, however, easy to make an offering to a sacred crocodile, for he evidently had his revenge by showing a preference for the tourist. Therefore the priests were always ready to exhibit a skill taught by long experience. They would wait until the creature was asleep in the sun, when, stealing up to him, they would quickly pop the fish and the honey-cakes into his jaws and leap back before he had time to bite them.

6

Egypt is a land without twilight. The sun sets. There is a brief expectant hush in whose vast stillness it seems that Time itself has stopped. The hills turn black against a lemon-coloured sky. A star burns. A bat flies. And the wings of darkness swoop down upon the world.

As the light goes out of the sky, life goes from the fields and the rice-meadows, from the crops of maize and sugar-cane: and each mud embankment is the scene of a homeward procession, black against the last streak of the afterglow like figures on a temple frieze.

Barefoot girls in bright gowns of red and blue drive goats before them, brown boys smack the angular flanks of water-buffaloes as they hurry on in the dusk; and from every patch of cultivation the red-brown *fellah* strides noiselessly on thin bare legs to his village in the palm-grove.

He is driven to rest by the weariness of his body and by his fear of the dark. Well can I understand his fear. This uncanny darkness, following on the heels of a golden day, must have inspired the weird pictures of the underworld which the people of ancient Egypt painted in their tombs. The ancient Egyptian believed that death would be like the night of Egypt, a death haunted by strange creatures of the imagination, half man and half animal, like creatures moving at night in the sugar-cane, and the shapes seen for a moment flying against the moon.

So silence and blackness settled over Egypt. The *fellah* and his family curl up on mats spread on the mud floor. Wolf-like dogs prowl about the villages, barking furiously at the little jackals who creep from the maize-fields to yap in the moonlight.

It is the hour when anything might happen to a lonely man on the roads, when anything might rise from the fields, from the water, or from the earth under his feet; it is a time when four mud walls protect a man from all the powers of darkness. It is eight o'clock. In nine hours the world will come to life again. . . .

I stand on my balcony to watch the sun rise. Stars still shine. Lake Karoun lies below, a wide sheet of silver. Date-palms in the garden rise black and motionless in the morning hush; there is a silence, as if the evil creatures of the night are flying before the coming day, back to the earth and to the waters of the earth and to the parched desert spaces.

A breath of wind springs up, just strong enough to move the palm fronds, and a grey light comes into the east. It is the breath of life, the beginning of a new day. The light spreads. The small stars fade and go. The greyness turns to yellow, to orange, to red, and suddenly the sun leaps over the world's edge and Egypt is wide awake.

Instantly the cocks crow, donkeys bray, camels bubble, and the red-brown men of Egypt set off to the fields. Some sing and laugh as they go, some walk prematurely bowed with labour and stiffened by a life spent in mud and water. In the early morning shadows of the palm-trunks which the sun draws aslant mud walls, women sit and nurse their babies, while little long-eared kids with coats like black velvet frisk about them in the dust.

There is an air of happiness about each new day in Egypt, as if all ugliness and injustice had been washed away in the night; as if Man were starting his pilgrimage afresh in a perfect world, with the sun to warm him and a blue sky overhead.

I went down to the lake-side to see what the fishermen had caught during the night. They alone of all the people in the Faiyûm are not bound body and soul to the black earth. They are nomad Arabs of Bedouin stock, whose ancestors came long ago across the gold rim of desert lying on the northern shore of the lake. They erected their black tents and learned to fish, and their descendants have been fishing ever since.

Their boats are stout, canoe-shaped craft made on the lake-side, their oars are thick pieces of wood, and they use drag-nets, and also the hand-net, which has been known in the East for centuries. It is the same kind of hand-net that was cast by the Apostles in the Sea of Galilee.

Although the sea is one hundred and fifty miles away and the lake is land-locked, the fish are sea-fish. Lake Karoun is well and regularly stocked by the Egyptian Government with Mediterranean and Red Sea fish, brought in tanks by air.

At about six o'clock every morning the fishing-boats come slowly to the shore, where the morning market is held. Buyers, who have been squatting on the sand, rise and go down to the edge of the lake. Has Allah filled the nets? Yes! The All Merciful has filled the nets to the point of breaking, indeed so generous has he been that only a giant could carry his bounty to the shore.

Curiously enough, such optimistic accounts—so typical of fishermen all over the world—were instantly contradicted when one small boy lifted his *gallabîa* and, leaping into the water, waded to the land with a basket on his head. Sometimes two men came ashore with the catch, but it never required the strength of more than two; at least, it never did while I was watching.

Spreading out the fish on the sand, buyer and seller plunged into those protracted arguments which complicate the purchase of even a shoe-lace in the East. They laughed. They frowned. They simulated indignation, anger, sorrow; but eventually a bargain was struck—a matter of a few shillings—and everyone was happy. How good it is to see a fisherman happy, for in other parts of the world he is the victim of price rings and middle-men.

At Lake Karoun the merchants load the fish in baskets, sling them on either side of waiting donkeys, and go off to do business in the villages. The fishermen buy themselves a handful of dates or a pinch of green tea, and spread out their nets to dry.

The strangest thing I heard about these fishermen is their method of catching duck. During the winter great flocks of migratory wild fowl come to Lake Karoun. They are exceedingly shy and the fowler must disguise a punt with reeds and hide himself in it, sometimes for hours, before he gets a shot. But the fishermen have devised a method which perhaps only a Bedouin fisherman could have invented.

They get a decoy and place it in about five feet of water, among reeds near the shore. Then they scatter rice on the water and, slipping their feet into stone stirrups, crouch waiting under the water, breathing through a blowpipe. They remain submerged sometimes for half an hour at a time.

As soon as a duck flies down and swims up to the rice, the Arab underneath the water grasps it by the legs and pulls it down; and he does it so swiftly and so quietly that often four and five birds are pulled under before their companions notice that anything is wrong.

If you look across the lake when the sun has set, you will see the fishermen putting out again for their night's work. How different are fishermen from men of the fields. All over the Faiyûm, except on these twenty-five miles of water, darkness means the end of work and the shelter of home. The fisherman alone goes out to brave the perils of night. But that is not really surprising, for, as every *fellah* knows, no *afrît* would dare to

come near him, because the ghosts and spirits and night creatures go in fear of a fisherman and his nets. And I have been told
that should you be caught after dark some distance from home
—which Allah forbid—you are safe if you can persuade a fisherman to walk beside you.

7

The Captain of Police and the Captain of Coastguards called
to present their compliments and to hope that I was enjoying
Egypt, and the particular portion of Egypt which lay under
their charge.

"Let us sit down and drink coffee, unless you would prefer
a stronger drink," I suggested.

"Coffee is good," they replied.

So we sat on the terrace of the little hotel beside Lake Karoun,
where green lizards flash in the sun and where the hoopoe,
which is the jay of Egypt, flies busily from tree to tree.

When the coffee came, we talked of many things, but the
most interesting were our own particular jobs in life. They
asked me questions about newspapers and books, and I answered them as well as I could. Then I turned to them.

"What is the worst crime you have to deal with?" I asked the
Captain of Police.

"Murder," he replied, sipping his coffee.

"How many do you have in a year?"

"About seventy or eighty," he replied.

"And the population of your province is about five hundred
thousand?"

"Yes, that is so. Many of our murders are—what is the term
in English?—family squabbles. They are handed down from
one generation to another, and when a murder happens for no
reason that you can tell, it often means that two great-grandsons have . . ."

He paused for the word and made the expressive Egyptian gesture of finality: a sudden wiping of the palm of one hand across the palm of the other.

"Another difficulty," he continued, "is that everyone in a village knows who did the murder except the police. This makes murderers very difficult to trace. You have to watch. You have to listen. No one will help you to find the murderer. They know nothing. Nothing!"

"But why does it take so long to work off a family squabble? Why should great-grandsons commit a murder because their great-grandfathers quarrelled?"

"Ah, that is not so easy to answer. There is a tradition among the *fellahîn* that a murder of this kind must be committed with the same kind of instrument as the original murder, and on the same spot."

"The law of atonement?"

"If you like. But you can see how carefully men avoid the place where their fathers were murdered! Years—generations —may pass before such a meeting happens. But when it does happen—skh!"

"What crimes do you deal with?" I asked the coastguard.

"Nowadays I have no real crime," he replied, "except when the fishermen make their nets of too close a mesh. This is a very simple matter. I collect the nets and burn them once a month. This happens to be the day for burning. You can see the smoke over there."

We looked along the lovely foreshore and saw three coastguards, men in blue blouses, wide Turkish trousers, and tarbushes, poking at a fire on the sand.

"Why do you say that you have no crime *nowadays?*" I asked.

"Because until recently I was stationed on the Suez Canal, where I had much crime. Oh, much. . . ."

He paused and made the gesture of abundance which is used

all over the near East.

"In those days," he continued, "I caught the smugglers of cocaine and hashish and heroin. And they are indeed clever people. There are some who drop packages of drugs worth thousands of pounds from steamers in the canal. These packages are wrapped in oil silk and are weighed down with salt. As the salt melts, the packages float to the top of the water, where men who have been watching from the banks row out and pick them up. But there are many, many tricks. There are men with false tops to their tarbushes. There are men who walk with hollow canes. There are men who hide drugs most skilfully on donkeys and camels."

The police captain looked at his watch and said:—

"If you are ready, shall we go and pay some calls?"

I had no idea what he meant, but I took my place in a limousine driven by a police orderly. Off we sped over the mud embankments, hooting loudly to warn camels, oxen, donkeys, and buffaloes of our approach.

We came to a peaceful little village among palm trees where the omdah, or mayor, a dignified elderly man, was waiting for us at his garden gate. He led the way into a bower of roses, the big red roses that bloom all through the Egyptian winter. There were banks of purple bougainvillæa and masses of honeysuckle falling from trellis-work arches.

We sat enjoying the shade, while the hot Egyptian morning lay in blinding whiteness beyond the tunnel of leaves. Servants appeared with coffee and with oranges plucked from the trees around us; the best oranges that I have ever tasted.

A hoopoe flew to a bough near us, lifting his cockade of feathers, and called for his mate to come and see what queer people had invaded the garden. Mrs. Hoopoe flew down and also sat watching, with an eye like a gold boot button.

"Do you know," asked the omdah, "how the hoopoe got the crest of feathers on his head? Well, I will tell you. Solomon was once making a journey across the desert. The sun was hot and there was no shade. Suddenly the king found himself moving in shadow, and looking up, he saw that the hoopoe was flying above, shading him with his wings. All day the hoopoe flew thus, and upon the next day he was there also, flying above the head of the king. When the journey was ended, Solomon, who, as you know, could speak the language of the birds, called the hoopoe before him and asked what he could do to reward him for his kindness. 'I should like a crown of gold, O king, like the crown you wear,' answered the hoopoe—for you can see what a cheeky little bird he is! 'O, hoopoe,' replied Solomon, 'I think you are a foolish bird, for a crown will not bring you happiness; nevertheless, if that is your wish, you shall have a crown of gold.' And Solomon waved his hand, and a gold crown appeared and settled upon the hoopoe's head.

"Some months later the hoopoe appeared before Solomon, and the king said, 'O, hoopoe, what is it you wish this time?' And the hoopoe answered, 'O king, take from me this crown of gold, for the sons of men covet it and my life is in peril. I have no peace from the sun's rising until the dark.' And Solomon smiled in his beard and waved his hand. The gold crown faded from the hoopoe's head; but in order that the bird might not go unrewarded for his service, the king replaced it with the beautiful gold crown of feathers which he wears so proudly. That is the story as it is written and as it is told. . . ."

The omdah turned to me with a charming smile, and the hoopoes nodded their crested heads. We said good-bye to our host and plunged again into the heat and dust of the roads.

But I shall always remember that garden with its running water, its green shade and quiet voices, for it is the peculiar genius of Moslem peoples to make an oasis on the other side of any garden wall.

"I have noticed," said the police captain as we were driving away, "that women cause much trouble in the world; and it

was like that with the hoopoe, only the omdah did not tell the
story properly."

"Well, what is the real story?"

"When Solomon asked the hoopoe what reward he would
like, the hoopoe said he must fly home and ask his wife. The
hoopoe's wife said: 'Ask for golden crowns so that we may be
richer and grander than all the other birds.' When the crowns
came, she was so proud that she refused to speak even to her
cousin, the bee-eater. But one day a man put some looking-
glass in a snare, and the hoopoe's wife walked into it because
she wanted to look at herself. As soon as men knew how valuable the crowns were, no hoopoe was safe, so the King of the
Hoopoes had to go to Solomon and ask for them to be taken
away."

8

When a town is compared to Venice, it generally means that
a few turgid canals creep unwillingly through its streets. I
have every feeling of sympathy for the dismay with which the
Venetians learn from time to time that this or that unlikely
place has been compared with their own incomparable city.
The big town of the Faiyûm—Medînet or el-Madîna—is sometimes called the "Venice of Egypt," though I have never in my
life seen a place less like Venice.

It is a typical Egyptian provincial town, some of it modern,
bits of it ancient, lots of it falling down; and the whole roofed
with a sky of brass. The main canal that links the Faiyûm with
the Nile, and ensures the fertility of the oasis, is the Bahr Yûsuf,
the canal of Joseph; for the Arabs believe that the ancient
reservoir of Pharaonic times was the work of the Biblical Joseph, in Arab legend the "Grand Vizier" of Pharaoh.

I went to el-Medînet with my friend the police officer. In
one of the streets I noticed a shop whose window was a confused mass of dusty, broken antiquities. In a moment of op-

timism the owner had suspended the blackened hand of a mummy from a nail, where it dangled horribly, slowly revolving with any breath of air, as if inviting the passer-by to enter.

In the old days the Faiyûm was a rich source of antiquities found in the neighbouring ruins of Crocodilopolis, the largest ruins of a town in Egypt. Nowadays the natives are forbidden to dig for treasure and must report any finds to the Government.

The interior of the shop was an incredible confusion of worthless and mostly shapeless relics of Ptolemaic Crocodilopolis. There was a dark room at the back piled to the ceiling with reddish clay figurines, lamps, Ushabti figures of the roughest kind, broken pots, scraps of mummy wrappings, and a hideous pile of dust and decay in which I was able to identify a human head and the tail of a mummified crocodile. Every time I dislodged an object the whole pile threatened to avalanche to the floor, and each dislodged object brought with it a puff of horrible dead dust.

On our way to the ruins of Crocodilopolis I stopped to watch men working in a brickyard. They looked like men made of mud. It had caked on their faces, arms, and chests, and it covered their legs to the thighs. Their method of brick-making has been in use in Egypt since the earliest times, and is the same process which created a labour dispute among the Hebrews. I noticed that these Egyptians were making bricks without straw, and doing it with conspicuous success. They told me that chopped straw is sometimes mixed with the mud to bind it, but most brick-makers use only mud mixed with a little sand to prevent cracks.

It is extraordinarily quick and simple work. The mud is first mixed and well trampled in a pit near by. The brick-maker takes up a sufficient quantity, roughly smoothes it on the ground and presses over it a wooden mould, which he removes, leaving behind a wet oblong of mud. He makes the next brick one, two, or three inches away, and soon has several rows drying in the sun. In four days the bricks are dry enough to be turned on end, and in about a week they are ready for building.

What, then, was the cause of the famous grievance among the Hebrews? They wanted the straw, not to mix with the mud, but to dust the moulds or the ground in order to prevent the mud from sticking. Thus our English proverb about the impossibility of making bricks without straw is clearly wrong and based on a misunderstanding: for bricks are made without straw in the brickyards of Egypt.

The ruins of Crocodilopolis stretched in hills and hummocks and pits which on examination proved to be the remains of mud-brick houses. There were fragments of pottery mixed with the churned earth, and in one place I picked up a bright blue bead. We encountered a *gaffir*, or watchman, with a gun slung on his back, who was guarding the site on behalf of the Government. He showed us the way to the site of the temple lake where the jewelled Petesuchos once accepted the offerings of Greek tourists. There is nothing to be seen now but a slight declivity in the hills of hard black mud.

We were glad to sit down and mop our brows, for the heat was beating fiercely upon the ruins. As we smoked cigarettes, I thought, as one is always thinking on archæological sites, how capricious are those chances which preserve knowledge when a civilization has crashed. It may seem incredible to some of us to-day to think that a future age might have no knowledge of Watt's steam-condenser save from an essay written by a school-boy, which happened to be used to line a steel box for some reason or other; or that all the works of Shakespeare might disappear except ten lines of *Hamlet*, which some eccentric admirer had caused to be carved in marble on a library mantelpiece. Far-fetched and impossible as this may sound, much the same sort of thing has happened to a civilization as great as ours; and in these days of Air Raid Precautions who would dare to say that they might not happen again?

When the late Lord Carnarvon was digging at Thebes some years ago, he found a wooden palette which a school-boy had used as a copy-book. On it was written what was evidently an inscription from the walls of a now vanished temple, and it told the story, hitherto unknown, of the expulsion of the Hyksos under the last king of the XVIIth Dynasty. Who could have dreamt that an idle school-boy, unwillingly fulfilling some task with the fear of a caning in his mind, would be chosen by fate to fill a blank in history and to write on wood words destined to survive ages after the stone temple, from whose walls they were copied, had fallen into oblivion?

In much the same way the sacred crocodiles of the Faiyûm were chosen as fate's safe deposit. When Grenfell and Hunt were digging in the Faiyûm for papyri, which they eventually found in such splendid quantities, they were disgusted to turn up nothing but mummified crocodiles. The disappointment spread to the workmen, one of whom in his rage dashed a sacred animal to the ground, where it burst open and out fell papyri! There was a rush for the other crocodiles, which proved to be libraries in disguise, for the priests had packed them with all kinds of old manuscripts: fragments of ancient classics, royal ordinances, private letters, land accounts, surveys, and petitions. It is by means of such fantastic chances that an age sometimes makes itself known to another across the silence of centuries.

Saying good-bye to my friend, I returned to Cairo by another route, a road that lies parallel with the Nile. It touches the river now and then before running, high and embanked, among fields of maize and sugar cane. High above the palm trees shone the white slanting sails of Nile boats as they drifted noiselessly up and down the river. Camels passed in file, donkeys trotted in the smothering black dust, geese cackled, turkeys gobbled, cocks crew, pigeons cooed, dogs barked, children cried and shouted, the *sakiyeh* groaned its age-long lament, and in the black mud of the canal banks half naked *shadûf* men lifted their dripping burdens.

If only the villages of Egypt could be freed from malaria and ophthalmia and a hundred other plagues and afflictions, they would be the most idyllic in the world. They look so lovely lying in the striped shadows of the palm groves, the flat-roofed houses so perfectly grouped together, white minarets rising above them, reflected maybe in the still blue water of a canal, and on the houses, or built apart in the fields, the white towers above which thousands of pigeons catch the sunlight as they wheel in flight.

In the Faiyûm, where these white towers sometimes look more important than the houses of men, I was told that the pigeons are kept for the manure, which is the best-known fertilizer for melons. It is interesting to connect this with II *Kings* vi. 25: "And there was a great famine in Samaria: and behold, they besieged it until an ass's head was sold for four-score pieces of silver, and the fourth part of a cab of dove's dung for five pieces of silver." It would appear that this fertilizer was sold in the days of Elisha exactly as it is in Egypt at the present time.

I came to the ruins of Memphis, mysterious in a palm grove. Even less of Memphis than of Babylon remains to tell the world that the mightiest city of its time once stood there. Darkness was beginning to steal through the wood like an old witch, and it was eerie to walk under the trees, where the colossal figure of a pharaoh lies prostrate, gazing at the sky, and to come upon a bland, indifferent sphinx whose lips are curled in a faint smile, sitting white and silent.

A shed has been built over the gigantic figure of Rameses II, and the attendant leads the way upstairs to a balcony from which you may gaze on the prostrate king. He lies like a captured Gulliver, with his face to the roof. The guardian whispers that his ear is over a foot long. He is so enormous that his shape is lost when you are so near to him. A child could slide on his lips as on a banister. His nose is a little hill jutting out of his immense, smooth cheeks.

I suddenly told the guardian very gravely that the place was haunted by a thousand *afrîts* and demons, and from the ensuing look of horror in his eyes, I gathered that I had struck the nail on the head. And the last thing I saw of Memphis was the pale sphinx smiling in the wood.

9

At eight o'clock on a Sunday morning I went to Old Cairo to attend the Korbân, or Mass, in the church of Abu Sefain. There was to be a christening in the middle of the service, for it is the ancient rule of the Coptic Church that infants must receive their first communion immediately after baptism. This rule was general in the first age of Christianity, when converts were usually adult persons, and it is typical of the rigid tradition of the Egyptian Christians that they should not have modified it to fit different circumstances. So every Coptic baby is baptized to-day with the same rites that admitted grown-up and aged pagans into the Church of the First Century.

When I arrived, the dark old church was already half full of men and women. The long offering of the morning incense had filled the building with pungent fumes. The haikal screen shone in the light of candles and through its open door I could see the priest moving about the sanctuary beyond, where more candles burned on the altar.

Every now and then men and women would enter and fall on hands and knees in front of the haikal screen, picking up the hem of the curtain and carrying it to their lips. Some of the more devout would remain praying on hands and knees, bending their bodies forward and touching the threshold with their foreheads.

It is an attitude which suggests Islam, and I have read accounts of Coptic ceremonies in which Western observers invariably comment on this prostration as a curious invasion of Moslem ritual into a Christian church. It is really the other way round. The Moslems adopted the act of prostration from the Christians, for when the Koran was compiled, Christian saints and hermits might be seen performing their daily prostrations in all the deserts and mountains of the East, as indeed we are told St. Simeon Stylites did upon his pillar in Syria.

The writings of the Early Fathers contain many a reference to prostration, and to the kissing, of even the porches and pillars of churches. Coptic monks still attach great importance to such acts, and the ordinary worshipper in a church, as I saw for myself in Abu Sefain, still approaches the altar on hands and knees, as our Christian forefathers used to do in ancient times. The only survivals of this custom in the West are the genuflection to the Sacrament, the "prostration," which is kneeling on both knees, and the Roman "prostratio," which is lying full length on the ground.

The congregation was composed of poor people from the streets around. The men wore their tarbushes in church—a truly Eastern touch—while most of the women sat cross-legged on the floor, with black veils drawn over their heads. I was charmed to see how the children, some of them hardly able to walk, were allowed to sit on the steps of the haikal, and how their little faces would peep into the sanctuary beyond. Gravely watching and peeping, they sat there while the priest prepared the altar for the Korbân. On one occasion, when he had to leave the altar for a moment, he was obliged to step over two or three infants, and once a little brown boy strayed into the sanctuary, to be gently removed by the priest with a reproving pat on the head. These Copts, though some have said how deeply they are sunk in ignorance and superstition, have at least not forgotten that Jesus said: "Suffer the little children to come unto me."

While I was watching this interesting congregation, and thinking how well the Copts have camouflaged themselves among their conquerors, for there was nothing about their dress to distinguish them from a Moslem crowd, I felt a gentle pull at my sleeve. It was my friend, the young son of the sacristan, whom I had met during my visits to this church. Beckoning me from my seat, he led the way into an adjoining courtyard, where I smelt the sweet warmth of baking bread.

"My father prepares the holy bread," he whispered, and pointed into a dark bakehouse where an old man in a *gallabîa*, and wearing a tarbush, was muttering the Psalms in Arabic while he tended a brick oven.

Every time the Korbân is celebrated, the eucharistic bread must go straight from the oven to the altar, and it must always be baked by the sacristan on church premises on the morning of the Mass. The loaves, of which he had baked perhaps twenty, were light brown in colour and were beautifully even and smooth, about three inches in diameter and an inch in thickness. Each one was stamped on top with a design of crosses.

When we returned to the church, the priest was vested for the Liturgy. He wore a tunic opening down the front, a long vestment that almost touched the ground, and was worn un-girded. It was made of cream-coloured silk and was undeco-rated. He did not wear the *shamlah* on his head, the primitive amice which Copts sometimes twist round the head like a tur-ban, but a new-fashioned cap rather like a mitre, except that it was not cleft, neither was it as tall as a mitre. This cap was richly embroidered with crosses, and from it a long veil hung down the back to the wearer's heels, decorated only with a single cross. He wore nothing to correspond with the Western alb, cincture, maniple, or stole. His deacon was a barefoot young man dressed in an ungirded alb, with a stole crossed on his left shoulder and a white skull-cap on his head.

A choir of fourteen dark young men entered, wearing white linen vestments with stoles crossed on the left shoulder. One man carried cymbals, another held a triangle. Seeing them like this, without tarbushes and isolated from an Arabic background, I was immensely struck by their resemblance to the Egyptians and the Græco-Egyptians whose portraits are to be seen on the Faiyûm mummy cases.

The Liturgy began with the long sanctification, or oblation, of St. Basil. The priest intoned the prayers in Coptic and the congregation made their responses in Arabic. The choir sang in Coptic in a high nasal tone, seeming at times to tear the words out of the air, their heads lifted and their eyes closed. They were accompanied now and then with a touch of the triangle or a clash of cymbals.

Here again, is it right to call this enharmonic chanting "oriental," in the sense that it has an Arabian origin? Surely it is more reasonable to believe that the Arabs took their music from the Egyptians. As I listened to this Coptic choir, I wondered if this church music might not be the last relic of the music of the Pharaohs, as the language of the Coptic Liturgy is the last relic of their language.

The sacristan brought in the Korbân bread. The priest came to the haikal door and examined each loaf minutely, turning it over and over; selecting the most perfect, he returned with it to the altar and placed the bread on the paten. Raisin wine was brought to him. During the Moslem conquest the cultivation of the grape was forbidden in Egypt, and Christians were obliged to make their sacramental wine secretly in the churches, using raisins instead of grapes. He poured wine into the chalice and added a little water from an ordinary clay *gulla*. He placed the chalice in the painted box that stands on every Coptic altar, and on top of the chalice he placed the paten, covering them both with a veil of yellow silk.

Repeated processions round the altar now filled the sanctuary with a mist of incense. There was no sound for some time but the regular chink of the swinging thurible and the voice of the priest intoning prayers in the language of ancient Egypt. He appeared suddenly at the sanctuary door and came down into the church with the thurible, to pass among the people and swing a puff of incense towards each person. He also touched each member of the congregation on the head in blessing.

And now a disagreement arose on the question of the correct lessons for the day. A layman in a tarbush went to the haikal screen and called to the priest. A long and excited consultation took place, in which two or three leading members of the congregation joined. Books were produced, pages turned, and eventually the dispute was settled. This air of casual improvisation went strangely with the deep reverence and the general punctiliousness of the ceremony.

The lessons were read, first in Coptic and then in Arabic, and they were followed by the Liturgy of the Faithful.

"Come, stand with fear, look towards the East!" cried the deacon.

"Mercy, peace, and a sacrifice of praise," chanted the priest.

While the words of institution were spoken, the people continually cried "amen," which they pronounced "armeen"; and a deep hush went through the church as the priest broke the bread and uncovered the chalice. The people prostrated themselves and cried out, "Amen, amen, amen, we believe and confess and glorify Him." Incense was swung all the time and the priest covered the elements with a veil of crimson silk.

During the prayers of intercession, the names of Egyptian martyrs who died in Roman times were mentioned, and also saintly hermits of the Thebaid; and a prayer was offered for the fruits of the earth, including vineyards, which have not been cultivated in Egypt since the Tenth Century.

The fraction and the institution followed. The priest broke

the holy bread into five pieces, and, dipping his finger in the chalice, signed them with the Cross. He took the central portion of the Korbân—the *isbodikon*—and placed it in the chalice, crying: "This is in truth the Body and the Blood of Emmanuel, our God." And the people, uncovered and prostrate, answered: "Amen. I believe, I believe, I believe and confess until the last breath."

The deacon meanwhile took up his position at the opposite end of the altar, facing the priest and looking westward down the church. It is a position which was first adopted during the Egyptian and Greek riots after the Council of Chalcedon in 451 A.D., when Melkite mobs would enter the Monophysite churches and try to interrupt the Mass. Now, centuries after, every Sunday the deacon still takes up his position facing the church door, to give the priest warning of an attack.

As the priest knelt in adoration, the choir broke into a quick, triumphant anthem, a loud and victorious song of praise that was accompanied, not by the slow clash of cymbals, but by the quick, metallic sound of these instruments being hit rapidly rim against rim. Incense drifted in clouds through the church, seeping through the haikal screen and winding like a blue mist from the door of the sanctuary. In the candle-light of the altar the priest communicated and sank on his knees in silent adoration.

Two or three people began to tiptoe towards the dark little side chapel to the right of the altar. Among them was a woman holding a small child in her arms. The baptism was now about to take place. Rising, I followed them through the side chapel and came into a dark, whitewashed baptistry where a stone font, not standing clear as our fonts stand, was built into a corner of the wall.

Leaving the deacon to guard the Holy Eucharist, the priest entered the baptistry with a lighted candle and two phials of oil. The font held about three feet of cold water, and the unfortunate infant, as if aware of the complete immersion awaiting it, began to whimper and cry as its clothes were removed. The mother was a poor woman from the adjacent tenements, and the child was a three months old girl.

The priest first said prayers of purification over the mother and anointed her on the forehead with oil. As if addressing an adult First Century convert to the Christian Church, he prayed that all remains of the worship of idols should be cast out of the infant's heart, and that she might prove worthy of the new birth that now awaited her. The small brown girl, by this time crying bitterly, was sent into a paroxysm of fear and rage as the priest grasped her wriggling body and touched it on the breast, hands, and back with oil.

Strangely enough the devils appeared to be, if not completely exorcised, at least severely startled, for she suddenly ceased her ear-splitting screams and looked round quietly with tear-dimmed eyes. One of her god-parents held her up while someone else lifted her tiny arms in the form of a cross. In this position the infant was made to renounce Satan and all his works.

"I renounce thee, Satan," (said the infant by proxy) "and all thy impure works, and all thy evil angels, and all thy wicked demons, and all thy power, and all thy vile service, and all thy wicked wiles and deceits, and all thy army, and all thy authority, and all the rest of thy impieties."

The priest then asked the baby three times: "Do you believe?"; and three times the god-parents answered on her behalf: "I believe."

The priest then anointed the infant with the second oil, or chrism, more thoroughly than the first time, making the sign of the cross on the child's eyes, nose, mouth, arms, hands, knees, back, and heart. He then went to the font and consecrated the water. He knelt down and offered one of the most beautiful prayers I have ever heard—a prayer for himself.

"Thou who knowest the evil that is in me, do not laugh me

to scorn, nor turn away Thy face from me, but let all sins flee away from me at this hour, O Thou who dost forgive the sins of men and lead them to repentance. Wash away the stains of my soul and body, purify me perfectly by Thy invisible power and Thy spiritual right hand, that I may not call upon others to seek absolution at my hands, and give it to them, namely the Faith which Thy great and unspeakable love for mankind has prepared, and be myself a castaway, as a servant of sin. Nay, Lord, let not the humble be put to shame, but be to me a Pardoner. Send down from on high Thy power; give me power to perform this service of great mystery, which is of heavenly origin. Let Christ take form in those who are to receive the baptism of new birth from me, vile as I am. Build them up upon the foundation of the apostles and prophets; and do not scatter them abroad, but plant them in the true plantation of Thy one only Catholic Apostolic Church, so that they may grow in piety, and that Thy Holy Name, glorious before all ages, may be glorified in every place, O Father, Son and Holy Ghost."

The priest then offered a prayer for the Pope (of Alexandria), and after the Creed had been said, he took holy oil and poured it into the font, which the Copts call "the Jordan." He burnt incense and then, bending down, breathed three times on the water, making the sign of the Cross with his breath. This is the act of insufflation, and it is employed to-day in Egypt as it was in the earliest days of the Church. The chrism was then poured on the water.

Taking the naked child, the priest first laid his hands upon her and breathed upon her to exorcise any evil spirit, precisely as Tertullian, who lived in the Second Century, described the act of Christian exorcism. His method of holding the infant interested me, because the few writers on this subject have generally disagreed on the Coptic method of holding a child at baptism. Vansleb, the Dominican missionary, wrote in the Seventeenth Century that in order to make the form of a cross the priest takes the child's right wrist and left foot in one hand, and the left wrist and right foot in the other, a position which Butler thought sounded like "a species of torture." This priest grasped the infant firmly by the nape of the neck with his left hand while with his right he held together the left wrist and left ankle, thus leaving the child's right arm and leg free to make whatever commotion was possible to them.

The squirming infant was now plunged firmly into the cold water as far as the waist, the priest saying in Arabic:

"Sabaat is baptized in the name of the Father. Amen."

He lifted her dripping and crying, and held her ready for the second immersion. Down she went again, this time up to the neck in water.

"In the name of the Son. Amen," cried the priest.

Sabaat's cries became louder. The third time she went in over the head and emerged howling.

"In the name of the Holy Ghost. Amen," concluded the priest.

While the mother dabbed at the waving legs of the now Christian Sabaat, the priest deconsecrated the water and, taking the chrism, came to Sabaat again and confirmed her, anointing her for the third time and breathing upon her, saying, "Receive the Holy Ghost." He laid his hands on the child and blessed her and gave her back to the mother, who clothed her in new garments: a dress of white, with a blue bonnet edged with white lace.

The priest meanwhile had returned to the altar, where the Holy Eucharist stood under a crimson veil. He took the chalice and advanced to the baptistry. Sabaat, now in her mother's arms, was carried forward. She was too small to receive the bread and wine together in a spoon, as the Copts receive communion, so the priest, dipping his finger in the chalice, placed a single drop of wine on the child's tongue. A deacon was standing near with a *gulla* full of water. He poured water on the priest's hand, and the priest swiftly dashed it in Sabaat's face. This made the child gasp and, in opening her mouth to cry, she received her first Communion.

While this was taking place, there was a movement in the church, and I saw what appeared to be a dying woman carried into the baptistry. She was one of the nuns from the convent of Mari Girgis. Supported by three sisters, dressed like herself in black, she was carried in and placed on the floor of the baptistry near the haikal, where she lay moaning and crying. I was told that she was desperately ill with dengue fever. The priest administered the Sacrament with a spoon, and the woman, now quiet except for her exhausted breathing, was carried out of the church.

The priest drained the chalice, rinsed it and drank the rinsings. The paten was washed and rinsed, and the deacon drank the rinsings. When the spoon had been washed, the deacon quickly laid it upon his eyes, a custom mentioned by St. Cyril of Jerusalem in the middle of the Fourth Century.

The congregation now crowded round the haikal screen in readiness for the surprising moment which concludes the Coptic Mass. The priest came to the door of the screen attended by the deacon, who held a *gulla* of water. He poured a stream of water on the priest's hands and the priest instantly tossed it up towards the roof. There was a wild scramble as men and women pressed forward to receive a drop on face or body. Three times the priest tossed water into the air, and three times the congregation rushed for it. When they looked up from their last scramble, the priest had vanished, the haikal door was closed, and the sanctuary curtain had fallen back into place.

As the people left the church, they were given a fragment of the bread which had been baked for the Korbân but had not been chosen. As a stranger, I was given a complete loaf. Here again I felt that I was touching some dim hand from the past, for the gift of unconsecrated bread—*eulogiæ*—to the faithful after the Mass was a custom in the Western Church fourteen centuries ago.

I returned to modern Cairo bewildered by the ghosts which haunt a Coptic altar. It would require long study to see them clearly for what they are. An interested passer-by can, however, see their vague shadowy forms moving in the incense; and, having seen them, it is impossible not to feel respect for these Christians who, heresy or no heresy, have kept faith with Christ through twelve difficult centuries, and who have preserved in the secrecy of their churches much that is beautiful from the bright morning of Christianity.

CHAPTER VI

I set out for the Oasis of Siwa in the Libyan Desert. At Mersa Matruh I meet Greek sponge-fishers. I cross the desert to the Oasis, see what remains of the temple of Jupiter Ammon, visit the Fountain of the Sun, and make a few friends. I drink green tea, attend a dance, and return eventually to Alexandria.

I

THE train from Alexandria pounded along the flat north-western coast of Egypt. It is a train that travels only once a day, at a steady twenty miles an hour, along a track laid on sand and liable to be washed away every year when the rains fall.

I think I was the only European on the train. My fellow-passengers showed a partiality for the floors rather than for the seats of their compartments. At every wayside station we took on a few more of them, some carrying wooden crates full of indignant turkeys and philosophic hens, others with their teeth sunk in green and purple stems of sugar-cane.

It became hot, and I resisted the temptation to pull down the shutters with which all Egyptian railway carriages are fitted. I was in a strange country and I wanted to see as much of it as I could, even though it was as dull as this relentless desert proved to be. A thin khaki dust as fine as talc found its way even into my packet of sandwiches. Now and again the tedium of the journey was relieved by a glimpse of the sea, lying hard and blue like a sapphire in the hot light.

I was going to a place which, since I was a boy at school, has lived in my imagination as one of the most mysterious spots in the world: I was going to the Oasis of Siwa. It was there in ancient times, far off in the wastes of the Libyan Desert, that the Oracle of Jupiter Ammon uttered prophecies and gave advice to those who journeyed from ten to twenty days across the wilderness to consult him. I wonder what really happened in the darkness of the sanctuary, when the travellers who had journeyed across sea and sand came at last face to face with the ram-headed god. Did his statue speak with a human voice? Did it move its arms or head?

Even in an age like ours, which is not without its superstitions, it is difficult to understand the oracles of antiquity, those supernatural spas scattered about the world where the divine wisdom bubbled from fathomless sources to issue from the mouths of mediums like the Pythia of Delphi, or the statue of Ammon at Siwa. That men of the greatest intellectual attainments consulted and believed in these oracles seems evident; and we cannot dismiss them all as superstitious fools.

There must have been something singularly impressive about Ammon, something in addition to the remoteness of his desert home and the mystery with which the priests no doubt surrounded him, which made cities despatch embassies across the seas in order to ask his advice on affairs of state, and to make men like Hannibal and Alexander present themselves humbly at his shrine.

The most famous of Ammon's visitors was Alexander the Great, the young conqueror of Egypt. He went there with a small retinue, and every school-boy who has read Arrian knows that on the way Alexander was nearly lost in the waste of desert, but was led onward by two crows which flew ahead of the army, though some say he was guided by two serpents. The result of Alexander's visit was his formal proclamation as Pharaoh, the divine Son of the Sun, the successor to a long line of Ammon's sons. While there is no reason to think that Alexander believed in his own divinity, such fictions were credited in his time. But whether he did so or not, Alexander was aware of its political significance and the interview with Ammon had an important influence on his life, as indeed it had on the future history of kingship. It was from this remote African oasis that the theory of the divine right of kings eventually crossed the Mediterranean into Europe.

After Alexander's visit, the Oracle at Siwa became the foremost oracle in Egypt, and, at one period, in the world. With the coming of the Romans to Egypt, however, its influence began to wane, until gradually the wells of prophecy became dry and the lips of Ammon no longer spoke; after Diodorus Siculus described the Ammonium about 20 A.D., the oasis disappears from history for nearly seventeen centuries.

There is something more fascinating than any tale of buried treasure in the emergence, after centuries of oblivion, of a place once known throughout the world. Siwa owes its rediscovery to a brave, rather prosy Englishman called W. G. Browne, who went there in disguise with Arab merchants in 1792. He was the first European to set eyes on the Oasis of Ammon since the days of the Romans, but he was not a welcome visitor.

Browne found that Siwa was inhabited by a fanatical tribe who penetrated his disguise and stoned him; and he was obliged to make what observations he could under difficult circumstances and leave the oasis after a stay of two or three days. Twenty-one years afterwards Browne was murdered in Persia when, disregarding the advice of people on the spot, he insisted on entering that country dressed as a Turk.

Once Siwa was replaced on the map, it exercised a fascination over a small group of travellers. But the fanaticism of the people was so great, and the journey so difficult, that few men attempted it. Until the war not more than twenty travellers had visited Siwa.

When the war broke out, the Germans and Turks were quick to see in the Senussi an admirable instrument for attacking Egypt. It was their "Revolt in the Desert." British forces consisting of Yeomanry, Territorials, Australians and New Zealanders, with a detachment of Indians and Egyptians, operated against the tribesmen from November, 1915, until the early part of the following year. There was a further outbreak of fighting in 1917, when Siwa was the scene of a spirited armoured-car engagement which finally broke the power of the Senussi. Since that time Egypt has been able to exert her authority over this wayward oasis, which is now part of the Western Desert Province.

When I proposed to go to Siwa, the efficient Frontiers Administration in Cairo, which looks after the Libyan and Arabian deserts, advised me to take the train from Alexandria to a desert outpost on the coast called Mersa Matruh; from there I could cross the two hundred miles of desert to the oasis by the way of the date convoys. This, incidentally, was the route taken by Alexander the Great.

I was given a letter to the officer commanding at Mersa Matruh, for there was a chance that he might be able to send me across in a military patrol car. Knowing that there are times when military patrol cars are not available, I decided to have a car fitted with desert tyres in Cairo and sent on by road to Mersa Matruh, to make certain of my transport. This car was owned by a polite but hard-bitten Syrian who, like most Syrians, was called Mikhail. He looked slightly shattered when I told him where I wanted to go, but raised no objections. He promised to fit the car with desert tyres and to take chains and other tackle with him.

All through the hot afternoon the train shed portions of its inhabitants at desolate desert villages whose houses were made of old kerosene tins. The entire population would stand at the station to greet the travellers and the home-comers would step from the train bearing the strangest loot from the great city. Some wrestled with gigantic packages which might have contained anything from a bicycle to a new wife; others walked sadly down the platform, carrying a bunch of carrots or even a few lettuce leaves.

As dusk fell the train gradually emptied, and I seemed to be travelling alone through a moonless night of stars. I could smell the sea at one window. The cool air was blowing in over hundreds of miles of Mediterranean. Eventually the engine gave a long mournful whistle, and we arrived at the end of the railway line—and Mersa Matruh. A military car, driven by a Sudanese, was waiting for me. We shot across a sandy track and came to a lonely building standing among sandhills. I could hear the sea quite close.

I was prepared for an hotel with no curtains on the windows and sheets bearing the imprint of the last occupant. Instead I entered a little hotel which might have flown over from the South of France. The hall was lit in the most modern French manner, and I could hear a petrol engine popping away somewhere, making electricity. The rooms were well furnished, and although there seemed to be no other guests, a man in a white jacket stood behind an American bar. I asked how it was possible that such a place could exist away out in the Western Desert. He told me that rich Greeks from Alexandria came there to bathe in the summer time.

As I was wandering round the empty lounge later that night, I learned that the British Air Force is also no stranger to the place. Aeroplanes often descend on frontier defence work. I discovered the following curious exiles on a table, among the unreadable technical literature which is distributed free to all hotels, no matter how remote they may be.

A Window in Thrums, by J. M. Barrie ("From Ethel. Aug. 2, 1918," on the fly-leaf), *The Countess Dubarry* (R.A.F., Jerusalem), *Self Help*, by Samuel Smiles, *The Judgment of the Sword*, by Maud Diver (Station Recreational Library, R.A.F., Uxbridge).

What a queer, lost company to discover on the edge of the Libyan Desert.

2

Although I knew that I had arrived at a lonely and romantic spot, no one had told me that Mersa Matruh is one of the most beautiful places in Egypt. When I opened the shutters in the morning, I looked out on a scene that sent my mind back over the years to Ballantyne's *Coral Island* and Stacpoole's *Blue Lagoon*. Here was the perfect desert place of romantic fiction: white breakers curling in the morning sunlight on a half-moon of gold; sandhills, white as snow, rising above lagoons as blue as grape hyacinths; and far to the east a little harbour where a few ancient rigged ships rode at anchor.

A land-locked lagoon lay about twenty yards from my balcony. Even in Iona I have never seen such colours. Light, striking through the lagoon, turns the water in its deepest parts to the colour of an emerald, and in the shallows to a delicate shade of apple-green. And there were many other colours: sudden vivid streaks of mauve and purple, where beds of weed were lying, and curious, pale patches of amethyst, and even touches of amber, as if dyes had been poured on the water. And beyond the coloured shallows and white hills, a hard line of Prussian blue was drawn across the sky: the deeper waters of the Mediterranean Sea.

The hotel stands by itself, about a mile from the village, and after breakfast I set off to explore. The treeless little outpost cowered in the sunlight, on the edge of the sea. It reminded me of those wild-west townships of the early films, where horses were always tethered to posts until their owners slouched out of a saloon easing the pistols in their holsters. But someone has ambitions for Mersa Matruh. Wide and optimistic roads with firm, rectangular convictions run here and there, but only three or four little bungalows stand along them, smiling nervously behind their garden fences.

The most permanent-looking structures are the shops of Greek grocers, for the wily Ulysses sells soap, biscuits, chocolate, tea-pots, and always *ouzo* and *retsinata*, where even a Jew would starve. He is to-day, as he has been since Hellenistic times, the enterprising commercial adventurer of Egypt. Above some of the Greek shops I noticed the half-effaced words in English, "Out of bounds," a memory of the Abyssinian trouble, when British troops were stationed at Mersa Matruh, which is only two hundred miles from the Italian frontier of Tripoli.

I was surprised to see a small modern Greek church and a Greek cemetery. The half-dozen Greek grocers of Mersa Matruh must be extraordinarily devout men to build such a church, I thought. It was so surprising that I went into a Greek shop to find out. Before I knew where I was, I had bought some chocolate, a tin of biscuits, a supply of matches, and a fly-whisk. I believe these up-country Greeks are the best salesmen in the world: no wonder they grow rich in the desert. The man in this shop was a square little brown man from Andros. He wore a felt hat on the back of his head, and he stood in his shirt-sleeves among a truly amazing stock which not only covered the counters and shelves, but was also suspended from the ceiling like the astrologer's crocodile. He gazed at me with brown eyes full of an uncanny intelligence, and was delighted to show off his English.

"This church," I asked, "why is it here?"

"Ah," he replied, "it is the church of the sponge-fishermen. Mersa Matruh is a famous place for the sponge-fishing. Greeks come from the islands every year—many, many ships—and fish for sponges as far up the coast as Sollum. The best sponges in the world come from here, not the little brown sponges that men sell in the streets of Athens, but the big, soft sponges that make much money in England."

"Have you got any for sale?"

He put his head on one side, shut his eyes, and lifted up his hand with the palm held level with his shoulder, which in the Greek sign language, understood all over the near East, means "no"; but not a nasty "no": a soft, deprecating, apologetic "no"; a wistful "no," a "no" full of genuine regret.

"It is not permitted," he explained. "The merchants, they come and buy all the sponges and take them away to Alexandria. We cannot buy here."

He told me that the few rigged ships which I had seen from my balcony were the only sponge-ships left, for the season was over.

"And the cemetery?" I said. "It is for Greeks only?"

"Ah," he replied, "sponge-fishing is much dangerous. There are always much dead men."

And here again he made another of those signs which Greeks make everywhere in the world. He pursed up his lips and lightly fanned the air with one hand in the direction of his face. This means riches, abundance, much, many, and at this particular moment it meant "much dead sponge-fishers." When I left the shop, the little man bowed himself almost under the counter in humble gratitude.

The largest building in the town is the headquarters of the Western Desert Province of Egypt. This wonderful department, half military, half police, and entirely nursemaid, mother, doctor, and detective of the desert, was once a British organization, but under Egypt's new status it is now run by Egyptians. If the Bedouin's camels die, if his wife runs away, if his crops fail, if someone bewitches his donkey or his camel, he treks sometimes a hundred miles to tell the frontier post all about it. In fact he tells the frontier post everything, except the name of the man who murdered his best friend. That is something which everyone in his own circle knows, but the frontiers people must find it out for themselves.

Having heard a lot about the benevolent activities of this force, I was not surprised to find the headquarters surrounded by hundreds of Bedouin waiting for a free gift of barley. They had come from miles around.

I was told a sad story by the officer who was doling out grain. There had been no rain for six years. The tribes were famished. Their horses and camels had died of hunger and thirst. The people themselves were hardly more than skin and bone, as I could see for myself. And now the blessed rain had fallen and the Bedouin had come in from every part of the desert, crying for barley to sow. Soon, if the rain continued, the edge of the desert would be covered with green crops. The tribes would stay camped in the coastal areas until the barley was ripe in April or May, and then, their pitifully meagre needs satisfied, they would disappear southwards into the metallic blaze of heat.

I entered the Frontiers Office to pay my respects to the Governor of the Western Desert. He was a newly appointed Egyptian colonel, who had arrived only the day before to take up his duties. He had, however, received a letter about my journey to Siwa. A map of his district, an area about the size of Wales, hung on the wall. A Sudanese orderly appeared with cups of coffee and we began to talk of my journey.

He suggested that I should start at five o'clock on the following morning, if my car arrived in time, and he would send a desert-patrol wagon as escort. No car is allowed to cross the desert by itself. A young Egyptian officer who had been to Siwa was called in. He said that if everything went well, and we had no breakdowns, we should do the journey in one day. This surprised me, for I had expected to spend at least a night in the open. The journey which cars can now perform in one day used to take eight to ten days by camel.

In the afternoon I walked to the harbour to see the sponge-fishermen. I noticed in the low, limestone hills signs of ancient terraces on which vines and olives once grew, and many a

Greek marble pillar has been dredged from the lagoon or dug up from the white sandhills. Such relics are all that remain of the small Greek port of Parætonium from which Alexander set out for Siwa, and where centuries later Cleopatra is said to have had a summer-house on the lagoon. An admirable little guide-book, which I bought in Alexandria, contains the strange statement that "those immortal lovers, Antony and Cleopatra, repaired to Parætonium to be alone with their bliss, and a better place could not be found throughout the length and breadth of Egypt for a summer idyll." Unfortunately there was no bliss and nothing of a summer idyll about their stay in Parætonium. They arrived there in despair from Actium, the first ship to touch Egypt with news of the defeat. Cleopatra bravely left for Alexandria with her ships decked as if for victory, and minstrels playing, for it was essential that she should obtain control of the palace and the garrison before the truth leaked out. Meanwhile Antony paced the sands of Parætonium with two friends, and it was in this lovely place that he contemplated suicide when he learned that four legions which he had left in Africa had joined the enemy. But his two friends dissuaded him and prevailed upon him to join the queen in Alexandria.

Until a year or so ago every drop of water was brought by sea in large tankers, and it was puzzling to understand how a town could have stood here in Ptolemaic times. The mystery was solved by the recent discovery of underground tunnels half a mile in length, and full of fresh water. Twenty-five manholes give access to the conduit, and when first discovered, there was something like 78,000 tons of sweet water lying underground waiting to be used. This is the ancient water supply, and it is now being used again and still runs through the old channels.

I hired a rowing-boat and went out to look at the sponge-ships. The scene might have been an illustration from *Treasure Island*. The ships lay in a sheltered bay as if on a sheet of dark-blue glass. So clear was the water that I could see fish, coral, and living sponges lying on the sand and rocks thirty feet below. Four wooden sailing-ships lay at anchor, their rigging festooned with the crew's washing, a happy touch which reminded me that when pirates reach a hidden and sheltered bay, they always indulge in such cheerful domesticity! As I drew nearer, I saw men who might have sailed the seas with Captain Kidd, blue-chinned, hairy, and half-naked, lounging about the decks or sprawled in sleep. I noticed that most of the ships came from Rhodes and Ægina.

The men answered my questions with surly suspicion. I could see their Greek minds wondering why I had taken the trouble to row out to them in the heat of the afternoon. They told me that the season was over. Most of the ships had gone home.

Sponge-fishing is a dangerous occupation. The men told me that a sponge-diver does not often live to be over forty, but a hundred pounds for a few months' fishing is real money in the Greek islands. If a diver is not killed by a defective helmet—and both masters and men are criminally careless—he may get diver's paralysis, caused by working under the water.

The most primitive method of sponge-diving, and probably less dangerous in the long run than a bad diving suit, is to plunge naked into the clear water, roped to a heavy stone. In the few seconds while he is on the sea bed the diver detaches a sponge or two and, letting the rope go, shoots up to the surface of the water. Some divers are able to stay below water for several minutes.

Another method is to hack at the sponges with a spear or trident, but this method often damages the sponges. A third method is the use of a diving suit, but I was told some horrible stories of the badly-fitting helmets in use and the capricious supply of air.

The sponge-divers' cemetery at Matruh tells the tragic story eloquently enough. Hardly a season passes but some divers leave their bones in Egypt. Some are killed by sharks, others die of paralysis or of diseases caused by under-water pressure on lungs and heart.

Standing in this lonely little graveyard, I remembered the small brown boys who dive for pennies round the lovely islands of Greece. They swim beneath the water like seals and come up with a penny in their white teeth, shaking the water out of their eyes and laughing with triumph. That is how the sponge-divers begin their short and dangerous lives.

Later that afternoon, just as I was beginning to feel anxious, a tired, dusty Mikhail arrived with an incredibly dusty car. He had had a rough journey from Cairo. I told him to have the car overhauled at the Frontiers Force garage and then to go straight to bed, which he was only too ready to do.

3

A man came into my bedroom with a cup of tea. The stars were shining and waves were breaking on the sand below the window. It was cold, and I hated the idea of getting up.

In the darkness below two cars were waiting to set out across the desert: my car and a military patrol lorry driven by a Sudanese soldier. There were two other figures wrapped to the eyes in drapery, who were also attached to me: one was a Sudanese cook and the other a young Egyptian servant.

I was delighted to discover that the cook, the waiter, and Mikhail were as excited as I was at the prospect of travelling to Siwa. That lonely oasis was as strange to them as it was to me.

"Have you ever been there before?" I asked the driver.

He sloped arms, brought his hand smack down on the butt of his rifle, and said:

"Yes, sir. Me go one time."

"When do you think we shall get there?"

"If no breakdowns," he said, casting a reproachful look at

SIWA

Mikhail's car, "we arrive to-night."

"Right. Let's start."

The patrol car roared off in the darkness and we followed its tail light into the desert. In two hours the sun came up and we looked out over a high tableland as bare and featureless as the sea.

The Libyan Desert, or rather that small part of it between the coast and Siwa, must be among the most monotonous portions of the earth's surface. It is unlike the conventional idea of a desert. There are no picturesque, undulating hills of golden sand. No palm trees strike the horizon. As far as you can see there is nothing but a brown plain like an ocean bed, scattered with millions of stones. It is a dirty khaki colour.

At first we saw camels grazing on the thorn bushes that grow here and there; then life ceased; as we journeyed on into the wilderness there was nothing but the sun beating on thousands of miles of brown sterility.

The road was merely a track made by the wheels of lorries. The wheel ruts turned and twisted among boulders and would suddenly run off at a tangent to avoid dips in which water gathered in the rainy season. At more or less regular intervals we came across hard sandy stretches as flat as a race track, on which it was possible to travel at sixty miles an hour for a minute or so before the track began again with its jolts and sudden crashes on axle springs.

At first we looked forward to the crest of ridges, hoping that when we reached them there would be a different view, something—anything—on which the eye could linger with interest, but it was always the same: a stone-scattered khaki plain, treeless, shrubless, lifeless.

The fate of the fifty thousand Persians who perished in this desert on the way to Siwa is too awful to contemplate. They were sent out by Cambyses in 525 B.C. to sack Siwa and wreck the shrine of the Oracle. They did not arrive and were never seen or heard of again. It is conjectured that they were either overwhelmed in a sand storm, or, losing the way, wandered over the desert until they went mad or perished of thirst.

Will some fortunate archæologist ever solve the mystery of this lost army? Somewhere along the road to Siwa fifty thousand Persians lie beneath the sand with their armour and equipment, just as they fell five centuries before Christ.

Noon came . . . one o'clock, two o'clock, three o'clock, and we continued to journey through the same nightmare land. I called a halt so that we could eat our sandwiches at one of the five wells that lie at distances of about forty miles along the route. Although there is water, there is no vegetation.

As Mikhail stepped from the car, he gave a howl of real terror, and looking through the window, I saw that he had almost stepped on the most deadly snake in Egypt—the horned viper. It was long and thin, almost the colour of sand, with a small, flat head and a tail ending in a thin pale point. I have been told that its bite can bring death to a man in twenty minutes. It is one of the few snakes that will deliberately attack a man, and among its horrible peculiarities is the speed with which it can travel not only backwards and forwards, but sideways as well.

Fortunately for Mikhail, the reptile had been driven out of its hole during hibernation and was in a comatose condition. We shouted to the soldier to bring his rifle, but he did not understand. So taking the first thing that came to hand, which happened to be my photographic tripod, we took our courage in both hands and killed the viper. We then congratulated Mikhail on being alive and had our frugal lunch in the shadow of the cars.

We continued our journey: I to bump unhappily from side to side of the car and the patrol-wagon, with its better springs, to dart ahead with surprising speed. There were no birds. Incredible as it may sound, there were no flies. We were in a dead portion of the world.

Some thirty-five miles to the east of the track is a slight hill which the Bedouin call Jebel Iskander, the Hill of Alexander. They do not know that Alexander's guides lost their way to Siwa: the name has just come down from mouth to mouth through the centuries. After the war a British officer, who had been told by the Arabs that pots were to be found on this hill, went there and unearthed eight perfect amphoræ of the Hellenistic period. I saw one in a garden at Mersa Matruh. It was made of red clay, and was about four feet high, with a pointed base, a bulbous body, a long neck, and two handles. If these are some water-jars of Alexander's expedition, as it seems they may be, one wonders what other relics might be found on that lonely spot.

As the sun was setting, we left the plain and entered one of the most fantastic bits of country imaginable. I think the mountains of the moon must look like this. It seemed that nature, conscious of the bleakness of the past two hundred miles, had crowded all the fantasy of which she is capable into a small space. The valley was surrounded on all sides by weird dead hills, each one carved into some improbable shape, a cone, a cube, a queer isolated pinnacle, a ridge that from a distance looked like a battlemented castle with turrets. Other hills rose up like the ruins of old cities. In this strange valley we cried out:

"Look! A bird!"

It was the first bird we had seen since early morning, and a sign that we were approaching Siwa.

For an hour or so we travelled slowly downhill through the moon mountains: then emerging suddenly from the gorge, we saw below us thousands of date palms standing in the pink flush of the sunset.

As we drew near, the superb fantasy of Siwa revealed itself: a rock covered with mud dwellings piled up like skyscrapers, like some queer African Manhattan Island. The date-palms formed a green sea from which this hill of houses rose against the sky.

Soon we were running in the shadow of this hill, and we realized that there was something uncanny about it. No people came out on the roof-tops to look at us. There was no movement at the small square windows which pierced the high walls.

We learned afterwards that the old town had been condemned as unsafe a few years ago and is deserted. The inhabitants have built a new village round about it, a cluster of low, flat-roofed, white houses made of mud and roofed with palm branches.

I went to the police-station, where the Mamûr, the district Government official, was expecting me. The Mamûr, the doctor, and the officer of the local camel corps, all Egyptians, are the only resident officials. There are no Europeans in Siwa.

The Mamûr said that he had opened the Government rest-house for my reception, and off we went for about a mile through a palm-grove and came to a gaunt building of white-washed mud, standing alone on a hill. Every window was closely meshed with mosquito netting, which delighted me, for I am one of those people whom mosquitoes love.

A sad air of departed grandeur hung about the house. King Fuad had stayed there when he visited Siwa, and a memory of that visit remains in a hand-rope covered with frayed blue velvet which still hangs, though a trifle listlessly, beside the stairs. There is also a bathroom, doubtless the strangest sight in Siwa, but its capabilities would not deceive the most optimistic wanderer.

I was given the royal bed-chamber, where a brass four-poster rose in the shadows, and from this room a step led into a pleasant living-room furnished with a wooden table and two canvas chairs. The usual portrait of his late Majesty, wearing a tarbush and a frock coat, gazed from the wall. A long window covered in wire netting ran along one side of the room and afforded a superb view of Siwa beyond the palm grove.

Sounds of dismay and confusion from the courtyard below indicated that the cook, the waiter, Mikhail, and the patrol-car driver were attempting to coerce a reluctant paraffin stove in the kitchen. Glancing out of the window, I saw the cook walking below, holding a dead cockerel. Soon I smelt a strange chorus of smells which indicated that the cook, with the passionate enthusiasm of one who finds himself alone and on his mettle, was preparing a tremendous meal.

The sun sank and darkness fell upon this lonely place. Stars snapped above the palm trees, the bats were flying; and a mile away the weird outline of the dead town rose on its hill, grey and ghostly.

The waiter came in with a paraffin lamp, and a dinner was served which only a Sudanese cook could have prepared in this remote place. There was soup, an omelette, fish from Mersa Matruh, roast chicken, tinned peaches, a cheese savoury, and oranges.

As I went to bed that night, I saw a big gold moon sail into the sky and hang above the dark palm groves. No dog barked; no jackal cried; no night-bird called. The oasis lay in a pool of green light, frozen in silence like a land under snow.

4

In the early morning Siwa is like a Gauguin or a Van Gogh. It is a reckless exercise in hot colour: ochre-brown hills; golden sand; vivid green trees; a hard sky of blue untouched by any cloud. Heat throbs in the open places. Goats run in blinding light to the welcome shadow of the palm-groves. White pigeons rise from feathery tree-tops to wheel sparkling in the sun. All the sounds are little sounds: the note of a bell on a goat's neck, the lazy song of a man working in one of the water-gardens, the bright click of a donkey's hoof hitting a stone, and the padded sound of camels walking.

From the window of the guest-house I could see to the west a narrow lake of intensely blue water, streaked with bands of snowy white. This is a salt lake which dries up in summer, so that it is possible to walk across on bricks of sparkling salt. In ancient times the priests of Ammon exported this salt, which was used in the temples of Egypt and Persia. The natives say that the sword, the seal, and the ring of Solomon lie hidden on an island in this lake. One of Siwa's early explorers, the French engineer Colonel Boutin, took with him a collapsible canvas boat in the hope of reaching this island, but the Siwans would not let him use it. Had he gone there in the summer, he might have walked to the island along a causeway of solid salt.

As I was dabbing a mosquito bite with ammonia, I wondered how many people in chemists' shops all over the world realize that they invoke the name of the Oracle every time they ask for ammoniated quinine or salammoniac; for it was here in Ammonia, near the temple of Ammon, that ammonia chloride is believed to have first been made from the dung of camels. I wondered, too, as my nose approached too near the bottle, whether the asphyxiating fumes of this chemical had anything to do with the Oracle. The Delphic Oracle sat on a tripod directly over a chasm which was supposed to emit vapours, and Plutarch believed that the prophetic frenzy was stimulated by breathing the fumes, just as diviners among certain tribes of Hindoo Koosh, the Dainyals, are said to work themselves into a prophetic condition by first inhaling the smoke of burning cedar wood.

The Mamûr arrived while I was having breakfast, a large man in a suit of khaki drill and a sun helmet, and we sat down to talk about Siwa.

The population is about 5,000 people and there are more

women than men. There is no polygamy, but divorce is so frequent, and so little thought of, that a proportion of the female population is in constant circulation; and one Siwan has been known to divorce as many as forty wives. The Siwans still hold to the Senussi faith, but their fanaticism and hatred of outsiders have broken down since the war. Cairo does not seem so far away now that aeroplanes can reach the oasis in a few hours, and the motor patrol cars bring it within a day's journey of Mersa Matruh, instead of seven or ten days. But the Siwans are still difficult, and ready to quarrel among themselves.

They are riddled with superstition and firmly believe in all forms of witchcraft. The Government doctor has a hard time to convince them that his knowledge can be more useful than the spells and poultices of witch doctors and wise women. Much of the work is done by the descendants of Sudanese slaves and the poorer Siwans; they are not paid in money but in food, which is given to them every six months. The Government pays for work in money at the rate of 3s. 6d. a week. This is considered lavish. But there is nothing to spend money on in Siwa, except green tea, the only extravagance of the oasis. Coffee is forbidden to the Senussi, therefore the Siwans have taken to tea, which they drink in enormous quantities, and on every possible occasion. The only real value of money is to purchase a wife. The price of a wife has been stabilized for many years at 120 piastres, which is about twenty-four shillings. As women are in a minority and are always sure to find suitors, and as large numbers of the men receive no money from one year to another, there is a proportion of the population which is resigned to life-long bachelorhood.

The rulers of Siwa are the sheiks, who own large date groves. The oasis possesses 600,000 date palms, which produce some of the best dates in Egypt. Each tree is taxed, and the oasis pays an annual tax of just under two thousand pounds to the Egyptian Government. This has cost a certain amount of bloodshed in the past, but, like most people under the influence of civilization, the Siwans are now becoming resigned to taxation.

The dates are sold in an open market and are taken away by motor-lorry. The old date caravans, which once used to come to Siwa from Egypt every year, are no longer seen, although merchant caravans do sometimes come from Tripoli. The end of the camel caravan traffic has had one curious effect on the Siwan exchequer. One of the main sources of revenue was derived from the sale of the camel manure left on the public square during the date market season. This has now ceased and the budget is down accordingly. The only industry in Siwa is a Government date-packing factory, recently established, where the dates are dried, washed, and sent away in boxes to Cairo and Alexandria.

The absence of dogs and cats in Siwa is due to the fact that the Siwans eat them. They also eat the jerboa, the rat, and the mouse. They make an intoxicating drink from the sap of palm-trees, called *lubchi*. Under its potent influence they become violent, and, in times now past, the east and the west ends of the town, which have always been at enmity, used to drink *lubchi* and engage in pitched battles in the main square, which invariably ended in considerable loss of life.

We set off together to see the wonders of the oasis, and, as we passed through narrow streets between rows of mud houses, I asked the Mamûr why so many skulls, bones, and inverted pots were built into the walls and set over the doors.

"Everyone believes in the Evil Eye," he replied. "It is thought that any possessor of it will look at things like the skull of that donkey over there, and so avert it from human beings."

We came into the wide main square above which rise the fantastic battlements of old Siwa. Nothing more crazy has ever been erected. For many centuries house has been built on top of house in a casual, haphazard manner, until the outside walls are nearly two hundred feet high in places. The streets that tunnel through this human ant-heap run in complete darkness and wind up to the top, giving you an occasional dazzling snapshot of the sunlight outside.

When the old town was inhabited, it must have been an eerie experience to pass crouching along the dark, narrow streets, more like shafts in a coal-mine than anything else, and to hear nothing but women pounding corn in the dark, or the voices of invisible people in the houses on either side.

There were once nine gates to the town, which were guarded day and night, and when darkness fell all unmarried men were expelled to spend the night in huts outside. They were not admitted until morning.

I had heard that there was some excitement in Siwa, for a merchant caravan had arrived from Italian Tripoli, the first for many months. This sounded romantic, and I expected something rather spectacular. But when we came to a small market-house roofed with palm trunks and branches, I saw four Bedouin squatting on the floor, with knotted handkerchiefs in front of them. This, I was told, was the caravan from Tripoli. They opened their handkerchiefs and exposed a few poor silver trinkets. They had come all the way across the desert, for days and nights, moving from well to well, striking camp and moving on, to bring these pitiful little things to the oasis. I thought this was an insight into the grim energy of such primitive commerce. Archæologists often wonder how a silver ring should have got here or there. I suppose there have always been men like these merchants from Tripoli, who would bring a ring across the whole world just for the pleasure of having a cup of tea and a gossip at the end of the journey.

The market itself was an object lesson in the simplicity of life in this oasis. There were not more than ten merchants, and each sat cross-legged, with a sack in front of him. One sack would hold about four pounds of granulated sugar, another two or three pounds of tea; in a third would be a few beans or lentils. To people accustomed to such a frugal market, no doubt the handkerchiefs of the Tripolitan Bedouin must have looked like Cartier's window in Bond Street.

We entered the date market not far away, a large open space floored with dates drying in the sun: some a rich gold, some pale yellow, and some the colour of horse chestnuts. The Mamûr explained that the dates have various names, and are of different varieties. Some Siwans are so expert in date culture that they can tell from which garden a particular date has come.

It is a custom that anyone can enter this market during the date harvest and eat as many dates as he likes. But he must not put one in his pocket!

The date is to Siwa what the olive is to the Mediterranean. The poorer people live almost entirely on dates. The trunks of the date palm provide the builder with wood. Palm wood is used as fuel. Fences are made of palm fronds, and houses and huts are roofed with them. From the fibre of the palm tree the women make beautiful mats, and baskets so closely woven that they will hold water.

The Siwan donkeys, which are remarkable for strength and size, are said to owe their perfect condition to a diet of dates. In a corner of the market I saw a donkey eating his date ration with enjoyment.

We passed again through the streets of Siwa, and small brown girls about ten or twelve years old, each one like an ancient Egyptian statuette, stood frozen in curiosity as we approached, waiting until we were within a few yards before running to cover. They were the belles of Siwa. Their faces were mature, but their bodies were those of children. Their plaited hair gave them a curiously archaic look, as if they were wearing the festival wigs of the women in ancient Egypt. They part their hair in the middle, and wear it tightly plaited, a fringe of plaits falling over the forehead in a straight line. It is dressed with an oily, scented unguent in which fig-leaves have been pounded.

Each little girl wore round her neck a hoop of silver, to some of which were attached silver discs about the size of a saucer. These are "Virginity discs," which the girls wear until their marriage. On the marriage eve the bride, attended by girls, goes to bathe in one of the springs of Siwa. She takes the disc from her neck and flings it into the spring; then, slipping off her garments, she dives into the water. One small boy is generally allowed to be present at such ceremonies. As soon as the ritual is over, he dives down and retrieves the silver disc, which is preserved for the bride to hand on to her daughter.

When in full dress, these little girls are loaded with barbaric jewellery. Enormous earrings are attached to their hair, carrying long chains to which bells are fixed. Huge necklaces, often made of beads taken from mummies, encircle their necks.

I saw these children everywhere, but not once did I see a woman between the ages of sixteen and thirty-five. Nowhere are married women more rigorously secluded, and it is only when you glance up at the houses that you sometimes see an eye gazing down curiously into the street.

5

When I came to know Siwa better and could find my way about, I never became weary of sitting beside the springs. There are about two hundred, some of fresh water, some of salt, some sulphurous, some warm, and some cold: a little Harrogate in a setting by Gauguin.

This varied volume of water has been pouring itself through the desert sand for centuries, and the explanation I like best is the theory that an underground river from the Congo shoots up through cracks and holes in the desert's crust. Nearly all the springs look like circular swimming-baths full of green and blue water; for it is green in the sunlight and blue where palm-trees cast their shade over it. Most of the springs are lined with hewn stones, and have parapets on which you can sit and gaze through fifty feet of limpid blue-greenness to floors of tinted stalagmites.

Gazing into still water is the historical occupation of the vain, and there is not much to be said for it unless you are very fond of your own face; but in Siwa the springs hold your attention by the hour because they are alive with ascending strings of pearls. These quicksilver bubbles come at times in such numbers that the whole surface of the spring moves with the escaping air, as if hundreds of invisible fish are mouthing the water. Then, for no apparent reason, the movement ceases and you look down into still, green cellophane. I can understand how these springs excited the imagination of antiquity, as indeed they still excite the superstitions of modern Siwans, for there is nothing mechanical about their queer aerated vitality: the bubbles are blown as if at the whim of some underground giant who becomes tired and starts again, or who goes away for a rest and returns, sometimes blowing chains of little silver peas and sometimes sending up one as large as an orange.

The clearings in which these springs lie are hot, sunny openings in green jungles. All around, like masts in harbour, rise the jointed, matted boles of date palms. Bright green leaves are spotted with the flushed rind of ripe pomegranates, or the delicious green-yellowness of sweet limes. And as you look into these springs, you can see clusters of dates reflected from the trees overhead, lying in the water like swarms of polished brown bees.

Dragon-flies of red, green, and orange dart and quiver over the springs, and sometimes a hoopoe, which is tame here, as elsewhere in Egypt, will fly down and look at you with a speculative eye, head cocked sideways, its plume of feathers rising like a question mark.

The springs of Siwa are of course the life-blood of the oasis, and the little channels carry the water into the gardens. Each spring has a guardian, and each guardian has a book in which is written the amount of water due to every strip of land. The guardians preside over toy canal systems of water tracks, some of which are carried over others through hollow palm trunks. When the time comes for a certain garden to be watered, the guardian approaches the water channel leading to it and kicks down a mud dam, which thus allows the water to flow in the right direction. And that is how the Israelites watered their gardens in Egypt long ago, as described in Deuteronomy xi. 10: "where thou sowedst thy seed, and wateredst it with thy foot, as a garden of herbs." And the guardian who waters the gardens of Siwa with his foot has no watch. He knows by the position of the sun, and when the sun sinks he takes his time from the muezzin, whose clear call he can hear in the still air, and when there is no sound from the mosque, he has the stars.

The Fountain of the Sun is the most famous and the most beautiful of Siwa's springs. Herodotus said that it was cold at mid-day but grew warmer towards midnight, a story which the Siwans repeat. There is also a legend that black sightless fish once lived in the spring and were connected with the worship of the Oracle of Ammon, whose temple was not far away. While I was sitting by this spring, a dignified figure in a Roman toga, for that is how all Libyans wear their white robes, came towards me through the trees. He wore a little red cap from which hung a blue silk tassel, and he grasped a black umbrella. This was the Sheik of the village of Aghourmi, and he had come to show me the ruins of the temple of Jupiter Ammon.

6

First we went to see a ruin not far from the Fountain of the Sun, which must be the remains of the smaller temple mentioned by Diodorus. There is nothing left now but a few stones which once formed a gateway or a pylon. They are covered with figures who are making offerings to the god Ammon. It is clear, from the broken character of the ground, that a large building once stood in this place. Leaning gracefully on his umbrella, the Sheik told me that long ago a Turkish governor had blown up the temple with gunpowder to obtain stones for the police station.

We ascended a small hill towards the old village of Aghourmi, which I thought even more impressive and interesting than Siwa. Its mud houses completely cover a rock that rises abruptly above the palm forests. From a distance it looks like a brown, mastless hulk drifting on a sea of palm fronds and, like Siwa, this village is now abandoned as unsafe, and the villagers have built new houses some distance away.

The main street wound steeply up between mud walls, losing itself now and then in an incredible rat-run of narrow tunnels which led to dark little houses inhabited now only by jackals and snakes.

We emerged on the ramparts, where we had a superb view of the oasis. The feathery heads of the palm forests lay below us mile after mile, and beyond them the Libyan Desert stretched to the horizon like a gold ocean.

Climbing in darkness over steep piles of rubbish and fallen walls, my electric torch revealed the splendid stones of an Egyptian temple, and the remains of a massive gateway. Some of the stones were as large as the stones of the Pyramids of Gizeh.

This temple on the hill, lifted so high above the palm groves, was the shrine of the Oracle, and somewhere beneath the mass of mud buildings and tunnels is the place where Alexander the Great stood face to face with Jupiter Ammon.

The Siwans believe that an underground tunnel connects the temple at Aghourmi with the lesser temple near the Fountain of the Sun. They say that a monarch called King Meneclush lies buried with his horse underneath Aghourmi. Who Meneclush was they do not know. They say he was a king who lived long ago and kept four speaking statues in his palace. These images spoke when the sun touched them. This surely must be some old memory of the Oracle?

The oracular god of Siwa, like the Oracle of Amûn-Rē at Thebes, of which he was a duplicate, was a statue of a god with a man's body and the head of a ram. It was made so that the head, and, no doubt, the arms, could be made to move in answer to the questions put to it. As the ancient Egyptians thought of the sky as an ocean on which the sun and the moon sailed in their barks, the god was exhibited either standing or seated in the shrine, which was placed amidships of a slender canoe-like ship covered with plates of hammered gold.

At Siwa the god's golden bark was covered with silver discs which hung down on each side, and when the curtain was drawn away from the shrine the god was seen inside, shining with green malachite, which is often mistranslated as "emeralds." There were rings at the corners of the boat through which poles were thrust, so that on festival days the priests might shoulder boat and deity and carry them in procession round the temple.

It was a fiction from remote times that every pharaoh who came to the throne of Egypt was the divine son of the Sun God, and apparently it was a necessary preliminary of coronation, during the Eighteenth Dynasty, to be recognized as the legitimate successor by the Oracle of the God at Thebes. Apparently the God had also the power to depose a king and appoint a successor.

Why did Alexander go to Siwa? Any man who wished to legalize his conquest of Egypt would first receive recognition of solar descent from Amûn-Rē. But that this was not Alexander's intention seems clear from the fact that he did not immediately publish his interview with the Oracle when he reached Memphis, where it would have been received with re-

spect by an Egyptian audience. His silence on this matter in
Egypt and in Greece leads one to suppose that his visit to the
Oracle was entirely a personal affair: he went there from
purely romantic and private motives, and what these were it
is difficult to say.

When he arrived in Siwa, eighty shaven priests in robes of
white linen came to meet him, bearing to the entrance of the
temple the golden ship of the Sun God. The air shook with the
silver sound of sistra; and incense hung in clouds round the
statue of Ammon.

What took place in the sanctuary will remain for ever unknown. Alexander alone was allowed to approach the god,
dusty as he was from his ride across the desert. His retinue were
obliged to change their clothes and to wait in the outer court
of the temple. When he came out, Alexander had altered. He
had received something in the shrine at Siwa which affected
him powerfully for the rest of his life.

We cannot hope now to know what happened or what words
passed between the young conqueror of the world and the father of the gods. But that it was satisfactory goes without saying, for it was the business of the priests of Siwa, of Delphi, and
of Dodona to know all the desires in the hearts of men.

7

The Sheik invited me to drink tea at his house. I have already
said that the drinking of green tea is an inevitable act in Siwa,
so I rose and followed him through the ruins and into a palm
grove.

His house was a short walk away: a large, square mud house
from whose upper windows I caught a fleeting glance of curious feminine eyes. We climbed a flight of mud stairs and
emerged on a square roof exposed to the blaze of the sun. Several doors led from the roof to rooms built around it, and in one

A GIRL OF SIWA

of them we found a table covered with food. There were biscuits, sweet limes, pomegranates, a soft delicious kind of date, called Shengbel, which must be eaten straight from the tree, bananas, and little plates of nuts.

Two or three young men came in, the sons of the house, and after some polite conversation, I was asked to help myself to dates and pomegranates, while the Sheik performed the solemn ritual of tea-making.

I watched his preparations with interest. It is a great compliment to be asked to pour, but it is not etiquette for a newcomer to accept; he must throw up his hands in feigned dismay and say that he is unworthy to do so. The man who makes the tea is called the "Sultan," and when Siwans gather together on social occasions, they elect one of their number to be the "Sultan" of the party.

The Sheik first rinsed little glasses in boiling water from a kettle that stood on a brazier of charcoal. He then opened a chest containing several compartments. One was full of green tea, one full of black tea, a third held soft sugar, and a fourth mint leaves.

He carefully and judiciously measured a small quantity of green tea, added a pinch or two of black tea, and poured a little boiling water into the pot. He smelt the aroma and poured the whole brew away. His next effort was more successful. He added more boiling water and poured himself a small quantity of the tea, which he sipped critically once or twice. At the first sip he appeared doubtful, and again I thought he was going to pour it away; but a second sip reassured him, and he handed me a little glass full of the scalding liquid.

The ceremony was immediately repeated. A second glass was given to me, and this time the tea was sickly-sweet with sugar. When, with many compliments, I had drunk this, tea-making took place for the third time. The third glass was sweet and flavoured with mint.

It is etiquette always to drink at least three glasses. You must never refuse. The Siwans believe that tea is good for you; but should you feel ill after too much of it, they recommend the eating of sweet limes.

A gilded scimitar, which King Fuad had presented to the Sheik, was produced for my admiration. I sat with it across my knees and was given first a sweet lime and then a red pomegranate, a fruit I cannot remember eating since I was a child. It is a difficult and disappointing fruit. When you open it, you might have opened a box of rubies, but the ultimate result is a mouthful of pips and mildly scented water.

The Sheik sat fanning away flies with a palm frond and pressing upon me chocolate biscuits of English make, whose appearance in Siwa struck me as one of the romances of commerce.

Our conversation was so trivial that we might have been a couple of visiting kings on some formal occasion. I did not ask the questions about the oasis which I had intended to ask, and after a number of compliments, I departed at the moment which I felt was indicated by etiquette.

8

I looked out of the guest-house window one afternoon, and saw a group of men putting up what I thought was a gibbet. They told me that as I was departing in the morning, a dance had been arranged in my honour; and the "gibbet" was to hold an acetylene lamp.

About nine o'clock that night, with a moon silvering the palm groves and lying green over the desert, the sheiks and notables began to arrive on donkeys. I had sacked the guest-house for chairs, which I had arranged in a row opposite the "gibbet." The largest chair had been reserved for the Mamûr, and the three next best chairs for the doctor, the officer of the Camel Corps, and myself. On either side of us sat the sheiks and village notables.

I had already sent down to the village for a pound of tea, and by this time I knew too much about local custom to ask my cook to prepare it. When the sheiks had all gathered, I suggested that the time had come to elect a "sultan." There followed a ridiculous scene of pure social hypocrisy, first one sheik pretending to be unworthy of the honour, then another, and again a third, until, finally, it was necessary to lead the elected one—who happened to be the most important and would have been deeply insulted had he not been chosen—almost by force to the brazier. He wasted quite a lot of my pound of tea in concocting brews which he tasted and poured away, and I began to wonder if we should have enough to go around.

At last his palate was satisfied, and he produced a large tin pot full of bitter fluid which everyone seemed to think the best cup of tea ever brewed in Siwa. Holding little glasses, which I had borrowed from the police station, we sat in the moonlight waiting for the dancers to approach from the distant village.

Coming nearer across the stretch of sand we heard the beat of a tom-tom. Someone lit the acetylene lamp and it threw a circle of white light brighter than the moonlight.

As the dancers drew nearer, we could hear a flute as well as the tom-tom, and every now and then the dancers gave a wild cry, a rhythmic repetition of the same sentence, a wailing, plaintive sound which ceased as suddenly as it began. Into the circle of lamplight came a barbaric gathering escorted by a *gaffir* with a long whip and a policeman with a rifle across his shoulders, strange guardians for a dance party!

Before the Siwans dance, they drink deeply of *lubchi*, and these men and boys, for there were no women in the crowd, had evidently worked themselves up into a state of exhilaration. They advanced clapping their hands and gyrating as they surrounded the drummer and two flute players.

Seating itself on the ground, the band played a monotonous

but attractive air. I wished I had enough musical talent to write it down. I believe the technical term for such music is "hot jazz." This, however, was several degrees hotter than anything I have ever heard, even in Harlem. It had the pathos and savagery of the Libyan Desert, and also a plaintive beauty, and a hunger which is the hunger and splendour of the desert.

At a certain point in the tune the whirling dancers sang the verse which we had heard as they were approaching over the sand. It was in the Siwan language, which the Egyptian doctor could not understand. I asked one of the sheiks to tell me what it meant.

"It is a love song," he said. "The dancers say that the beauty of the loved one is so great that their eyes do not close at night. . . ."

The dance itself was the most barbaric posturing that can be imagined. The men circled round the musicians, suddenly leaping in the air with wild cries, or revolving in a curious crouching attitude. There was also a bounding forward step, and now and again the whole horde of dancers, as if animated by the same insanity, crouched and took three forward leaps.

It was done with a meticulous regard for rhythm, and none of the steps was essentially more ridiculous than the dance steps made popular in the last twenty years. During the war there was a step which consisted of three quick runs and a dip, that compares not unfavourably with the Siwan technique.

The dreary thing about this dancing, in London as in Siwa, is its monotony. As the *lubchi* began to work, the dancers became absolutely tireless. I was told that they could keep it up all night.

I began to talk to the young doctor. He was an Egyptian who had spent many years in the desert and had come to Siwa from the oasis of Bahariya, where, he told me, the women dance instead of the men. They dance a peculiar and ancient dance. Standing with backs to their audience, they move their hips in time to drums and flutes. The Bahariya women are kept in the strictest seclusion, except on dance nights.

"I remember," said the doctor, "that once I had to go to a sheik and tell him that unless his wife saw me she would probably die.

" 'All right,' he replied. 'See her; but as soon as she is well again, I shall divorce her.' And he did so."

"What impression have you formed of these desert people?"

"They are —— primitive man. If an anthropologist wants to study primitive man, why should he dig up skulls that are thousands of years old when he can come out to the oases and study the living human being? Customs and beliefs, going back beyond ancient Egypt into an unknown past, have been handed down in these places, and every doctor is up against witchcraft in some guise or other."

A touch of variety was given by the arrival of a remarkably coy, elderly woman. Her hair was dyed a bright auburn, her cheeks were rouged, and her hands were loaded with jewels. She was a shapeless bunch of rather garish garments, and her feet were encased in delicate little heelless Arab boots of soft crimson leather.

"Who is she?" I whispered to the doctor.

"She is a dancer," he replied. "She came from Tripoli long ago, when she was so very beautiful that men contended for her charms."

As soon as she arrived, a rival dance ring was formed. Another drummer and flute-player appeared and squatted in the centre. After many coy preliminaries, the dancer glided into the circle with a queer, undulating movement and with a black veil completely hiding her face. As she had appeared unveiled, I was surprised.

"No woman must dance without a veil. It is the custom," explained the doctor.

I was hoping that the beauty from Tripoli would infuse a

little charm into the proceedings, but her motions, which were just a rhythmic sideways movement of the hips, became as tedious as the movements of the rival dance ring. She kept this up for nearly an hour, after which a man leapt into the ring and danced with her.

I began to feel that the evening had outlived its first careless rapture, but the Siwans were as fresh as ever. The sand flies were now biting without mercy. I suggested that perhaps the time had come to break up the party.

The policeman with the rifle, and the man with the whip, instantly flung themselves into the dance, but the dancers declined to stop. They said that they would dance as long as the music went on playing. The band said that they would play as long as anyone wanted to dance. I seemed to have heard these sentiments before, but far from these desert sands!

Eventually a happy compromise was reached. The band was persuaded to return, still playing, to the town. As they moved away, the dancers clustered round them like a swarm of bees about the queen.

The sound of the tom-tom and the monotonous chant faded in the distance: but all that night the tom-toms beat in Siwa, and only in the hours before the dawn did the dancers fall down exhausted.

9

I was awakened at a quarter to five. The moon was still up and I could hear the servants packing in the courtyard below. Looking out of the window, I saw Siwa lying hushed in a wash of green light, the tracks running across the sand, the dark trees standing motionless, and the old village on its hill, silent and dark as a place of tombs.

We had managed to buy a couple of eggs the night before, and these came to the table in the light of a paraffin lamp. The moon was still shining when we started at six o'clock, though the first hint of dawn was in the air. A bird flying near in the darkness uttered a sweet note, but though I looked everywhere, I could not see it. Someone said that it was the Haj Mawla, a bird known only in Siwa.

The patrol car roared off across the sand, and we followed into the silent, sleeping village. We stopped at the police station, where the driver of the patrol car had left his rifle. The Sudanese cook and the waiter sat crowded together in the patrol car, their heads swathed in white cloths like people with tooth-ache. Their dark faces peered out at the fretted walls and the black shadows, and up to the old village which lay massed in inky darkness, its turrets touched with green moonlight; and they were strangely quiet. The driver came down the steps of the police station carrying his rifle and bandolier. He slung the bandolier across his shoulder, leaned the rifle against his seat, and climbed up. The police sentry sloped arms and wished us a good journey, and we sped off into the white moon mountains. I looked back and saw Siwa lying dark among its palm trees, with the stars burning in a sky that was growing lighter with approaching day. Then for some time we went on through the pass with the moon on our left and daylight coming in a pink pulsation on the right. Soon all the east was throbbing in livid incandescence, and when we reached the plateau we saw for one second a burning rim rise over the desert's edge, then the sun was shining and the air grew warm.

All that day we journeyed to the north through the heartless land. We saw the sun cross the sky. We became tired, hot, and thirsty. We saw the stars come out. In the first hour of darkness a camel ran across our headlights and we knew that we were nearing the end of the plateau and the long descent to the sea at Mersa Matruh. Suddenly we looked down and saw the lights of the town shining on the edge of the sea.

In the morning, while another dawn was rushing upward from the east, I got into Mikhail's car and we drove along the coast to Alexandria. The villages through which we passed rose treeless on a brown plain, and sometimes we saw to our left the blue line of the Mediterranean shining across a mile of sand. We bought petrol in a village made of petrol tins and inhabited by men who wore their *jurds* like Roman togas. The man who lifted the cover of our radiator was draped like a statue of Augustus.

As darkness was falling, we saw the lights of Alexandria covering the flat land for miles, and we were soon running through the confusion of its streets.

CHAPTER VII

I look at the remains of the Pharos, meet a man who believes that Alexander the Great is still buried in Alexandria, travel the desert road to Cairo, and see the ruins of the city of St. Mena. In the Wadi Natrûn I visit four Coptic monasteries where Christian monks have lived since the Fourth Century.

I

ALEXANDRIA was looking her best by night. Her pearl necklace of lights was reflected in still water, the air was warm, and palm trees in the gardens below rose in a windless silence.

The first act of the desert traveller is to call for a bath and a barber. My barber, it is perhaps unnecessary to say, was a Greek. Alexandria is still one of the largest Greek cities in the world, and if someone who had never seen Athens were taken there blindfold and told he was in the capital of Greece, it might be some time before he discovered his mistake. Names are written above shops in what is more or less the alphabet which Plato knew. Greek newspapers are sold everywhere, and you can try to read them in Greek cafés while you sip a glass of *ouzo* or *retsinata*.

My Greek barber was a brown, bright-eyed man who professed an undying love for England. I positively blushed as I listened to the virtues which he attributed to us. There was nothing to be done, for obviously a man armed with a razor is a privileged conversationalist. He had at one time worked in the shop of a London hairdresser not far from Piccadilly, and the fact that I had sometimes had my hair cut there seemed, to him, to establish a unique bond of sympathy between us. He talked of "dear old London." He asked me whether I had ever used a special kind of hair lotion sold in this shop, and I said that I had

237

done so. We agreed that ten shillings a bottle was a fantastic price to pay, but I explained that I was only in the habit of buying it in days when I was very poor; which is true. Suddenly, with a dramatic gesture, for the Greeks are among the most transpontine of people, he pulled open the door of a cabinet which revealed itself to be full of bottles.

"I have taken the recipe!" he cried proudly. "Here is the same mixture . . . exactly, sir! And—to you—three shillings!"

In every Greek I meet I seem to encounter some resemblance, though it may only be a faint distorted one, to Ulysses: of course I bought a bottle, and so far as I can tell it is indeed the same mixture.

Later in the evening I was sitting in the lounge of the hotel when a young Englishman sat down at the next table. I had an idea that, like myself, he was a stranger in the country and we fell naturally into conversation. As he told me about himself, I marvelled at the queer jobs some men manage to find. He was employed by a firm of chocolate manufacturers, whose name is known to everyone, to find out what kind of chocolate the Egyptians like, and why they like it. This, I suppose, is scientific salesmanship. But as we sat in the lounge in Alexandria, it seemed sheer fantasy that this well-dressed, educated, and expensive young man should be going about asking the Orient if it preferred nut-milk or plain. He had recently received a cable asking him to discover why the products of a rival firm were selling so well in Baghdad.

"Do you really mean to tell me," I asked, "that you are going all the way to Baghdad to find out?"

"Oh, it's not so very far," he replied. "I shall fly there."

"And what will you do on your return?"

"I shall fly over to Cyprus," he replied.

There was something ambassadorial about him, and I thought him every bit as strange as any character in the *Arabian Nights*.

One of the strange things about Egypt is that Alexandria, having been a ruin from the Middle Ages until a century ago, has risen from its grave, not Arab, but almost European. It never belonged to Egypt. It has always been a piece of Europe grafted on to Africa. In the Hellenistic Age it belonged to Greece and, to a great extent, to the Jews; and to-day it belongs to the Levant.

The statement so frequently made that "there is nothing to see in Alexandria" is untrue. What memories crowd round the shores of the Eastern Harbour: memories of Alexander, of Ptolemy, of Cæsar, Cleopatra, Antony; of the Seventy Rabbis translating the Septuagint; of St. Mark stepping ashore from his galley; of Bishop Alexander watching the young St. Athanasius playing at baptism on the edge of the sea.

Parts of Alexandria are beautiful, but it is a little difficult to understand why other parts should be so ugly. They might have passed unnoticed if my mind were not filled with a vision of the splendid city which has perished so completely. From a ship at sea Alexandria is entirely satisfactory, for then you might be looking at the marble city which Cleopatra knew. The pressed-concrete buildings and the buildings of stucco and plaster boldly group themselves until it seems that the great Pharos is once again standing out to sea, that the Museum is rising in pale marble above the city, and the Canopic Way, pillared from end to end, still sweeps in white majesty from the Gate of the Sun to the Gate of the Moon.

Nothing but legend is to be discovered of St. Mark's association with Alexandria. In early times there was a martyr's shrine dedicated to him near the Eastern Harbour, but even the site of this has been lost. When St. Paul and St. Barnabas quarrelled so bitterly on the question of St. Mark's fitness for the missionary life, these noble companions parted. St. Paul took Silas and went into Asia Minor; St. Barnabas and St. Mark went together to

Cyprus, where St. Barnabas received martyrdom. The Copts say that after his friend's death, St. Mark took ship to Egypt and founded the Church there.

He then accompanied St. Peter to Rome and gleaned from him those vivid touches of the eye-witness which distinguish his gospel. It was in Rome at this time or later that St. Mark again met St. Paul, then an old man, and became reconciled, possibly because of his work in Egypt. Coptic legends say that St. Mark then returned to Alexandria, where he had ordained as Bishop of Alexandria his first convert, Annianus, a shoemaker. The martyrdom of the Evangelist is said to have taken place in the reign of Nero, and was caused by his protest against a public procession held in honour of the god Serapis. Infuriated by St. Mark's condemnation, the worshippers of Serapis seized him, tied a rope round his neck, and dragged him through the city, repeating this on the following day until death ended his sufferings.

The Cathedral of St. Mark, which in time rose on the site of the place where the faithful had buried the saint, was burned during the Arab invasion, but was re-built in 838 A.D. The bones of St. Mark were at this time intact in the tomb. One of the caliphs is believed to have threatened to plunder the church, and, in order to save the relics, the Egyptians are said to have allowed two Venetian merchants, whose galley was in the harbour, to take them away. These two merchants, Buono Malamocco and Rustico de Torcello, placed the relics of St. Mark in a large basket covered with herbs and pork, which the Moslems, of course, abhorred. So, crying out the word "pork!" at intervals, they passed unquestioned by the customs to their galley. Hoisting sail, they were soon on their way to Venice, where the Cathedral of St. Mark, the glory of Venice, was built to enshrine the martyr's bones.

2

I took a walk one morning to the Isle of Pharos, which is known nowadays as Kait Bey Fort. It stands on a rocky promontory which forms the northern arm of the Eastern Harbour, and is joined to the land by a narrow causeway.

I was more interested in it than I thought I should be, for in the foundations of the Fifteenth Century fortress may still be seen what appear to be the remains of that wonder of the ancient world, the Pharos of Alexandria. The old fort is now uninhabited and ungarrisoned, and I walked through dusty cavernous rooms and peered through embrasures and descended stone stairways, all the time hearing the crash of waves on the north wall, which faces the sea.

The fort is built on solid rock, and some of the huge granite blocks which lie in the sea round it may have belonged to the older building. I believe there are many huge blocks of Aswan granite, invisible except from a boat.

When the Arabs conquered Egypt the Pharos was still in working order. It was said to be six hundred feet in height, which is nearly twice the height of St. Paul's in London, and was a stone building formed of several towers, each one smaller than the one below. The first story was square, the second was possibly octagonal, and the lantern was circular.

The stones were held together with molten lead, which was a better preservative than cement against the assaults of the sea. There are said to have been three hundred rooms in the Pharos, and an inclined roadway led to the lower half of the building, up a slope so gradual that chariots could be driven along it. Donkeys laden with fuel were constantly ascending, and, when they had dropped their loads, the wood was lifted to the top of the building by machinery.

Ancient writers say that ships could pick up the beam of the

Pharos nineteen miles out at sea, but no one has ever been able to find out whether the ancient Greeks had discovered the use of the lens. The classical writers were so eager to admire the Pharos that they never explained very clearly how it was constructed or how the light was worked. I suppose they thought that everyone knew this, and they were perhaps unable to imagine a time when not one stone of it would be left upon another.

The Arab chroniclers write with maddening vagueness about a "great mirror" on the summit of the lighthouse, which could be turned to catch the sun's rays so as to burn ships at sea. Another story says that when you looked through the mirror it was possible to see ships as far off as Constantinople! Putting these stories together, we seem to have a description of a telescope and also a lens. The mirror was reported to be made of "transparent stone," which must surely be a description of glass.

The end of the Pharos came about in this way. During the Ninth Century a Christian spy was sent from Constantinople to wreck the lighthouse because of its usefulness to Mohammedan shipping. He set about his task in a way which leaves no doubt about his nationality: he was evidently a countryman of Ulysses.

Insinuating himself into the confidence of the Caliph Al-Walid, he said that a great treasure of gold was concealed beneath the lighthouse. There has never been a surer way of wrecking a building in the East.

When the Arabs had almost demolished the Pharos, they appear to have detected the hoax. They tried to rebuild it in brick, but were unable to lift the great mirror back into position. This precious relic, whose existence to-day would have solved the mystery of the Pharos, fell from a height and was shattered to pieces.

Although neglected for centuries, the remains of the Pharos were still visible in 1375, and if an earthquake had not tumbled them into the sea, they might still be in existence to-day.

The Arabs called the Pharos *manar*—the place where fire burns—a word that is related to the Hebrew *menorah*—the place of light—which was the word used for the Seven-branched Candlestick. The word *manar* passed from the Pharos into *manaret* or *minaret*, and was applied to the prayer towers of the mosques. I have read somewhere that the Pharos was architecturally the parent of the minaret, but Dr. Creswell, the great authority on such matters, tells me that the earliest known minaret was a tower in Damascus.

3

I met a man in Alexandria who believes that the body of Alexander the Great is still lying under the city, and may some day be discovered. That this surprising theory is not as fantastic as it may sound, is indicated by the interest taken in it by a man who knows everything there is to know about the archæology of Alexandria, M. Breccia, once keeper of the Municipal Museum.

After Alexander's body had been brought from Babylon, it was laid to rest in a splendid tomb in Alexandria, where in the course of time all the Ptolemies, including the famous Cleopatra, were buried.

Alexander's tomb was the central feature of this extraordinary collection of defunct royalty, and was evidently a place which was freely visible. He was buried "in the Macedonian fashion"; that is to say, his corpse was placed on a stone plinth like a bed and laid to rest in a room with an open door leading to an apartment furnished with stone benches and a central altar, where members of the family would come from time to time to eat and make offerings, just as modern Moslems do today in the tombs outside Cairo. A number of Hellenistic tombs of this type have recently been unearthed at Chatby, near Alexandria, and these probably reproduce, though in a less splendid manner, the tomb of the great Conqueror.

Alexander's mummy was enclosed in a golden coffin in which it remained until Ptolemy IX had it melted down to pay his Syrian mercenaries. It was then placed in a coffin of crystal in which it was to be seen when Strabo was in Alexandria in 24 A.D. The Roman emperors showed reverence for this tomb. Augustus paid it a pious visit and Caracalla left there his mantle, his belt, and his jewels as an offering, so that even at this late period the body of Alexander must have been lying in its crystal coffin.

If the tomb were rifled during the revolutions and Wars of the Third Century, or when Alexandria fell into ruin some time after the Arab Invasion, there is no record left of it. And it is surely unlikely that a tomb venerated alike by Greeks, Romans, and Arabs, for Alexander figures as a hero in the Koran, could have been sacked in secret, or that no one should have put it on record.

That the tomb was lost among the ruins of the royal palaces is evident from a remark in one of the homilies of St. John Chrysostom. "Tell me," he asks, "where the Sema [the tomb] of Alexander is?" It is clear that he is asking what he feels to be the impossible. So at the end of the Fourth Century the whereabouts of Alexander's burial place had been forgotten.

Archæologists believe that the place known to have been occupied by the Sema of Alexander is to-day an ancient mosque dedicated to a deeply venerated saint said to be the Prophet Daniel. Those who support the theory that Alexander's body was never destroyed, but was merely lost, believe that Daniel is Alexander: "Everything goes to show that Alexander's Tomb was in the vicinity of the Mosque of Nebi Daniel, if not under the mosque itself," says M. Breccia in *Alexandria and Ægyptum*. The theory is that the Arabs discovered an imposing tomb containing an unknown body, which, for want of a better name, they called Daniel, and they built a mosque over it.

The ground under the mosque has never been disturbed, and

every time this has been suggested religious objections are put in the way. The idea that Daniel is Alexander is not a novel theory: it has apparently been in existence for centuries. When that delightful traveller, George Sandys, whose bones now lie in Boxley Church, near Maidstone, visited Alexandria in 1610, he was told of "a little Chappell within a tombe, much honoured and visited by the Mahometans, where they bestow their almes supposing his [Alexander's] body to lie in that place."

Seventy-eight years ago considerable impetus was given to the story when a dragoman named Schilizzi, in the service of the Russian Consulate, claimed to have descended into the tomb chamber of the mosque. He said that in 1850 he had penetrated into the vaults below the mosque and had come to a wooden door with a hole in it. Looking through this hole, he saw a "human body whose head was crowned with a diadem," preserved in a cage made of glass. The figure was not lying down, but was, so far as he could make out in the dim light, sitting bent on what looked like a throne or elevation of some sort. A number of books and papyri were scattered about.

This story has always been regarded as a dragoman's tale, and no importance has ever been placed on it. Even though we may dismiss Schilizzi as a liar, we must admit that he was voicing the tradition of centuries.

When I went to visit this mosque, which stands near the tramlines running down the Sharia Nebi Daniel, I found it closed on account of some feast day. It is an ordinary looking mosque with a minaret and several domes, as well as a pleasant little garden at the back where a few palm trees grow.

4

I decided to motor across the desert road from Alexandria to Cairo to see the four Coptic monasteries of the Wadi Natrûn, which lie half way between these cities. I started one morning at six o'clock and was soon driving rapidly across a Roman-straight ribbon of tar that in some miraculous way had been laid on the desert. This road looks like a black tape stretching to the sky, and on either side of it there is nothing but a gaunt, yellow emptiness. It is, however, a dangerous and deceptive road. The desert is never flat for long, and the result is that the road is full of sudden long dips which conceal an approaching car until it is almost on top of you. We had a pointed warning when a lorry driven at fifty miles an hour shot up in front of us as suddenly as a demon in a pantomime; and had we been following the fashion and driving on the wrong side of the road, nothing could have saved us.

After about ten miles a narrow track sprawls off to the west. It leads to the ruined city of St. Mena, or St. Amen, a saint who is not very well known in the West. I wanted to see what remained of this city, and we turned off and were soon alone among miles of sand and dunes.

Years ago my attention was first drawn to St. Mena in a small shop on West Hill, Wandsworth. It is the only one of its kind that I know of in London where you can buy fragments of the ancient world for an absurdly reasonable price. From a mass of pottery I drew out several small flat clay flasks, each impressed with a raised design showing a man in Roman dress flanked by two animals which looked like camels. After I had bought them, I discovered that they were pilgrim oil flasks from the Church of St. Mena in Maryût, and that the man was the saint himself.

Mena was born of Christian parents in the Third Century, in answer to a prayer which his mother addressed to an ikon of the Blessed Virgin. As she finished her prayer, she heard a voice from the ikon agreeing to grant her wish, and she caught the sound of the word "amen," which was pronounced in the Eastern manner as "amîn." When the child was born, he was called Amen, or Mena, which preserves the second syllable of the Eastern pronunciation. He grew up and entered the army, and was eventually promoted to be a military governor. When Diocletian persecuted the Church, it was the duty of Mena to imprison the Christians in his own district. This he refused to do. He wandered out in the desert to ask God's help, and while he was kneeling in prayer, he heard a voice saying: "Whosoever bears suffering for the name of Christ shall wear such crowns as these"; looking up, he saw a host of martyrs wearing crowns that shone with more than the splendour of gold.

He returned to the city and declared himself a Christian. He was tortured and martyred, and his body was buried at Cotyæa, in Phrygia. Some time after, when Christian troops were leaving this town for Egypt, they took the body of St. Mena and carried it along with them. Some accounts say that during the voyage strange creatures came out of the sea with heads like camels and attempted to lick the body, but flames came forth and drove them back into the water.

St. Mena was buried under the cottage floor where he had been born, beside the Lake of Mareotis. The time came when the troops were again moved and once more they gathered his bones with the object of taking them away, but the camel on which they were placed refused to move. Another camel was brought and he also refused; therefore the soldiers, seeing the will of God in this, buried the martyr where the camels had stood, and went their way.

The simple grave was quite forgotten until one day a shepherd passed by with a flock of sick sheep. There was a spring of water near and when a sheep had entered this water and rolled on the ground, the shepherd saw that it had been healed. The news of the healing spring began to spread itself about the world until it reached distant Constantinople, where the Emperor's daughter lay smitten with leprosy. It was decided to send her to Alexandria in the hope that the spring of water might do for her what all the doctors had failed to do. She arrived, and after mixing some dust with the water, rubbed her body with it and slept that night near the spring. While she slept St. Mena appeared to her in a dream and told her that he was buried in that place. She returned, cured, to her father, who erected a splendid church there as a thankoffering. In the Fourth Century the Emperor Arcadius added to this church.

By this time the shrine of St. Mena had become known over the Christian world. From the Fifth Century to the Seventh it was the Lourdes of Egypt. Pilgrims came from all parts to visit the tomb and to take away some of the healing oil, which was sold in small flasks of clay impressed with the image of St. Mena and the camels.

Like the other warrior saint, St. Sergius of Resafa, St. Mena crossed the Mediterranean, and churches were dedicated to him in Rome, Arles, and Cologne. The Roman church stood on the Via Ostia, not far from the bridge across the Almone and close to its junction with the Tiber. As recently as 1350 a hospital was attached to it which, says Dom Leclerq, was no doubt "the religious centre of the Alexandrian colony of sailors and merchants whose business transactions brought them to Rome." Both church and hospital have now disappeared.

We travelled for some ten or twelve miles across a sandy desert, along a track that was rarely used. There was nothing to see but flat brown country rising here and there in low ridges and lying beneath an arc of intense blue. As we went on, I thought how literally the Roman army in the first three centuries might be termed "soldiers of Christ." Saint after saint in Egypt's martyrology was a Roman soldier turned Christian, who suffered death for his Saviour's sake. Common soldiers and officers stand together in the ranks of Egyptian sainthood in such numbers that it would seem almost as if the mantle of the apostles had been changed into a military cloak.

Mikhail, suddenly pointing ahead, said "Abu Mena!" Looking into the yellow glare, I made out the ruins of a large city lying uninhabited and desolate in the desert. I was soon climbing over the ruins, looking at shattered roadways, and gazing from the immense piles of débris which shone here and there with chips of snow-white marble. I went into the largest of the three churches, the superb basilica of Arcadius. What a lovely church this must have been, a building sheeted with every colour of rare marble, a pavement of tinted polished stone stretching its whole length, and its roof upheld by fifty-six columns with richly carved capitals, of which only the bases and an occasional fallen capital now remain.

The ruins are confusing until you realize that three large churches of different periods have been built together, east end to west end, forming one enormous building but at the same time still retaining their own separate characters and purposes. The first church is a beautiful octagonal baptistry; even in its ruin, I think it is the most beautiful I have ever seen. In the centre of the marble pavement stands a long marble font designed for the total immersion of a great number of converts. It is level with the floor and those to be baptized descended marble steps and walked through the water, ascending a corresponding flight of marble steps at the opposite end.

The next church is of the same early period. It is the original church, in whose centre, just as the column of St. Simeon Stylites occupies the centre of Kala'ât Si'mân, rises the marble balustrade from which steps descend to the burial crypt of St. Mena. The third church is the huge cruciform building erected by Arcadius, with a pillared nave leading to a high altar placed at the meeting of the wide transepts. The altar stood beneath a marble canopy lifted on marble columns and behind it there is trace of a tribune, and behind that are the ruins of a round marble apse.

All round the church lie the remains of the guest-houses, the shops, the baths, and the potteries where the small clay flasks of St. Mena were made. Here in Egypt, fifteen centuries or more ago, crowds of invalids and those who had made a pilgrimage for the sake of someone they loved, who was too ill to travel, gathered to pray at the shrine of the saint and to take home the precious oil, or water, in the little flasks with their effigy of a Roman soldier and two camels.

I wondered how such a solid town as this could have tumbled so quickly into ruins. Its later history is not completely known, but it seems clear that disaster after disaster came upon it after the Moslem Conquest, culminating in the destruction of the whole town to provide stone for the new buildings which the Caliph Mu'tasim erected at Samarra, near Baghdad, about 836 A.D. I suppose if one looked carefully among the buildings at Samarra in that stoneless country, one would discover many a trace of the once glorious marble sanctuary of Egypt's soldier saint.

Yet Christianity in Egypt is extraordinarily resilient, and as you turn the pages of history after a major disaster to the Church, you see that candles are still burning in the sanctuary, that incense still ascends before the altar. It was so with Abu Mena.

After the Caliph's destruction of the town, after thousands of tons of marble had been carried to Irak and after the very pavement had been prized up and carted away, the church was quietly rebuilt; and it was flourishing in the Eleventh Century. An Arab writer, El Bekri, is our sole authority. He was travelling in the district at that time, and says that he came to "a great church which contains statues and sculptures of the greatest beauty. The lamps burn day and night, without ceasing. At one end of this building is a great dome containing the image of a man standing with each foot upon a camel, one of his hands is open and the other closed. This group, all in marble, represents, they say, Abu Mena."

He also gives us a curious piece of information. He says that part of the church was a mosque! In one portion men prayed to Christ; in the other to Mohammed. So the Lamb lay down with the lion, as indeed happened once in the Monastery of Mount Sinai, where to this day a mosque is to be found within the Christian walls, side by side with one of the oldest churches in the world.

Mr. Anthony de Cosson, who has studied the Maryût district of Egypt, and whose book *Mareotis* is the only one of its kind, tells me that he believes the final blow was given to Abu Mena by the Black Death. He thinks that plague fell upon this place of healing and even Abu Mena was powerless to help. Desolate and deserted, the town fell into decay. Earthquakes shattered it. Year after year the wind drove the sand over the stones until even the name of the town was forgotten. But from time to time little flat flasks were dug up on which St. Mena was seen standing beside his camels. It was not until 1905 that Monsignor Kaufmann of Frankfurt, searching in the desert, identified the mounds which the Arabs called Tell Abôma as the pilgrimage town which had been lost for something like five centuries. He received permission to dig there, and what he found now lies open to the blue sky of Egypt.

5

We were travelling again towards Cairo when we came to the only sign of life on the roadside: a tent, a petrol pump, and a stone building in the process of erection. A Greek emerged from the tent and presented his card, on which I read with appreciation the name D. Xenophon. As I ate lunch in the tent, Mr. Xenophon explained that the new road to Alexandria had seemed to demand some public-spirited effort in the matter of rest and accommodation, and he had therefore decided to build an hotel in the desert. It was the unfinished building I had seen.

We climbed all over it after lunch and, perilously mounting ladders, reached the roof. The view over the desert was superb.

Mr. Xenophon is not aware perhaps that he has made it easy to visit one of the most interesting sights in Egypt, the last four inhabited monasteries of the Wadi Natrûn. The few travellers who visited them in the old days, and Robert Curzon is, perhaps, the best known, describe weary journeys by camel before they could be reached. It was necessary to take a tent and to camp out there, and so to move, camping from time to time, until all four monasteries had been seen. But to-day you can reach them in two or three hours from Alexandria or Cairo, and, if you want to see them in a leisurely and comfortable way, you will be able to stay with Mr. Xenophon.

The desert begins to slope down to the west immediately behind the hotel, and this slope descends into a valley about twenty miles long, and is seventy-six feet below the level of the sea. This is the Wadi Natrûn—the Natron Valley. In the deepest part of the valley are lakes which almost dry up in summer, but are filled again by the infiltration of Nile water during the inundation. During the hot weather the water evaporates, leaving plentiful deposits of natron behind; this chemical is a compound of sodium carbonate and sodium bicarbonate, which the water brings up from the beds of the lakes.

The natron in this valley has been gathered for thousands of years. The ancient Egyptians used it in the process of mummification, for the manufacture of glass, for cooking, and in medicine. Modern Egyptians use it for glass and soap making and the bleaching of linen, and some of them are in the habit of mixing it with tobacco and chewing it.

Bidding farewell to Mr. Xenophon, we motored down the sandy slope and slowly descended into a hot, windless valley, and with an eagerness which I cannot exaggerate, I looked forward to seeing the four monasteries which have been in existence in the Wadi Natrûn since the Fourth Century.

A DESERT MONASTERY, WADI NATRÛN

Egypt is the home of the monastery, and monasticism is Egypt's gift to the Church. The first Christian monks and nuns were men and women of the Fourth Century who turned their backs on life and went out into the desert to be alone with God, and to lead lonely lives of prayer and fasting. What made this movement so extraordinary was its national character. Within a generation the land was covered with monasteries and cells in which a large proportion of the population was segregated. Young and old, rich and poor, went out with gladness to seek a spiritual life. Whole towns like Oxyrhynchus were inhabited by monks and nuns. Everywhere up and down the Nile the temples of the old gods had been turned into monasteries. On the slopes of desolate and inaccessible mountains, and on flat wastes of burning sand, stood still more monasteries; and caves and tombs were tenanted by hermits who gazed with fear and horror at the pictures which their ancestors had painted on the walls.

Towards the end of the century the Government was seriously embarrassed in its attempt to raise levies, because so great a proportion of the young manhood of the country had embraced the monastic life and claimed to be exempt from military service. Indeed, the administrators of that day saw whole cities and districts pledged to celibacy, and must have feared the possibility that the race might end, extinguished by its own fear of the physical.

This is a strangely blank period in Egyptian history. Everyone knows the story of the Pharaohs, which went before, and equally well known is the time that came after, the period of Arab rule. In between is this queer gap of something like four or five centuries, during which the Egyptian people are a mystery. It was at this time that the whole nation seemed to change its habits and its characteristics.

The ancient Egyptians whom we know so well were gay, laughter-loving people, who liked the easy comfortable things of life. We can see them depicted in the tombs, sitting in the shade of their vines, listening to music, and watching dancers; or grouped round the festive table, drinking, sometimes too much, and eating large quantities of delicious food. Then the curtain falls on them. We see nothing for a time but Greeks and Jews in Alexandria. The curtain rises on the Egyptians again—but is it possible that these are the descendants of the old Egyptians? It is a most remarkable transformation. Here is a nation in sack-cloth and ashes. Here are half-naked hermits lifting emaciated arms to God in the lonely places of the land. Here are thousands of men and women vowed to poverty and hardship. Here is a nation striving to stamp out all the desires of the body in order that the soul may rise triumphant. Such is the Egypt of the Desert Fathers.

The ancient Egyptians believed, as the moderns do, that the desert was haunted by evil spirits and that was one of the reasons why the hermits went to live there: they deliberately entered Satan's country in order that they might pit the strength of their faith against the evil which they felt to exist all round them. It is wrong to think that these men entered the desert to escape temptation. It was the exact opposite, for to an Egyptian of that time, the desert contained infinitely more temptation than a city and, as the tempters were supernatural, they were more difficult to fight.

The hermit guarding his soul in the desert might not relax his vigilance for one instant, or the devils would be at him. He was on perpetual sentry duty, pacing the ramparts of his soul, ever on the watch for the enemy and for the spies of the enemy, for Satan was always sending out scouts. They came in disguise, sometimes even in the habit of holy men and speaking in a voice of hypocritical sanctity; therefore it behoved every hermit to look beyond the exterior and the fair face of words into the soul of things, if he would not be lured away. A dangerous adversary was Satan's daughter, in whose existence the early hermits firmly believed. She was a woman, more than presentable, who, like all the fiends of hell, had the freedom of the desert and would often be sent out by her parent when other more obvious troops had failed to carry an objective.

There was only one way to keep evil at bay: by unceasing prayer. All the fiends together, led by Satan himself, were powerless against the pure soul of a truly holy man. Thus the great hermits, though they were encompassed by clouds of devils, remained safe and secure in the strongholds of their sanctity. Every hermit was surrounded by a wall of prayer which grew higher and stronger with the years. Every day and night spent on the knees in communion with God added another stone to the protective rampart.

St. Anthony, though so mighty a man of prayer, was one of the most devil-pestered of all hermits. And this, of course, was natural, for the greater the man the greater Satan's triumph in his capture; the higher, the more impregnable the fortress of faith, the greater the satisfaction of the enemy in the fall of such a citadel of God. The name of Christ and the Sign of the Cross were two infallible protections against the attacks of devils. When St. Anthony saw them prowling round the ramparts, looking this way and that for a possible breach in the defences, he would often blow a puff of wind at them and make the Sign of the Cross, and, lo, they would vanish into thin air, although a moment before they had seemed solid creatures of the earth.

In order to become a monk, it was necessary to take nothing into the desert but love of God, humility, and a determination to stamp out every bodily desire. "As the body groweth the soul becometh weak; the more the body becometh emaciated the more the soul groweth," was a saying of Anba Daniel, and another holy man, Anba Poemen, used to say, "the Spirit of God never entereth into the house wherein there are delights and pleasures."

Dry bread, baked perhaps once in six months or a year, and

softened in water before use, salt, and herbs, were the diet of a monk, but the more advanced ascetics did not eat every day. An ordinary monk would eat in the evening, but he would strive to subdue his appetite until he could go without food for two days, then perhaps for three days, and so forth, until eventually he would be able to fast without difficulty for a week. Some of the more severe Fathers considered that even dry bread inflamed the passions. Theodotus said, "Abstinence from bread quieteth the body of a monk." Others declined to touch herbs that had been cooked, and took as their ideal the saying, "eat grass, wear grass, and sleep on grass," a maxim which some actually put into practice.

Silence was another rule of the monastic life. Arsenius said that even the twittering of a sparrow would prevent a monk from acquiring repose of heart, while the sound of wind in the reeds would make it absolutely impossible. A naturally talkative monk named Agathon only learned silence by holding a stone in his mouth for three years. Sleep also had to be conquered. Arsenius trained himself until one hour's sleep a night was enough for him. Anba Sisoes was in the habit of spending the night standing on the very edge of a precipice, so that one moment of unconsciousness would have hurled him to death.

Yet when the great Macarius visited a sick brother and asked what he wanted, and the brother replied, "I want some honeycakes," Macarius, without a word, set out for Alexandria, sixty miles away, and procured them. Love and charity were as important as humility and endurance. Once when the holy Bishop Ammon visited a community, he was asked to take disciplinary action because one of the monks had harboured a woman in his cell. The others, outraged by this offence, asked Ammon to expel him from the community. The bishop entered the cell with a search party, knowing full well that the woman was hidden all the time beneath a large water-jar. He sat on this while the monks searched here and there for the emissary of Satan, and after they had gone away, the bishop said to the erring monk, "Take heed to thy soul," and quietly departed.

The childlike charm of desert life is beautifully illustrated by a story told by Rufinus in his *Historia Monachorum in Ægypto*. Two ancient hermits had lived peacefully together for years. "At last one of them said to the other, simply, 'Let us have a quarrel, as other men have.' And when the other answered that he did not know how to quarrel, the first replied, 'Look here, I will place this stone in the midst between you and me; I will say it is mine, and do you say that that is not true, but that it is yours—and in this manner we will make a quarrel.' And placing the stone in the midst, he said, 'This stone is mine!' And the other said 'No, it is mine!' And the first said, 'It is not yours, I say, but mine!' And the other said, 'If it be yours, then take it.' And, in short, they could by no means contrive to quarrel, being so accustomed to peace."

Another beautiful story—told by Palladius, who lived for years with the monks—is that of the drudge of a convent, a woman who waited on all the sisters and performed so many duties that, as Palladius perfectly terms it, she was the "broom of the whole nunnery." She wore over her head a piece of roughly cut cloth instead of the well-made veils worn by her sisters. The others would not let her sit down with them, and when she was eating, they never looked at her. She never touched an unbroken piece of bread, but was content to eat the scraps left by the others, and she drank the rinsings of the basins.

Now while the holy Anba Piterius, "that man of wonder," was living in the Mountain of Porphyry, an angel appeared to him and told him that in the nunnery at Tabenna was a woman who was his superior in saintliness. He was rebuked (and no saint is too great to suffer such rebukes) and told to go to the nunnery and look for a nun with a piece of rough cloth cast over her head. "Her whole heart is set upon God," concluded the angel, "whilst, as for thee, though thou dwellest here, thy mind wandereth about in many countries."

When the holy man arrived, all the sisters gathered to receive his blessing, save only "the broom of the whole nunnery." Looking round, and unable to see a nun wearing a piece of rough cloth, Piterius asked for her. "Master, she is of no account," he was told. Piterius said, "Bring her that I may see her also." The nuns went out and returned dragging the protesting sister, snatched from some rough labour. As soon as Piterius saw her, he bowed down before her, saying, "Bless me, mother," and she fell at his feet, saying unto him, "Bless thou me, master." When the sisters, struck with wonder, ventured to interrupt, saying that the nun was a person of no account, the holy Piterius turned on them in anger, crying, "Ye yourselves are creatures of no account, but this woman is your mother and mine, and I entreat God that He will give unto me a portion with her in the Day of Judgment." Then the sisters fell at her feet and implored her forgiveness for their conduct towards her.

This is not the end of the story. The ending seems to me truly characteristic of the desert. Palladius tells us that unable to endure the penitence and the praise to which her companions subjected her from that moment, the humble sister quietly disappeared and no one ever discovered where she went—"and where she died no man knoweth."

The founder of Christian monasticism was St. Anthony, whose temptations are so celebrated. Although there were isolated hermits before his time, he is regarded as the founder of monastic rule because he was the first saint round whom other monks grouped themselves in a desire to follow his way of life.

He was the son of well-to-do Egyptian parents and was born in Middle Egypt about the year 250 A.D. He was a shy, delicate boy and did not go to school because he disliked the roughness of the other boys. He grew up without a knowledge of Greek and unable to read or write. When he was twenty years of age his father died, leaving him the possessor of property and the guardian of a small sister. One day when he was in church, St. Anthony heard the voice of God: "If thou wilt be perfect, go and sell all thou hast, and give to the poor, and thou shalt have treasure in heaven: and come and follow me."

St. Anthony sold his possessions and leaving his sister in the care of a pious woman, retired to a ruin not far away, where he lived in solitude for twenty years. His austerities, his temptations, and his triumphant life of prayer spread his fame throughout Egypt, so that he became much troubled by visitors. He escaped into more remote solitudes. Other men who desired to be like him gathered about him and he was obliged to make the choice either of escaping from them or of coming forth and leading them. It was an historic moment when Anthony came out of his cell and decided to teach his brethren; for in that moment monasticism was born.

Even so, it was necessary for the life of his soul that he should live alone. Joining a caravan, he journeyed across the Arabian desert and found a cave high in a steep mountain, where he lived until his death. The monks would visit him for guidance and he would visit them in return at frequent intervals, to supervise their way of life. At least twice he went to Alexandria, where his appearance caused a sensation. The first occasion was during the persecution of Maximin, when he comforted those in prison, and the second was to support his friend, St. Athanasius, against the heretic Arians.

He died aged one hundred and five years, leaving two sheepskins as his sole possessions. He left one to St. Athanasius and the other to Serapion, Bishop of Thmuis. All his life he had been haunted by a horror of mummies and mummification, for it was still the custom for Egyptian Christians to mummify their dead and to keep the mummies in the house for some time, in order that the deceased might be visited by friends and relatives. The aged Anthony, pledging the two disciples who tended him in the last years to bury him in the earth in some secret place, fell asleep in God with a blessing on his lips; and no man knows where he lies.

Though the inspirer of monasticism, St. Anthony was not the organizer. He had all the charm of a dreamer and an idealist, but he was not a practical man. His monks were solitaries who were subject to no rules save those of conscience, and who performed no tasks save the austerities which they copied from those of their master. The man whose genius organized monastic life was Pakhôm, or Pachomius, an Egyptian born of pagan parents about the year 285 A.D. He is said to have been converted to Christianity while watching the endurance of martyrs during the persecutions under Diocletian. He served in the army during the reign of Constantine, and there can be no doubt that the order and discipline which he introduced into the individualistic life of the desert were due to this military training. When he left the army, he went for instruction to a hermit in the Thebaid, and then began to found monasteries with a definite rule of life. The monks had to work for their living at the various trades to which they had been accustomed. Houses were set apart in which were grouped men of various trades: a "House of Bakers," a "House of Potters," a "House of Weavers," and so forth. Each monastery was under the rule of an abbot and each house under that of a prior. Like a true soldier, he prescribed a uniform for his monks, and he invented the cowl. They wore a rough tunic tied with a girdle, with a hood hanging at the back which could be drawn over the head during meal times. Monks had to sleep three in a cell and to eat in a common messroom, or refectory. Each monastery was as orderly and as organized as a camp. It was surrounded by a wall, and contained a church, a refectory, a library, kitchens, workshops, wash-houses, an infirmary, and a garden.

Newcomers who wished to enter the Pachomian monasteries

had to wait outside the gate for some days, while they were coached in the proper psalms and prayers under the care of the doorkeepers. There was then a long period of probation before they could become monks. Chastity, poverty, obedience, and work, were among the rules of the Pachomian System. The work undertaken by the monks were handicrafts which were taken at intervals to the nearest markets and sold, the proceeds going to the upkeep of the monasteries. Discipline was strict and punishment was administered to offenders by the abbot.

This system brought the ideal of monasticism from the clouds down to earth, and continued side by side with the older method of monastic life. They were in no sense rivals. There was room for both of them. St. Anthony had heard of the Pachomian System and thought highly of it, and was sorry that he never had the chance of meeting its originator. Although a much younger man than St. Anthony, Pachomius died ten years before that saint.

The solitary type of monasticism was, however, always more popular in Egypt than organized monasticism, and it was the *Life of Anthony*, by St. Athanasius, which introduced the monastic ideal to the West. If the life of Pachomius had been circulated instead, perhaps the world would not have waited so long for St. Benedict.

There are only seven monasteries in Egypt still inhabited by monks. Four of them are in the Wadi Natrûn, the famous holy district of Scetis; one is at Asyût; and two are in the Arabian desert, not far from the Red Sea, Dêr Anba Bulos, the Monastery of St. Paul, and Dêr Anba Antonioûs, the Monastery of St. Anthony.

These monasteries have a history which links them with the Fourth Century, and they are the oldest Christian monasteries in the world. You may imagine with what keen interest I now found myself descending the sandy slopes of the Wadi Natrûn to find out what the modern monks of Egypt are like, how they live, and what resemblance, if any, they bear to their famous predecessors.

6

The desert slopes gradually to the natron lakes, where the red chimney of a chemical factory lifts itself in a great expanse of sand. A factory in the desert is an unusual sight. It looked to me rather like a prehistoric monster that had come to drink the turgid natron water; a creature that, aware of its vulnerability in open country, was lifting its tall red neck with a certain apprehension.

The factory workers live in a village near by, in which there is also a post of the Frontiers Administration. Hearing the sound of a car, the post, and that part of the village which was not at work, which included all the children and dogs, turned out to greet us. The captain of the post politely asked where I was going, and then offered to send the local sheik and a sergeant with me. The sheik was a middle-aged man with the moustache of a Guards sergeant-major. He had a heavy gold *egal* binding his *keffieh*, such as I have seen before only on the brows of Arabian royalty, and at his belt was a weather holster from which protruded the butt of a revolver. The sergeant was a six-foot Sudanese in khaki, who grasped a long hide camel-whip.

These two climbed into a desert patrol lorry and led the way across the slopes of sand which rise into the bare fastness of the Desert of Scetis, a desert which stretches without a break westward to the boundary of Tripoli, and then, still westward, into the Sahara, with its three and a half million square miles of desolation.

As we mounted the sandhills, we saw three touches of white on the desert, about four miles away: one was standing by itself, and there were two close together. It was like sighting ships at sea, for there was nothing else to attract the eye. These were the walls of the desert monasteries. Stopping the patrol car, the sheik pointed towards them and told me their names. That to the right, standing by itself, was Dêr el-Baramûs; then, six miles to the left, Dêr Anba Bishôi and Dêr es-Syriani stood together, a mile of sand separating them. To which should we go first? I told him to go to Dêr el-Baramûs. But where was Dêr Macarius, the most famous monastery of them all? The sheik pointed to the left and said that it was twelve miles away, out of sight.

For a time we had all three monasteries in view, and I could see that they were built on the same plan. Each one lay within a high, rectangular wall, and each had only one gateway. There was absolutely nothing round them but the flat desert stretching as far as the eye could see. No roads led to the gates, no wheel-tracks, no footprints of man or beast lay around them. A remarkable air of alertness was given to them by the absence of any kind of outbuildings. They were three white boxes on a brown table.

At first I saw only the walls shining against the sand, but as we approached Baramûs, squat white domes and the tops of buildings and a few palm trees showed above the ramparts, for ramparts they were. Each monastery proclaimed itself a fortress built to endure siege and assault, and to their history is due their permanent air of watchfulness. The buildings fell back within the enclosure as we drew into the long shadow of the wall.

The sheik pulled a bell-rope that hung from the top of the wall. A faint tinkle sounded on the other side. But nothing happened. The monastery remained as silent as the tomb. An earthenware pot of water stood on a flat stone near the gate, and the sheik told me that it was the custom—"from old, old times"—for the monks to place water outside for travellers and Bedouin. Every monastery, he said, had its water-jar. Thus at the gates of my first monastery, in the last abode of the Desert Fathers, I encountered a relic of that charity and thoughtfulness of others which the hermits and monks prized so highly in their Golden Age.

I was impressed not only by the strength of the wall, but also by the vast archway which formed so strange a contrast to the gate itself. The archway was made for giants, but the gate for dwarfs. There was no need to ask the reason for this narrow postern: it spoke eloquently enough of desert raids.

At last we heard a voice, and we saw above us a brown old man gazing down from the top of the wall with a puzzled expression. He wore a white skull-cap and a dusty black shirt. Did we want to come in? Who were we? He asked a lot of questions and at last said that he would come down and open the gate. Eventually we heard the noise of many keys turned, of many a bar shot back, and the tiny gate opened gingerly to reveal our ancient friend of the ramparts, holding three or four immense keys, one of them a wooden toothed *dabba* about two feet in length.

Although I was impatient to see the inside of this queer place, I spent some moments examining the door. Never have I seen one so loaded with chains, bolts, locks, and wooden cross-bars. It looked as though the inventors of such things had been practising on it for the past ten centuries. As if this were not enough, the narrow passage behind the door could be filled with stones, thus sealing up the entrance to the monastery; and in this way has the last glimmer of Christianity been kept alive in the Desert of Scetis.

The old man led the way towards a remarkable collection of buildings, shining with a blinding whiteness in the hard sunlight. Some were roofed with clusters of domes like white button mushrooms, and all were crowded together without plan or method. There was a central square, an overgrown garden where palm trees and a few orange trees in fruit rose from a mass of shrubs and plants. We passed several cells. The door of one was open. A monk sat cross-legged on a mat inside, busy with pen and parchment as he copied a liturgical book in Arabic. Like the old man, he wore a skull-cap and a black *gallabîa*.

I was led towards the guest-house, a modern, half-French-looking house with a verandah on the upper story and wooden slatted shutters to all the windows. A number of monks, some of great age, emerged like blackbeetles from their cells to look at me. There was no question about their poverty and it was also evident that, like the first Desert Fathers, they scorned soap and water as a pandering to the flesh.

Upstairs in the guest-house was a plainly furnished room where I was asked to sit down. Divans ran all round it. A photograph of the present patriarch, and of an equally bearded and ancient man who may have been his predecessor, hung framed on the walls. Curtains of some dark material were more or less attached to curtain poles, and it occurred to me how lifeless a room can become when it has never known a woman. It is probably natural for a man to live in a cave, but not in a room. As soon as he has a room, it demands a woman to choose a colour for it and to keep it clean, and to see that all the inanimate things, which obey women, such as rugs, carpets, chairs, tables, and fabrics, keep their proper place. The curtains of this room, hanging so reluctantly, seemed to me pathetic, perhaps a distant memory of some monk's home in Asyût; and I wondered if the Desert Fathers ever find themselves obliged to seek the advice of the youngest brother, as the one last in touch with the lost world of womankind, on the correct method of hanging curtains and the right way they should be looped back.

My reflections were interrupted by the entrance of a man not much more than five feet in height, who wore a round black turban, a black gown, and a pair of slippers. As he came forward and shook hands, I knew that he was the abbot. I suppose visitors to Dêr el-Baramûs in the course of a year might be counted on the hands, yet the abbot greeted me as if he had been expecting me, and asked no questions; which is one of the most ancient rules of courtesy. I could tell that he wondered why I should have come, so I satisfied his curiosity to the full; and we were soon talking about the great ones of the past. A brother entered with little cups full of scalding hot tea.

When I visited the other monasteries in the days that followed, I was to discover that I had been fortunate in my first abbot. He was more alert and intellectual than most Coptic dignitaries. He told me that there are thirty-five monks now in the monastery and that the word Baramûs is an Arabic corruption of Pa Romeos, the cell, or monastery, of the Romans. When I asked him who the Romans were, he told me an interesting story.

About the year 380 A.D., two holy young brothers, famed for the miracles they had worked, came from Palestine to live in the Desert of Scetis. The monasteries were not yet built, but the desert was full of anchorites living in caves and in huts of reed and matting. The young men were St. Maximus and St. Domatius.

The two brothers were known to their fellow hermits as the "Young Strangers." St. Maximus "achieved perfection," but St. Domitius, though an exceedingly holy young man, was not quite . . . and here the abbot fluttered his hand up and down to indicate that the brother saint fell short of absolute perfection only by so much as a flutter.

Whether they were carried off by the plague or by the severity of their austerities is unknown, but both young men died not long after their arrival, and "all the saints gathered to welcome them into heaven." Soon afterwards the hero of Scetis, the great St. Macarius, passed that way, and he told the monks to build a church in memory of the "Young Strangers" and call it Pa Romeos.

At my request the abbot first took me up to the sentry walk that runs round the wall on the inside. Here, forty feet or so above the sand, we looked out over miles of desert, and over the vaults and domes of the monastery buildings within the walls. All the monasteries of the Wadi Natrûn are essentially the same: fortified walls with one gate, and inside them churches, cells, a refectory, a bakehouse, a mill, various outbuildings, and, most prominent of all, a high square keep called a *kasr*, or fortress, standing by itself and provided with a wooden drawbridge. The monks would barricade themselves in these keeps if the monasteries were invaded, pulling up the drawbridge behind them.

I asked if he had any swords or muskets from the days of the Arab raids, and he was astonished to think that monks should fight with arms. For something like fifteen centuries, it appears, they have repelled their enemies with boiling water and stones. The last time this monastery was attacked by the Bedouin was during the Eighteenth Century.

To look at these monasteries to-day, one naturally imagines them to have been organized Pachomian monasteries from the start. But this was not so. In the Fourth Century Scetis was one of the most famous haunts of the cenobite, or individualistic, monk. Thousands of them lived alone, or grouped about a leader, in cells which were made of stone or of reeds dotted all over the desert. Many are even said to have lived in caves, but they cannot have been really convincing caves in this flat desert.

Churches were built, which the monks attended on Sunday for Mass; after eating a common meal, they returned to their cells to work out their own plans of salvation. During raids by desert tribes in the Fifth Century, towers were built beside the churches—the predecessors of the modern *kasr*—to which the monks fled for safety in time of trouble. I wondered whether the mysterious Round Towers of Ireland are connected with the monks' towers of Egypt; for if the wagon-vault went from Egypt to Ireland, why not the tower?

The next stage in the development of the desert monastery

was the building of fortified walls round churches and towers, when the raids became continuous during the Ninth Century. At this period life was so dangerous for the monks that they retired inside the walls, and thus became enclosed communities by force of circumstance.

It took me some time to realize that the characteristics of the modern Coptic monk which offend the unsympathetic observer (the words "dirty," "lazy," and "useless" convey these characteristics) are really a direct survival of the cenobite attitude to life of eighteen centuries ago. The ideal of the modern Coptic monk, as of his predecessors of the Fourth Century, is still that of individual salvation. He is interested only in the preservation of his own soul. This will seem to many people a deplorable creed.

The very squalor which repels and revolts so many Western Christians is in itself entirely in accord with the teaching of the first hermits. When the godly matron, Melania, saw a young deacon, who afterwards became Bishop of Askelon, washing his hands and feet in an attempt to keep cool during the height of summer, she rebuked him with these words: "Believe me, O my son, for I am this day a woman sixty years old, from the time when I first took upon myself this garb water hath never touched more of my body than the tips of the fingers of my hands, and I have never washed my feet, or my face, or any one of my members. And although I have fallen into many sicknesses, and have been urged by the physicians, I have never consented nor submitted myself to the habit of applying water to any part of my body; and I have never lain upon a bed, and I have never gone on a journey to any place reclining on a cushioned litter."

The dirtier the body became, the cleaner, in the eyes of the hermits, became the soul. All the tortures endured by the hermits, Stylites on his pillar, Macarius bitten into an unrecognizable state by mosquitoes, and a hundred other self-inflicted pains and humiliations, were designed simply to degrade the body and elevate the soul. We in the West have long forgotten the ancient association between dirt and sanctity which can be dated to the age of the Desert Fathers, but it seems to me that the Coptic monasteries have still got this tradition of saintly dirt in the blood. Our maxim "Cleanliness is next to godliness" would have sounded in the ears of St. Anthony with the ringing clarity of Satan's voice! Until we understand this, I think we are always in danger of saying unjust and cruel things about these Eastern monks. In all my contacts with them I tried to remember that I had no right to judge them by any standards known to the modern world.

The abbot took me down to a cool, dark church like a colossal tomb, standing in a confused huddle of buildings. It is dedicated to the Blessed Virgin and stands on the site of a church built in the Fourth Century. Some parts of the building probably date from that church, although most of it is, I imagine, of the Eighth Century and later.

The light filtered through small windows high up near the wagon-vaulted roof. Everything was covered with an indescribable veil of age. It was grey with antiquity as a tree grows grey with lichen, and the old men who wandered in drifted about like ghosts. A great mound of corn was heaped to a height of six feet in the nave. The monastery receives corn and oil from Cairo, the product of the monastery property at Tanta, in the Delta.

The church was divided by the wooden screens common to all Coptic churches, and one end was occupied by the customary three altars. In a recess on the left I was shown the bodies of St. Maximus and St. Domatius, sewn up in leather bolsters, and also the relics of a saint with the strange name of "Moses the Robber."

Passing through a door at the end of the church, I entered the most venerable-looking room imaginable: it was lighted by openings in the bays of the vaulted roof, and a stone table over fifty feet long and four feet wide occupied the centre.

A stone bench ran the length of the table and there was a stone lectern at the end of the room. This was the refectory. Plaster was peeling from the walls, dust and dirt had collected everywhere, and the table was piled with lumps of rock salt and a mass of round brown objects as hard as brick, which might have been bread.

When I asked if it was bread, the abbot took up a handful of the brown stones and pressed them on me, telling me to soak them in water as the monks did. That is how St. Anthony ate his bread sixteen centuries ago, and St. Athanasius, in mentioning this, explains that it was the Egyptian custom to bake at one time enough bread even for a whole year. That the monks of Egypt should still eat this hard bread, and flavour it with rock salt, precisely as the first hermits did, is surely an astonishing piece of conservatism.

We next entered the *kasr*, crossing the drawbridge and climbing a massive stone staircase. The two floors of the tower are occupied by a number of vaulted chambers, most of them empty, some in pitch darkness, and many of them badly in need of repair. The most interesting is a chapel dedicated to Michael the Archangel, which, I was told, is a feature of all monastery keeps. On the roof of the keep is a small cell built about twenty years ago for the last of the hermits, a monk called Serabamum, a grand survival of the Egyptian name Serap-amûn. Like a true hermit, the monastery did not suit him and he lived in a cave about half-an-hour's walk away. He would arrive at the monastery for Easter Week or for Christmas, but his presence cannot have added to any gaiety which Coptic monks allow themselves at such times, for he refused to speak to anyone or to inhabit any of the numerous vacant cells. Instead, he insisted on living on top of the tower. During one of his infrequent appearances a small pumping engine, which had been procured in a rare moment of enterprise, went wrong, and, to the astonishment of the community, he was the only person who knew how to put it right! Some of those present no doubt regarded this as a miracle. Having exhibited this unsuspected knowledge of the Twentieth Century, the hermit gathered his rags about him and disappeared with every appearance of relief into the Fourth Century. Whether they ever sent messengers to his cave from time to time, as to an electrician or a plumber, begging him to come and look at the engine, I was unable to discover.

The whole community accompanied me to the gate and waved me along the track to Bishôi and Syriani.

7

We went first to Syriani and pulled the bell-rope.

While we waited for a response I had plenty of time to remember that this was the monastery where, just a century ago, Robert Curzon persuaded the abbot to sell the collection of Coptic and Syriac manuscripts which now adorns the British Museum. Towards the end of the century A. J. Butler rode up to this gate wearing a belt full of gold, hoping that Curzon had left something behind. It proved a vain hope.

We were admitted to the same white glare of clustered buildings as at Baramûs, the same dark shadows, the same unruly gardens, the same shabby, dusty figures emerging from their cells, some leaning on sticks and nearly all of them barefoot. I was taken to the guest-house, where the abbot arrived, a thin, tall man with, I thought, more than a touch of Abyssinian blood. Unlike the abbot of Baramûs, he was almost totally ignorant of history and spoke only Arabic.

I sat on the verandah while a monk, whom I had seen crossing the courtyard with a kettle, prepared tea. With charming courtesy, an old monk came forward and, groping in his dusty garments, produced a packet of cigarettes. I think St. Anthony, while he might have censured his indulgence in tobacco, would have commended his generosity, for cigarettes were obviously a great luxury in this place.

There are twenty-five monks in the monastery at present, and they are obviously less prosperous than the neighbouring community in Baramûs.

As the abbot led the way across the drawbridge into the keep, I remembered that it was in one of the rooms on the ground floor that Curzon made his great discovery. He found it covered to a depth of two feet with loose vellum pages and complete manuscript books, and so full of dust that the monks took turns to hold the candle near the door while he examined the treasure. There is nothing there now to interest even the most ravenous church mouse.

From the roof we had a wonderful view of the desert and the monastery of Bishôi, standing about half a mile away. We looked down into the crowded monkish village with its haphazard architecture; it was not a square enclosure like Baramûs, but a narrow oblong, and even more congested with buildings.

The history of Syriani is different from that of the other Wadi Natrûn monasteries. The site it now occupies was originally scattered with the cells of monks from Anba Bishôi. In the year 535 A.D. the peace of the desert was interrupted by what an early commentator calls "an impure heresy," which rose out of the "blasphemy of the impure imagination of the accursed and detestable Gaianites." These were the followers of a monk called Gaianas, who at this time had seized the Patriarchate of Alexandria, but was eventually sent into banishment. His followers in the desert monasteries were expelled by the other monks and proceeded to found rival monasteries near those they had left. The Gaianite monks from Bishôi founded their monastery within sight of the parent building. All these duplicate monasteries fell on evil days and became ruins, with the exception of this one, which was bought in the Eighth Century on behalf of the Syrian monks who were scattered about the desert. It is from these Syrians, who came to live in it so many centuries ago, that it takes its name.

There is a church dedicated to the Blessed Virgin, and also one to "Our Lady Mary," as well as several disused churches which are now in ruins. In the first church, a gaunt, dark building which contains some fragmentary early frescoes, I was shown the leather bolster containing the body of St. John Kame —John the Black—an Ethiopian saint who died in 859 A.D. He retired to the desert and gathered round him three hundred monks, who lived under his rule, and when their monastery fell into ruin in the Fifteenth Century, the saint's bones were brought to Syriani.

This monastery also contains a superb but uncared for refectory, with a stone table running the whole length of it. I have never seen anything like these tables. They were obviously built in the days when large numbers of monks visited the monasteries from their cells in the desert, and it would not surprise me if they are the most ancient relics in these monasteries. A small door leads from this refectory to a cell which the monks call the Cell of St. Bishôi, which they claim was there before the monastery was built. They say that, in order to keep himself awake, the saint was in the habit of tying his hair to a nail in the wall, so that if he began to sink into repose, a warning tug would bring him back to his devotions.

This was the cell in which St. Ephraem the Syrian visited St. Bishôi at some time in the Fourth Century. St. Ephraem left his stick outside the cell and when he had concluded his interview and went to take it, he found that it had sprouted leaves. While they were telling me about this, one of the monks standing on the fringe of the crowd became very excited and insisted on leading me to another part of the monastery, where he pointed to a colossal tamarind tree. That, he said, was the staff of St. Ephraem.

This tree was seen by travellers in the Sixteenth Century and was even then a venerable relic. I measured its girth as well as I could, and it is about seven feet round the base of the trunk. Saying good-bye to the monks, we went on towards the next monastery.

The white walls of Bishôi were soon above us, and we entered another of these Christian strongholds. This monastery seemed even less prosperous than its companions, and the strange figures of the monks even more scarecrow.

The abbot, after the kindly inevitable tea, courteously took me everywhere. We entered dark churches, and a refectory containing two stone tables placed end to end, with a total length of over eighty feet, surely the longest table in the world. This one was so low that the monks must either have squatted on the ground or reclined in Roman fashion.

I wish someone would examine these wagon-vaults and explain their resemblance to the same feature in the early churches of Ireland. In every monastery of the Wadi Natrûn I was reminded of ancient Celtic churches. I asked the abbot if he had ever heard of a country called Ireland, but he shook his head reluctantly, for he was instinctively polite and hated to disappoint me. It was no good telling him that in the Bibliothèque Nationale in Paris there is an ancient guide-book for the use of Irish pilgrims to these very monasteries, and that probably his remote predecessors of the Fourth and Fifth Centuries had given shelter to Irishmen. It is interesting to think of such pilgrims making the regular journey which pious pilgrims made in those days to the famous anchorites and the monasteries, and transferring, as I am sure they did, the fervid austerity of Scetis and the Thebaid to the mountains of Wicklow.

The abbot was anxious for me to see the most precious possession of the monastery: the relics of the founder, Anba Bishôi, and of his companion hermit, Paul of Tamwah. He pulled aside a cloth from a wooden case and revealed the usual long leather reliquaries. He told me how Bishôi and Paul had lived together in the desert, wrapt in contemplation, and how God had revealed to them that even in death they should not be separated.

After both had died, the Bishop of Antinoë was anxious that the relics of Bishôi should be taken to his city, and they were accordingly placed in a boat. The boat refused to move and lay becalmed on the Nile until an aged hermit came forward and told the bishop that it would remain stationary until the body of Paul of Tamwah was also taken aboard. This was done, and the saintly cargo was placed in a shrine at Antinoë. Centuries passed and at length the bodies of the two saints were taken up and carried to Scetis, where they have remained ever since.

I remembered that when the French engineer, Sonnini, was passing this monastery in 1778, he described in his travels how the monks of Bishôi came out and asked him to enter and see a saint "as fresh and rosy as if alive"; but Sonnini, who had been robbed by the Bedouin and had quarrelled with the monks of Baramûs, was in no mood to accept, and passed angrily on his way. I asked the abbot if he knew of such a saint. He was astonished that I should have heard of this and excitedly patted the leather bolster which contains Anba Bishôi, saying that the saint was not only fresh but unwrinkled. He was so curious to know how I had heard about Anba Bishôi's incorruptibility, and I am so bad at being mysterious, that I cast away my easily gained reputation for omniscience and told him about Sonnini's book. I should not have done this. I have a feeling that I forfeited his respect.

After we had wandered round the monastery, entering rooms that had collapsed from sheer old age and others that were on the verge of collapse, I said good-bye, and recrossed the desert to the natron lakes. It was now too late to think of visiting Dêr Macarius, but I arranged to return in a day or so and go there.

While we ran along the excellent road towards Cairo, I thought that I could have borne with the dirt and the personal squalor of the monks if only their altars and their liturgical vessels and furniture had been clean. A dirty monk may be excused on the theory that he is punishing his body for the sake of his soul, but there can be no excuse for an altar spotted with candle-grease, a dusty altar-cloth, and a neglected church. But no matter what their failings may be, these monks have preserved Christianity in the desert for sixteen centuries, they have died for their faith century by century, and, if necessary, they would certainly do so at this moment.

They are ignorant. They are squalid. Their ways are not our ways. But in face of the fact that they have within them the making of martyrs, the sword of criticism is blunted before you draw it. One dirty but sincere saint may be more acceptable in heaven than a well-washed, but nominal, Christian.

8

St. Macarius, to whom the fourth monastery in the Wadi Natrûn is dedicated, was the founder of the monkish settlements in Scetis. He was born about 300 A.D., and had been dead only a short while when Palladius arrived in the desert about 391 A.D. to visit the famous anchorites and write the lives of the Desert Fathers.

Like so many monks and hermits, Macarius was a peasant; he was by occupation a camel-driver, whose work took him to the Wadi Natrûn for loads of salt. He married to please his parents, but, like many another early Christian, agreed with his wife that their union should be one in name only. After her death he decided to devote his life to God, but as few hermits except Anthony had at that time penetrated to the outer desert, he began by inhabiting a hut near a village. Here a village girl made a charge against him, whereupon the enraged villagers dragged him from his hut and tied pots and pans round his neck, covering him with abuse and with bruises. The saint meekly returned to his cell and set about weaving baskets to earn money for the support of the girl, but divine interference is said to have compelled her to tell the truth and confess that she had made a wicked and false charge against the saint. After this unpleasant interference with the contemplative life, Macarius moved into Scetis, the first hermit in the Wadi Natrûn.

He became so famous, and was besieged by so many visitors, that he was frequently obliged to fly from his cell and seek refuge in a cave half a mile away. He was evidently pursued above ground, for we are told that in time he dug a tunnel from cell to cave and would go to earth when he did not wish to be disturbed, travelling underground to the cave so that no one could see him. "As he was going from his cell to his cave he used to recite four and twenty antiphons, and, as he was coming back, four and twenty also."

Every sympathy will be felt for the saint's occasional flight if many of his visitors were as distracting as the man who arrived one day leading a saddled mare, which he said was his wife. He explained that another man, who was in love with her and had despaired of receiving any response from the lady, had consulted a sorcerer. He had asked that the wife should be made unpleasing in the eyes of her husband. The magician, evidently using the recipe known to Lucian, did his work so well that when the husband went home he was surprised to see a woeful-looking mare lying on the bed.

"Then he lifted up his voice in a sorrowful cry, and he wept tears, and heaved sighs; and he spake with her, but she made no reply unto him, and she answered him not a word."

He took his trouble to the sheik of the village, and after they had tried the wife with dried grass and a little bread, both of which she sorrowfully declined, it was suggested that perhaps the saint should be consulted. The man saddled her and took her off to the desert. Macarius made short work of it with holy water and some Korbân bread, and sent man and wife away with an injunction to attend church more regularly.

A study of Palladius suggests that the hermits were besieged by the sick and the ailing until the desert resembled a vast free Harley Street. The greater a saint's reputation for sanctity, the greater became the number of his visitors; and no doubt the more difficult he was to find, the more determined became the searchers.

Palladius is interested only in the miracles attributed to the Desert Fathers, but if you read him carefully, you come to the conclusion that many of the visitors were the ordinary consulting-room characters known to any modern doctor.

So great became the fame and sanctity of Macarius that the Desert of Scetis, which had been empty when he went there, was covered with the cells and the caves of hermits by the time he died at the age of ninety. Its fame had spread far beyond the Nile Delta. Pious and curious travellers arrived in Egypt simply to tour the hermit country and to see the new way of life that was going on there. All of those who came had heard of Macarius, and many visited the church founded in his memory, which has grown into Dêr Macarius.

The monastery of St. Macarius lies at the southern extremity of the natron lakes. The glare of its white walls was blinding as we drove up one early morning.

An old monk answered the bell and led me to the guest-house down dusty paths between white buildings. I sat on a divan under a window which gave me a view of the clustered mushroom domes, the wilted green of the poorest of all the monastery gardens—I learned afterwards that here there is salt in the earth—and on the groups of monks who stood in the sunlight like black crows, gazing up at the guest-house windows. The silence was broken by the discreet explosions of a petrol-engine which was pumping water. The sound contained a surprising energy. It was the beat of the modern world and was quite out of place in these surroundings. I remembered that I had seen electric-light bulbs in the other monasteries, but I had never heard an engine running or seen a light switched on. I imagine that all the plants are out of action except at Macarius.

The abbot came in, followed by several of his monks. He could speak only Arabic and seemed more of a countryman than some of his companions. While we were talking after the tea had been brought in, a young monk, whose cheeks were covered with silky hairs like those of a black spaniel, came up and whispered to me. Would I take him back to Cairo? I wondered whether he was trying to escape. I felt as a visitor might feel at a school if a preposterous pupil suggested running away. The young monk was earnest and insistent. I said we should have to ask the abbot. Oh, that was all right, he said. He explained that he was in priest's orders and could leave the monastery with special permission, as long as he went back there to die. He particularly wanted to go to Cairo and take a train to Zagazig, where his father was ill. I asked him what he would have done had I not happened to come along. He replied that he would have walked across the desert to the main road and have waited for a lift on a lorry.

We went out through the pitiless sunlight into the welcome darkness of the churches. There was a church dedicated to the Forty Martyrs, called by the monks the Forty Sheiks. These were forty monks who refused to flee during a raid on the monastery in 444 A.D., and, indeed, went out of their way to encounter death. They are buried under a raised platform in the church.

I inspected the reliquary which contains the body of St. Macarius, and in a church so dark that it was impossible to see anything clearly, the place was pointed out where many patriarchs of Alexandria lie together in death.

We climbed to the platform running round the wall of the monastery. On the opposite side, some distance off, were the roofs of a cluster of cells, bare flat roofs like those of any Egyptian house in the Nile Valley. I noticed a movement on the roof and observed a gaunt-looking monk kneeling there, making prostration after prostration. I was told that he has not spoken to anyone for seven years. Isolated in an uninhabited corner of the monastery, he lives there, a hermit in the desert. He leaves his cell only to attend church and to collect a few scraps of the hard bread on which he lives. He is thirty years of age.

I was told that he wears a variation of the hair-shirt, called an *askîm*. This is a cross-belt made of untanned leather cut into the shape of crosses. It is worn next to the skin, and those who wear it are vowed to severe mortification of the flesh. They must make three hundred prostrations each day, keep silence, and fast all the time, taking just enough bread to keep themselves alive.

I asked if any other monks in this monastery wore the *askîm*, and was told that, in addition to the hermit, three others wear it. Now here is evidence, as direct as one can have it without living for a long time with these monks, that, despite all appearances to the contrary, spiritual fervour does exist in these monasteries, and it is of the same kind which caused the first saints and hermits to perform those exercises in hardship which justified their proud title to be the "athletes of God."

We climbed the stone stairs of the *kasr* to the finest of all the monastery keeps. It is higher, larger, and contains even more cavernous vaulted chambers than the others. There is a large disused church, with three altars, and walls showing traces of frescoes.

The monks said that the castle was built with money sent by "King Zenoun of Athenia." They told me an admirable story, hideously confused in the telling, but by going over it point by point and word by word, I managed to sort it out. King Zenoun of Athenia had a daughter who wished to become a "monk." She was named Hilaria. Leaving Athenia disguised as a man, she arrived in the Desert of Scetis and was given a cell where she lived, wearing an *askîm* and practising the most severe austerities. She became known as Hilarion the Eunuch, and she was eventually admitted as a monk into the monastery of St. Macarius.

Now King Zenoun had a second daughter, who became mad and was sent to the monastery of St. Macarius in the hope that one of the holy men of the desert might be able to drive the devils out of her. Hilaria recognized her sister at once. Going to her one night in the guise of the monk Hilarion, she took her in her arms and kissed her, whereupon the madness left her. The princess did not know that she had been kissed by her sister, and returning home, she described the cure to King Zenoun, who became furiously angry. He wrote to the abbot demanding that the young monk who had shown such familiarity to his daughter should be sent to him in Athenia. Hilaria was therefore sent home, where she received her father's rebuke with meekness until, stung, I suppose by his insinuations, she cast back her cowl and revealed herself. The astonished king tried to persuade her to remain with him, but she told him that only in the desert could she find peace. She returned to St. Macarius with "a great caravan of presents," including much fine wheat and oil. Hilaria —or Hilarion as the monks knew her—died in the monastery, and it was in memory of her that the king built the *kasr*. He continued to send wheat and oil every year.

That is the story told by the monks of St. Macarius. Although history does not record any daughters, I discovered later that "King Zenoun of Athenia" was the Emperor Zeno, and that he did endow the monastery of St. Macarius with an annual grant of wheat and oil.

As I was saying good-bye to the abbot, a stately figure carrying a small attaché case was seen advancing between the mud walls. The monk in priest's orders, who had previously worn an old *gallabîa* and a pair of down-at-heel slippers, now appeared robed in glistening marocain, a pair of elastic-sided boots, and a shining black turban on his head. I was taken aback at the thought of arriving in Cairo with such a spectacular dignitary.

He sat next to Mikhail, and apart from a pardonable flinching when we passed another car at the usual Egyptian rate of progress, there was nothing to indicate that a hermit was re-entering the world.

CHAPTER VIII

I go to Luxor and see the mummy of the Pharaoh Tut-ankh-Amûn. I descend into the tombs of kings and nobles, visit temples, and see a Luxor sunset. I go to Aswân and see the ruins of a desert monastery, and make a voyage on the Nile.

I

A TRAIN of white sleeping-cars leaves Cairo every night to go south to Luxor and Aswân.

When I glance from this train in the early morning, I see that we are steadily pounding along an embankment high enough above the surrounding land to lift it clear of the Nile's inundation. The sun is up; the sky is blue; the villages are awake. Donkeys come along the embankments with a mincing quick-step, bearing on their backs shrouded and rotund forms. At the corner of a patch of sugar-cane I see a fox stealing home to his lair. Women in trailing robes stand at the wells, their waterpots held on head or shoulder; and in the villages among the palm trees, young and old sit warming themselves on the sunny sides of walls now streaked with the black, gigantic shadows of early morning.

No sooner does the warm light pour itself on Egypt than the whole land begins to wheeze, protest, and whine with a hundred aged voices like the sighs and groans of over-burdened men, for under tattered roofs of palm-matting oxen slowly revolve as they make a circular journey which must have known a beginning perhaps before the Pyramids were built, but seems to know no end. And as they travel thus, without a hope of arrival, the wheezing, whining *sakiyeh* wheels turn as slowly as the mills of God, and a number of poised water-jars discharge their minute contribution to the welfare of the land.

Someday a learned man digging in the eloquent sands of this
ancient country may come upon a carved stone bearing the design of the first *sakiyeh*, that most involved yet most simple of
all man's inventions. With a gasp of delight, he will discover in
the neat language of hieroglyphs the name of the inventor—
He-âth Rob-in-Son. For who can doubt but that the *sakiyeh*
is really a joke that was taken seriously?

Men whose skins are the colour of mahogany and shine with
a polished glow like Chippendale furniture, stand in mud
trenches and pull down the slim, curved mast of the *shaduf;*
dipping the bucket in blue water, they lift it dripping to the
channel above. In a few hours' time, when the sun grows
stronger, they will throw off their clothes and work like living
statues of bronze.

Now and again, as the train presses southward, the Nile is
seen hushed and windless in the golden morning, lying among
the emerald embroidery of maize and sugar-cane like a broad
ribbon of palest blue. Upon the western bank the Libyan Desert
rears itself in wild hills, sometimes the colour of a lion's skin,
sometimes the colour of an orange; and in the valleys between
these hills, and in their clefts and corries, the light is mauve,
deepening to the misty blue of lavender in bloom.

The Nile twists and turns through the green land, often losing itself for a mile or two in groves of palm trees, then shining
clear again, only to disappear into the green, its presence proclaimed by the tall sails of the *giyasât*, like the wings of white
birds poised above the palm trees.

And now a man passes down the train, knocking at the doors
and crying "Luxor!" Tourists crowd to the windows, first at
one side, then at the other, for they are nearing the great moment of travel in Egypt: Thebes, the Valley of the Tombs of
the Kings, the Tomb of Tut-ankh-Amûn, the great Temple of
Karnak.

I step from the train and select a smart little *'arabîa* drawn by two dapple-grey Arab ponies. We pass with a jingle of harness and a tinkle of bells through the streets of this growing town, dreary streets even in the eternal sunlight, and we come at last to one of the most exquisite places in the world—the banks of the Nile at Luxor.

There are two hotels on the bank, one hidden in a scented garden, the other on the riverside, like a ship in dock. A row of little shops faces the Nile: souvenir shops, shops full of fake antiques, English book-shops, and a pharmacy kept by a Scotsman who used to be a chemist in Chelsea.

I go to the big hotel on the river-front. From the balcony of my room I look down on the river, which is twice as wide as the Thames at Westminster, but so smooth that the ferry-boat which is crossing to the west bank appears to be moving on a pale mirror.

The pink Libyan Hills shine against the sky on the other side of the river, their valleys and corries filled with blue shadows as if an artist who had been painting the bluebells at Kew had taken his brush and made a series of delicate little downward strokes on their tawny flanks.

It is that hour of the morning when the sound of Luxor is the prickle of water on tough leaves. I see gardeners directing hoses on exotic flowers that might be stamped from red velvet, on trailing banks of blue bougainvillæa, and on thousands of red and yellow rose trees. If they stopped for a month, the garden would wilt and go back to desert. Rain does not fall sometimes for sixteen years at a time, yet the constant effort of the men who pour Nile water on the garden makes it one of the greenest places in Egypt. No rain for sixteen years! Can you imagine what the sun is like at Luxor; how it springs into a clear sky every morning, bringing long, golden hours, day after day, year after year, sinking to rest in the evening behind the Valley of the Dead, in a symphony of red, orange, lemon, and apple-green?

The certainty that to-morrow will be as lovely as to-day explains the sense of happiness and well-being which steals over you in this place.

2

When I was at Luxor fourteen years ago, I used to step into a boat on the east bank of the Nile, sail across to the west bank, and, mounting a donkey, ride for an hour up into the Valley of the Kings to the tomb of Tut-ankh-Amûn. It is different now. The Nile has thrown up a sandy island between its banks, and you must leave your boat, walk across this island, and take a second boat to the west bank. And—what a change awaits you!

Instead of the donkeys and sand carts, about twenty old Ford cars now stand with engines running, turned in the direction of the Valley. The drivers lean out of their seats and shout:

"You go to the Valley of the Kings, sir, jump in, sir, and on the way back I take you to the Ramesseum, or Dêr el-Bahari, as you wish! Jump in, sir, this is the best car!"

It is a pity that the donkeys have almost disappeared, because the slow ride into the Valley of the Dead, the gradual approach to that fiery cleft in the hills, every yard becoming more grim and more desolate, was, I think, a better approach than the rush in a car over a bumpy road.

The Valley widens, the road ends, and the orange-yellow mountains become higher and rise more steeply on every side. Their lower slopes are covered with small limestone chips, the refuse flung out three thousand years ago, when the tombs were tunnelled. In the sunlight this limestone is as white as snow.

Sixty-one tombs have been found, but only about seventeen are open to inspection. How many more remain to be discovered no one can tell. Most of the existing tombs were rifled in ancient times, and the only untouched royal burial which has ever been found is the tomb of Tut-ankh-Amûn.

There is no sound in the valley but the insistent stutter of a small petrol engine which makes electric light for the tombs. Gaffirs paid by the Government, and armed with guns and buck-shot, guard the tombs day and night. There is a certain poetic justice in the fact that these guardians are descended from the tomb robbers who until recent times spent their lives searching for mummies, ready to tear them limb from limb for the gold which they hoped was concealed about them.

The entrances to the tombs are all the same: a flight of lime-stone steps leading down into the mountain, and a black opening hewn in the face of the rock, protected by a grille like the door to a safety deposit vault. One of the first tombs on the right is that of the young Pharaoh Tut-ankh-Amûn, the smallest and the plainest tomb in the valley. That its position had been forgotten when the architects tunnelled the later tomb of Rameses VI, immediately above, is well known. Had their tunnels deviated only a yard or so in some places, they must have broken down into the golden treasury which, all unknown to them, was lying below.

As I descended the sixteen shallow steps into this tomb, I remembered the last time I had done so fourteen years ago, when the burial-chambers were piled almost to the ceiling with the treasures which are now in Cairo.

It was a queer experience to stand beside the two guardian statues of the king and to know that when Alexander the Great was born they had already been there for over a thousand years, grasping their thin wands of office, and that their incredible vigil had lengthened to nearly two thousand years by the time William the Conqueror set foot in England. The awe which dawns in the mind at such a moment is partly due to the feeling that Time, whose inexorable demands cease not even when we sleep, had somehow spared this hidden cave

under the mountain. That the gold and the wood had not perished did not seem so wonderful to me as that wreaths of flowers, brown with age and tender as ash, had still retained their
shape; and from these I turned to thoughts of the hands which
had plucked the flowers and had cast them in the places where
they still lay.

I remembered, too, how I had sat waiting on the wall outside and had heard, muffled by the rock, the sound of hammers
and chisels breaking in upon the king's silence. Bit by bit the
wall which separated the ante-chamber from the tomb-chamber
was broken sufficiently for those who were watching to see, in
the darkness beyond, the tall, gleaming tabernacle which rose
over the nest of coffins in which the mummy of the king was
found.

I stood again in the tomb of Tut-ankh-Amûn. By the pale
radiance of an electric light I mounted a wooden platform and
looked down into another chamber, where I saw a beautiful
sarcophagus of red granite. Inside is a gold coffin shaped to the
human figure, which encloses the badly preserved mummy of
a youth of eighteen; for that was the age at which death over-
took Tut-ankh-Amûn.

The gold face gazes calmly with open eyes towards the roof
of the tomb. The king is portrayed wearing a close-fitting war-
helmet of gold, with the symbols of his country, the Vulture
and the Cobra, rising from his forehead. His gold hands are
crossed on his breast; in the right he grasps the Flail, in the left
the Crook, emblems of royalty. Tall figures painted on the wall
show him, followed by his Ka, or spirit, embracing the mummified figure of Osiris, the God of the Dead.

In this silent tomb, where many thoughts crowd into the
mind, one thought perhaps comes first: gladness that the dis-
coverers have not taken the mummy of the king away to Cairo,
but have left it in the tomb where it was placed over three thousand years ago.

3

I spent the morning descending into the tomb of pharaoh after pharaoh. Painted corridors slope gently into the rock so that the king's mummy could be dragged downward on a sledge. The passages end in lofty halls whose walls, seen by a dim light, are a theological tapestry of figures and scenes still as bright as on the distant day when they were painted. Ever downward the shafts lead, and into an ever stuffier darkness until, at last, you stand perhaps five hundred feet from the tomb entrance, in the burial-chamber of the pharaoh.

The floor is inches deep in black dust and it is scattered with chips of stone. Some are fine white limestone, others are red granite or alabaster; and they tell you that at some time treasure-hunters smashed everything in their frenzy to reach the gold. The electric light casts only a pale glow, leaving the corners in shadow. It is switched on and off as it is required, and when it goes on suddenly various dark objects, like black rags attached to the ceiling, swiftly detach themselves and go flapping noiselessly in the hot, still air.

The big bats in the tomb of Amenophis II, which filled me with such horror fourteen years ago, are still performing their *danse macabre* above the dead face of the king. He who was once master of all this fair land now lies in the dark hall, gazing up through a sheet of plate-glass at the flickering of bats.

While I was exploring one of the royal tombs, the light which fell from the shaft was obscured by the bodies of two descending human beings, one an American and the other his dragoman. When the American had mopped his brow and removed his coat, he turned to me and said:

"How do you suppose they painted these pictures on the walls? Had they gotten electric light, do you think?"

Many people have wondered how the artists painted these exquisite scenes deep down in the earth, without leaving behind a trace of lamp-smoke. I told him I had read that a smoke-less oil was used, and there is a theory that sunlight was trained round corners into the darkness by means of a series of reflect-ing discs.

"And now, gentlemen, if you please," chipped in his guide, "here is the Eye of Horus and over there you see the sacred ape. . . ."

I stayed just long enough to observe on the face of the visitor the bewildered but attentive expression which the features of Herodotus probably wore on such occasions; and leaving him to follow the explanations of his guide as best he could, I climbed up into the sunlight. Hardly a day passes now on which you may not stand above a pharaoh's tomb and know that in the darkness below stands a perplexed Christian, an inaccurate Moslem, and all about them the confident theology of ancient Egypt.

I decided to go to El-Qurna and see the Tombs of the No-bles. Instead of the puzzling and conventional glimpses into the Underworld, here are amusing and infinitely touching little pictures of real life. You can see people who lived in Egypt thirty centuries ago, dressed in their best clothes, seated at ban-quets, listening to music, watching dancers, fishing, hunting, gathering the harvest, and sitting together in affectionate hap-piness, with their families around them.

What an astonishing gulf separated the pharaoh from or-dinary men. The convention that he was divine is nowhere more obvious than in the Valley of the Tombs of the Kings. He was not allowed to take with him into the other world any charming reminders of his past life. His wife could not sit be-side him, hand in hand. No children were allowed to play about the throne. The lovely days he had spent in his garden, or boating on the palace lake, were not considered fit subjects for his soul's comfort. He was obliged to walk, a god among

gods, his soul nourished by no memories of earth, but by the
grim comradeship of forbidding fellow-deities who, having
asked for his credentials like passport officials, passed him onward to the chill realms of the Osirified. Even home-sickness,
so common with the ordinary soul, was denied the pharaoh. A
god was simply returning home, and could not therefore retain
any interest in his sojourn on earth. But how different it was
with common men. How clearly the walls of ordinary tombs
—those snapshot albums for the soul—express the belief that the
lonely Ka would return many times to dwell upon the days
that were gone.

I think the most attractive couple in any of the tombs are
Ramose and his pretty little wife at Qurna. They sit together
at a feast. She places her left hand on his shoulder and grasps
his right arm in that affectionate and charming pose seen so
frequently in the marital couples of Ancient Egypt. He grasps
the badge of his rank, a wooden baton, and they both gaze
sedately in front of them towards their guests.

What a delightful pair they are, and what a model of con-
jugal companionship to have come down to us from 1300 B.C.
It is not until early Christian times that we are again privileged
to see the lord and his lady sitting together in their hall in dignity and in peace; each supreme in their own spheres, as, no
one can doubt, Ramose and his wife were in theirs.

It seems so strange to me that tourists spend many heated
hours exploring the royal tombs of Thebes, when they might
see something so understandable and so human in the lesser
known tombs of the ordinary citizens of ancient Thebes.

4

When I came out of the tombs at Qurna, and before my eyes
had become used to the light, I was aware that people were
running towards me. One of the first to arrive thrust something

into my hand. I looked down and saw that I was holding the hand of a mummy. I did not wonder to whom it had belonged, or whether it had once been a beautiful hand or an ugly one: I was anxious only to get rid of it. It was dry, black, and claw-like, and was even more hideous than it need have been by the loss of one finger.

The man to whom it belonged refused to take it back, be-lieving that as long as I held it there was a chance that I might give him the shilling he asked for it in preference to all the other things that old and young were thrusting on me. While I was wondering what to do, I saw a man who looked as old, as brown, and as horrible as any mummy I have ever seen, coming slowly in my direction, leaning on a staff. Although his eyes were closed and he seemed to be blind, he found his way nimbly over the stone-scattered ground, and when he came near he cleared a way for himself by making savage swings with his staff at the legs of the crowd. Several children ran away howl-ing, and I noticed that not one of those who received his blows showed any resentment, for such is the respect for age in the East.

The old man evidently had something important to say to me. When a few yards away, he slowly opened his eyes; and they were white. A desire to get away from this terrible old man came over me, but I waited to see what he wanted. Slowly he thrust his hand into the body of his shirt and drew forth a piece of coffin. It was horrible to see this old man, himself a walking mummy, trying to sell me a bit of coffin, and a nausea for this disgusting trade in tomb relics swept over me until I was ready to put distinguished archæologists and all others who have dug up Egypt's dead on the same level with this dreadful apparition.

I looked down at the mummy's hand, which I was still hold-ing, and decided to buy it for a shilling and bury it, or get rid of it somehow to put it out of its misery. My purchase seemed to astonish the crowd, and especially the man who had sold it, and they all disappeared shouting into the sandhills, leaving only the terrible old man standing in a bewildered, half-witted way, holding a piece of yellow coffin wood.

I had no newspaper in which to wrap the mummy's hand, and when I tried to put it in my pocket it clawed at the edge of the cloth and refused to go in. I began to feel sorry that I had bought it. To have buried it where I stood, or to have slipped it behind a rock, would have been futile, for it would have been re-discovered within a few hours and offered to some other visitor. There was nothing to do but to walk about hand in hand with it until I could find some safe place to bury it.

I had promised to take coffee with the sheik of Qurna, and while I did not relish the idea of appearing at the house of the most important man in the village holding this grisly relic, I thought it best to offer no explanations, but to behave as if I were in the habit of carrying such things about with me. The sheik led the way into a bare room on the ground floor of his house. It was teeming with animal life. A group of hens made way, rather resentfully I thought, in the passage; crickets were trilling somewhere in the mud walls; and a line of ants, like one's conception of a military expedition in Afghanistan, was proceeding along what was, to them, the mountainous inequality of the floor. In a corner of the palm trunks which served as rafters a swift had built a nest like a small yellow sponge. Every now and then he would fly into the room over our heads, flatten himself against the nest for a second, and curve out into the sunlight.

A barefoot boy entered with a tray of Turkish coffee, and while I was helping myself to a cup I thought I saw a movement in the corner, but I could not be sure. Looking again, I saw an extraordinary mouse. He was the size of four English mice, and his coat was of the pale fawn colour worn nowadays only by royal coachmen. His ears were large and almost round and all his characteristics were those familiar to admirers of Mr. Walt Disney. I was astonished that a creature as large as a rat, and so nearly related to it, should have retained all its mousy charm. There was nothing sinister and rat-like about it. It came running merrily in as if on wheels, busily nosing here and there, looking round intelligently all the time, and then darting away again. The sheik saw my interest in this creature, but neither of us made any remark about it, just as we accepted in silence the mummy's hand, which lay between on us on the divan.

While we sipped our coffee in the cool, dark room, I asked him if he had ever met 'Abd er-Rasûl Ahmad. He looked at me sharply, for I had plunged from the harmless triviality of polite conversation into reality. I had touched the deathless story of Qurna. He replied that he remembered 'Abd er-Rasûl well as a man of over ninety, and also the old man's mother, who used to walk about on two sticks, until she died at the age of a hundred and ten years. This story of 'Abd er-Rasûl of Qurna is one of the most romantic that I know.

A little over sixty years ago a number of wonderful antiquities were sold quietly to tourists in Luxor. Many of them were objects associated with kings and queens of Egypt whose mummies had never been found. The authorities, realizing that a discovery of great importance had been made, set men to watch, and eventually an Arab family, whose ancestors had lived in an old tomb at Qurna since the Twelfth Century, came under suspicion. Arrests failed to drag the secret out of them, but, as usually happens in the East, someone made a clean breast of it; and so the whole story came out.

It appeared that one day in the summer of 1871, 'Abd er-Rasûl Ahmad, when climbing the hills behind Dêr el-Bahari, discovered a shaft which went down into the earth for forty feet. When he descended to the bottom, he saw that a tunnel, which proved to be two hundred and twenty feet long, led from it into the mountain. He crawled along and emerged in a rock-cut chamber. As the light of his torch flickered over its contents, he caught his breath in astonishment, for he saw a scene which even he, the descendant of a race of tomb-robbers, had not considered possible in his most optimistic dreams. The cave was piled to the roof with coffins, mummies, and funeral furniture, whose gold decoration glittered in the light which he held aloft. He did not know it at the time, but he had stumbled by chance on a secret cache in which the priests had hidden about thirty royal mummies in 966 B.C. to save them from the thieves who robbed the tombs of Egypt even in ancient times.

His joy must have ended abruptly as he realized that, in order to move the heavy sarcophagi and to prize open the cartonnage cases, he would need help; and that meant admitting others into his astounding secret. After thinking it over, he confided in his son and his two brothers. These four men then began to visit the cave of treasures at dead of night, to rifle the mummies and to remove the small and easily portable objects, which they unloaded gradually on the market. Their fortunes grew, and it was necessary for them to observe great self-control in order to prevent others from guessing that they were sitting on the greatest gold mine which it had ever been the good fortune of tomb-robbers to discover. But such treasures could not remain hidden. As soon as the purchasers had shown them in Europe, their value and interest roused such curiosity that it was only a question of time before the secret of the cave was made known.

It was a bitter day for 'Abd er-Rasûl Ahmad when, having made his confession, he was ordered to lead Emile Brugsch Bey, of the Antiquities Service, to the cave.

"It is true that I was armed to the teeth, and my faithful rifle, full of shells, hung over my shoulder," wrote M. Brugsch, in describing his adventure, "but my assistant from Cairo, Ahmed Effendi Kemal, was the only person with me whom I could trust. Any one of the natives would have killed me willingly, had we been alone, for every one of them knew better than I did that I was about to deprive them of a great source of revenue. But I exposed no sign of fear, and proceeded with the work. The well cleared out, I descended, and began the exploration of the passage.

"Soon we came upon cases of porcelain funeral offerings, metal and alabaster vessels, draperies and trinkets, until, reaching the turn in the passage, a cluster of mummy cases came into view in such number as to stagger me. Collecting my senses, I made the best examination of them I could by the light of my torch, and at once saw that they contained the mummies of royal personages of both sexes; and yet that was not all. Plunging on ahead of my guide, I came to the chamber, and there, standing against the walls, or lying on the floor, I found even a greater number of mummy cases of stupendous size and weight. Their gold coverings and their polished surfaces so plainly reflected my own excited visage that it seemed as though I was looking into the faces of my own ancestors."

Among the mummies discovered in this cache were those of the most famous kings and queens of the New Empire: Seqenen-Rē, Amenhotep I, Queen Nefertari, Thutmôsis II and Thutmôsis III, Seti I, Rameses II (who was once identified as the Pharaoh of the Exodus), Rameses III, and many others. It was a whole catacomb of ancient Egyptian royalty, and nothing like it had ever before been known.

A special boat was sent from Cairo, and three hundred Arabs laboured for six days, carrying the mummies of the kings and queens aboard. As the boat sailed down the Nile, an extraordinary scene took place. The banks of the river were lined by frantic crowds on both sides, from Luxor to Quft, the women wailing, tearing their hair, and casting dust on their faces, the men firing rifles into the air, in salute to the dead Pharaohs.

I learned from the sheik that 'Abd er-Rasûl Ahmad, like

many another who has presided for a while over unlimited wealth, died in abject poverty, an old man of nearly a hundred. He was haunted for the rest of his life by the dream that came true, only to vanish as his fingers were stretched out to grasp it. He would never consent to approach the shaft after the departure of the mummies, until, when ninety years of age, a visiting archæologist, Robert de Rustafjaell, persuaded him to go there and be photographed at the entrance. But when the old man reached the place, he was so overcome by emotion that he fainted.

The sheik accompanied me in the polite Arab way to the edge of his territory, and then left me to the heat that beat upward from the rocks. As I passed down to the place where I had left my hired Ford, a small group came racing towards me with the usual collection of relics. It was led by an eager child holding the hand of a mummy. I recoiled in horror and passed on. A second group was waiting behind some rocks. A young man ran up and drew from the pocket of his *gallabîa* another mummified hand. I waved the claw I was carrying threateningly at him, but he followed, pestering me, and I heard in the conversation of the crowd behind me the words "Abu yadd." So they had given me a name. I was "Father of the Hand." The news had gone round that at last a man had come who was willing to pay good piastres for the hands of mummies, and every person with such a relic had produced them. There were many more, which I refused to notice as I strode indignantly to the car.

As I was stepping into the boat to cross the Nile, a youth who had been sitting in the shade of a rush hut came racing down to the water's edge, and, of course, I knew that he had another hand for me. I left him standing on the sand with an expression of bewildered disappointment, as, thrusting the mummy's hand into the folds of his garments, he walked slowly away.

With the feeling of futility which must occasionally come to all reformers, I managed to sink the hand in the depths of the Nile, in whose mud, I trust, it will find a decent oblivion.

5

It is difficult to convey to anyone who has not been there, the extraordinary beauty of the Nile at Luxor. The words "blue," "hot," "calm," and "yellow," no matter how you use them, do not really convey the true atmosphere of this place. By some fortunate accident of light and climate Luxor greets each sunrise with a hushed serenity which, although every morning is precisely the same as the one before, never becomes monotonous.

I love to step out on my balcony in the early morning and to find that everything is exactly as I knew it would be. The Nile, lying below, is untouched by any wind, and I can tell what time it is by the way the light is lying on the Libyan Hills opposite. The rising sun touches first the crests of the tall mountain behind the Valley of the Tombs, lighting its ridge in a slender bar of warm, pinkish light which, even as I look, begins to travel down the mountain as the sun mounts into the sky. This line of light pours downward over the hills, turning lower ridges and peaks from lifeless sulphur into glowing gold. Then a cascade of light pours itself over the trees in the garden like a warm shower; and I can feel it on my hands and face. A ship, with white sails lifted, moves slowly in a wind that is just strong enough to fill the tall canvas without rippling the water; and it moves forward, as if in blue oil, making a path in the smoothness and sending out two expanding lines on either side, which travel slowly to the banks. It is so still that I can hear an Arab boy singing far across the Nile, in the sugar-cane near Qurna. I know that he is singing at the top of his voice, with his head flung back and his mouth wide open; but still it is a long way for sound to travel. Hawks hang in the sky, hoopoes come and cock their heads, and bring their wives to look at me in the most impertinent way, and the old gardener walks out carrying a length of water hose, which he directs at the flaming flowers and the burning earth.

In the evening, when the sun goes down behind the Libyan Hills, an enchanted hush repeats the spell of early morning. And there are evenings when the whole western sky turns to a sheet of orange flame shot with thin tongues of crimson, and behind the massed colour you can see the throbbing vitality of fire blazing in mid-air. The natives think nothing of these sunsets, indeed they hardly look at them, but a visitor, arriving at Luxor in the middle of one, might well fear that he had arrived during the opening moments of Judgment Day.

Minute by minute the fierceness of the colour fades from angry crimson into pink. Feathery wings of light ascend the sky like flocks of heavenly flamingoes, and hang there glowing; then the fires fade in dull metallic bars of red and gold which lie upon a background of apple-green. There are perhaps ten minutes of stillness, in which, it seems, one should be able to hear the stars getting ready, and then darkness, like an overdue assassin, swoops down upon the world.

6

The horse carriage stops at the avenue of ram-headed sphinxes which guards the entrance pylon of Karnak. Sand is everywhere. It lies in hills and hummocks and in drifted dunes. Date palms and villages are planted on it. But this temple, the mightiest ruin of antiquity, lies in a hollow. It was built ages ago in an Egypt that was twenty to forty feet lower than the Egypt of to-day.

I enter the temple by a gateway that leads to a vast court scattered with drum and capital, with shattered sphinx and broken god, and the stone limbs of unknown kings.

Dark temples roofed with massive slabs of stone lead from this court. They reek of bats. When I walk into the darkness, the bats squeal and I hear the beat of wings; looking up, I see these creatures flapping against the roof.

Dim temples and open halls lead on, one after the other. The Hypostyle Hall, against whose forest of fantastic columns a man becomes less than a midget, would alone be one of the world's wonders; but here it is only one of a series of halls, all vast in conception, all covered with stiff pictures of men, gods, wars, tribute, and devotion.

You can wander all day in Karnak, trying to discover a pattern. It is a pious architectural competition that lasted for centuries. Each pharaoh, from the virile Eighteenth Dynasty to the Ptolemaic decadence—a period of fifteen hundred years— either pulled down a bit of it or added something new; and frequently he did both. It is as if every king of England from William the Conqueror to George VI had added something to Westminster Abbey, until a labyrinth of church buildings began at Charing Cross and ended in pious confusion somewhere near Victoria Station.

To call Karnak "the temple" of Karnak is obviously absurd. Even if one called it "the temple town" of Karnak, it would hardly describe the wilderness of ruins which testify to the devotion of the pharaohs to the great god of Thebes—Amûn Rē.

After seeing Karnak, with its insistence on sheer power and size, and all the implications such things suggest—the mighty vested interests, the army of priests and nobles, the lip-service of centuries—you wonder what kind of man Akhnaton was, that queer, consumptive-looking, almost feminine creature, who yet had the strength to revolt against the god of Thebes, to remove his capital to El Amarna, and to head the most remarkable religious revolution of ancient times.

The story of his revolution means little until you have walked through Karnak and have seen the institution that he defied.

If Karnak is beautiful, it is with the beauty of golden pylons slanting back against a sky almost the colour of a violet. It is the beauty of an absurd, inquisitive hoopoe shaking his crested head on the statue of a god, or cracking a dung beetle on the walls of an apartment where long ago the high priest of Amûn changed his vestments.

7

When I was an earnest young reporter at the tomb of Tut-ankh-Amûn, there was a lot of fuss and bother about the freedom of the Press and the moral right of a certain great journal to control the news of this discovery. But control it, it did; for the news was at the bottom of the locked tomb and at the top of the tomb was a platoon of infantry with ball cartridge.

Now the other newspapers, righteously indignant that this famous freedom of the Press should have been endangered, and anxious that their readers should have that something extra which every newspaper feels only its own special correspondent can provide, sent three men out from England with instructions to break the monopoly by any means which seemed proper to them. These villains, or champions of freedom, whichever you prefer, were the late Arthur Weigall, Valentine Williams, and myself. Between us, we represented more newspapers than any three men have probably ever represented. My own allowance was ninety-six journals all over the Empire.

If you wish to read how the monopoly was broken, you will find the story well told by Valentine Williams in his admirable autobiography, *The World of Action*. He did most of the work; Weigall was always ready to share his archæological knowledge; and I did only two things on which I look back with any pride: I suggested that the three of us, instead of working in rivalry, should unite against the combine, which we did, and once, in the interests of the cause, I stayed out all night in the Valley of the Tombs.

This was a silly thing to do. Rumours of the gold in the tomb had brought together into the Libyan Hills a record collection of murderers, thieves, and bandits from both deserts, and visitors who stayed out after dark on the west bank were in danger of being robbed and murdered. One tourist was found dead in the sugar-cane at Qurna, and another was discovered at daybreak floating in the Nile; and this brought down on Luxor a detachment of the camel corps under a cheerful officer named, if I remember rightly, Mitchell, who forbade anyone to cross the river after sundown.

Now I had got it into my head that the tomb was to be opened secretly on a certain night, when everybody was safely tucked away on the other side of the river, and I felt that someone should keep watch on it. So, telling my allies that if anything should happen, I would find some way of summoning them, I arranged to be ferried over the Nile at about ten o'clock with my donkey and its boy. It was a dark night and cold. I remember feeling dangerously alone as, astride my reluctant mount, I climbed slowly out of the belt of cultivation into the solitude of the Valley of the Tombs. I was interested to discover that the cold night air of the river was left behind as I travelled through the defile, for the rocks still held the stored warmth of the day.

Mounting the hills that rise up sheer behind Dêr el-Bahari, we came out on a high ridge; there was nothing above us but the stars; to our right lay the sombre shadow of the gorge. We descended to the brow of a hill whose slopes fell straight down to the Valley, and from here I could see, through night glasses, a dark oblong which was the doorway of the tomb of Rameses VI; below it were the limestone walls of the tomb I was watching. I remember ordering the donkey boy to lie down so that his white garments would not be seen. So we stayed there in the appalling silence.

Suddenly the donkey, horrified by such unorthodox behaviour, lifted his head and gave forth a long and blood-curdling hee-haw, which I think must have been heard, as he intended it to be, away back in Luxor. I leapt to my feet frantic to stop him. But how do you stop a braying donkey? Every time he uttered his cry I saw the darkness creeping with advancing forms of assassins, drawn towards us by the noise; and finally, in despair, I removed my braces and bound them tightly round his muzzle.

The hours passed, as such hours do, with inconceivable slowness. This night seemed twice as long as any other night. And nothing happened. Once I saw a movement in the valley below, but it was only the tomb sentries. Now and again the donkey-boy, who was even more jumpy than I was, would pull my sleeve and ask if I had heard something, and we would turn together, scanning the stone-scattered crest behind us, fortunately in vain.

After three o'clock the time began to speed up in an unaccountable manner, but the feeling of anticlimax grew with every moment. When four o'clock came, I was sure that nothing would be attempted, but I continued to lie there, unwilling to go. Towards five o'clock a pearl-grey light began to come into the sky, and I saw myself no longer the romantic watcher in the darkness of the hills, but an absurd figure lying out in the morning sunlight with a pair of glasses. So unstrapping the donkey, who revenged himself instantly for his long silence, we slowly descended the hill.

Although the value of my deed was non-existent, I have often looked back on it with considerable pleasure. I shall never forget the indescribable silence of the Valley, with the tombs of the pharaohs gathered darkly in its shadows.

I made my way on a donkey up the same path to have a look at the place where I had spent the night fourteen years ago. I am sure no one has hidden there since, and probably no one ever will again. And after one of those wistful appointments with the past which become more frequent as one grows older, I descended by the steep hill-path to Dêr el-Bahari, where all that fiery beauty bursts suddenly into view, lying eastward to the Nile.

I rode my donkey over the sandhills, where the heat trembled in a white distortion, and into the great temple of Queen Hatshepsut. This is the only temple in Egypt which relies for effect not on massive bulk, strength, and repetition, but on line and balance, so that its air, almost of lightness and happiness, seems like a promise of the Parthenon.

Dêr el-Bahari means "the northern monastery," a name that perpetuates the memory of an early Christian settlement, all trace of which has been lost. The first Christians took over the immense halls, erected partitions in them, covered the pagan inscriptions with a coat of plaster on which they painted saints, and made the first Egyptian churches. So one generation worshipped Christ there as its fathers had sacrificed to Osiris and bent the knee to the Blessed Virgin in the halls of Isis.

8

The road runs for some way out towards Karnak, and then shoots off into the desert, taking you in time to a white wall standing among palm trees. Several low white domes rise above the parapet of the wall. This is the Church of Dêr Anba Bakhûm, the only survivor of all the saints of Luxor.

There was a time when, as a Copt in Luxor expressed it to me, "the church bells rang at Luxor and were answered all the way down the river until all Egypt was ringing with them"; but the evidence of that time has now been largely destroyed. Egyptologists have swept away the remains of Christian churches in order to discover the ancient temples underneath, or they have torn them down in order to see the halls and courtyards in which they were built. There are still a few traces of coloured saints on the pillars of the festival hall of Thûtmosis III, at Karnak, and in several tombs in the Valley of the Kings I noticed the writing, in Coptic and in Latin, of hermits who once lived in them. But of the once mighty Thebaid, whose saints were so famous in the early centuries of Christianity, there is hardly a vestige left. We can only imagine that every temple contained many churches, and that the desert around was scattered with an unknown number of hermitages.

A Moslem dragoman told me about the Church of St. Bakhûm, and I asked him to take me there. He said that Moslems as well as Christians revere this saint, and attend his annual feast, the last public Christian ceremony in the district. Its character, however, seems to have relapsed into paganism, for he told me that every April six or seven garlanded oxen, escorted by a great crowd of people, are led to the saint's tomb and are there slaughtered. The followers of Christ and Mahomet then sit down to feast together side by side.

He could tell me nothing about Anba Bakhûm beyond the fact that he was a Roman soldier who became a Christian and came to Thebes, where he died.

When we entered the enclosure in which the church stands, I could see that it had been a walled monastery in ancient times, but the monastic buildings are now turned into squalid dwellings. Donkeys, goats, and the ubiquitous flock of turkeys, roamed about the courtyard among piles of fodder and dung. Huge copper pans were lying about, which are used every year to cook the sacrificed oxen at the Feast of St. Bakhûm. The church which we now entered is a curious structure, and I have not seen another Coptic church quite like it. There are five altars in a row, the central one dedicated to the saint, and his tomb is said to lie beneath it. The altar on the left is dedicated to St. George, or Mari Girghis, as the Copts call him, but the *fellahin* who crowded into the church could not tell me, or rather could not agree among themselves, on the dedication of the other three altars.

I have never entered a more disgraceful Christian building in the whole course of my life. I was ashamed to stand there beside a Moslem and for him to see into what incredible and disgusting squalor Christians can allow their place of worship to sink. No attempt can have been made for years to sweep out the church. Those altars which were not dismantled and falling into ruin were in a horrible condition of filth, and, in addition to the natural dirt of the place, someone was using it as a store for chicken baskets and a dump for rags and bones. It would be better for this church to fall into complete decay and achieve the status of a ruin, for at the moment it is an insult to the saints to whom it is dedicated.

I could not find a priest or any responsible person, and when the villagers saw that I was displeased, they shut up like oysters or faded away. The building is beautiful and unusual, and even if there is not enough Christianity in Luxor to look after it, perhaps some society interested in Coptic architecture could spare it some attention.

My dragoman told me that it is a custom both of Copts and Moslems to go there and swear to fulfil their obligations on the saint's tomb; an oath that is never disregarded, because it is believed that terrible ill luck will dog a man who utters a falsehood at the tomb of Anba Bakhûm.

Wandering round the courtyard and picking my way over the confused farmyard litter, I came to a roofless outbuilding in which a few brown boys were sitting against a mud wall, murmuring a lesson like a swarm of bees. A young schoolmaster stood before them, beating time with a stick and holding a book in his hand. I asked what the boys were repeating, and was told that they were learning the Bible by heart, as Moslems learn the Koran. After the hideous sight of the church, I was astonished to discover this spiritual effort in the place. The young schoolmaster had that quick, intelligent willingness which I have noticed as a characteristic of the Copts. I felt that this young man was worthy of a better schoolroom and that he deserved also the help of those, whoever they may be, in authority over him. I was touched by the fact that the Bible he was using had been illuminated by himself, every word carefully copied from some old manuscript and the initial letters picked out in colour.

The young schoolmaster told me that St. Bakhûm ruled a monastery containing four thousand monks and that, in order to keep himself awake during his protracted devotions, he used to cover his chair with nails. That was all he knew about him.

9

On the edge of the desert, overlooking the Nile at Aswân, is the ruined Monastery of St. Simeon. Its local name is Dêr Anba Hadra. I had taken the train to Aswân, which is a hundred and thirty miles south of Luxor, in order to see the monastery, and I found myself in heat that glitters and trembles over the rocks even in winter.

I sailed across the Nile one morning and, after a good half mile's walk over soft sand, climbed up into what must at one time have been a magnificent fortified Coptic monastery. The man who went with me was a Copt who knew something about the history of the monastery. He said that no monks have lived there since the Thirteenth Century. St. Hadra, to whom the church is dedicated, was a Fourth Century saint. He was the son of Christian parents, and was married at the age of eighteen. On the day after his wedding, Hadra followed a funeral procession to a church and became so impressed that he decided to leave the world and become the disciple of a hermit. After studying austerity for eight years under a saint called St.

Baiman, he asked permission to go away and seek a cell of his own in the desert. During his life in the desert, stories of his holiness spread abroad and he diligently strove to model himself on that lodestar of Egyptian monasticism, St. Anthony. The time came when the Bishop of Aswân died, and the citizens went out to his cell and took Hadra by main force to make him bishop.

His monastery at Aswân was, I think, a community which followed the rule of Pachomius, for among the few recognizable buildings is a dormitory in which three monks slept together on hard stone couches, and that was one of the Pachomian regulations. The church itself, roofless and ruined, still preserves a few interesting frescoes showing several raven-haired figures in hieratical attitudes. The Copts always portray our Lord with a jet-black beard and eyes dark and flaming, and it is unusual to find an ikon or a fresco painting in which the colouring is not a striking contrast to the traditions of the West. The earlier the ikons or frescoes, the more European are the figures, but, as you come forward in time, the Hellenistic tradition grows fainter and fainter, until the Christian saints and martyrs, could they speak from their wood or stucco, would undoubtedly use, not Greek, but the language of Islam.

10

Someone in Cairo had said to me that "Unless you travel on the Nile, you have not seen Egypt," and the remark lingered in my mind. I decided to hire a motor-boat and spend two days travelling slowly down the river to Luxor.

The suave emissary, who is always ready to do one's most reckless bidding for a consideration, came to see me and said that the very boat was at that moment available: it was a superb motor-boat with a reliable engine, and a cabin in which I could sleep at night. I could have it to take me to Luxor "for a sum."

When we had cut this sum in two, thrown them both away, made another one, and drunk five cups of coffee, I went to see the vessel. She was moored to a wooden landing-stage and, as I know nothing about boats, I can only say that she was more or less white in colour, about thirty feet in length, and there was a cabin with glass windows right astern; and on its roof was a small upper deck with a foot-high rail round it, approached by a short flight of steps.

It was arranged for the launch to come round to the hotel landing-stage at five o'clock on the following morning. I rose at four and was slightly startled to find that the polite Swiss hotel manager had actually risen at that unearthly hour to say good-bye. As we walked down through the dark garden by the light of an electric torch, we heard the sound of a few sharp explosions on the Nile. Each explosion seemed wrung in agony from whatever piece of machinery was responsible for it.

"That, I think, is your boat," said the manager with uplifted finger.

A faint tinge of uneasiness came into my mind. Was he being very gentle and kind to me, as if he never expected to see me again? As we passed under the dark palm trees, I shivered, for I seemed to see him standing neat and well-groomed in a morning coat, saying to somebody: "Yes, I saw the poor fellow off. Such a nice man, and so keen on this unfortunate voyage. Ah, well! Will you take dinner in your apartment?"

We stood at last on the big, smooth rocks near the landing-stage, and watched a white blur with a lantern hanging to it detach itself from the shadows and approach the pier in a slow, uncertain way. It would give an occasional cough like a horse with a bad cold, and then dark arms would be seen punting it along with poles from rock to rock. Once it gave a series of quick coughs and shot ahead for a few yards, and then sidled up to the steps with a bump.

"Good-bye," said the manager, "and—good luck!"

"Good-bye," I replied with tremendous heartiness. "I am looking forward to this immensely."

I stood on the deck and waved my hand in farewell, hoping that the crew would get her smartly out into the river; but instead a man in a white shirt, still grasping a pole, came up to say that the chief engineer was missing. I asked where he was. The man said, "He sleeps."

I told him to go and wake him and bring him instantly. He returned to the forward portion of the boat, where a cavity revealed the faces of three dark persons who were crouched there like men in a trap. A heated quarrel took place, which ended in one of these men being pulled out of the cavity by his shoulders and kicked ashore, where he shambled off in the darkness.

"Don't you think it would be better to come back and have a cup of coffee?" asked the manager.

"I beg of you, go back to bed, my dear sir. You have been more than kind, and we shall be off in a minute."

So we parted with many handshakes, he into the shadows of the garden and I to sit fuming impatiently in the cabin, which smelt strongly of insect-powder. This was, however, a sign that meant well. One of the tragedies of the East, by the way, is that everybody means so well.

In ten minutes or so, a sleepy figure wearing a tarbush and a suit plastered with grease came aboard and silently let himself down into the cavity. The sound of hammering followed and continued for some time. The three other members of the crew squatted on the deck, humming and smoking cigarettes. As the man with the hammer was obviously our engineer, I went forward to ask why we could not be away. The captain, who was the man with the pole, rose respectfully, and said that the man who had been sent to wake up the chief engineer had not returned and it was impossible to leave without him. I said that a crew of five for a small motor-boat seemed to me unusual, but the captain said that it was always so. However, just as I was contemplating the advisability of stepping ashore and continuing by train, the lost man appeared, bringing good fortune with him, for the engine set up a shrill hysterical cackle, and we parted from the landing-stage.

We described a graceful curve outwards on the Nile, missing one of the rocks by a yard or so (the captain prodded it as we went by), and, seeking the centre of the river, we exploded northwards with great rapidity, the boat trembling and shuddering with every revolution of the propeller. I sat in the cabin watching the sun rise, thinking how cruel and wrong it is to blame these excellent fellows simply because they do not go about things as we do. They have their own amazing way of making things work.

An appalling smell of oil began to spread around us, while dense oily clouds passed overhead and lay drifting in our wake. The engine began to miss badly, but the man in the tarbush gave it a smart rap and brought it to its senses; and so, with the sun in the sky and this lovely land passing in review, I felt that everything was wonderful.

We had been going for perhaps two hours when I climbed up to the roof of the cabin. I saw a member of the crew sitting there at his ease and flicking cigarette ash on a pile of petrol tins which contained our fuel supply. There were nineteen tins. He accepted with good grace the suggestion that he should smoke his cigarettes somewhere else. The only other object on the roof was an extraordinarily homely-looking basket armchair, which had thoughtfully been provided for me. It was the sort of chair that should have been at home in England, with a cat asleep in it, instead of standing up ridiculously above the waters of the Nile. When I sat down in it, I realized that the slightest list to one side or the other would precipitate the chair and myself straight into the river, for the rail was too low to prevent our departure. Still, it was good to be there in the sunlight, watching the green strip of land which is Egypt narrow almost to nothing, and noting how in places the belt of cultivation becomes so slender that the desert peeps over the tops of the palm trees. Women with pots on their shoulders, donkeys, camels, and walking figures, all clear-cut, strode along the high embankments, bearing a remarkable resemblance to ancient Egyptian friezes.

Suddenly the engine stopped! The boat gave a hideous list to port and stayed there. The chair began to tilt, and I leapt to my feet only just in time. The engine started again, and stopped. This time we were in a current, and the boat began to turn slowly round in the middle of the river. It was a sickening, horrible movement, and I began to wonder whether the cabin below was filling, for its windows were only about six inches above the water. We now began to drift, and the captain stood ready with his pole in a magnificent attitude of defence, though what he intended to do I have no idea, because the Nile is a wide river and we were in the middle of it. I called him up and told him that the engine was in a shocking condition. He said it was really a very good engine, but it had been lying idle for a year. There was a lot of rust on it. The engineer was a very clever man, and he would soon make it go—whoof!

I went down to have a look at it, and peering into the cavity, I saw the engineer playing about with petrol in a way that terrified me, so I decided not to watch. Sitting aloft in lonely isolation, observing our steady drift, the thought came to me that we really might sink or founder, or do whatever a boat of this kind does as a last gesture of defeat.

Happily the engine started up again and we straightened ourselves, but our progress now was desperately slow. Every hour the same breakdown occurred, the same sickening list, the same humiliating drift. I got out a map and looked for the nearest railway station. It was at Edfu. With any luck we might be at Edfu before dark. I wondered if the night train from Aswân

THE TEMPLE OF KOM OMBO

would be there before us, and I decided to abandon ship and make my escape.

To my astonishment the temple of Kom Ombo came into view on the eastern bank of the river. The sight of it encouraged me enormously. We really were getting somewhere. We had done about twenty-five miles in nine hours, which is almost three miles an hour. This was better than I had imagined.

I stepped ashore at Kom Ombo and explored a perfect Ptolemaic temple of the crocodile god. What interested me about this temple was its curious air of revivalism. The stone-masons, it is true, were still good at their work, but the artists who covered the walls with figures and hieroglyphics no longer believed in themselves or in what they were doing. They were attempting to revive something which had expired.

The old strength and, above all, the old conviction, are absent, and instead of figures inspired by a mighty sense of power and stability, we have a number of almost Parisian profiles, weak and exotic, masquerading as the deities and monarchs of Egypt. There is nevertheless a charm and a sophistication about this Ptolemaic art which easily degenerates into superficiality and self-consciousness, and as you look at these figures, it almost seems as if Greek art were attempting to force its curves into the rigid angularity of Egyptian tradition. And it may be that the artists of this time, who were born into the Hellenistic world, admired Greek art and despised their own as an old-fashioned relic of a faith in which they no longer believed. It is interesting to see how an art, which at its best shines with a hidden life, can find its way eventually to such a graceful death bed.

Returning again to my unhappy boat, we pushed off and were soon making our way northward. It would be tedious to relate how many times we stopped, it seemed for good, and how hope quickened with every renewed beat of our now heroic engine. As the sun was setting, we arrived at Edfu with wild cries and waving arms, bumping heavily into the steps of the landing-stage. There was a train leaving in about two hours. In the meantime I explored the temple of Edfu, which is the best preserved in the whole of Egypt. Its courtyards, its halls, and even the dark little holy of holies in which the statue of the God Horus was kept, are in perfect preservation; the granite pedestal on which the sacred barque of the God reposed is still in position in the centre of the sanctuary. To the Christian archæologist this chamber is interesting, because a corridor surrounds it which bears a close resemblance to the ambulatory of a church.

I had to leave all this ancient splendour and return to inform the crew of my decision to proceed no further with them. I expected an explosion which, oddly enough, never occurred. The captain merely sighed, and the clever engineer lit another cigarette. As for the rest of the crew, they seemed to have vanished. Anyhow we parted the best of friends, and I caught the night train up to Luxor. A tourist guide to Egypt was lying in the carriage, and as I idly opened it, my eyes fell upon the following sentence: "Navigation along the Nile, the oldest method of transport in Egypt, is also one of the most delightful. To sail or steam between its fertile banks is to realize that . . ."

But such words were not for me.

II

I took the morning train from Luxor, and left it before noon at a large market town called Sohâg, the capital of the Province of Girga. It is a clean, pleasant town with a fine river-front. On the opposite bank are the mud houses and minarets of Akhmîm, a town on which Europe has made no impression, and from whose mounds and cellars rise relics of the Greek Panopolis, to delight the hearts of dealers in the antique.

I had come to Sohâg to see the White and the Red monasteries, two of the most interesting Christian buildings in Egypt. I called on the Bishop of Sohâg, an impressive, bearded figure, with a gold pectoral cross on his chest and a black, melon-shaped turban on his head. He was a very different type of ecclesiastic from the simple monks I had met in the desert monasteries, a man of refinement and culture. We drank coffee together, and I thought that if all Coptic priests possessed his broad outlook and education, his church might experience the spiritual revival which is several centuries overdue.

He told me a story about the origin of the White and Red monasteries which is interesting, because little is known of the early history of these buildings. The Coptic tradition is that they were founded by St. Helena, the mother of the Emperor Constantine, when she was "on her way back" from Jerusalem, after her discovery of the Holy Cross. The Copts say that she came to Egypt with a military escort and went straight to El-Manshâh, which is on the same bank of the Nile as Sohâg, and about nine miles south of it. Here she is believed to have founded a small monastery. She then moved north to Sohâg and camped in the desert, on roughly what is now the site of the White Monastery, which she founded; and, keeping her bodyguard in the hills, she founded also the Red Monastery, about four miles to the north-west.

This story seems to me a likely one. Some authorities believe that St. Helena arrived in Jerusalem in December, 326, and others think in January, 327. The Empress was then in her eightieth year. She arrived escorted by a large number of soldiers and accompanied by wagons full of coined silver. Her first act was to pull down the temple of Venus, which Hadrian had built on the site of Calvary, and to discover in a pit near by the relics of the True Cross. She then founded the Church of the Holy Sepulchre in Jerusalem and the Church of the Nativity at Bethlehem; and in about a year's time, when these buildings were advanced, she left to rejoin Constantine in Nicomedia.

It is therefore possible that St. Helena visited Egypt, not, perhaps, "on her way home," as the Copts say, but during her year's sojourn in Palestine. An interesting point is the mention of El-Manshâh as her destination in Egypt. No one who had invented a story about St. Helena since the Middle Ages could have chosen this one squalid town of *fellahin* as the scene of a royal visit. But in the time of St. Helena, El-Manshâh was the Greek city of Ptolemais Hermiou, which Strabo says was "the largest town in the Thebaid and not inferior in size to Memphis, with a constitution drawn up in the Hellenic manner." Therefore, this now unlikely town was just the place to offer hospitality to the mother of the Emperor sixteen centuries ago.

A car took me along an embanked road to the White Monastery, and in about twenty minutes we left the cultivated fields and came to the edge of a sandy, hilly desert. On its extreme edge stood an extraordinary building. At first sight, it looked like an Egyptian temple. The white walls, made of huge blocks of limestone, were about eighty feet high, and leaned inwards like the walls of the old pagan temples. The cornice curls over and outwards with the effect of a breaking wave, which is a characteristic of Egyptian temples and is known to architects as the "cavetto cornice."

If you saw it only from the outside, you might well imagine it to be an ancient Egyptian fortress. Narrow slits are the only openings in the high wall, and at first there seem to be no doors to the building, for these have been blocked up.

Entering the monastery by a postern gate, I saw what at one time must have been the most majestic church in Egypt. It has been repeatedly attacked by raiders (when Denon passed with Napoleon's army in December, 1798, it was still smoking from a raid by the Mamelukes), and its nave is now uncovered to the sky, and broken pillars lie here and there. Houses of mud brick have been built in what was the body of the church, and a few old monks linger in them, celebrating the Korbân once a week in a small church formed in the apse of the building.

It is confusing to call this building the White Monastery: it should be called the White Church. The monastery once lay all round it, but its buildings—cells, granaries, store rooms, mills, and kitchens—were made of mud brick and have now disappeared. The White Church rose in the centre, behind its high wall, and the plan of the settlement must have been the same as an ancient Egyptian town: the stone temple, or church, standing up in the centre of a mass of mud-brick dwellings.

Sir Flinders Petrie, who excavated the site of the monastery in 1907, came to the conclusion that a first church of the time of Constantine lay to the south of the present building, which supports the Coptic story of St. Helena. The existing White Church is a later building, erected about 440 A.D., in which many of the pillars and decorative sculpture of the earlier church have been used.

What remains of the decoration of the church is remarkably rich. Magnificent classical columns with intricately moulded capitals still adorn the apse, and the semi-domes are still covered with mediæval frescoes. But it must always have been one of the most incongruous buildings imaginable. The idea of a big, blank Egyptian wall embracing so much delicate Græco-Romanism is fantastic. Yet it is also a marvellous illustration of Egyptian Christianity. The Christian hermits lived in the mummy chambers of the tombs, and the first churches of Upper Egypt were formed by putting up partitions in temples once used for the worship of Amûn-Rē and other deities. I am not aware that anyone has ever explained how the White Church, this Greek kernel, became embedded in its Egyptian shell. In my opinion we may find the solution in the life of the only great man associated with the monastery, Shenoudi, one of the most remarkable characters in the history of Egyptian Christianity. He was born in the Akhmîm district about the year 334 A.D., and he was a pure Copt, untinged by any Greek influences. At an early age he began to show a fitness for the religious life and became the pupil of his uncle, Anba Bgoul, who was head of the first White Monastery, the community founded by St. Helena. The Copts say that when the young Shenoudi was led as a boy to his uncle, the saintly old man, realizing that he was in the presence of a saint greater than himself, knelt down and, placing the child's hands on his head, asked for his blessing.

His uncle died when Shenoudi was about fifty, and he succeeded to the headship of the monastery. He had developed into no wraith-like hermit or pale ascetic, but combined a fervent piety with a violent temper. Shenoudi had become the greatest figure in Coptic literature. He made his own dialect of Coptic, the Sahidic, into a literary language, and his works, of which many survive, are as fiery as he was himself. He made violent war on the relic worshippers of the time and condemned the veneration of spurious relics. He then set himself the task of reforming the monasteries and drew up new and stricter standards of conduct and discipline. He entered into all the great church questions of his day, and attended the Council of Ephesus in 431 A.D., where he became violent in his conduct towards Nestorius. He also attended the Council of Chalcedon, and saw the Church of Egypt take its own way into heresy and isolation.

We are told that he came to rule over twenty-two thousand monks and eighteen thousand virgins. Even allowing for exaggeration, it is clear that he was the spiritual leader of an enormous community. About the year 440 A.D. it became necessary for him to enlarge and re-build his uncle's monastery, and it is perhaps natural that a man so completely Egyptian in birth, training, and outlook should have surrounded his new and still Greek church with a wall modelled on the temple walls of his native land. This would explain why we find a Greek church inside an Egyptian enclosure.

But it is as a saint and as a monastic leader that he is venerated in Coptic history. Although his rule was so stern, he drew round him immense numbers of followers. He himself relates that he was in the habit of beating errant monks, and on one occasion, when civil authorities claimed the right of entering the monastery, the high-handed abbot kicked them off the premises and nearly strangled the chief official. But it is necessary to remember, before we condemn Shenoudi as a brutal man, that the majority of the monks were *fellahin* and that numbers of them were merely disobedient children. No doubt, like many another hot-tempered extremist, Shenoudi exaggerated his own violence and, in the succeeding moods of equally violent repentance, saw himself in a worse light than others would probably have done. His *fellah* monks came from a class which had been disciplined with the stick since the Pyramids were made, and it was probably the only argument they recognized.

His failings, to which he freely confessed, were balanced by piety and tenderness. He believed that the Redeemer had come to him in visions and had gone everywhere about the monastery with him.

"There is no foot of ground in this monastery," he once wrote, "which the Saviour has not walked leading me by the hand. Whoever cannot visit Jerusalem may make his offering in this church. This monastery *is* Jerusalem."

I went on to the Red Monastery, less than four miles away. Unlike its companion, this building does not stand alone on the desert, but lies partly concealed by houses and palm trees. It is called the Red Monastery because it is built of reddish baked brick.

As in the White Church, the only portion of the building which is in a tolerable state of preservation is the east end of the church. This undoubtedly is the most ornate Christian relic in Egypt. Hellenistic in style and perhaps rather over-decorated, the building has a grandeur and a dignity even to-day. It belongs definitely to the classical tradition, which makes it such a strange sight in the stronghold of native, Coptic-speaking Christianity. Some believe that it was built with pagan columns from a neighbouring Greek city but this is not con-vincing when you remember that the monks who were gathered round this church not only spoke no Greek, but detested the Greek Church. It is difficult to believe that the Egyptians should have built themselves a Greek church just when the Monophysite heresy had split the Church from top to bottom, but there must have been some unusual reason for it. If we ac-cept the Coptic tradition that St. Helena built the Red and White churches, they would be hallowed by two centuries of religious observance, and thus it follows naturally that the monks would wish to rebuild them and to preserve their orig-inal features when the time came to reconstruct them.

That evening I caught the train from Sohâg, and was in Cairo in the morning.

CHAPTER IX

Describes a journey to the Greek Monastery of Mount Sinai. I travel through the wilderness of the Exodus and stay for a few days with the monks in their lonely retreat. I see the Church of the Transfiguration, the relics of St. Catherine of Alexandria, and climb Mount Sinai.

I

THE Greek monks who live in the lonely fortress Monastery of Mount Sinai will not receive a traveller unless he brings with him a letter of introduction from the Archbishop of Sinai, who lives in Cairo. When I went to the Archbishop's house, I was taken to an upper room where a Greek monk told me that His Beatitude, Cyrillos III, would see me in person. The Archbishop's position is a notable one. He owns no superior, as Adrian Fortescue puts it, "but Christ and the seven councils," and, as head of the smallest of the autocephalus Greek churches, is the absolute ecclesiastical master of Sinai.

The Archbishop entered, a bearded Greek dignitary who wore his authority with grace and gentleness. He told me that as he was on the point of leaving for the lonely retreat, we should meet again, God willing, in the shadow of Mount Sinai. Until recently he was obliged to set out by camel caravan, and this slow journey always took from seven to eight days. Nowadays, however, he hires a Ford car in Suez and always completes the journey within a day.

He gave me the necessary letter of introduction, and we wished each other God speed.

Most travellers who have explored the Peninsula of Sinai have been anxious to identify the sites mentioned in *Exodus;*

but I was interested in the Christian history of the Peninsula, and there is less known about it. Like the deserts of Egypt, Sinai began to receive its first hermits and anchorites during the great monastic movement of the Third and Fourth Centuries. Instead, however, of Egyptian hermits, the mountains of Sinai attracted the Greeks. This, I think, was natural, because Sinai was at that time a portion of the Greek-speaking world. When Sir Leonard Woolley and the late T. E. Lawrence made a journey across Sinai before the war, they discovered that this now barren land contained the site of many a Byzantine city, church, and monastery, and that a trade route crossed it from the Red Sea northward through Beersheba to Gaza. Therefore the Greeks who sought solitude in Sinai fifteen centuries ago were turning to a portion of their own world, leaving the deserts of the Nile Valley to be inhabited by the Egyptians. A Greek hermit, who would have felt himself among foreigners in the Wadi Natrûn, would have been at home in Sinai, although both Greeks and Egyptians belonged to the same church; and this underlines the deep national rift in the Alexandrian Church long before Monophysism brought about complete separation.

The first hermits settled on a romantic mountain called Serbal, which many people believe was the original Mountain of the Law, and also twenty-five miles away, in a desolate gorge where a bush was pointed out as the Burning Bush in which the Lord appeared to Moses. The Serbal settlement flourished and overflowed into a pleasant little valley called Pharan—now the Wadi Feiran—which was eventually made a bishopric. The Bishop of Pharan was the head of the monastic movement in Sinai, and had under his care several square miles of trackless mountain honeycombed with the caves and cells of his flock. When the government weakened and Arab frontier raids became frequent, the monks of Sinai were massacred with appalling frequency. Legend has it that St. Helena listened to the pleas of the hermits and built a church and a tower of refuge for them at the place of the Burning Bush, but the main monastery of Pharan was left to take care of itself as best it could. In the Sixth Century life became so dangerous in Sinai that the Emperor Justinian enclosed the little church of St. Helena and the tower with a massive fortress wall. In the meantime the unprotected settlement of Pharan broke up under repeated Arab attacks, and the bishop sought refuge within the walls of the Monastery of the Burning Bush. As his successors continued to live there, the title gradually died out, and after 630 A.D. the bishops called themselves Bishops of Sinai. It is possible that with the transference of the see, a good many traditions took flight from Mount Serbal and alighted on Mount Sinai; but of this it is difficult to speak with any certainty.

Through the dangers and ups and downs of fourteen centuries Justinian's monastery has stood on Sinai, the only Christian outpost in a waste of mountains. The Empire which protected it passed away, and this monastery saw the first Moslem hordes go westward into Egypt. Although they swept so much before them, the stout Byzantine walls withstood the Arabs. The monastery was already ancient, and was venerated all over Europe, when the Crusaders carved their names upon its walls. Napoleon repaired those walls and, as years went by, another campaigner in the East, the late Lord Allenby, accepted hospitality within them.

Through change of scene and fortune, the Monastery of Mount Sinai has stood firm, with its roots not in Byzantine Constantinople, but in the Church of Alexandria, whose Greek sons first went out into the deserts of Sinai to live that life which Procopius called "a careful study of death."

2

I motored to Suez one morning to make arrangements for my journey. I had a letter to a Greek garage proprietor named

Michael Vallinis, who seemed to be the man I was looking for. He had been to the Monastery of Mount Sinai five times, and I had been shown, by way of encouragement and recommendation, some graphic photographs of him standing in his shirt sleeves energetically pushing enormous boulders from the path of a disheartened-looking limousine. There were also pictures of him standing with pick and shovel, with the words "en route à Sinai" written beneath them. He evidently knew the road.

Suez is a hot little town at the north end of the Gulf of Suez, notable only for the fact that liners appear to travel towards it across the sand. Their propellers just tick over as they crawl along, trying not to cause a wash that will damage the banks of the Canal. Sometimes they come through with their bands playing, while cheerful people dressed in white clothes wave down to the camels on the canal banks, thus adding to the air of improbability in which Suez lives its life.

I went to see Mr. Vallinis, who is just the kind of man I like. His energy was terrific. His knowledge of the country was profound. His zest for adventure appeared to have no limit. He was forthright, stern, and quick.

He said that we should have to take a spare car in case of breakdowns, for that is the rule in the Egyptian desert, and we should also have to carry enough food and water for six days, the time I proposed to be away. We needed a cook, which Mr. Vallinis would provide.

I agreed to leave everything to him. This is not my usual practice, but I flatter myself that I can tell a good man when I see one. Later in the afternoon, however, when I was killing time in Suez, I suddenly thought that perhaps it was rather rash not to tell Mr. Vallinis the kind of food I dislike.

"Food?" he cried. "You wish to know what food I shall take? You come and see."

We went to the back of the garage, where an American saloon car, fitted with desert tyres and big springs, was having a sandboard, two spades, a pick, and several such accessories of desert motoring strapped to it.

Mr. Vallinis opened a black fixture at the back of the car which I thought was an abnormal type of luggage boot. It was a chest made to take a slab of ice. The first object that came out was a turkey, plucked and trussed. Then came several chickens, pigeons, a large piece of veal, a leg of mutton, and several lamb cutlets.

He groped about angrily among the bodies.

"What are you looking for?" I asked.

"Oh, miserable, miserable!" he cried. "They have forgotten the guinea-fowls and the quails! You see what it is, unless you do everything yourself!"

I told him not to worry about the guinea-fowls and the quails, because I thought we should have enough to eat. I did not dare to tell him that, earlier in the day, having no idea of his conception of a journey to Sinai, I had innocently bought two tins of bully beef and some baked beans, thinking that these would be luxurious additions to our pantry.

But Mr. Vallinis had not done. He dragged from the spare car a huge case, and, diving into it, produced artichokes, cabbages, potatoes, French beans, tins of *petits pois*, and new carrots.

"Is it good?" cried Mr. Vallinis.

He gazed earnestly at me and, mistaking my expression of bewilderment for one of disappointment, he gazed with a deepening frown. Then a thought lit his face, and he gave a cry of inspiration:

"Ah!" he cried, "*Maybe you like caviare!*"

I went back to the little hotel near the station with the feeling that things were not working out properly. Here was I going to Mount Sinai contemplating every kind of hardship and privation and—Mr. Vallinis was worrying about the caviare!

3

At five o'clock on the following morning my Ulysses arrived to take me to Sinai. Two cars were drawn up in the grey light, and soon we were on the way. The first car contained Mr. Vallinis, who drove it, myself, my luggage, and our huge sybaritic ice-chest. In the second car were blankets, a tank of fresh water, boxes, a young Greek driver, and a plump, cheerful individual in riding-breeches, who turned out to be Yûsuf, the cook.

The sun rose as we approached the chain ferry across the Suez Canal. Although you could fling a stone from Egypt across the canal into Sinai, the country on the opposite bank seems already a different land. There is no nonsense about it: it is plainly and definitely the Sinai Desert.

The man at the ferry told us that we were the first to cross that morning. We bumped across to the Sinai shore, where a detachment of the camel corps was encamped on the edge of the desert, which creeps right up to the banks of the canal. The camels were tethered to stakes driven into the sand, fine, light-coloured trotting camels, as different from a transport camel as a racehorse from a dray horse. Two or three Sudanese in smart khaki uniforms came to the tent-flaps to watch us go past, a foretaste of the curiosity which every traveller arouses in the desert.

Our road lay southward. But the word road is misleading, for, as I had discovered on the way to Siwa, there are no roads in the desert. There are only tracks in the sand and in dry torrent beds made by cars and desert lorries. When the Governor of Sinai announces that all roads are closed, it means that rain in Sinai has washed these tracks away and covered them with boulders swept down from the hills. Repair parties are sent to move the stones and to blaze a new trail. Then the roads are said to be open once again.

As the two cars bumped over the sandy track, I felt that we had said good-bye to civilization for a while. We saw a signpost in the sand. One arm pointed to the north, the other to the east. The northern arm said "Jerusalem"; the other arm said "St. Catherine's Monastery." Soon afterwards, we arrived at the Wells of Moses, where a few dense clumps of palm trees grow round pools of brackish water.

Some Bedouin were camped there with camels. I asked them where they had come from, and they replied that they had been travelling from the Wadi Feiran for six days, with charcoal for Suez. This is the only money-making pursuit open to the Sinai Bedouin, and what a pathetic job it is, in a treeless wilderness. But make charcoal they do, by burning any stray fragment of wood that is capable of carbonization. Having gathered a few sacks full, they trek for days to earn a few shillings at Suez, where the charcoal is used for braziers and for the bowls of hookahs.

Tradition says that Moses and the Israelites journeyed this way into Sinai, but we shall probably never know the exact route of the Exodus. It is impossible to say where the Israelites crossed the Red Sea, or what happened to them after they had crossed it. There is no reason, however, to doubt the tradition that localizes the Exodus in some part of Sinai, and certainly no country more like one's Sunday school impression of the Wilderness could be imagined.

Hour after hour the track ran on over a plain which was not actually featureless, because there was always a gentle rise of ground ahead. To the north lay a blue line of great mountains which grew yellow as we approached it.

We had been travelling for two hours or so when we saw four swift desert lorries approaching. Who could these be?

They were military lorries. They stopped. We stopped. All travellers stop in the desert, and they always ask the same questions: Where are you going? and What is the road like?

A tall man in a tweed suit leaped out of the first lorry and came towards us. He was the Governor of Sinai. He had been patrolling his roads. They were not very good, he said, but we should get through. He had spent the night at the Government rest-house at Abu Zenîma and had ordered it to be kept open for me. We shook hands and parted. The dust of our wheels met and mingled in the air and slowly settled down over the desert.

Shortly after mid-day we passed through a mountain range, and ran an erratic course along dry torrent beds. I have never in my life seen such colours on mountains. Some were rose-red, some pale blue, others dark blue. The coloured summits towered into the sunlight. After an hour we came suddenly to a sight of the Gulf of Suez, a broad strip of dark blue lying beyond golden sand, and we pulled up at a lonely little bungalow about twenty yards from the water. This was the Government rest-house. It contained a sitting-room and three bedrooms furnished with camp beds and chairs.

Yûsuf produced an amazing meal. He set out on the bare little table a bowl of soup, sardines, a roast pigeon, cold ham, turkey and beef, a bottle of English pickles, a potato salad, Brie cheese, French bread, butter, and a bottle of beer. And this was the Desert of Sinai!

I spent the afternoon walking along the lonely half-moon of sand, collecting the strange and beautiful shells for which this stretch of the Gulf is so famous. Some are conch shells of enormous size lined with pink mother-of-pearl, others are delicate pink shells like flowers, and if you look carefully, you can find delightful little polished brown shells which you will probably keep until you reach home; but, as everyone knows, it is the sad fate of shells to be gathered with tremendous enthusiasm only at some time to be heartlessly thrown away.

About half a mile from the rest-house are the hutments and quay of a manganese mine, the only touch of modern life in Southern Sinai. The manganese is mined far away in the coloured mountains at the back, and carried to the quay in trucks on a mountain railway.

After the sun had set, the waters of the Gulf became a cold lemon colour, and the mountains turned black and seemed to grow taller. Three Arab fishermen were launching a boat. They and their craft, even to its smallest rope and to the ragged fringes of their garments, were etched sharply in black against the yellow water. One man drew off his clothes and stood ready to push out the boat. He leaned against it, moving it slowly, and, swinging a leg over the boat's side, sprang aboard and stood upright. I felt that I had seen something as old as the world; and it was strange that a poor Arab going off to fish at night should have deserved for an instant the attention of Phidias.

The stars came out one by one, and Yûsuf carried in a paraffin lamp.

4

The rest-house *sufragi* came in with a cup of tea. It was four o'clock. He said that breakfast would be ready in ten minutes and the "caravan" was getting ready to depart. I dressed and went into the sitting-room, where Yûsuf had prepared the kind of breakfast which perhaps John Mytton might have eaten on a hunting morning. It was still dark and the stars were shining.

Yûsuf had evidently had to do with military and official Englishmen, because from some corner of the rest-house he had unearthed an old copy of *Punch*, which he placed with proper reverence beside my plate. I dutifully read it by the light of the paraffin lamp, and had I not been conscious that it represented English Literature, in fact world literature, in Abu Zenîma, I

might have taken this happy glimpse of my native land onward
to the Monastery of Mount Sinai.

We started into the cold morning, Mr. Vallinis radiating
that Greek enterprise and dogged determination which plants
grocery stores from Alexandria to the Sudan. No one, except,
maybe, an Irishman, can be quite as theoretical as a Greek in
his own country, or as practical when he steps out of it. It was
interesting to compare this tornado of Greek energy which
was carrying me into the Sinai Peninsula with the temperament
of the excellent Mikhail, whose activity, although it was of the
best Syrian kind, was really underlaid with fatalism. Mr. Vallinis, if suddenly faced by a horned viper, would never wait
for me to hand him a photographic tripod: he would jump on
the viper, or pulling out a hitherto unsuspected revolver, shoot
it accurately. He was that kind of man.

And now, as we journeyed towards the mountains, the sun
jumped over the high ridges and the world was alive. The blue
water sparkled. The glare from the rocks hurt the eyes, and
we turned this way and that, now driving into the face of the
sun and the next moment with the light behind us. In a little
while we left the foothills and ran outward to the shores of the
Gulf, with a great plain before us, about twelve miles long, a
flat plain tufted with scrub and camel thorn. This has been
identified by some with the Wilderness of Sin, the place where
the Israelites, longing for the fleshpots of Egypt, began to mur-
mur against the Lord and to blame Moses for having led them
into the desert.

It is difficult not to imagine Israel moving through this country, where water lies hidden under the rocks; where great
flights of quail come down exhausted and may sometimes be
picked up by hand; where a substance believed to be manna
is still pricked by insects from the tamarisk stems.

In addition to happy memories of bread, onions, and melons,
the Israelites took with them out of Egypt the mummy of

Joseph. That Joseph was mummified in accordance with Egyptian custom we know from *Genesis* l. 26. "So Joseph died being an hundred and ten years old: and they embalmed him, and he was put in a coffin in Egypt." That the departing Israelites took this mummy with them is proved by *Exodus* xiii. 19: "And Moses took the bones of Joseph with him."

There is a firm tradition that this mummy was eventually buried in the Cave of Macpelah at Hebron, beside that of Jacob; and the information that Jacob was also embalmed in the Egyptian fashion is to be found in *Genesis* l. 2. This cave is to-day lying beneath the mosque at Hebron, and no one is allowed to enter it.

We crossed the plain and turned eastward into the entrance of a mountain gorge that rises gradually between towering heights. This was the beginning of the Wadi Feiran, which runs for about thirty miles into the mountains and drains the whole of the Serbal Range. Walls of rose-red and mauve granite rose up sheer into the sky, where they hung with bare and jagged peaks, shining against the blue; and side by side with them were mountains of pale amber and sulphur-red, streaked with plum-coloured veins of porphyry and black bands of diorite. All the beauty which we normally associate with the colours of grass, heather, and flowers was here poured recklessly over a fantastic wealth of geological formations. Never for one moment did the eye become weary of this wilderness. There was some new beauty to be seen along every yard of the way. As if nature were not content with the natural colours of the rocks, the light filled each hollow and cranny and the long, downward gashes of the mountains with blues so pale and delicate that I was reminded of the pale blue of the Connemara hills, and blues so deep and definite that I compared them to the darkness of the hills of Skye. How different is this Desert of Sinai from the terrible monotony of the Libyan Desert, with its meaningless contours and its stone-scattered plains, which take the very heart out of one.

We continued for four hours or so in this exquisite fantasy of rock, climbing all the time, picking our way between scattered boulders and rushing the soft, sandy portions of the track, so that we might avoid becoming stuck. Small birds with a curious swooping flight were the only living things we saw until, many miles up the wadi, we came on camel foals eating thorns, and we knew that, somewhere in a crook of the hills, or behind the giant boulders, was a Bedouin tent lying like a black bat spreadeagled on the ground.

At the climax of the gorge we came to the only oasis in the whole of Southern Sinai, the Oasis of Feiran, the "Pearl of Sinai"; but in any other part of the world it would pass as a pleasant, shady spot with a few trees, a bit of grass, and a stream. In this wilderness the Oasis is a paradise, and, after four or five hours of stark mountains, it was good to see green avenues beneath palm trees, and to hear the sound of goat-bells and the thin tinkle of water.

The only inhabitants are a few Bedouin and one Greek monk, Father Isaiah, who lives in the capacity of watch-dog and gardener in a house belonging to the Monastery of Mount Sinai. Mr. Vallinis had told me about the old man, who grows vegetables for the monastery. I thought it would be courteous to pass the time of day with him, and we pulled up at the mud wall surrounding his dwelling, and hammered on a door which had a small wooden cross nailed above it.

Through a crack in the door we saw a white-bearded Greek monk, half patriarch and half bandit, come in a crouching, defensive attitude down the garden path, wearing a dusty cassock over a pair of khaki trousers and grasping a gun. His long grey hair was pinned up in a tight bun at the back, and on top was the high black hat of a Greek priest.

"Who is it?" he called from the other side of the gate.

"Thieves and robbers," promptly replied Mr. Vallinis, who

THE TRANSFIGURATION: DOME MOSAIC IN THE CHURCH OF THE
TRANSFIGURATION, THE MONASTERY OF MOUNT SINAI

never lost an opportunity of chaffing another Greek.

There was a long silence. Looking up, we saw the solemn face of the old monk gazing down at us from the top of the wall. He lowered his gun.

"You should not joke about such things," he said. "It is wickedness. Have you any tobacco? I have been smoking dry weeds for many months. Come inside . . ."

We went into a shady garden. A pergola led from the gate to a bare little house where the monk lives. He explained to me that his job is to keep order among the Bedouin and to see that they do not squat on the monastery land.

"Isn't it very lonely?" I asked.

"Why should it be lonelier than anywhere else?" was his admirable reply.

"From what part of Greece do you come?" I asked.

But I was never to know, for the old man gave a cry, grasped his gun, and ran off into a belt of sugar-cane, where he was lost to sight. We heard an alarming explosion. He came back in a bad temper. He had missed a hawk that was raiding his pigeon-loft.

"May I look at your gun?" I asked.

He handed me an old flint-lock muzzle-loader whose barrel was bound with bands of brass. It was an English gun with the word "Tower" and the date 1859 engraved on it. What a strange fate for an old English muzzle-loader made nearly eighty years ago. It was obviously an old army gun and I suppose the word "Tower" referred to the Tower of London, in which this now terrifying weapon had at some time been proofed.

The old man asked in a wheedling way, like a little boy asking for sweets, if we had any cartridges to give him. We had a gun with us and more cartridges than we could possibly require, and so we gave him a good big fistful; but I asked what use they could be to him, for they were obviously no good for the muzzle-loader. He gave a delighted cry and, biting through one of the cartridges, poured the powder into a little powder-flask. He explained that he can make his own bullets by melting lead and dropping it into a pan of water; but he cannot make powder. He has to rely on the generosity of passing sportsmen, whose cartridges he tears up. He showed me some of his home-made shot, and very nasty-looking shrapnel it was. He packs the charge with dead leaves and uses the old ram-rod which, despite all the adventures through which this gun has passed, still remains in position.

I asked the old man how much property he was guarding. He answered by pointing round to several square miles of mountains and to an adjacent ruin, which I recognized as an old church. I saw on nearly every summit piles of stones which looked like cairns but when I looked through glasses, I realized that they were the remains of cells. The old man was guarding the ruins of the hermit city of Pharan.

I should dearly like to go back to this oasis and spend a fortnight exploring those hills. They are honeycombed with the caves of the first hermits and with their graves. From this point, right up to the summit of Mount Serbal, the remains of the churches and dwellings of the anchorites are waiting to be investigated; and they have remained untouched since the Arab raiders destroyed them during the first six centuries of the Christian era.

The ruins of the church in the monk's garden are evidently the remains of the cathedral church of Pharan. His pergola is supported by broken Byzantine columns which once belonged to this church, a building that preceded Justinian's Church in the Monastery at Sinai. It was evidently in the ruins of this building that Palmer, when travelling with the Ordnance Survey Expedition to Sinai in 1869, found a curious little stone figure of a sitting man with uplifted arms, evidently intended to be Moses at the Battle of Rephidim.

No wonder the monks and hermits of Pharan eventually migrated to the Monastery at Sinai, for a more hopeless place to defend than Pharan cannot be imagined. It is ideal guerilla country. The Arabs could just sit behind rocks and shoot their arrows down into churches and hermitages. I was reminded of a vivid account of a massacre which was written about 380 A.D. by a travelling Egyptian monk named Ammonius. After making a pilgrimage to Jerusalem, he decided to ascend the holy mountain of Sinai. He arrived during one of the periodical raids. The aspect of the monks, he thought, "was that of angels, for they were pallid and, so to say, incorporeal, owing to their abstaining from wine, oil, bread, and other foods that tend to luxury, living on dates only, just enough to keep themselves alive."

A few days after his arrival Saracens suddenly attacked the hermits in their cells and slew them, "so that," says Ammonius, "I, together with the superior Doulas, and others, sought refuge in the tower while the barbarians slew all the hermits who were in Thrambe, Choreb, Kedar, and other places." It is interesting to note that the monks of Sinai had their towers of refuge just as the monks of Wadi Natrûn had at the same period.

While Ammonius and the hermits were sheltering in the tower, the Saracens were frightened away and the hermits sallied out to view the damage. They found thirty-eight anchorites lying dead in their cells. A messenger arrived to say that a neighbouring settlement had also been raided, not by Saracens, but by a wild Nubian tribe, the Blemmyes, who were probably ancestors of the shock-haired Bisharin of Aswân. This had been a much fiercer affair than the raid of Pharan. The Blemmyes rushed to the refuge tower, and ran round it screaming while the hermits prayed inside. Paul of Petra, the father of this settlement, was a saintly man of courage:

"O athletes of God," he cried, "do not regret this good conflict; let not your souls be faint, and do nothing unworthy of your cowl, but be clothed with strength, with joy, and manliness, that you may endure with a pure heart, and may God receive you into His kingdom."

In the meantime the Blemmyes had piled tree-trunks outside the tower and burst in the door, which suggests that these towers, like the Round Towers of Ireland, had their doors high up in the masonry. They rushed in, calling for the Superior. Paul of Petra stepped out and declared himself. The raiders demanded his treasures and he replied, "Forsooth, children, I own nothing but this old hair-cloth garment that I am wearing." They stoned him and split his head in half with a sword. Then the man who was describing these events to Ammonius said, with a candour which rings so truly down the years:

"Then I, miserable sinner, seeing the slaughter and the blood and viscera on the ground, bethought me of a hiding-place. A heap of palm branches lay in the left-hand corner of the church. Unnoticed by the barbarians, I ran to it saying to myself, 'If they find me, they can but kill me, which they are sure to do if I do not hide.' "

From his hiding-place he watched all the hermits being murdered in the church and saw the barbarians searching everywhere for treasure, except, presumably, under the palm branches; finding none, they rushed wildly from the place.

Raids such as these filled the Coptic and Greek calendars with saints centuries before the birth of Mohammed. There was no religious hatred at the back of these raids: they were frank outbursts of savagery.

We said good-bye to Father Isaiah, who gave us an important message about beans to the *œconomos* of the monastery, and continued our journey through the oasis. For a few minutes we travelled through green shade, a shade of palm-fronds pierced by shafts of light, and beyond the filigree of branches we could see the red rocks burning all around. When we left the last palm tree behind us, the heat of the desert leapt at us again like a tiger.

"Oh, I shall be the popular one to-night," sang Mr. Vallinis, "and the monks will say to me, 'Michael, you are a good man and a good Greek, for you do not forget your friends.' I have something good for them. . . ."

He crouched over the wheel in happy anticipation of forthcoming popularity, and lifting one hand, joined thumb and forefinger and lightly moved his hand to and fro in a way that is understood from Chios to Athens and from Athens to Salonica.

"Behind us on the ice is a great basket of sea-crabs from Suez," he explained. "I bought them yesterday morning before the market was open. The monks love sea-crabs. Such things are not found in the desert."

Then a worried look came into his face.

"Is it, maybe, a time of fasting?" he asked himself, then his natural optimism banished such a thought. "No matter, we shall see. . . ."

And the sun moved to the west. Mountains that had been in shadow now lay in gold light. Others, recently in sunlight, were now blue in shadow. The blue turned to black. Slowly the light moved upward over the stone walls, and the shadows pursued it, until only the highest crests and ridges were barred with light, so that we moved in a valley of twilight with the mountain-tops shining far above. There came a moment when the sun slid away from even the highest peak, and a star burned in the sky. It was suddenly cold; for the valley that leads up into Sinai is several thousand feet above the sea.

5

Without warning the monastery came into view round the shoulder of a hill.

It lay in a valley enclosed by immense dark mountains, whose feet were in shadow, whose summits were in starlight. Towering ridges and peaks dwarfed the monastery, making it seem like a child's toy on the floor of a room. There were scores of cypress trees, pointing their dark fingers in the twilight, and there was a timid burst of green in the garden, lying against the thirsty wall of the mountains.

Mr. Vallinis switched on the headlights and shattered the silence of the valley with the hideous scream of a klaxon horn, to warn the monks of our arrival. Before the horrid noise had flung itself from side to side of the gorge, first one black figure, then another, then two or three, appeared on the battlements, all gazing down at us and pointing.

They wore black gowns and black stove-pipe hats. We could see their black beards as they turned excitedly to one another before disappearing to unbar the great door.

Darkness came down swiftly on the world, and the stars were burning above the monastery, snapping and winking in blue electric fire. The building, now that we were beneath its walls, was immense. A few more monks appeared on the wall.

"With God's help we have come to the Holy Mountain," called Mr. Vallinis in Greek towards the ramparts, "and we have brought you a basket of sea-crabs from Suez!"

We craned our necks and saw the black figures nodding and chattering above us like startled necromancers.

"It is Kyrios Vallinis," we heard one say, then another called down to us: "What is it you say you have brought from Suez?"

"Sea-crabs!" shouted Mr. Vallinis.

There was a burst of slightly unmonkish merriment from the ramparts. How cold it was! The air was now icy. How long they took to unlock the gate! It is barred each night as if the Saracens might still come. I looked up at the stupendous walls and saw the pent-house, like the projecting loft-door of an English barn, standing out from the wall. Had we come here a century ago, we should have been hauled up into that pent-house in a boatswain's cradle. It is only in comparatively recent times that the monks have grown sufficiently confident to have a door.

At last we heard them at the locks and bars; at last the gate opened; and we were soon shaking hands with a number of pal-lid young men, for it was the younger monks who had rushed down to greet us. Their long hair was bunched beneath rimless birettas, and their pale cheeks were fringed with incipient beards like the down of black swans. The two cars were to be left under the walls, guarded by the monastery Bedouin. Mr. Vallinis shouldered his gun and we walked across a courtyard in the starlight, into a space crowded with whitewashed buildings.

We passed through a narrow alley from which cavernous archways led here and there. One side was in starlight, the other in deepest shadow. Above us white towers and roofs, all on dif-ferent levels, and clustering together, rose into the serenity of the night. Standing behind a door was an old cannon on a wooden gun-carriage; a white cat sprang out of a shadow and crossed our path. The silence was unbroken except for the sound of our steps on the stones. I could smell incense and knew that we were passing the church, Justinian's church; then we ascended steps into an open space. Turning to the left, we as-cended a long wooden staircase to an outside gallery which re-minded me of the New Inn at Gloucester. The monk who was leading us tapped on a door, and I found myself in a small room full of yellow lamplight, in which the Archbishop of Sinai was sitting behind a knee-hole desk.

Seated with him in the room were the four elders of the mon-astery, big, black-bearded men with brown, rugged faces like those of the peasants who live in the hills around Delphi. They all rose as we entered. The Archbishop bade me welcome and asked how we had found the road and how long our journey had taken. When I told him that we had spent a night at Abu

Zenîma, he ran a ringed hand down his soft beard and nodded indulgently, saying that he had come through in one day from Suez. I complimented him on his prowess as a motorist, and all the dark figures nodded and smiled in admiration and agreement. A lay brother entered with glasses of *arak*, which the monks make from dates, and with saucers of jam. After a little more polite conversation, I was shown to my room, which was three doors away along the wooden gallery. Before going inside, I turned to look down on the clustered buildings below, a pattern of starlight and shadow. All around, wherever I looked, I saw gaunt mountains shouldering the stars.

My room was bare, yet crowded. An ancient iron four-poster, heavily encumbered by lace frills and a mosquito net, occupied most of the space not taken up by a couch, two chairs, a marble-topped table, and a washstand on which stood two tin jugs of cold water. The only picture was an ikon of the Madonna, which hung in a wooden shrine on the wall, with a sprig of dry basil lying in front of it on a little shelf. The outer wall of the room was that of Justinian's fortress, and from a small window punched in its massive stones I looked down into the entrance courtyard, and over the cypress trees in the garden to the mountains of the gorge. The bedroom ceiling had been painted green somewhere about the year 1860, by a monk who had released his knowledge of contemporary decoration in a flowery and not unpleasing wreath.

Near the bed was a framed copy of the Monastery Regulations in Greek, Arabic, French, and English. I gathered from the following rules that the monks have been obliged to place things on a firm financial basis.

Each visitor desirous to pass the night in the monastery must pay for food and lodging one Egyptian pound daily, and without food half a pound only per day.

Passing the night outside the monastery (under a tent he

should bring with him) he has to pay Piastres 25, for entrance fees to visit the monastery.

Any person wishing to visit the Mount of the Decalogue and the Mount of St. Catherine must be accompanied by a monk, and has to pay Piastres 25 for camel fares to the Mount of the Decalogue, Piastres 30 for camel fares to the Mount of St. Catherine, and, moreover, Piastres 50 to the monk who will accompany them.

Times, it seems, have changed since scholars invaded the library of the monastery and went off with ancient manuscripts under their arms. The monastery now demands a fee of two gold francs for every page of manuscript photographed, and persons who wish to work in the library must first pay a fee of five pounds.

I went along the gallery and discovered that Mr. Vallinis was living in a less ornate apartment at the end of it, while Yûsuf had been given the freedom of the guest-house kitchen, an incredible place built against Justinian's wall. Like all good cooks, he was complaining bitterly of the uncouth, alien oven. He looked cut to the heart when I asked only for two boiled eggs. After supper I retired to my four-poster and tried to sleep. I read for some time by the light of two candles, but more than once I got up and stole over to the door to make certain that I was not dreaming: there, sure enough, was the Monastery of Mount Sinai, lying hushed and white beneath the stars.

I was awakened by a dull, resonant sound. It was still dark. When I glanced at my watch, I saw that it was three o'clock. The sound went TAK-tak-tak-tak—one long note followed by three short—as if a gigantic woodpecker were at work in the night. I tiptoed over to the door and looked out. In the shadows below I could make out the figure of a monk hitting a wooden semantron. This is a large plank of wood which has been in use since the earliest times in the Greek Church, to call monks to prayer: it is hung up by chains, and is struck with a wooden mallet. By hitting different portions of the plank, varied sounds can be made.

This insistent staccato, unlike a gong and unlike a drum, a sound with a strange quality entirely of its own, carried into the remote recesses of the surrounding mountains an impression of astonishing venerability: it was the ancient, unchanged voice of the Monastery of Mount Sinai, calling the brothers to prayer as it used to do when Justinian was emperor.

I went to sleep, and was again awakened, this time by a cheerful riot of bell-music that went gambolling wildly through the air. It was broad day. I lay for a moment listening to the curious rhythm that the Greeks put into their bells:

> *Ling-tow, ling-tow, ling-ling-tow,*
> *Ling-ling-tow, ling-tow*
> *Ling-ling-tow, ling-tow.*

I opened the door and saw a young monk standing in the bell-tower, which was almost level with my balcony; he grasped a rope in each hand. Two bells were flying this way and that, sending their urgent, triumphant call over the monastery, over the desolate plain of El Râha, and up the slopes of the great mountains which still lay in their own vast shadows, although the sun had risen. With the bell-ringing, monks hurried from their cells to the church. I could see them on the way, always ascending or descending steps, winding in and out of passages, each one coming in time to the place where Justinian's church lies below the level of the modern pavement.

6

In broad daylight the monastery looked more than ever like a fortress. Or perhaps one should compare it with a miniature town of the Middle Ages, with its crooked streets, its mass of buildings of different heights and styles, its delightfully haphazard plan, all telling of centuries of readjustment in a walled space.

A breast-high sentry-walk runs round the wall, in which embrasures have been made so that a few antiquated cannon, of the kind seen in the gardens of retired naval men, may peep down at the rocks. I believe these squat, dangerous-looking objects are still fired during feast days, when their brisk Eighteenth Century detonations add to the excitement of the chiming bells and the thudding semantra.

While I was having breakfast in a room on the gallery, five or six cats of various colours, no two of them alike, crept up and crouched expectantly round the door. They sprang on any scraps of food flung to them, but vanished instantly like so many witches when I invited them to come inside. If you could imagine a cat belonging to anything so plebeian as a herd, I would say that Mount Sinai has a herd of cats, for these animals are everywhere: cats that have never known the thrill of being chased by a dog, have certainly never tasted the joys of fish, and know nothing of the pleasures of milk or the abandoned ease of the fireside. The kittens are the only young things that ever enliven this place with their beauty, and the mother cats are the only representatives of their sex who dwell, or have ever dwelt, within the walls. The cats of Sinai share with those of London an abundant and never-ending roof-line. It should be possible for a cat of agility to make his way overhead from end to end of the monastery, while for those with a fondness for tiles, there are tiles without number. But the cat of Sinai has his work to do: he is there to keep down the rats and snakes.

A pale young monk, wearing powerful spectacles, arrived on the abbot's instructions to show me over the monastery. His name was Brother Gabriel. As we descended the gallery stairs, we saw twelve old monks seated at a trestle-table in the earliest patch of warmth which the sun casts over Mount Sinai. They were engaged in the daily task of sorting grit from corn. They smiled as we came down, and some of them came forward and shook hands cordially. Most of them said "Kalí méra," one said "Bon jour," and another said "Good day."

Their task is simple. Each monk sits with a pile of grain before him which he sifts by the obvious but time-wasting process of picking out the grains one by one and adding them to a separate pile, thus leaving behind all the grit.

We passed from the warmth of this golden corner into chill shadows as yet untouched by sun. I suppose when a monk has lived in the monastery for some time, he knows it as a place mapped out in patches of sun and shade, of warm places and cold ones, for, so high are the surrounding mountains, that the sun gives the monastery only a passing attention, and after two o'clock vanishes for the day behind the tall peaks of Mount Sinai.

I asked the brother to take me as far round the wall as we could go, and we went on, sometimes bending our heads in low stone tunnels and now coming out on the sentry walk with a grand view below us of the distant rocks. When the embrasures were first made in this wall, they were not for culverins or muskets, but for arrows. We came to a dark chamber in which stands a windlass of such gigantic size that it must require the combined strength of the monks to push it round.

This is the machine that was used to pull visitors up in a boatswain's cradle from the year 1600 until the British occupation of Egypt. It is still worked, said Brother Gabriel, when anything heavy has to be introduced into the monastery, or for anything too large to be carried round the narrow lanes. While we were looking at it, two lay brothers arrived with a sack of what appeared to be brown stones, but, having been in Coptic monasteries, I recognized it as that hard bread which must be soaked before it can be eaten. They opened the pent-house door and arranged a rope over a pulley. Looking down, I saw a number of

TAKING UP FIREWOOD, MONASTERY OF MOUNT SINAI

Bedouin standing at the foot of the wall and gazing anxiously up at us.

"They have come for their bread," explained Brother Gabriel; "we give it to them every morning."

I was fascinated to see this ancient custom still being observed in Sinai. The Arabs below were all attached to the monastery, and are known as the Jebelîya. Their tribe has nothing to do but wait near the monastery and tackle any outdoor jobs that have to be done. It is said that these people are not Arabs by blood, but are descendants of a hundred Roman slaves from the Black Sea, and a hundred Egyptians, whom the Emperor Justinian transferred, with their wives and families, to protect and look after the monks when the monastery was first built. The monks have fed them for centuries and, as I was about to witness, still do so every morning at nine o'clock.

First, bundles of firewood were pulled up at the end of a rope, and in return bread was let down to the poor ragged creatures at the foot of the wall, who leapt up to receive it and frequently quarrelled over it. I was told that no Arab is supposed to receive the bread dole two days running.

It seems strange that the monks still hold all commercial relations with these Arabs by means of a rope and pulley, for surely all danger of an attack is now over. Though the Jebelîya are now Moslems, their ancestors were once Christian, and perhaps a relic of Christianity is an hereditary reverence for the monks, whom they believe to be magicians gifted with the power to bring rain or to withhold it. This belief is as strong to-day as it was when Burckhardt visited the monastery in 1816 and heard a good story about it. It seems that the Bedouin believe that the rain of Sinai is caused by the opening and the shutting of a book which the Lord gave to Moses on the summit of Mount Sinai, which book, they think, is in the possession of the monks. One day, says Burckhardt, a Bedouin, whose camel and sheep had been washed away in a torrent, rode up to the monastery and fired his gun at it, and when asked the reason, indignantly exclaimed: "You have opened the book so much that we are all drowned!"

The rules of the monastery allow only three of the Jebelîya to enter at one time, and no Bedouin is allowed to sleep inside the walls. They live mostly in the garden and the sheds outside. I had a good look at these people, wondering if any trace of their peculiar origin still remained in their faces, but I failed to see any: they looked to me much like other Bedouin, though one of them, the man who carries the mails to Tor, is the best-looking man I have seen in the desert. If ever a hero was lost to the films, he is the man who spends his life crossing the mountains on foot from Sinai to Tor twice a month.

The monastery is ruled by the Sinai Assembly, composed of the non-resident Archbishop and four archimandrites, all resident monks. There are generally from thirty to forty monks in residence, some of whom hope to end their days there; others spend five years or so and leave for other monasteries. There is a mill where corn is ground, a wheelwright's shop, like a dungeon in the Tower of London, and a vaulted bakery in whose windowless gloom stands a stalwart monk with a white apron tied round him, mixing the bread and dispatching the loaves to the cavernous ovens. Shut in by granite walls is a pathetic little garden in which I was surprised to see a few rose trees.

"We grow flowers for Christmas," said Brother Gabriel; and, searching about this heroic patch of earth, I came on snapdragons, narcissi, and iris.

I asked Brother Gabriel to show me his cell. We ascended several steps to a group of wooden buildings rather like almshouses, built against the monastery wall. He pushed open a door and led the way into a clean little room where a few sacred pictures hung on the walls and a few Greek books stood on a shelf; there was a bed and a chair. As cells go, it was almost luxurious, and he said he was happy there.

Next to the church stands a whitewashed mosque whose square minaret rises beside the bell-tower. The monk told me that centuries ago a Turkish general was marching to destroy the monastery, and the abbot and a deputation of monks went out to meet him and so affected him by their eloquence that he promised to save the monastery if he could. Unfortunately, he said, the temper of his troops was up and they were thirsting for Christian blood, and, though he himself had no desire to harm the monks or their monastery, it would be difficult to control them. "Go back quickly," he said, "and build a mosque beside your church inside the walls, and when we come, say to us that in days gone by the Prophet himself visited the monastery, and the ground is therefore hallowed by his feet." The monks returned, and every pair of hands in the monastery was engaged in building a mosque against time, with the result that when the attacking army arrived, they saw a minaret standing above the walls side by side with the church.

7

We now descended the steps to the Church of the Transfiguration, which is generally believed to date from the reign of Justinian and may therefore be about one thousand and four hundred years old. It is remarkable not only as one of the great pilgrimage churches of Christendom, but also as a Byzantine church in the desert which has never fallen into ruins.

I have mentioned the legend that the first church was built by St. Helena to enshrine the Burning Bush, which in the earliest Christian period was the most sacred object in the valley. She is also believed to have built near this little church a tower of refuge in which the monks might gather during attacks by the Saracens. No date is given for these foundations, but, if the legend is true, it must have been in 327 A.D., when she was in Jerusalem seeking for the relics of the True Cross. If she travelled to

Egypt at that time, as the Copts believe she did, and founded the
Red and the White monasteries near Sohâg, there is, perhaps,
nothing improbable in the thought that she should have built a
church and a tower in Sinai. Even if a personal visit to Sinai
were too exhausting for a woman then in her eightieth year, St.
Helena would readily have provided the necessary money. Indeed it is difficult to believe that the hard-pressed hermits of
Sinai, learning that the generous Christian Empress was within
a few days' journey, did not approach her with the tale of their
woes and beg her patronage.

The original church of the Burning Bush had been standing
for two centuries when Justinian built the fortress walls around
it in 530 A.D. At this time, or shortly afterwards, the Church of
the Burning Bush was enlarged into the present church, which
was then called the Church of the Transfiguration, from the
exquisite Byzantine mosaic which still decorates the dome
above the high altar. The apse of the older Church of the Burning Bush was retained and still stands beyond the present east
end of the Church of the Transfiguration, obviously part of an
older, smaller building, and on a lower level.

Until the Middle Ages, pilgrims continued to visit the
Church of the Transfiguration, to pray beside the Burning Bush
but the translation there of the relics of St. Catherine of Alexandria created a new chapter in the history of Sinai's church.
The church now not only changed its name for the third time,
but the whole monastery became known popularly as the Monastery of St. Catherine, by which name it is still called to-day,
although the church is not dedicated to this saint, but merely
preserves her bones.

The association of St. Catherine with Sinai is a remarkable
story, and from this remote mountain fastness the fame of the
saint went out over all Europe, particularly to Belgium. St.
Catherine was a virgin of Alexandria who died for her faith during the reign of Maximianus. Among the tortures devised for

of Sinai. Outside the monastery it is never possible to forget your surroundings for a moment, but when you stand in this church you might be in any fine Greek cathedral in Europe. It is, perhaps, the most spectacular of all the gifts which the Greek Church has offered to God; a gift held up to heaven for fourteen centuries by men whose lives have often been in danger and have always been lives of hardship and privation. It may be that heaven does not need so much gold paint, but it is man's poor way of showing love, and perhaps the spirit that placed it there finds its way to the Throne of God.

The twelve pillars that divide the nave into two side aisles are tall Byzantine columns of granite, covered with stucco and painted an unhappy shade of green. Some day, when the church is redecorated, the stone may be allowed to remain in its own simplicity. It is difficult to imagine why some writers have described these columns as "lotus capitals," for there is not one lotus capital in the church. They are all typically Byzantine capitals, and each one is different. Brother Gabriel explained to me that each of the twelve pillars contains the relics of a martyr, one for each month of the year.

An *ikonostasis* loaded with a wealth of ikons conceals a beautifully rounded apse, in which stands the high altar. In the dome above is the famous Justinian mosaic of the Transfiguration. There is probably no early mosaic that is less known than this. It belongs to the same period, certainly to the same style, as the mosaics in the Church of the Holy Wisdom (St. Sophia) at Istanbul, and those at Ravenna and at Salonica, all of which are among the earliest in the world. On the flat wall space above the inward curve of the dome are mosaics which show Moses beside the Burning Bush and receiving the Tablets of the Law, but these are obviously by a later hand and have not the exquisite quality of the mosaics on the dome itself.

The beautiful group of the Transfiguration is framed by a series of thirty-two circular medallions with silver backgrounds, against which glow the heads and shoulders of saints and prophets. There is a Greek inscription running along the inner curve of the dome: "In the name of the Father, and of the Son, and of the Holy Ghost, the whole of this work was executed for the salvation of those who have contributed to it by their donations, under Longinus, the most holy priest and prior, by Theodore, the priest." The mosaic itself shows five figures grouped round the central figure of Jesus, who stands in a mandorla, or almond-shaped space, formed of several blending shades of blue. Our Lord is clothed in a cream-coloured mantle of Byzantine pattern which falls in graceful folds to His feet, and the clavus, or band of colour on His garments, is shown in gold. The nimbus is of silver, and at the back glows a cross. He stands with a scroll of writing in His hand, while from His body issue five rays of faint silver light towards each of the five figures, who stand or kneel in attitudes of fear and amazement. Underneath the mandorla St. John lies prostrate, covering his face from the glory of God; on either side kneel St. Peter and St. James, and above them stand the figures of Elias and Moses. The mosaic is an exquisite blend of dark blues, greens, and browns, against a background of dull gold glass mosaic. The Saviour's hair and beard are of a deep, rich brown, and He is the Christ familiar to the art of the West.

The light is so faint in the apse that it is never easy to see the details of this work, and after about ten o'clock in the morning the sun moves away from the two small windows overhead, the only source of light.

To the right, as you face the altar, is a marble shrine upheld by four slender Byzantine columns of marble. From its domed roof nine hanging lamps are suspended above the small decorated sarcophagus of marble in which lie the relics of St. Catherine. One of the senior monks came in with a bunch of keys and offered to display the relics. Candles were first lighted upon the altar, and all the monks who were present reverently removed their birettas as the archimandrate unlocked the coffin. The space inside was crowded with objects, but I was shown only two, both of them in caskets of gold. As the first was opened, the monks crossed themselves and I looked at a skeleton hand covered with rings. Emeralds, rubies, and diamonds sparkled on the finger-bones. The wrist had been padded with cotton-wool to enable it to take a sparkling gold bracelet.

The next casket contained a skull whose smooth brown dome was alone visible. Various precious gifts were attached to it, notably a Victorian gold sovereign. There were other relics of St. Catherine in the chest which I was told are never shown. As the relics were replaced, the candles were extinguished.

I was then asked to remove my shoes before entering the Chapel of the Burning Bush, which lies behind the church. I was tremendously interested in this tiny dark apse, for there can surely be no doubt that it is the last relic of the church which stood there before the Church of the Transfiguration was built. It is on a slightly lower level than the later church, and the masonry of the walls is hidden everywhere by blazed tiles. In the centre is a windowless domed recess in which a small altar stands, upheld by four thin marble columns. Three lamps hang beneath the altar, above a small silver plate which is said to mark the site of the Burning Bush.

The monks told me that on a certain day once a year, a ray of sunlight finds its way into this dark little church. The surrounding mountains are so high that except on this particular day, the Chapel of the Burning Bush is in almost complete darkness.

8

Possibly the most tactless thing an Englishman could do in Sinai would be to inform the monks that he had subscribed to the purchase of the Codex Sinaiticus, which is now in the British Museum. I am thankful to say that no one mentioned this subject to me, for I understand that the monks have strong feelings about it. They say that Tischendorf took away the Codex in 1859 to copy it, and that the Tsar retained possession of it by unfair means. Apparently they think it wrong of us to have bought at great cost what they regard as stolen property.

Whatever may be the rights and wrongs of this question, the subsequent fame and financial value of the Codex have caused the monks to guard their Library with the eyes of a lynx. The books are no longer neglected. They are stored in a stone room rather like a bank vault, and the more precious volumes are kept behind a locked grille. The books repose on shelves, and most of them bear paper labels on the spine, on which titles are written in Greek and Arabic. I was shown the famous Codex Aureus with its illuminated pages, and many other ancient and valuable manuscripts, now rightly kept under lock and key.

Not far from the Library is the ancient refectory. This is a stone vaulted room with a small altar in a domed recess at the east end. The walls are covered with modern frescoes showing saints in medallions. The most remarkable decoration is the fresco over the altar, which was executed by a monk of Sinai. With a wealth of detail worthy of Brueghel, it pictures the confusion of the Last Judgment, and, whatever its defects may be, lack of action and realism are not among them. At the top, God is seen enthroned in the heavens in the central seat of a curved tribunal; on either side of Him sit the Apostles and Saints, waiting to pronounce judgment on the souls of men. On the right of the picture Hell is ready to receive the wicked, some of whom have already arrived and may be seen writhing in great distress, while serpents, horrible beasts, and devils chase them here and there. On the earth below, the tombs are opening and the dead are coming forth. A black St. Michael clothed in full Roman armour is slaying the dragon; a group of jet-black devils are escorting Anti-Christ; and, most remarkable of all, an army of saints has opened the door of the Holy Sepulchre, from which our Lord walks, bearing His Cross. It is an extraordinarily sincere and decorative piece of work, and I was sorry that I could not discover the artist's name.

The walls of the refectory are covered with many coats of arms, scratched on the stone by Crusaders and pilgrims of the Middle Ages. Unfortunately many more, which were painted on the stone, have been recently obliterated by a coat of distemper.

Brother Gabriel told me that it is the custom for the abbot to sit with his back to the east wall, while the monks occupy each side of the tables. During meals, which usually consist of black beans, oil, and bread, a monk reads selections from the lives of the saints, his words regulated by a hand bell which the abbot rings to tell him when to stop or when to resume his reading.

The monks used to wash the feet of pilgrims in the refectory, but now that Russian pilgrims no longer come to Sinai, this ceremony is seldom observed. When Pococke was at the monastery in 1739, he said that it was usual for pilgrims, soon after they arrived, to have their feet washed by the monks. Pococke's feet were washed by the abbot. "One of the monks, after this ceremony is over," he said, "holds a basin and urn to wash the hands, and then sprinkles the pilgrims with rose-water; if it is a lay person, one of the lay monks performs these ceremonies, the whole society sitting in the hall and chanting hymns."

I think the beauty of the monastery garden has been exaggerated by some visitors, but it is not possible to exaggerate its rather touching character. It is an arboreal counterpart of the monastery: a group of exiled European trees and shrubs sheltering behind a wall in an alien land.

When you open the little wicket gate, you enter a garden where cypresses, a few olive and almond trees, and many other fruit trees cast their shade on the yellow rocks. To me, it was a curiosity, but to the monks it was a piece of their native land.

No matter whether a monk comes from Salonica, Crete, or Cyprus, he can see in this garden a reminder of his home, and it may be that the ability to look at it without emotion is a sure test that a man has made his peace with God.

I should not say that the monks are great gardeners: they seem to leave all the work to the Bedouin. Among their most prized products is an exceedingly hard kind of pear that will keep from one harvest to another. Though it is so hard, it is not woody, and the flavour is curiously scented, unlike any pear I have tasted in Europe.

I was walking round the garden one morning when I happened to meet Brother Gabriel and another young monk. As we were passing a white building among the trees, which I knew was the bone-house of the monastery, one of them asked whether I should care to see inside. He unlocked the door and we walked into a vaulted room which was piled almost to the ceiling with human bones. To the left, as I went in, was a pile of skulls, and opposite were thousands of arm-bones; in other parts of the vault were similar neat stacks from which skeleton hands and feet protruded.

I was so occupied by this gruesome sight that I did not notice what my companions were doing until the smell of incense caused me to turn round. They stood together, one holding a lighted candle, while the other swung a censer towards the hideous figure of a skeleton clothed in the dusty garments of a monk. It was strapped to a kitchen chair, from which it leaned in a ghastly parody of life, a wooden cross and a rosary dangling from its bony fingers.

This is the skeleton of a monk called Stephen, who died in 580 A.D. He was a hermit on the slopes of Mount Sinai, and they say of him that he caught a panther cub and taught it to protect his cell from hyænas. When he died, his body was carried down to the monastery to mount guard as porter of the bone-house;

THE MONASTERY OF MOUNT SINAI

and so for thirteen hundred years Stephen has presided, still dressed in a hermit's robes, over Sinai's dead.

It has always been the custom of the monks to exhume their dead after an interval of time and stack their bones in one part of the crypt and their skulls in another. Only bishops and arch-bishops are allowed to have boxes, which lie round the vault with tickets on them, giving the names and titles of the skeletons within. It is obvious that in the plain of El Râha, with rock everywhere around, this rather grisly custom has been forced on the monks. If every monk who is represented by a skull in the bone-house had been interred in a rock-hewn sepulchre, the mountain would by this time have been honeycombed with tombs.

Among the curiosities is an iron belt which had been taken from the body of a dead hermit. There is also a hair shirt and, strangest sight of all, two skeletons linked together by iron fet-ters. Romantic and inaccurate stories are told about these skele-tons, which are obviously those of two penitents who died, still fettered, while fulfilling a pilgrimage. Many such penitents must have come to Sinai in the course of its history, and we know at least of two brothers called Fromont, of Rennes, who committed murder in the Ninth Century and were sentenced to go fettered on pilgrimage to Rome, Jerusalem, and Sinai. They were received by Pope Benedict III, who gave them his blessing. After spending some years in Jerusalem, they went to the The-baid and lived with the Egyptian monks, coming at last, and still in fetters, to the end of their pilgrimage at Sinai. They re-turned to Rennes by way of Rome, where, after all the hard-ship they had endured, death struck the fetters from one brother: but the other continued to wear them until at length, his penance over, they were taken from him. It was a common thing for such fetters to be made from the weapon with which the murder had been committed.

The monks were willing to show me more of this bone-house, but I was only too ready to make an excuse and go out into the warm garden.

9

Brother Gabriel and I, accompanied by a lean and tattered Bedouin, set off early one morning to climb Mount Sinai.

The enormous wall of apparently perpendicular mountain at the back of the monastery was lying in cool shadow. The head of Mount Sinai remains remote and hidden by the heights leading to it. It is eight thousand feet above sea level—or almost twice the height of Ben Nevis—but this gives an exaggerated idea of the climb, which, although exhausting, is neither dangerous nor difficult. The monastery itself is nearly four thousand feet above the sea, therefore you have to climb not much more than three thousand five hundred feet, a task made theoretically easier by some three thousand steps cut in the mountain-side in the time of the great Sinaitic pilgrimages.

After we had been climbing for about three-quarters of an hour, I found the granite steps more tiring to my leg muscles than an ordinary straight climb would have been, for some of them are as steep as a ladder set against a house, and you rarely find two together of the same depth. It is this lack of uniformity in the steps which makes them so wearying; in fact I regard the stairway up Sinai to be more of a penance than a help.

We climbed slowly from the cool shadow of the lower slopes into sunlight; then, as the shape of some mighty height obscured the sun, we plodded upward again in welcome shade. Every now and then we would look back to admire a view which became grander with every step.

We stopped to rest beside a small rock spring where, say the Arabs, Moses once tended the flocks of Jethro. Although Brother Gabriel was thin, with a face the colour of candlegrease, he was as tough as a mountain goat, and I believe he could have run all the way up Sinai and down again without fatigue. He was an outstanding example of the virtues of a spare diet. I asked him to give me an hour by hour account of his day.

"Take yesterday," he said. "I rose at three-thirty, and was in church until six-thirty. I had a cup of coffee at seven o'clock, but nothing to eat, because it was a fast day. From eight o'clock until one we were looking at the monastery. When I left you at one o'clock I had something to eat—black beans, bread, and oil. I then went to sleep for half an hour. At two o'clock I called for you and we were out on the mountain until five. After this I had a plate of vegetable soup and went to bed. I was in church again at three-thirty this morning."

That is typical of life at Sinai. The food is of the most frugal kind, and the duties of the monks consist chiefly of attending long services in church.

As we talked, the tattered Arab brought from the folds of his rags an object which had once been a briar pipe, and it was now almost entirely bound with bands of brass. Into the bowl of this precious pipe he crammed a mixture of the chopped green herbs, which Sinai Bedouin smoke instead of tobacco.

He then produced a flint, which he held in his left hand with a piece of soft rag placed against it. He took a piece of iron, gave the flint a quick slanting blow and blew down on the rag, which at once began to smoulder. His pipe was soon alight, and the process of lighting it had been as neat and quick as if he had used the most modern kind of petrol lighter.

"Would you like a cigarette?" I asked.

His eyes widened. Swiftly he knocked out the green herbs and took two cigarettes, which he packed into the bowl.

We plodded onward and upward like characters in *The Pilgrim's Progress*, until we entered a gorge where the stairway ascends through a crack in the mountain. There is a small stone chapel dedicated to the Virgin Mary, which is locked except on a certain day in the year.

"There is a story about this," said Brother Gabriel. "In ancient times food caravans once failed to come from Egypt, and
the monks suffered not only from lack of food but from a
plague of fleas. It was decided to forsake the monastery and find
somewhere else to live. Sad at heart, the monks paid a last pilgrimage to the holy mountain. When they reached this place
they saw the Holy Virgin, the Mother of God, sitting with the
Child in her arms. 'Go back,' she said, 'and your troubles will be
ended.' Wondering and amazed, they descended to find camels
loaded with food standing under the walls, and—all the fleas had
vanished!"

As the stairway climbs the ravine, it passes under an arch. At
this gate Stephen used to sit, the monk whose skeleton guards
the charnel house at Sinai. His task was to examine pilgrims to
see whether they were spiritually worthy to ascend the mountain. If he passed them, they went on to another gate where a
friar waited to hear their confessions and to give them absolution.

The steps then led to a curious little plain, the only stretch of
level ground on the way up Mount Sinai, where a tall, solitary
cypress stands like a sentinel. They say that this tree is five hundred years old, and the engraving of it in Laborde's book,
which was published in 1838, shows it looking just the same a
century ago as it does to-day.

There are two buildings on the plain: an old stone chapel
dedicated to Elijah and a little Grimm's fairy-tale house which
stands near an abandoned garden. These buildings, the tangle of
garden, and the lonely cypress tree, were living, like all deserted
places, in an atmosphere of conspiracy. I felt that had we arrived just a minute before, we might have seen something—or
someone—but now tree, buildings, and garden were pretending
to be asleep and waiting for us to go away.

It was here, in front of the Chapel of Elijah, that we encountered a mild disaster. Brother Gabriel groped in his robes for the key and discovered that we had left it far below in the monastery. He told me that the chapel is built over a cavern in which, it is said, Elijah concealed himself when he was flying from the wrath of Jezebel, as described in I *Kings* xix. 9. While he was living in this cave, the Lord appeared to him and told him to return and elect Elisha as his successor; and from this cave he returned and sought out Elisha "and cast his mantle upon him."

The chapel is opened only once or twice a year, when a few monks climb up into the solitude and celebrate Mass there, spending the night in the little fairy-tale house and returning to the monastery on the following day.

From this point the climb, although steeper than ever, is easier because the air is like iced wine. It blows over the roof of the world, driving the ache from one's knees and the heat from one's face. And as I went on, I kept turning every hundred feet or so to look back at the mountains, which an hour ago were gigantic and now lay below me; and over their brown heads I saw more mountains lying behind them. Even these, as I climbed higher, lowered their craggy crests and offered a view beyond them of a world as dead as the mountains that cover the face of the moon.

Like many other great heights, Mount Sinai remained withdrawn and invisible until I was within the last few yards of the summit. Looking upward, I saw at last, at the top of a rock-cut stair, a little stone chapel lying against the sky. The cross on its gate was outlined upon an immense blueness of space, and when I had climbed the last few yards, I looked down upon the distant earth.

I have climbed many a high mountain in my life, but never before have I seen a view like that from Mount Sinai. Everywhere I looked, I saw range upon range of mountains lying far below, like the waters of a frozen sea. Only to the south-west did the dark shoulder of Jebel Katherin close the view. A storm at sea turned into stone is perhaps the only imagery that may convey some idea of the stupendous spectacle. Crests of mountains, sharply pointed; long ridges, like waves about to break; blunted masses of rock, like waves that have collapsed; enormous, sweeping, scooped-out valleys, like a backwash of water arrested in the moment of gathering itself to re-mount the heights; all these lay spread below, hungry, savage, and desolate. On this cloudless day, and in the clear air, I could see great distances. To the east, the golden sands on the Sinai side of the Gulf of Akaba were plainly visible, edged with blue water which stretched eastward to the country of Ibn Saud. Northwards, I surveyed the terrifying barrier of mountains that runs into the heart of Sinai; and to the north-west these giants lowered their flanks and descended gently towards the Gulf of Suez. In the Wadi below, the Wadi Seba'îyeh, I could see camel-tracks lying like grey threads. As I was looking at the blue mass of Jebel Katherin, whose twin peaks are slightly higher than Mount Sinai, I saw a bird fly from a rocky ledge several hundred feet down and come slowly across the space between the two mountains. He was joined in a few moments by his mate, and those two great birds, slowly moving above the distant earth, were the only signs of life. I am almost sure they were golden eagles.

Lifted above the world, on the highest point of the mountain's summit, is the small Chapel of Mount Sinai; within a few yards of it, and separated from it by a low stone wall and a rail of barbed wire, is a single-roomed mosque which the Arabs visit once a year to sacrifice a sheep to Moses. Both chapel and mosque are built of massive blocks of granite. The chapel, which is modern, replaces one whose history goes back perhaps even further than that of the monastery in the valley. The ground round about is strewn with finely hewn stones, bits of marble, and traces of Byzantine carving, the remains of the first chapel. Many sculptured stones from this early building have been built into the walls of the present chapel.

I was asked to sign a vellum visitors' book which is kept in the little vestibule of the chapel. The last visitor, I noticed, was here about two months before, and nearly everyone who has signed this book boasts about the time he took in ascending the mountain. Two hours is supposed to be good going.

The chapel is adorned by a series of vividly coloured Old Testament scenes which are not yet finished. We saw the monk's paint-pots and brushes in a corner of the church. To the right side of the altar a portion of the bare rock has been left exposed, as in the Mosque of the Dome of the Rock in Jerusalem, and this rock is the place sanctified by tradition as that on which the Commandments were given to Moses. The first chapel on Mount Sinai was built over this rock centuries ago, and the bones of St. Catherine were brought to it from the neighbouring mountain and kept for many years.

The monk lighted a taper on the altar, and it remained burning while we were on the mountain. On the other side of the chapel is a low cavern in the open air, large enough to take a human body; it is said to be the place where Moses covered his face from the glory of God.

I do not know whether monks have ever lived up on the summit of Mount Sinai, or whether they used to climb up with the pilgrims and unlock the church as they do to-day. There was a tradition that if anyone slept on the mountain he would be disturbed and driven down by unearthly rumblings. One of the earliest references to the holy sites of Sinai is the travel journal of a woman who made a pilgrimage there nearly a hundred years before the monastery was built. She was a pious Spanish nun named Etheria, and she is believed to have set out about the year 460 A.D. to identify the places she had read about in the Bible. Her description of climbing Mount Sinai throws a flood of light, as indeed her whole diary does, on the conditions of Eastern Christendom at a time when pilgrims were still uncommon. She says of the mountains of Sinai that "you do not go up them slowly and slowly like a snail, but straight up you go, as if it were a wall, and you are obliged to descend each of these mountains till you get down to the very root of that middle mountain, which is specially Sinai. And there, with the help of Christ, our Lord, aided by the prayers of the monks who accompanied us, I accomplished the ascent, and with great labour, for I was obliged to ascend on foot, as I could not go up in the saddle; nevertheless this labour was not felt, because the desires I had I saw fulfilled with the help of God."

In four hours' time Etheria reached the summit of Sinai. "And in that spot there is now a little church, because the said place, which is the summit of the mountain, is not very large. But nevertheless the church has of itself great grace. When, then, with the help of God we ascended to that summit, and arrived at the door of that church, behold the presbyter met us, coming from his monastery, which is considered to belong to the church, a healthy old man—a monk of what is called the ascetic life here, one moreover who is worthy to be in this place. . . . But no one dwells on the summit of the mountain, for there is nothing else there save only the church and the cave where St. Moses was. Having read in the very place all from the Book of Moses, and having made an offering in due order, and we having partaken of the communion, just as we were going out of the church the presbyters of the same place gave us thank-offerings, that is, gifts of apples which grow in the mountain itself."

Looking down on the mountain tops of Sinai fourteen centuries ago, Etheria wrote: "This I would have you know, ladies, venerable sisters, that the mountains which we had at first ascended without difficulty, were as hillocks compared with the central one on which we were standing. And yet they are so enormous that I thought I had never seen higher, did not this central one overtop them by so much."

nowned saints and solitaries of the desert. One day, when he was climbing the mountains of Sinai, he saw a man who was clothed only with a girdle of leaves and whose body was covered with hair. At the sight of him Paphnutius hid himself, under the impression that the man was mad. But it was the hermit St. Onofrius. Taking Paphnutius to his cave, the hermit told him that seventy years ago he had belonged to a monastery in Egypt, but, wishing to emulate St. John the Baptist, he had been consumed by a desire to live in the uttermost recesses of the wilderness. He found his way to Sinai, where gradually his habit fell into rags until there was nothing to cover his nakedness. Even while he was describing his life a pallor grew in his face, and it was obvious to the visitor that the saint was dying. He died blessing Paphnutius, who tore off a portion of his own cloak and, wrapping the body in it, left it in a cleft in the mountain.

Another name mentioned by Brother Gabriel was that of "the holy Nilus." The monks claim to have his skeleton in the bonehouse, although I am sure I have read somewhere that these relics were taken to the Church of the Apostles in Constantinople at some remote time. However, Nilus was one of the great literary hermits, and his writings serve to illuminate the darkness of the distant days in which he lived. A man of wealth and position in Constantinople in the time of the Emperor Theodosius II, he burned with desire to seek God in the lonely places of the world. Leaving his wife, he took his young son, Theodulos, with him, and went on a long journey, possibly about 390 A.D. He tells us that the desert was full of savage Saracens who worshipped the Morning Star and sacrificed comely young boys on altars of rough stone. If they could not sacrifice boys, they forced a young white camel to kneel, a beast without blemish, which the sheik despatched with a sword-thrust in the neck. The Saracens would then fall upon the victim and devour it, and it was their rule that every portion of the sacrifice had to be consumed before the first rays of the sun appeared on the horizon.

While Nilus and his son were living in a hermit community, a band of these Saracens descended on the church and seized the food which the hermits had stored in their cells for the winter. They then ordered the hermits to strip off their clothes and line up according to age. Some of the older hermits were killed, and the young boys, among them Theodulos, the son of Nilus, were seized and taken away.

"O why had the miracles of Sinai ceased?" cried Nilus, "and no thunder rolled, no lightning flashed to scare them in their wickedness!"

After the dead had been buried, the hermits met together and decided to make a complaint to the king of the local barbarians, who apparently was responsible to the Roman Government for the safety of the mountain passes, just as the local sheiks in Sinai were responsible until the establishment of the Frontiers Department. The king told the hermits that he would follow up the Saracens and exact vengeance for the raid, and Nilus, anxious to recover his son, asked if he might go with them. The king agreed, and Nilus travelled with the pursuing force for twelve days across Sinai. He then met a man who said that he had encountered the Saracens and that the boys had not been killed. Nilus was overjoyed to hear that Theodulos was still alive. He had, however, been sold into slavery in the Greek town of Elusa, which Sir Leonard Woolley and T. E. Lawrence have identified with the ruins of a place called Khalasa, some fifteen miles south of Beersheba.

Nilus went to this town and searched for his boy. He discovered that the Bishop of Elusa had made him doorkeeper to the church there. Theodulos told his father how he and the other captives had lain all night on the ground, bound with thongs, beside an altar on which was a sword, a basin, a phial and incense. But the Saracens had over-drunk and over-slept, so that in the morning, and for days afterwards, the captives were hurried along, until it occurred to their captors to turn them into ready money. The Bishop of Elusa was so struck by the piety of father and son that he ordained them.

Nilus and Theodulos then returned to Sinai to make their lives with the hermits there. They distinguished themselves by their austerities, but Nilus was not an extremist, and found time to criticize what he considered to be the evils of the ascetic life of his time. His writings, and especially his letters advising and correcting fellow-Christians, are among the most intimate and instructive which have come down from that remote day.

Discussing these great ones of the past, we came down from Mount Sinai by the camel road into the Wadi Shu'aib, where we saw the monastery lying before us in the shadow of the hills.

"Look," I said, "who is that?"

Far off on the opposite gorge a black figure was descending the mountain side. He was so far away that it was difficult to see him unless you kept your eyes on him all the time. Father Gabriel, whose eyes were not strong, was unable to see him at all, but the Bedouin picked him out at once and mentioned a name to the monk.

"Ah," said Brother Gabriel, "he is an old monk who spends all his time climbing the mountains to fix crosses on the high places. You have seen the crosses everywhere around. He puts them there in memory of the glorious martyrs and hermits who once lived and died here."

II

It was my last night in Sinai. As I sat alone after supper, in the little room next to my bedroom, a monk brought in the visitors' book for me to sign. As I turned its pages, famous and interesting names revealed themselves in the light of the lamp. It is strange that many a bad hotel in much frequented portions of the earth has a visitors' book bound in precious vellum, while the monks of Sinai, whose visitors are as unnumbered as the sands and include pilgrims of all ages and of all countries, content themselves with an exercise book.

This visitors' book is a modern touch in Sinai, for it begins only in the year 1860. Burckhardt has told us that when he visited the monastery in 1816 he found the walls covered with scraps of paper on which visitors had written their names, so that the present book is evidently what is termed "a long-felt want."

The first entry is that of Johan Thomas Olaf Neergaard of Copenhagen, who stayed there from March 19–21, 1860. The first English entries in that year are those of C. M. Nickels, S. H. Moore, and William Howard Doughty, who left sixty francs for the benefit of the monastery.

There is an entry in French dated March, 1868, by a large party from the Suez Canal Company, in which appears the signature of a Marie Voisin. Written on the same page, but on September 30, 1935, are the words "The son of Marie Voisin, wife of Jean Micard, has the happiness to visit this holy spot sixty-eight years after the pilgrimage of his mother and his grandfather. Gaston Micard."

On April 5, 1871, was this item:

We beg to acknowledge with many thanks the kindness and courtesy received from the monks during four days visit to the convent.

CUNNINGHAME GRAHAM,
Scotland.

At an unspecified date in 1875 the book was signed: "Charles M. Doughty."

There is a delightful letter dated October 7, 1888, which reads as follows:

I am the under-signed Staff Officer, Headquarter's Office, Egyptian Army, in charge of the eastern part of the country. Have come to this convent after inspecting El Tor accompanied with Ismail Agha Ahmed Baluh, Bashi of El Akaba. I beg to inform the reader that the way of El Akaba, Wadi Musa and El Khalil, is quite safe. Sometimes the sheiks of the Arabs say a falsehood on a special purpose of their own benefit, that the said way is unsafe. I wish if any lady hears such falsehood will kindly inform the Government, that we may do the needful about the lying man. We left this convent after a stay of three days with very many thanks to the monks for the respect, kindness and attention we received from them. They provided us with food, forage and all that we wanted. I am very sorry I had no time to visit Jebel Musa and Katerina but I hope I could visit them next year. I have seen everything in this convent and found it quite correct. I am going to live at Suez.

Staff Capt. IBRAHIM EFFENDI
ZOHNI, H.Q.E.A.
BALUH, Bashi of Akaba.

On March 1, 1894, the book was signed "Pierre Loti."
On May 10, 1903, the following entry appears:

We were the first Franciscans to come here to this holy spot after many·centuries, and were delighted with everything we saw. We had the happiness to venerate all the sacred places and the holy relics, and we do not know how to express our thanks to the good fathers of this monastery for their kindness and charitable reception. We shall never forget to remember the delightful days we spent here, and write these few words in thanksgiving for all the kindness we received here. May God bless this holy house and all who dwell therein.

F. GODFREY, O.F.M.
W. MOWBRAY
FRA FIDELIS DA BOSTON.

On November 16, 1922, the late Lord Allenby visited Mount Sinai and wrote these words:

On leaving the Convent of Santa Katerina, where I have had the honour of being the guest of His Beatitude, the Archbishop of Mount Sinai, I must express my deep sense of appreciation of the hospitality and generosity that I and my staff have received. I was profoundly touched by the thought of the Archbishop to celebrate a solemn mass for the repose of the soul of my beloved mother; at which ceremony it was my privilege to be present. We carry away with us reverent and happy impressions of our stay at this centre of sacred memories.

ALLENBY, FIELD-MARSHAL.
16–18th November, 1922.

Although I have copied only a few of the entries which interested me, there is hardly a nation in the world that will not find its language represented in this book.

12

The bells were rung as usual at three-thirty in the morning. It was still dark and the stars were brilliant. I descended four stairways and crossed white-washed courts, all so silent, so hushed, and so cold, and before I entered the church I could hear, in the stillness of the morning air, a deep rumble of voices coming from it. I stopped to listen.

"*Agios-agios-agios-agios-agios-agios-agios* . . ."

Then a higher voice would break in with:

"*Kyrie eleison* . . ."

And a third, deep as a bassoon:

"*Kyrie elei-soon* . . ."

The last syllable would be carried fathoms deep into the ultimate pits and caverns of the voice.

I entered by a side door into a mist of incense. At first I could see nothing but pin-points of candlelight and two green sparks and one ruby-red, hanging in the darkness; but soon my eyes could make out the forms, darker shadows in a world of shadows, of the great candelabra hanging from the roof of the nave. It was like wandering in some vast cave hung with stalactites.

I tip-toed to a choir-stall and stood there unseen. Near the east end of the church was a faint glow of light in which the top of the lectern was visible. Bearded faces would appear out of the darkness and shine for a moment in the glow, to disappear again smoothly into the dark. Only a rustle indicated that a face would appear in this glow, just a faint scraping on the floor, as an invisible body approached, then suddenly a new face, pale and bearded as all the others, would be shining like the ghost of Banquo.

Slowly, almost imperceptibly, dawn began to steal like a grey veil into the church, but it seemed impossible that light could ever invade that solid darkness. Then across the nave, in the stalls opposite, I saw monks standing; I saw the nave pillars going up like grey shadows, and the high outline of the *ikonostasis* with its rampart of saints. A door in the *ikonostasis* opened. A priest in a vestment, which I could now see was red, came out with a large book in his hand; a monk in black stood beside him holding a candle near the book. His voice sounded for a long time in the cold church. The light grew. I could see the faces of saints gazing long-bearded from the gold of ikons. The priest and his attendant moved through the door; there was a bright sound of curtain-rings running along a brass rod, and a sheet of red brocade filled the doorway. The service, which had been in progress since half-past three, had ended with the dawn.

On the steps outside a few monks were standing in the grey light before sunrise. The Archbishop of Sinai invited me to his room to see the ceremony of the first day of the month. Sinai still uses the Julian Calendar, which is thirteen days behind our Gregorian Calendar. We went together to the room on the wooden gallery, followed by the priest whom I had seen in the church, still wearing his red vestments. He held a brass bowl of holy water, a sprig of basil, and a silver hand-cross. When we came to the Archbishop's room, the priest offered the basil and the hand-cross to his superior. Holding them together, the Archbishop dipped them into the holy water, held them against his forehead for a moment, while he uttered a silent prayer, and then shook the water over the room, using the basil as an aspergillum. This ceremony over, the priest took the bowl, the basil, and the cross, and went throughout the monastery sprinkling every room and every monk's cell with the holy water.

And as he was bringing that message of peace and grace to his brothers, the sun came up over the mountains and the monastery was bathed in light.

An hour later I said good-bye to His Beatitude and to the monks who had been so kind and helpful. Brother Gabriel came down to the gate to see me off, and when I asked him what I could send him from England, he thought seriously for some time and asked for pictures of London and some stamps of King George VI.

The cars roared, and the Jebelîya came running with their children, so that it was through a crowd of wondering faces that we lurched off over the rough road. Turning before we lost sight of the monastery, I saw it embattled in the mountain pass, and upon its ramparts a few dark figures stood gazing like magicians from the towers.

13

We reached Suez before dark that night, and at five o'clock on the following morning I set off again with Vallinis, Yûsuf, and the two cars, to travel along the western shore of the Gulf to a monastery which is as little known as Sinai is well known. This is the Coptic monastery of St. Anthony—Dêr Anba Antoniûs—which claims to be older than Sinai.

I know of only two brief descriptions of it, for the great explorers of the Nineteenth Century, diverted, perhaps, by nearer sites, never penetrated to the remote desert in which it lies. Unlike Sinai, the Monastery of St. Anthony has no history of pilgrimage and no European associations. Its claim to fame rests on its connection with St. Anthony and on its extraordinary antiquity; for it was founded by his followers near the cave in which the saint suffered his celebrated temptations.

The road along the west shore of the Gulf is rough and difficult, and the road to Sinai is safe and easy in comparison. This western road presents continual obstacles in the form of wadi beds full of enormous boulders carried down by mountain torrents. Every fall of rain alters the track by redistributing the boulders and adding new ones. The optimist who thinks he can discover an easy way round by making a détour, will inevitably find trouble and be obliged to retrace his steps. The lesser evil is to move the boulders from the path of the car, which we did in several places. I have never seen a road which offered greater peril to the back axle.

As we continued our journey, I noticed a peculiarity of the west bank of the Gulf which may have been due to wind or tide, or some such temporary cause, or may be a permanent peculiarity. It is that all the bamboo baskets, chicken crates, oranges, spars of wood, and such-like things cast overboard from ships in the Gulf, drift to the west bank, which was strewn with them every inch of the way. The path to Abyssinia seems to be marked by empty Chianti bottles, for I was told that these had been flung over by Italian transports passing through into the Red Sea. What bad luck it is for the Bedouin of the east bank if nothing of this treasure ever finds its way over to his shores!

When the mountains recede, there are long stretches of soft, deceptive sand, especially between Abu Derega and Râs Zafarana, in which it is almost impossible not to become embedded. Both our cars stuck in this sand within a mile of Râs Zafarana, and nothing we could do prevented them from sinking to the back axles. Even the dodge of putting out stretches of canvas with struts of wood nailed along them failed to give the tyres a grip, and we were forced to appeal to that noble force, the Frontiers Department, which has a small white police post at Râs Zafarana. This post, by the way, gazes across the waters of the Gulf of Suez to Abu Zenîma.

Six lusty privates in charge of a Sudanese sergeant arrived quickly in a police car. These Sudanese non-commissioned officers do everything at the double. This sergeant lined up his men, called them to attention, and came running over; he saluted like a guardsman, and asked permission for the troops to advance. In half an hour they had lifted the cars out of the sand by sheer man power, and when, in the most tactful way possible, I attempted to give the sergeant a slight token of gratitude, he again came to attention and asked to be excused as a servant of the Government who was merely doing his duty. I well understand why men who have served in Egypt and the Sudan admire and respect the Sudanese. They seem to be natural born soldiers and are a tribute to the men who trained them.

We struck inland behind Râs Zafarana, and after several hours' hard going through rising desert, came within sight of the bare range of mountains at whose foot the monastery is situated. Inexpressibly wild and remote, this lonely place lifts its fortified white wall amid miles of stony desert, and when we drew nearer, I saw how precipitous are the mountains which rise immediately behind it.

We drew up before a great white wall and pulled the bell rope beside the gate.

The Coptic Patriarch in Cairo had been kind enough to give

me a letter of introduction to the *kummus* or abbot. The monks opened the door and told us to drive the cars into the enclosure. We entered a walled space that looked to me like any Egyptian village, except that there were no women or children. The ground fell away steeply to the left and was full of bushes and palm trees. In front of us ran a regular street of square mud houses, some of them six storys high, with the ends of palm-trunks protruding from their walls; and above each door was the Sign of the Cross. This street ended at a central square where two modern bell-towers were standing. Behind the square, another narrow street of mud houses ran to a white building with a drawbridge, which I recognized as the customary *kasr*, or keep, of a Coptic monastery. In the background were a cluster of flat mud roofs and low white domes, which I knew indicated a church.

The Monastery of St. Anthony is larger than any of those in the Wadi Natrûn, and although there is ample space within the walls, all the buildings are grouped closely together. Unlike the stone and limewash buildings of the Natrûn monasteries, most of the houses and outbuildings are primitive constructions of brown mud brick.

A young lay brother conducted me up a flight of steps, and across a paved courtyard where several immense pans of bees-wax were cooling, to a building of some size which looked like a prosperous shopkeeper's house in a small French country town. I entered a dark cool hall furnished with divans. It was obviously the guest-house and was beautifully clean and swept.

I had been sitting there for a few moments when two men entered. One was extremely handsome, with European features, a fine forehead, a straight nose, and a brown beard; he wore a black turban and a maroon-coloured gown. His companion was a short, dark man with a black beard, and was dressed in black; he was just as quick and animated as the other was slow and reserved. The first man was the *kummus*, who spoke only

Arabic, and the other was a visiting priest who had been secretary to the Metropolitan of Abyssinia, and had recently come from Addis Ababa. He spoke some French.

They were interested to hear that I had come straight to their monastery from Sinai. On clear days, said the *kummus*, when you climbed the hills at the back of the monastery, you could see right across the Gulf of Suez to the mountains of Sinai, and southward towards the Red Sea.

Turning to the lively priest, I asked him one or two questions about Abyssinia. We were soon discussing the history of this church, which has remained a dependency of the Coptic Church since the Fourth Century, when the great Athanasius, then Patriarch of Alexandria, consecrated St. Frumentius as the first Bishop of Ethiopia. It has always been the custom for the Coptic Patriarch of Alexandria to appoint the head of the Ethiopian Church, but the Italian conquest of Abyssinia has now created certain difficulties about it.

A lay brother came in with coffee, and after the formalities had been observed, the *kummus* himself showed me to my room. It contained a high, hard bed, a chair, a table, and a washstand; and the barred window gave me an admirable view of the circular mounds of cooling bees-wax waiting to be made into candles. The door opened and a lay brother came in with a basin and a jug of water. I held out my hands and he poured a thin stream of water on them. I used soap, and he poured again in the ancient way which is common all over the East, where our habit of washing in still water is considered inexpressibly dirty. Clothed in his dusty black gown, and with a pair of heelless slippers on his bare feet, he would have passed without notice in any Egyptian village in the Nile Valley, but his eyes had an unusual earnestness and there was nothing dull or stupid about his expression. I was astonished when he suddenly addressed me in English.

"I take first-class English certificate in Coptic school," he said. "Ah, English, I like much, very much. It is a language of courage. I ask the *kummus* to let me serve you because you come from England."

"How long have you been here?" I asked.

"Now, one year," he replied.

"And are you happy?"

"Oh yes, I am happy."

"Did you always wish to become a monk?"

"No; not always. I did want to enter Government employ, but . . ."

And here, at the most interesting part, he stopped and looked confused; and I saw that the cheerful little priest was standing at the door. I determined to resume the conversation as soon as possible.

"We have," began the little priest with a lifted forefinger and an incredibly waggish expression, "we have killed a chicken for you." He broke into a ripple of merriment. "It is our custom that the guest eats with us the first night." He then became carried away with the humour of his thoughts. "But it is not possible for us to eat with you, because we are fasting!" He then grew serious. "Your servants down below do not understand. They wish to give you dinner. But it is our custom that you eat with us."

I ran downstairs to the place where the cars were parked, knowing well what I should see. Yûsuf, whose baseless conception of me was still of one who traverses the desert in a condition of Gargantuan and epicurean repletion, was kneeling in the glare of a headlight, selecting from the ice chest pigeons, eggs, a tin of caviare, a bunch of carrots, some onions, and a box of Camembert cheese. A group of astounded monks stood by, gazing down on this floodlit exhibition of man's greed. When I told Yûsuf that dinner was cancelled, he gave me the mournful look of an unjustly chastised dog.

"Sir, you eat nothing," he cried with his arms outstretched, an egg in one hand and a bunch of carrots in the other. "You not like my cooking!"

"I love it, Yûsuf," I told him, "and to-morrow you shall do what you like."

"As you say," he replied with gloomy fatalism.

It was then too dark to see the monastery. I returned to sit in the guest-house and wait for dinner. The odour of a boiling fowl began to find its way about the place, and I could hear close by the confused sound of many cooks tripping over each other in a confined space. An hour passed and nothing happened. I began to feel ravenously hungry. I ventured to tiptoe to the room opposite and look inside. Beyond a bedroom was a kitchen in which at least seven or eight persons were moving about in the combined light of a paraffin lamp and two brown church candles of unbleached wax (as ordained, I thought unhappily, for the burial of the dead). Mr. Vallinis, in his shirt sleeves, sat on a stone bench cheerfully bandying words with the monks; Yûsuf sat in a corner gazing cynically at five black figures who stirred a cauldron in turn and ran about the place in search of things. It was a strange scene. I tiptoed away without being seen, realizing that to have shown myself would have flung whatever organization existed into an ecstasy of speedless haste.

At last the lay-brother came to say that dinner was ready. He took me to a bare, white-washed room lit by one brown candle in a sconce. A small table bore a steaming hash of chicken and rice. The little priest entered and sat down with me, and I told him that I would not eat unless he joined me. He shook with laughter, and his eyes shone like two illuminated sloes.

"I tell you what I will do," he said. "I notice that your man has brought oranges with you. I will eat one orange, because this is a special occasion."

So while I ate the excellent hash, Father Anthony, for that was his appropriate name, slowly peeled an orange and ate it

DÊR ANBA ANTONIÛS

with many a merry laugh.

About twelve miles over the mountains to the south-east, and a few miles from the shores of the Gulf of Suez, is another monastery, Dêr Anba Bulos—the Monastery of St. Paul—which contests St. Anthony's claim to be the oldest Christian monastery in the world and is regarded as the premier monastery of Egypt because of its association with the founder of monasticism. Father Anthony told me that in his opinion St. Anthony's is the older monastery. It was once the privilege of St. Anthony's to provide the head of the Coptic Church, a monk chosen for his simple and pious qualities. The more simple and pious he was, the less he desired to become Patriarch, with the result that it was the custom to take the elected dignitary bound in chains to Alexandria, weeping and bewailing his fate.

St. Anthony left the Nile Valley and sought the greater solitude of the mountains about the year 312 A.D. He found a cave, which is still to be seen, in the cliffs that rise steeply behind the monastery. When he arrived on this mountain, he discovered that he was not the only inhabitant. St. Paul (Anba Bulos) was already living in a cave twelve miles away, near the monastery which is now named after him. The two hermits met, but Paul, unlike Anthony, never laid down any rules of conduct for his fellow-hermits: he lived in complete isolation. When he died at a great age, about 340 A.D., he bequeathed his tunic of stitched palm leaves to St. Anthony. Sixteen years after Paul's death, St. Anthony, then one hundred and five years old, died in the company of two faithful disciples, Macarius and Amatas. It was Amatas who provided St. Athanasius with the material for his *Life of St. Anthony*, written about 356–7 A.D., and addressed to the "monks abroad" in Italy and Gaul.

St. Anthony, it seems, was not only the founder of monasticism but also psycho-analysis, for he believed in keeping a diary in which the most secret thoughts of the mind should be entered, on the principle, well known to modern exponents of this art, that it is better to expose them to the light of day. He was not a bookman, though he entered fully into the church disputes of his time and corresponded freely with those who sought his advice, among whom were the Emperor Constantine and his sons. He was not outwardly a morbid hermit; in fact, he seems to have greeted those who came to see him with courtesy and cheerfulness. It was difficult to arrange an interview with him unless it were on behalf of some suffering human being. Rich people tried vainly to lure him from his cell, and he always replied: "As a fish dies out of water, so a monk out of his cell."

His food was dry bread and water, and he fasted sometimes for four days together. He never ate until sunset, even on days when he was not fasting, and he never washed. He was not a tall, commanding figure, as he is generally pictured by artists: he was a small man, yet there was something about him which made men turn to look at him in a crowd. When he went to Alexandria at the request of St. Athanasius, to preach against the Arians, crowds followed him through the street shouting "The man of God!"

He was visited by periods of ecstasy which lasted sometimes for an hour. At such moments his disciples used to wait for him to come back to earth, and he himself believed that, to be perfect, prayer should be ecstatic. When he died, as I have mentioned elsewhere in this book, he charged his disciples to bury him secretly, and his tomb has never been discovered.

The monks believe that their monastery is dated from the death of St. Anthony in 356 A.D. There is even a legend that the Church of St. Anthony, the chief church in the monastery, was originally an oratory erected by the saint at the foot of the mountain.

I said good-night to Father Anthony and walked on the terrace before going to bed. An almost full moon hung over the desert. The monastery lay like a ship becalmed at sea, its white walls shining in an emptiness of earth and sky. I stayed some moments listening to a silence so deep that my ears invented sounds which were not there.

The lay-brother had placed at my bedside a brown ecclesiastical candle three feet in height. It burned with a great guttering of soft wax. No sooner had I snuffed it, than my eyes seemed to open again to the daylight.

14

The monastery contains two chief churches, each one roofed with twelve low white domes. These domes are all the same size and they lie in four rows, three domes to each row. One of these churches is dedicated to St. Anthony and the other to St. Marcus, who seems to have been a monk of the monastery long ago.

The Church of St. Anthony lies at the back of the main group of houses near the *kasr*, and is on the highest part of the ground. It is a large, square, limewashed building with a bell-tower at the west end. This slender campanile ends in a squat dome, and there is an open arch near the top in which you can see the bell hanging.

When Father Anthony and I approached the church door, I saw a row of slippers standing outside as if it were a mosque, and therefore I removed my shoes. I found that this was expected of me whenever I entered this church. We passed into a narthex which led into one of the strangest and most primitive churches I have seen, even in Coptic Egypt. It would not surprise me to learn that it is the oldest church in the country.

It is a small building about forty feet long and a little more than half that in width, and anyone unacquainted with ancient Coptic churches might imagine at first that he had entered some venerable stone farm-building which had been badly whitewashed and filled with a large assortment of objects: wooden screens, ikons, rugs and carpets. There is no artificial lighting in the church and few candles. Several ostrich eggs hung from the roof in the choir.

The nave is a single massive room of irregular shape, with a vaulted roof. It is divided from the tiny choir by a wall four feet high, with a gateless opening in the centre.

The choir stands under one of the domes, and the two pillars which divide the nave from the choir are primitive and rough, and may be mud with centuries of white-wash on them, or stone pillars embedded in plaster. Both nave and choir were covered to the steps of the haikal with carpets and camel rugs put down over reed matting, as the Moslems lay rugs in their mosques.

Two pieces of wood nailed across the length of the choir carried five crude and decayed ikons. The central ikon depicted the Blessed Virgin with the Infant Christ; the ikons on either side were of winged angels, and the two others showed mounted saints, one of whom was Mari Ghirgis—St. George. The sanctuary itself was an almost completely dark space under another dome, and was separated from the choir by doors formed of a number of wooden spindles rather like Jacobean chair-legs.

The whole church had once been covered with frescoes. The dome bore blackened traces of painting all over it and the south wall still carried a series of scratched and almost invisible saints, standing stiffly under a continuous arcade. But the most interesting features of the church were the ancient painted crosses visible in those places where the plaster had fallen away. These are obviously old, and are very beautiful. Each cross is about twelve inches high, Greek in shape, and is surrounded by a conventional wreath. Above the arms of the cross are the Greek letters I.C. X.C., and, beneath the arms, NIKA, the well-known Greek monogram meaning "Jesus Christ the Conqueror." Each cross is painted a deep shade of red, on a cream ground, and the wreath is green. The paint of these crosses is hard and glossy, and some of them lie at least a quarter of an inch beneath the repeated coats of whitewash and plaster.

I was anxious to pick away a small piece of plaster to see the lower letters more clearly, but no sooner had I touched it with my nail than a monk came up and said politely that the last time someone had attempted to do such a thing, a thunderbolt had killed him. These crosses are probably dedication crosses and prove how venerable the church is, for many a century has gone past since Greek influence was felt, or Greek spoken, in this desert.

An archway in the south wall leads to a windowless chapel called the Chapel of the Revelation. Its dome is decorated with frescoes showing the symbols of the Four Evangelists: the Lion for St. Mark, the Ox for St. Luke, the Eagle for St. John, and Man for St. Matthew. These creatures of the Apocalypse are shown holding out a crown. Father Anthony did not apparently connect them with the Evangelists.

"The Ox asks mercy of God for all animals," he said, "the Eagle asks mercy for all birds, the Lion asks mercy for all wild creatures, and Man for Mankind. So all creation begs mercy from God."

Near this church, and connected to it by a narrow dark passage, is a church dedicated to the Blessed Virgin. There was a huge pile of olives drying in the nave; an extraordinary sight, for wherever you see olives in Egypt you can be sure that they are a relic of Hellenistic agriculture.

We climbed steps and crossed a drawbridge to the *kasr*, where we entered the Chapel of St. Michael. Father Anthony produced a key, and, with one of his waggish laughs and a lifted forefinger, whispered that he was going to show me the Library. He seemed to imply that I might be another Curzon and that I must be good and not go off with the precious treasures. After wrestling for some time with a difficult lock, he opened the door of a room where hundreds of volumes stood entombed in wooden book-cases. What a depressingly uninviting sight a library can be when it belongs to people who rarely read books and take no interest in them.

The volumes were packed tightly together as if by the relentless hand of a charwoman, and books for which no place could be found in shelves were harshly tucked away on top and wedged in anywhere. They looked, indeed, as forbidding as a lawyer's library, and the air of the room was stuffy with paper and parchment which have been locked away for months on end. I should like to have had enough knowledge to have examined this collection for rare manuscripts.

With Father Anthony leading, I made a tour of the monastery. We went to a vaulted bakehouse where two lay-brothers were kneading dough and stoking a great furnace. I saw a corn mill worked by the monastery horse, a docile creature on whose muzzle the lively father implanted an affectionate kiss. An interesting feature of St. Anthony's is a large roofed cistern full of clear water that wells up from springs at the foot of the mountain. This endless supply of good water explains the luxuriant plantation of date palms, olives, and vines; probably the only vines in Egypt which have survived the Arab ban against them in the Eleventh Century.

A few Trappists from Mount Melleray in Ireland would transform the monastery garden in the course of a year, but that is not the Coptic attitude to life. Here, as in the Wadi Natrûn, I detected that loose organization as of a number of hermits gathered together rather than of a community inspired by one ideal. I like to think that this is not due to slackness and laziness, but to the individualism which has always inspired Egyptian monasticism. While it would drive me, or any man from the West, mad to live in such an atmosphere, it is natural for these monks to give all their energies to long and exhausting vigils in church, and to live so sparely that they literally have no energy left for manual labour.

The monks get their supplies from a town called Bûsh, on the Nile. Camel caravans deliver them every two or three months, and the journey takes four or five days.

The monks are inspired by the lives of the remote hermits and monks of the Fourth Century, and they do not realize, or wish to realize, that any better way of life could be devised than that laid down in ancient times. All monks who enter the monastery swear to renounce every possession, never to marry, and to forget all ties of relationship. They swear to eat no meat and drink no wine, to live a life of fasting and prayer and wear only their monkish habits, never changing them. They must also say the canonical hours and make a stated number of prostrations every day, falling flat upon the earth and making the sign of the Cross as they rise.

I asked Father Anthony how many of them wore the *askîm*, and he appeared astonished that I should have heard of this. Many, he replied, wore it. He said, as I had already heard at Dêr Anba Macarius, that monks of the *askîm* are vowed to longer fasts and more exhausting prostrations.

Huddled against the eastern wall of the monastery is the twelve domed Church of St. Marcus, whose bones rest there. It is a large white building and contains his tomb.

15

I found it impossible to sleep, and at half-past two I decided to get up. Moonlight was pouring through the bars of the window. I rose furtively, for the monastery was lying dark and silent, and went out. It was a wonderful night. I could see every house, every palm tree, standing in clear light. I walked up the street towards the Church of St. Anthony and was astonished to see rows of slippers outside the door. The monks were inside at this unearthly hour! How easy it is to misjudge these Coptic monks as you see them strolling about in the day-time. I tiptoed inside and saw a sight I shall never forget.

The church was lit only by a few pricks of light in the choir, where wicks floated in olive oil. The building was full of dark, murmuring figures. Some leaned against the wall, their eyes shut, their lips moving in prayer; others stood in the nave, leaning on the T-shaped staves which they carry to their interminable offices; a few knelt on the ground, bending forward in prostration. Most of them had covered their shoulders with a wrap, because the night was chilly. They did not notice me. They were all lost in prayer, and here again I noticed that it was all individual prayer: they were not praying together like monks of the West: they were so many individual hermits addressing their own prayers, in their own way, to God.

Curious pallid men, lost to the world, dreaming only of finding their own paths to heaven, denying themselves in this world in order to reap the reward of a life to come: and as I watched them, I knew that I was seeing the devotions described by Palladius and Pachomius so many centuries ago. No matter what we may think of such an ideal, so different from the vigorous missionary ideal of the West, we cannot withhold from these Egyptians the credit which must be accorded to a triumph of individual conscience. Who, travelling across this desert by the light of the moon and seeing the walls of this retreat at the foot of the mountain, could imagine this scene going on behind them at half-past two in the morning? Who, having blundered by chance upon this silent nightly gathering in the desert church, could ever find it in his heart to scoff at these fellow-Christians?

A dark figure rose in the choir and prayed aloud. Responses came from the shadows. The voice went on and I heard the language of ancient Egypt. He was praying in Coptic, the tongue of St. Anthony, the tongue of Ptolemy, the tongue of Pharaoh himself.

was the pillow of St. Anthony. He told me that once a year all the monks from the monastery climb the mountain in solemn procession, with tapers lighted and swinging thurible, and celebrate the Korbân in the place where the saint lived and died.

I asked if he had ever read of the temptations of St. Anthony. He had done so, and I thought that probably in twenty years' time it might be possible to discuss them with him. He knew, exactly as we know it in the West, the story of St. Anthony's meeting with St. Paul: how one day when the saint was thinking that surely no man had ever served God for so long, and in such solitude, he heard a voice say: "There is one holier than thou, for Paul the hermit has served God in solitude and penance for ninety years." St. Anthony took his T-shaped staff and set off to find St. Paul. He discovered him in a cave in the mountains and the two saints embraced. They became friends and were together when St. Paul felt death approaching. Wishing to spare St. Anthony the pain of watching his death, he sent him on an errand, and when St. Anthony returned to his friend, he saw the soul of St. Paul ascending through the high air, white as driven snow, and round about him a great company of saints and angels rising with him into Paradise. St. Anthony then wrapped the body of his friend in a cloak and buried him. He returned to his own cave and lived there until he too was called to join the company of God's elect.

We descended the mountain and returned to the monastery.

"Are you sure," I said, "that you will never regret entering this place?"

And no sooner had I said it than I felt how strangely like an utterance of Satan it was. It was just the sort of sly thing the devil would have said.

The young man looked at me with the uncompromising fixity of a small child.

"Never," he replied. "I am even now longing for the time

when I shall go to my cell and pray."

I thought that Sinai was like a clear page of illuminated Byzantine manuscript which a man could read and understand,
but this queer place in the desert was shrouded in an impalpable
mist, almost like the mist of legend, and out of it gazed no emperors and no pilgrims and no kings, but pale, bearded men of
long ago, kneeling to God upon the mountains of the world.

17

We were away early in the morning. The grave, courteous
kummus, the lively Father Anthony, and the young lay-
brother came down to the gate to see the cars go out into the
desert. They waved to us for a time, then a rise of ground hid
the monastery from sight.

We crossed the Arabian Desert to the Nile at El Wasta, a
journey of eighty miles. Here we struck the high embankments
and the flying black dust of Egypt, and went on through a ribbon of land over-populated with donkeys, water-buffaloes,
and camels, until the lights of Cairo dawned on us. Except that
the desert track was as good as desert tracks can ever be, I remember only one thing about that journey. We were in the
middle of the desert, plodding along hour after hour and seeing nothing but the burning ridge ahead, when suddenly about
thirty camels crossed the horizon, and eventually our ways met.

It was a caravan with Bedouin walking beside it with sticks.
We thought that it must be the monastery caravan moving
eastward from Bûsh, and it occurred to us that it would be
amusing to send back something to Father Anthony, some
message or some little gift, that would make him go into one
of his peals of laughter. We drove the cars up and spoke to the
Bedouin.

"Are you going to the monastery?" asked Mr. Vallinis in
Arabic.

A COPTIC MONK WITH PRAYER-STAFF, DÊR ANBA ANTONIÛS

The leader of the caravan, a long, lean man, with brown feet in toe-thong sandals similar to those found in the tomb of Tut-ankh-Amûn, came up and looked at us, then looked away.

"No," he replied, addressing the desert, "we are taking nothing to the Christians. We are for the Bedouin."

He shouted to the camels and ran on waving his stick.

I said good-bye that night to Mr. Vallinis and Yûsuf, two good companions, one an Ulysses, the other an artist whose dream it is to make the desert blossom like the Ritz. And in the morning I said farewell to Egypt and caught a boat to Europe.

CHAPTER X

I end my journey in Rome, where I visit the places associated with the Apostles, and descend into the catacombs. I attend a solemn ceremony above the tomb of St. Peter, and go out to see the ruins of Ostia.

§ I

FACING the Piazza di San Pietro in Rome is a small café that survives in the roadway, its precarious territory marked out by trees in green tubs.

I have sat there many a time drinking coffee or San Pellegrino faintly flavoured with the dust raised by passing omnibuses and cabs, by the feet of monks, friars, nuns, monsignori, pilgrims, and ordinary tourists like myself. I have an affection for this modest café, and when it vanishes in some street improvement scheme, as all one's favourite landmarks must if one lives long enough, Rome for me will have lost one of those sentimental anchorages which make us say that we love cities. No one could really love a city: what we really love are the appointments with ourselves which we keep at their street corners.

The first thing I did when I found myself in Rome again was to walk to the Tiber and make my way across the Pont San Angelo to the little café in the Piazza Rusticucci. With a glow of satisfaction I saw that nothing had altered: it was as dusty and as much in the road as ever; the same little tables were dotted about and apparently the same waiter was flicking at invisible flies with a napkin. Sitting there, I looked straight out to the most superb open space in the world. In the centre rose that obelisk of Aswân granite which witnessed the death of St. Peter, on either side were the fountains, blowing whitely

394

like the plumes of a Life-guard's helmet, and in the background rose St. Peter's, touched by the sunlight of early morning.

The whole square was alive, for it was Holy Week. Every tram-car and omnibus and car that drove up to the end of the piazza let loose a crowd of pilgrims. Some were independent and others were in charge of the village priest. The good man would emerge, earnestly grasping an umbrella, and prudently feeling the ground from the high step of the bus with the toe of an elastic-sided boot; then, safely on terra firma, he would marshal his chattering flock, gaze round in search of a missing pilgrim, and eventually march off across the mighty square to become a gesticulating dot on the vastness of the distant steps. There were nuns in starched coifs who exhibited remarkable organizing ability in marshalling crowds of small, agile girls; there were numbers of square-faced, Teutonic-looking Poles (for a Polish martyr was to be canonized on Easter Sunday), and there were others whose nationality was baffling. They all marched across the square, where the shadow of the obelisk lay in a black bar like the pointer of a sun-dial; and mounting the long flight of steps, they disappeared into the basilica.

I sat there watching them, thinking that they are the most continuous procession in the history of Mankind: they are the end of a procession that I had encountered in deserts and mountains of the east, beside old rivers of the ancient world, and in cities now fallen into dust: the great procession of Christian pilgrims which has been moving over the world for nineteen centuries. The city of Resafa, now lying silent and dead under the Syrian stars, once echoed to their prayers; the ancient shrine of St. Mena in the sands of Mareotis once gave them precious water in little oval flasks; the God-trodden mountain of Sinai has known them; and in the awful fastnesses of the Egyptian desert they have knelt side by side with the saints.

It was like watching a river still flowing on, a river that, like the Nile, dries up here and there or changes its bed, but never ceases to find its way to the sea. And I thought that could one awaken from his long sleep a primitive Christian of Antioch, Jerusalem, or Alexandria, this procession up the steps of St. Peter's would probably be to him the one entirely comprehensible feature of modern Rome.

2

All Christian pilgrimages must end in Rome, because only in Rome is it possible to descend steps into the depths of the earth and stand in buildings whose walls may have echoed to the voices of St. Peter and St. Paul.

Alone of all the ancient patriarchates of the once Universal Church, Rome has preserved unbroken contact with the Apostolic Age. Even Fifth Century Christians, in an age before the Islamic invasions, when all their holy sites were intact, looked with reverence upon Rome for this very reason. The learned Theodoret, Bishop of Cyrrhus, in Syria, wrote to St. Leo about 450 A.D., saying:

"Your city possesses the bodies of Peter and Paul, the fathers of us all, our masters in the faith, whose tombs illumine the hearts of the faithful. These blessed two, inspired by God, have arisen in the East, and spread on all sides their rays: but it is in the West they have found their setting, it is from the West that they illumine the world. It is they who have given to your seat an incomparable glory: they are the most precious of your possessions."

And one of the wonders of the world, which cannot perhaps be fully appreciated by those who have not travelled the stricken battlefields of Eastern Christendom, is that the shrines of Rome, which were the goal of the earliest pilgrimages, are still being visited to this day.

At the outset of my journey, while I was on the road to Kala'ât Sim'ân, my thoughts had turned, not to the mediæval pilgrim, but to his distant predecessor, the Greek or Roman pilgrim, who set out while the Roman Empire was yet unfallen to follow in the steps of Jesus and to visit the places associated with His holy Apostles.

Pilgrimage began within the life-time of those who had known Christ and the Apostles. St. Paula and St. Eustochium, who lived in Bethlehem in the Fourth Century, state that Christians, anxious to see for themselves the scenes of the Crucifixion and the Ascension, came to the Holy Land from the earliest days of the Primitive Church. Among the first recorded pilgrims was the great Origen, who was born in Alexandria about 185 A.D. He visited Jerusalem about 238 A.D. to "seek after the footsteps of Jesus and His disciples and prophets." This was about a century before St. Helena uncovered the site of the Holy Sepulchre which was then occupied by a temple which the Emperor Hadrian had built, possibly to stamp out the sacred associations of the site. He had also rebuilt the city of Jerusalem as a Roman city.

Origen could not have seen Calvary or the tomb of Christ, because they were not uncovered until about 335 A.D., but he was shown a building in which the piety of all early pilgrims was centred until later times. This was the Cœnaculum, the House of the Last Supper. It lay, as the Gospel narrative infers, just outside the wall of the city, and thus escaped the destruction under Titus. The upper chamber, the meeting-place of the Apostles after the Resurrection and the scene of Pentecost, was, says St. Epiphanius, a small church as early as 135 A.D., the date when Hadrian transformed Jerusalem into a Roman city. Thus the grandfathers of the Christians who were worshipping in this church in the time of Hadrian might have been present at the Crucifixion. In a country where stone is the common building material, it is possible that the Cœnaculum visited by Origen and the other early pilgrims was actually the house of Mary, mother of Mark, and not a later building erected on the same site. In later ages a more impressive church was built there and was standing when the Moslems captured Jerusalem. They turned it into a mosque, and as a mosque it exists to-day.

Another of the earliest holy places in Christendom was the Cave of the Nativity at Bethlehem. Origen saw it a hundred years before Constantine's basilica, which stands over it to-day, was erected. Writing of this cave, Origen says: "Everyone in the country knows it, and the pagans will tell again and again to him who cares to hear it, that in the said cavern was born a certain Jesus whom the Christians admire and adore."

The full tide of pilgrimage set in after St. Helena had made her journey to Jerusalem in 335 A.D. and had uncovered the sites of the Crucifixion and the Nativity, and had built churches there. Pilgrims now converged on the Holy Land from all parts of the world, and holy sites became multiplied in a not always satisfactory manner. The Fathers of the Church were in two minds on the question of pilgrimage. Some advocated it as an aid to piety; others condemned it, dwelling on the sins of the cities through which the pilgrims were obliged to pass. In 393 A.D. St. Jerome wrote to dissuade a pilgrim, saying that "access to the courts of heaven is as easy from Britain as from Jerusalem, for the kingdom of God is within you."

Pilgrimage to Rome began as early as pilgrimage to the Holy Land. All over the world Christians were aware that the Church in Rome treasured intimate memories of St. Peter and St. Paul, which it prized above all its possessions. There were secret meeting-places in Rome which were hallowed by memories of the Apostles in times when the Church was persecuted, and in the catacombs outside the city the Christians of the First Century had a wonderful record of their earliest history. Fully a century before St. Peter's was built, pilgrims went to Rome to pray beside the Apostle's tomb, which was to be found beside the road on the Vatican Mount, and beside the tomb of St. Paul on the Ostian Way. The great churches which now stand in these two places are like an answer to their prayers; for Christians had knelt there in times when there was no vault above them but that of the open sky.

It was often dangerous to be found at the tomb of St. Peter. The *Acts of St. Sebastian* mention that St. Zoë, surprised on her knees at the tomb, was arrested and led away to martyrdom. Nevertheless, even at this remote period, when the Church was living furtively in the catacombs, pilgrims came secretly to Rome to pray with the faithful and to draw strength from the corporate memory of the Church. St. Paternus was there in 252 A.D.; St. Marcius travelled from Persia with his wife and sons in 269 A.D.; and St. Maurus came from Africa in 284 A.D.

There was no St. Peter's and no St. Paul's, no St. John Lateran, and no Vatican. What, then, did these pilgrims see? They saw the tombs of the two Apostles, and certainly the catacomb of St. Callixtus, in which Christians at that time prayed and celebrated the Mass, and no doubt they saw also the buildings which became the churches of St. Pudenziana, St. Clement, and St. Prisca. All these places are to be seen to-day. They have been handed down from Christians of the First Century through all the adventures and disasters which the early Church suffered in its precious infancy and youth. Nowhere else in the world is there such a satisfying and undeniable continuity with a remote past. It is that continuity which must cause every Christian to gaze with awe and reverence upon the ecclesiastical antiquities of Rome.

3

I entered St. Peter's, where the tomb of the Apostle stands beneath Bernini's splendid canopy at the western end of the basilica.

Every time I enter this church, I am amazed by its size and by what Goethe called the ability of art as well as nature to set aside every standard of measurement. Even Karnak is not so daring an exercise in size as St. Peter's; but I would willingly forego the sight of so much magnificence for one glimpse of old St. Peter's, with its lost mosaics and its nave of columns.

Kneeling pilgrims surrounded the marble balustrade of the Confession. Each one gazed downward, past the curving marble steps and the praying statue of Pius VI, to the bronze doors leading to the sepulchral crypt in which lie the bodies of St. Peter and the early Popes. The relics that are within have never been disturbed. A great church was built over them in the Fourth Century. It was pulled down in the Sixteenth and an even larger church was erected; and still the hallowed bones lay untouched in the secrecy of their rocky sepulchre, while mountains of rare marble were piled above them.

When the pilgrim has made his devout prayers in this sacred place, it is perhaps right that he should remember the faithful ones who long ago took up the bodies of the martyrs and gave them burial, thus handing them down through the centuries as the sacred possession of the Church.

The Vatican is believed to take its name from the Latin word *vates*, a prophet or soothsayer, for on Mount Vaticanus once stood an Etruscan oracle which told the future. In the First Century, the Emperor Caligula built a race-course there and imported from Egypt the obelisk, which now stands in the middle of the Piazza di San Pietro, to mark the centre of the *spina*, the narrow central platform around which the horses and the chariots turned in their courses. When Nero became emperor, he chose this race-course as the scene of his hideous tortures of the Saints, when Christians steeped in tar were burned as torches in the arena. There, probably in the year 67 A.D., St. Peter was crucified.

On the night of St. Peter's death, those who loved him presented themselves before the civil authorities and made the same request that Joseph of Arimathea made to Pilate for the body of our Lord. We can be certain that among them were St. Linus, St. Anacletus, and St. Clement, the three immediate successors to the pastorship of the infant Church. Their request was one that was never at this period refused. It was the Roman law that when sentence of death had been carried out, the bodies of those put to death must be handed over to the relatives.

In the darkness of that night a scene must have occurred in Rome which reproduced in nearly every detail the scene in Jerusalem on the night of the Crucifixion. Like his Master, St. Peter was taken from the Cross and swathed in fine linen; he was then placed with sweet-smelling herbs and spices in a sepulchre hewn from the rock. This tomb, which is now beneath the high altar of St. Peter's, was, in the year 67 A.D., an open cemetery on the side of the Via Cornelia. On the left of this road rose the north walls of the Circus; on the right, in the very shadow of them, was this cemetery, which later excavation has proved to be full of pagan and early Christian burials. Possibly a member of the Church offered his own tomb, as St. Joseph offered his for the body of Jesus. And in this place St. Peter was buried.

The first shrine was erected over the grave of the Apostle by St. Anacletus, who had been ordained a presbyter by St. Peter and became the third Bishop of Rome. This shrine was the usual *cella memoriæ*, and was no doubt above ground, clearly visible to everyone who passed along the Via Cornelia. It was probably made by carrying the walls of the tomb upward and forming a chamber above. Below this, and round the grave of the Apostle, were buried the Popes for the first two centuries, from St. Linus, who succeeded St. Peter, to St. Victor, who reigned probably from 189 until 199 A.D.

When the Emperor Constantine became Christian and the persecutions came to an end, he granted the request of Pope

Sylvester that a great church might be built above the ancient Papal cemetery in the Via Cornelia. According to the custom of the time, the original grave was not touched and old St. Peter's was built round it in such a way that the tomb lay beneath the high altar. Constantine used the north wall of the old Roman Circus of Nero as the foundation for the south wall of his basilica, so that the south side of old St. Peter's occupied nearly the whole northern portion of the Circus from whose tiers of seats the Roman crowds had watched the burning and crucifixion of the martyrs over two and a half centuries before.

The early pilgrims entered a church very different from the present St. Peter's. Five and thirty steps, which pilgrims ascended on their knees, led to the façade of the entrance court, or atrium, a large marble court open to the sky and surrounded by cloisters. In the centre of this court marble columns upheld a bronze canopy beneath which was a colossal gilded pine cone that gushed water, an ablution fountain for the use of those about to enter the church.

Crossing this court in the sunlight, the pilgrims passed into a vast, dim church of pillars, where seven hundred lights burned day and night before fifty-two altars and chapels. The walls and arches glowed with gold mosaic, and the floor was of white marble taken from Nero's Circus. Towards the west end of the church twisted columns upheld a canopy; beneath this lay the tomb of St. Peter. The church ended in a western apse and a wide, semi-circular tribune with a central throne for the Pope, and on the arch of the tribune was the famous mosaic, now lost, showing the Emperor Constantine on his knees, offering a model of his church to the Saviour.

Had we visited old St. Peter's at the time of the Saxon pilgrimages, we should have knelt at the Confession as pilgrims do to-day, but we might have been able to see the tomb of the Apostle. It was the custom for pilgrims to lower kerchiefs or other small objects on the end of a stick kept there for the purpose, so that they might be hallowed by contact with the sarcophagus of St. Peter. There was a deacon of Tours called Agiulphus, who visited the tomb about the year 600 A.D., and on his return gave a detailed description which St. Gregory of Tours quoted in *De Gloria Martyrum:*

"St. Peter is buried in a church called from ancient times the Vatican," he wrote. "His sepulchre, which is placed under the altar, is very rarely entered. However, if anyone desires to pray, the gates by which the place is fenced are opened, and he goes in above the sepulchre and then, having opened a little window, puts his head within, and makes request according to his needs. Nor is the result delayed, if only the petition is a just one."

The deacon also refers to the practice of lowering cloths into the tomb, and this is also mentioned by certain bishops who, during the reign of St. Hormisdas, asked that cloths might be laid actually upon the tomb of the Apostle. St. Gregory the Great also alludes to the custom, in a letter replying to the innocently audacious request of the Empress Constantina for the head of St. Paul. "I am distressed that I neither can nor dare do what you enjoin," wrote St. Gregory, "for the bodies of the Apostles Peter and Paul glitter with so great miracles and terrors in their churches, that one cannot even go to pray there without great fear. Moreover, let my most tranquil lady know that it is not the custom of the Romans, when they give relics of saints, to presume to touch any part of the body; but only a cloth is put into a box and placed near the most sacred bodies of the saints. . . ."

The custom survives to this day. Behind the bronze doors of the Confession is a niche where the *pallia*, which the Pope sends to newly consecrated archbishops, are kept in a gold casket. The proper description of a *pallium—pallium de corpore sancti Petri—*"from the body of St. Peter"—preserves the early meaning of this custom. The *pallium* is a strip of white lamb's

wool which is worn round the neck, over the chasuble, by archbishops on certain occasions, and is always buried with them.
It is assumed that the gift of a *pallium* represents the custom of
handing the mantle of a dead teacher to his disciples; and in
Egypt it was the custom for the new Patriarch to take the *pallium* from the dead body of his predecessor and place it round
his own neck, an act which constituted succession to the headship of the Egyptian Church.

It will be seen from the references I have given that in remote
times it was possible to approach, and possibly to see, the tomb
of the Apostle in old St. Peter's. It is generally believed that the
tomb was walled up during the barbarian invasions in order to
protect it from the Goths, the Vandals, and the Saracens, and
it has not been seen since that distant time, except by chance
during the rebuilding of the basilica in the year 1594.

Constantine's church began to show signs of age long before
the Sixteenth Century. Its wooden roof was eaten by rats and
the south wall, which had been built on the wall of Nero's Circus, began to subside. It was therefore decided to erect a new
church. In the year 1594, while the architect, Giacomo della
Porta, was working above the tomb of St. Peter, the ground
gave way and he was able to see into the vault, which thus became visible for the first time for about eight hundred years.
Pope Clement VIII was instantly informed, and calling three
cardinals, Bellarmine, Antoniano, and Sfondrato, he went at
once into the basilica. While the architect held a torch above
an opening in the tomb, the Pope and the three Cardinals
looked down and saw the gold cross, as high as a man, which
Constantine and Helena had placed on the tomb of the Apostle
in the year 326 A.D. It is said that by the light of the torch they
were able to make out the legend: *Constantinus Augustus et
Helena Augusta hanc domum regalem simile fulgori coruscans
aula circumdat*—"Constantine Augustus and Helena Augusta
surround this royal dwelling with a court shining with like

splendour." One account says that the Pope ordered the opening to be securely sealed with cement in his presence; another states that he considered the possibility of exposing the crypt to view as in primitive times, but was opposed everywhere by the superstition that any alteration to the tomb of St. Peter would be followed by terrible misfortunes.

This same superstition was roused so violently thirty-two years later that it spread beyond the Vatican to every corner of Rome. The erection of Bernini's heavy canopy had made it necessary to find firmer foundations for the four pillars, and in June, 1626, when Bernini began to excavate in the crypt, he discovered human remains almost at once. A superstitious crisis was caused by the deaths, one after the other, of several men closely associated with the work, and when Pope Urban VIII became indisposed, Rome said that the reconstructions should cease. It was the Pope's duty—not an easy one in the face of such general superstition—to decide whether to abandon the erection of the canopy, or to continue with the work; and he, "since he knew his intention to be most upright and that the action itself had no other object than the honour and glory of God," decided with courage to continue the excavations. These proved that beneath the high altar of St. Peter's, and grouped round the body of the Apostle, are layers of tombs in which lie not only the skeletons of martyrs, but bones of early date which bear the signs of fire. Fortunately a detailed account of these discoveries was written at the time by R. Urbaldi, a canon of St. Peter's, and lay hidden away in the Vatican archives until Professor Armellini discovered it in 1891.

"Two of the principal coffins were uncovered," wrote Urbaldi, "and each of them was seen to contain two bodies. The shapes and forms could be distinguished, and also that their heads were towards the altar. They were clothed with long robes down to the heels, dark and almost black with age, and were swathed with bandages like infants; the bandages also passing over the head. These bodies were placed side by side with the utmost care. Both these and all the others in the coffins, as soon as they were touched and moved, were resolved into dust, and except some portions of clothing, nothing resisted the touch. It was not possible to form any particular or individual idea of either the names or size of these bodies, but the tradition is very clear and certain that close to the body of St. Peter there were buried those first patriarchs and fathers of our Church, whose blood was the seed of this holy and great republic. . . ."

Such quantities of remains were discovered as the work went on that they were reverently reinterred in coffins of cypress wood as each excavation was completed, places being found for them as near as possible to those which they had occupied so many centuries before.

"They began to excavate for the second foundation opposite the first, in front of the confession," continues Urbaldi. "Not more than three or four feet down there was discovered at the side a large coffin made of great slabs of marble, but since this did not interfere much with the site needed for the foundation, it was thought sufficient only to cut it back. When its end had been cut off they were surprised to see within ashes with many bones, all adhering together and half burned. These brought back to mind the famous fire in the time of Nero, three years before St. Peter's martyrdom, when the Christians, being falsely accused of causing the fire, and pronounced guilty of the crime, afforded in the Circus of the Gardens of Nero, which were situated just here on the Vatican Hill, the first spectacles of martyrdom."

During the digging of the fourth foundation, on the Gospel side of the altar, a tomb was found which contained two bodies.

"Their faces could be distinguished and their clothing seemed large and full and reaching to the feet. In one could be seen the shape of the vestments open over the shoulders, and in both the fine texture of the albs, which were worked for a space of two fingers from the bottom with a small arabesque pattern. The undergarments were large and full, and of monastic shape, dark and almost black in colour. Everything was almost dust except only the hair, which was long and hanging, of a chestnut colour, but straight, looking as if it had been recently cut. Some few bones were also found preserved in a box apart. Many conjectured these to be two of the first Popes, who were Greeks."

When a plan of the excavations was made, it was seen that the saints had been buried like spokes in a wheel, pointing towards a central place which contained the sarcophagus of St. Peter. "These bodies surrounded St. Peter," wrote Urbaldi, "just as they would have done when living at a synod or council."

Not the least of the miracles is that Rome, although more than once given over to pillage, should still retain what St. Jerome called "her coronet of martyrs."

4

I went down into the crypt, which is one of the most solemn places in Rome. If solemnity implies repose, the church above, with its stupendous vistas and its population of baroque angels and more than life-size popes, could never be called solemn. You might call it triumphant or exultant, or even militant. Every monument leans forward in action, surrounded by folds of swirling drapery, and every cupid bursts with health and faith.

But when you leave behind all this superb vitality, this almost riotous sacredness, and take the little winding staircase that leads beneath the church, you come into a silent place of shadows, of old walls, of low, vaulted ceilings where plain electric-light globes cast a faint glow in the darkness. Big stone coffins lie here and there, and, approaching them, you read the name of dead Pontiffs—Nicholas I, who died in 867, and Calixtus III, who died in 1458. In a dark corner are three plain tombs lying against the wall, with the plaster peeling and cracking; cheap plaster that is veined to look like marble. And you read that here repose the bodies of Francis James Stuart, "King James IV" of England; Charles Edward Stuart, "King Charles III"; and Henry, Cardinal York, "King Henry IX." The last Stuarts lie in the plainest tombs in the crypt, but rich in their nearness to the grave of St. Peter. Their beautiful memorial by Canova, in the church above, was placed there, not by those who would have drawn the sword for them, but by George IV; and while it reflects most creditably upon George IV, how its magnanimity underlines the bitter tragedy of the last of this brilliant, unhappy, and attractive line of kings.

While I was walking round this solemn vault, whose roof you can touch with a stick, I came across a red granite sarcophagus that contains the body of the only Englishman who ever sat in the chair of St. Peter. He was Nicholas Breakspear, who reigned from 1154 to 1159 as Pope Adrian IV. He was a poor lad, born at Langley, near St. Albans, whose father left him destitute. Nicholas begged his way to France, and, after studying at Paris, became a servant in the house of the canons regular of St. Rufus, near Valence. As time went on, his leadership, his piety, and his learning gained him admission to the order, and eventually he was made abbot. His discipline was so strict that certain of the canons complained to Pope Eugenius III, which served merely to bring to notice the stern virtues of the abbot, for the Pope marked him down for a higher position. He soon became Cardinal of Albano and was sent to Scandinavia, where he was so successful in strengthening the relations between the Holy See and the northern kingdoms that he was called the Apostle of the North.

His reign as Pope was one continuous battle with rebellion and an endless struggle against the ambition of Frederick Barbarossa. When Barbarossa came to Rome to be crowned Emperor, the Pope rode out to meet him at Nepi; but Barbarossa did not come forward, as he should have done, to take the bridle of the Pope's mule and help him to dismount, whereupon Adrian refused him the kiss of peace. The struggle between Barbarossa's pride and Adrian's firmness continued for several days, and ended only when Barbarossa consented to lead the Pope's mule by the bridle in front of the German army. The Pope then greeted him with the kiss of peace and they proceeded towards Rome. Six years of constant trouble followed, and Adrian died just as he was preparing to excommunicate Barbarossa. A more remarkable career could hardly be imagined than that of the poor English boy who begged his way from St. Albans and ended by sitting in the chair of St. Peter.

I noticed that the few visitors who were wandering round the crypt never looked at the floor, which is one of the most interesting and least thought of memorials in Rome. It is the pavement of Constantine's basilica. The ancient stones are worn and cracked, and it was on this level, if not actually on these stones, that our Saxon kings, that Charlemagne himself, and all the pilgrims of the Middle Ages, knelt in homage.

5

Rome is still a small city from whose streets you can quickly escape into the country. You pass out of the walls and after a mile or two find yourself travelling along country roads, with sienna-coloured houses and old farms lying here and there. Cypress trees stand in solemn groups and flowers grow from the hot earth. When the sun passes behind a bank of cloud, a swift shadow moves over peaceful distances enclosed by lines of faintly blue hills.

I drove out one afternoon to the Abbey of Tre Fontana, which is built over the traditional place of St. Paul's martyrdom. There has never been any doubt that St. Paul was be-

headed "at the third mile-stone" along the Ostian Way. No
other site has ever challenged the accuracy of this tradition. In
the reign of Nero the place was called Aquæ Salviæ—the Salvian
Springs. At a later time the picturesque legend sprang up that as
the Apostle's head struck the earth, it bounced three times and
at every meeting with the earth a stream of water gushed forth.

Passing the superb basilica of St. Paul's-Without-the-Wall,
where the Apostle's headless body is buried, I followed the Via
Laurentina, which runs across a stretch of country near a bend
in the Tiber. A narrow country lane led off the main road to
the left, and this ended at a tall archway over which bougainvillæa drooped in purple cascades. Eucalyptus trees, which
grow everywhere, prove what a malarial swamp this place must
have been at no distant date. Visitors who went there in the
early part of the last century speak of it as a horrible, fever-
ridden spot, deserted in summer except for a few pale monks,
listless and shivering in the quagmire. The anopheles mosquito
was so numerous at one time that the place became uninhabit-
able, and therefore Pope Pius IX gave it in 1865 to those storm
troops of agriculture, the Trappists.

Those grim, hard-working, silent men took the place over
and, with the help of prison labour, turned it into a semi-tropical
paradise. They have drained the swamps, planted the right kind
of trees, and the result is that you pass beneath the archway into
something like a botanical garden. Unfair as it was, I could not
help comparing this energetic example of monasticism with
the listlessness of the Egyptian monks, who would have died
steadily year after year in a place like this. It would never occur to them to drain it and make it habitable. God put the
mosquitoes there, they would argue, so why bother about it?
But they would never have abandoned the site, even though to
live there meant certain fever and death.

I walked under the eucalyptus trees, looking for someone to
show the churches to me, but the place appeared deserted.

There are three churches close together in the garden, one of them a circular baroque building on a slightly higher level to the right. The word "Silentio" was written everywhere, but there was no need for it: the only sound was the cooing of ring-doves in cages among the tall dark trees. Turning a corner I came upon a human being, a Trappist monk who was digging in the soil with a kind of violence. I felt that every spadeful was doing his soul good. He thrust the spade into the earth as if he were striking it into the heart of Satan, and he lifted it and shot the soil away as if he were shovelling sin. The sweat stood on his head and he gave himself no rest.

I wanted to talk to him, but there was a notice with "Silentio" within a few yards of him. I remembered Robert Louis Stevenson's disastrous attempt to talk to a Trappist monk, and thought it better not to risk a mutual embarrassment. Still, in the hope that he might be temporarily released from his vow of silence, I lingered near watching him, wondering why he worked with such unbecoming zeal. He turned and saw me, and with a slightly resentful expression continued to dig with fury. He was quite a young monk, and his face would have pleased El Greco.

I went into one of the three churches, which astonished me because it was that rare thing in Rome, an almost Gothic building. I stood in a long, bare, white nave that might have come from France. While I was wondering in whose honour this church was built, an elderly French Trappist, evidently one whose duty it is to show visitors round, came up and told me that it was the church of St. Vincent and St. Anastasius. He told me the story of St. Vincent.

"He was a deacon of Saragossa, in Spain," he said, "and was tortured and slain under Dacian during the persecution of Diocletian in 304 A.D. The Christians gathered his remains and eventually buried him in the cathedral at Valencia. In the Eighth Century, when the Christians of Valencia were forced to fly from the Moors, they took up the relics of St. Vincent and went by sea to a cape, now called Cape St. Vincent, where they buried his relics. In the Twelfth Century the relics were taken up from Cape St. Vincent and placed in the cathedral at Lisbon.

"Who was St. Anastasius? He was a Persian who became a monk at Jerusalem. One day he made a journey to his native land, and was martyred there by the Persians in 628 A.D."

When we came out of the church, we saw the young monk still digging.

"Why does he dig with such zeal?" I asked.

"It is always so with him," replied the monk softly. "He is like that."

"He looks as if he were digging a grave against time."

"That may be so," he replied. "Now, this is the Church of Santa Maria Scala Cœli—the 'Ladder of Heaven.' You think it is a strange name for a church? Yes; perhaps it is a strange name. But when I tell you the reason for it, I think you will say it is a beautiful name. Once when St. Bernard was saying Mass here, he had a vision of a ladder which rested on this church and went up into heaven. And as he looked, he saw souls ascending the ladder with white angels leading them upward, and he knew that these were the souls of those who had been released from Purgatory by his prayers. That is why we call the church by that name. You must now come and see the church of San Paolo alle Tre Fontane. . . ."

We climbed down the little hill and entered the church which is built over the Salvian Springs. It is not a beautiful church, but it is an unusual one. Three altars stand in a row, and beneath each altar is one of the springs. You can hear the water bubbling and gurgling beneath the marble. Steps lead down to one of the springs, where water can be seen moving darkly out of the earth. The monk told me that in the Sixteenth Century the church was built by Giacomo della Porta on the

MONASTERY OF THE THREE FOUNTAINS, ROME

site of an ancient church.

The Trappists made a number of discoveries when they put Tre Fontane in order, but perhaps the most remarkable was the finding of coins of the time of Nero among a number of almost fossilized pine-cones. As soon as these were discovered, it was remembered that in the Greek apocryphal Acts it is stated that St. Paul was executed beneath a stone pine.

The monk departed to lead a group of stolid Polish peasants through the churches, and I went out into the garden, where a strong smell of eucalyptus led me to a small building not far from the gate. Here I found a little shop full of chocolate, which the monks make, and also stacked with flasks and bottles of "Liquore Eucaliptina," a yellow liqueur made by the Trappists from eucalyptus pods. I bought a bottle of this, but I discovered the pleasure of drinking the liqueur was slightly marred by the memories it so vividly suggested of lying in bed suffering from a bad cold. Still it was worth buying for the delightful little decorative label on each bottle, carefully painted in blue and red by some Trappist father whose heart was in the library with the illuminated manuscripts.

Another of the products of Tre Fontane are rosaries of a substantial kind, made from eucalyptus pods strung together, each bead the size of a hazel nut and as hard as stone.

6

I spent a day descending into the depths of the catacombs.

They are apparently visited by every Easter pilgrim, for I found all the catacombs crowded and the churches above filled with people waiting to go down in batches.

In some churches a priest or a monk would ask what nationality predominated. As this was difficult to say without holding an examination, for we were a bewildering mixture of English, French, Germans, Italians, and Poles, it was generally the first person to speak who naturalized us, and a priest or monk, who spoke, or gallantly attempted to speak, the required language, was produced to lead us down into the earth.

I had never before systematically explored the catacombs, and as I went from one to another, I was astonished by their number and size. Apart from the fact that they are all, of course, dark, and all more or less like the shafts and workings of coal mines, there are hardly two of them alike. Some are well cut, with wide passages, some narrow and badly designed; some are vaulted and decorated, with a pretence at architecture, and some are rude undecorated tunnels in the volcanic rock. It would take weeks to explore every catacomb in Rome, possibly months, for only a few of them are open to the public.

An attempt was once made to measure the length of these underground workings and the total came to five hundred and eighty-seven miles! An Italian archæologist made an estimate that from the First to the Sixth Centuries at least six million bodies must have been laid to rest there. Five of the catacombs were in existence in Apostolic times, and the rest date from the Second to the Fourth Centuries. After the Peace of the Church under Constantine, only five or six small catacombs were excavated, for the necessity had then ceased to exist and Christians could be buried above ground.

It was once believed, and even now is still sometimes said, that the catacombs were old, worked-out tunnels, from which veins of sand had been extracted, and that the Christians found them ready when the persecutions of the Church made it necessary to hide the dead. But Father Marchi has proved beyond all question that no pagan so much as delivered a single blow with a pick-axe in order to make these miles of passages: they are entirely the work of the first Christians, who employed a special class of excavator—*fossores*, or gravediggers—to make them. These people were evidently a kind of minor clergy, and as time went on they exercised an administrative control of the catacombs and devised a regular scale of charges for those who desired to be buried there. In times of peace, it is unhappy to relate, some Christians lost their air of meek and attractive submission and became rapacious profiteers, willing to sell burial sites near the martyrs for as much as they could get for them. St. Gregory the Great stopped this disgraceful custom in 597 A.D., at a time when five gold scudi was the price for a tomb near that of a martyr.

The entrance to most of the catacombs is near a church, sometimes in the church itself. There is a little door which opens on a flight of steep steps leading into a pit of darkness. It was a strange experience to descend these steps with a crowd of men and women and to find oneself in a long tunnel, dank-smelling with wet, dead air, whose pitch-darkness was only partially relieved by the lighted tapers which we held. As we advanced in single file, sometimes with bent heads, we would try to keep together, haunted by the fear of dropping behind and becoming lost in the maze of awesome passages which lay to left and right. Now and then the person in front would allow his taper to go out and he would turn quickly and ignite it from the taper behind, as if hating to be without its comfort for a second in that gruesome place.

Once, in the catacomb of St. Agnes, I was the last person in the file. The blackness seemed to lie on my back like a weight, and, as we went on, I could see a long line of variously held yellow tapers ahead, their light wavering over square and semi-circular graves in the corridor. The person in front of me was a plump, blonde Polish girl with cheeks like a couple of ripe apples. In spite of the fact that we could not speak the same language, she kept turning with solemn, blue saucer-wide eyes and making remarks in a tone of voice which indicated that she was startled and appalled. Once, as we were turning the corner of a gallery, her taper lit the interior of a tomb in which, to her horror, she saw a considerable portion of an early

Christian lying in the soft dust. She stopped, and her taper went out! In her agitation she jabbed it in the light of my taper and put that out also; and the darkness came down on us like a hood. While I fumbled with a box of matches, I knew what a horrible experience it would be to become lost in the catacomb of St. Agnes, and by the light of my match I saw cheeks no longer apple-red but a very unripe green. Until we caught up with the glimmering line of lights, it was rather like wandering through several pages of Edgar Allan Poe at his worst.

I thought of St. Jerome, who as a youth wandered through these catacombs with the same feeling of awe and astonishment which is still visible on the faces of people fifteen centuries later. He would spend the week studying grammar under Donatus, or rhetoric under Victorinus, and then on Sundays he would go down into the catacombs and prowl about in the dark, discovering the tombs of the martyrs and reading the old inscriptions on the clammy walls.

"When I was a boy in Rome, being instructed in liberal studies," he wrote, "on Sundays, with others of my own age, I used to wander about the sepulchres of the apostles and martyrs; and I often went into crypts dug out of the depths of the earth, which have along the walls, on each side as you enter, bodies of the dead; and everything is so dark that those words of the prophet are almost fulfilled: 'They descend alive into hell.' Now and then a light from above modifies the horror of the darkness, but it seems rather a hole pierced to let down the light than a window, and as you advance step by step, and are immersed in the blackness of night, you are reminded of the words of the poet: 'The very silence fills the soul with dread.' "

St. Jerome wandered in the catacombs about the year 360 A.D., and his account might well have been written to-day.

The catacomb of St. Callixtus stands below a fine garden of the Trappists. Here everything was very business-like. Three monks were darting about behind a counter, selling an incredible number of post-cards, medals, rosaries, and replicas of the lamps found in the catacomb. As the visitors emerged from this shop, they were divided into language groups. My group consisted of about twenty English schoolgirls in charge of a nun, three Americans, and a Japanese. Our guide was a tall, thin Englishman—not a monk—who carried a wax taper twisted round the end of a long stick. He uncoiled a little piece of this taper whenever the wax began to burn down. At the door of the steps he handed each one of us a taper, and we followed him into the cold darkness.

This was the finest catacomb I had so far seen. I had the impression that it was probably one known to St. Jerome, for it had air holes which sent a pale green light into the main shaft. We groped our way towards a high crypt in which many of the Popes who had occupied the chair of St. Peter from 168 to 296 A.D. had once been buried. The walls around gaped with their empty tombs, for their bones were removed to other churches in Rome soon after the Peace of the Church. A narrow, dark passage led down to another crypt, where we saw the effigy of a young woman in white marble lying on her side as if asleep. This was St. Cecilia, who was martyred in 177 A.D. and whose remains, after lying here for some time, were taken to the beautiful church of St. Cecilia-in-Trastevere.

In the course of our journey we came upon a remarkable sight in the very depth of the catacomb. A small group of men and women were kneeling before a tomb, like early Christians. Candles were alight. A young priest was folding his vestments and placing them in a bag. He had just celebrated Mass on the tomb of a martyr. The guide told us that over fifty Masses had been said by visiting priests that morning in the Catacomb of St. Callixtus.

I noticed here, as in all the other catacombs, the absence of the Cross as a Christian symbol. The early Christians rarely used it: they used instead the Greek monogram of Christ. They loved to paint pictures of our Lord as the Good Shepherd, not the Christ of later art, but a youthful, beardless figure, sometimes holding a lyre or with a shepherd's crook in His hand. I noticed that one of the most frequent tomb paintings was the figure, generally of a woman, standing at prayer with extended hands, in the same attitude that I had seen the Copts adopt in their churches. These figures personify the soul of the departed.

I made a list of the New Testament scenes that were painted here and there on the tomb chambers, for I thought it interesting to see which particular incidents in the Gospel narrative appealed to the first members of the Church. There were several Baptisms, I saw one Annunciation, and a group that may have been the meeting of our Lord with His disciples after the Resurrection. The Raising of Lazarus was not uncommon, and there was one unmistakable picture of Jesus talking with the Woman of Samaria at the well of Sychar.

The dove is frequently seen on the walls of the catacombs, and so are the peacock and the pelican. The symbolism of the dove is well known, but the reason why the Christians adopted the peacock is not perhaps so familiar. This bird, which was sacred to Juno, was in pagan times let loose from the funeral pyre of an empress to signify her deification, and the Christians borrowed it as a symbol of immortality. The pelican represented the Redeemer, who gave His blood for mankind, for it was a common fable in ancient times that if a snake bit young pelicans the parent bird would tear his breast and revive them with his blood. This symbol again became popular in Christian art at a much later period, when St. Gertrude had a vision of Christ in the form of a pelican, feeding mankind from His breast.

Emerging again into the daylight, I walked along the Via Appia to the catacomb of St. Sebastian. We were taken down by a quick, enthusiastic little Franciscan, who kept whirling

round on us on steps and in narrow passages, pointing out something with the exclamation "Magnifique, hein?," and then
striding off again down the long, cold corridors. This catacomb
is lit by electricity, which makes it much easier to see, without
detracting from its impressiveness.

It was the only catacomb in Rome which mediæval pilgrims
visited. The others were lost and forgotten until they were
discovered in later times. The catacomb of St. Sebastian has
always been a pilgrimage place because of the legend, which
there is every reason to believe, that the bodies of St. Peter
and St. Paul were removed there for safety in early times, before their churches were built.

A new interest was given only a few years ago by the discovery of many tombs of the Apostolic period. The little Franciscan told us how one day—I think he said in 1919—a Brother
Damien was digging a grave when he suddenly fell through the
bottom into a First Century house, and only just escaped falling
into the well, which still contained water. When this building
was cleared, it was seen to contain the tomb of a First Century
Roman called M. Clodius Hermes.

"Magnifique, hein?" exclaimed the monk, leading us to this
astonishing fragment of Apostolic Rome, thirty feet down in
the earth.

"Who was M. Clodius Hermes?" asked the Franciscan. No
one answered him. Then in a dramatic way he lifted his arm and
began to chant these words from St. Paul's *Epistle to the Romans:*

" 'Salute Asyncritus, Phlegon, Hermes, Patrobas, Hermas
and the brethren that are with them. . . .' *Hermes!* This is the
tomb of Hermes!"

We looked down into the silent cavern of tomb niches, conscious that we were looking into a building which St. Peter
and St. Paul may have known; a building that existed in the
time of Nero. A few steps along the corridor, the monk pointed

to a skeleton in a long sarcophagus. The end had fallen out, exposing the feet.

"Look at those bones!" he cried. "Those feet may have walked to St. Peter; those knee-bones have bent to St. Paul! Here lies a Christian of Apostolic Rome. . . ."

He turned and led the way up to the church.

7

Thirty feet or so beneath some of the oldest churches in Rome are buildings of the First Century in which the Apostles may have preached, baptized, and celebrated the Holy Mysteries. Among these churches are St. Pudenziana, St. Clement, St. Prisca, on the Aventine, and St. Prassede.

St. Pudenziana stands in the Via Urbana, almost at the top of a gentle hill, with twenty-four steps leading down to its paved courtyard. There is nothing about the exterior to indicate the great age of the building, for it has been restored from time to time. Even when you enter the church, there is nothing remarkable; it is a square pillared building which has lost its character, the aisles having been turned into side-chapels. Then you see the mosaic in the dome over the altar, and you can look at nothing else. This is one of the earliest mosaics in Rome, and may perhaps be earlier than the year 400 A.D.

It shows our Lord seated on a throne, holding a book on which are the words "Dominus conservator ecclesiæ Pudentianæ"—"the Lord, Preserver of the Pudentian Church"—and at the back, as part of a scenic background, rises a terraced mound on which towers an immense jewelled cross. Seated to the right and left of the Saviour are the Twelve Apostles, St. Peter on the left hand—the place of honour in Roman times—and St. Paul on the right. The Apostles are in Roman dress, and behind St. Peter and St. Paul stand two female figures holding wreaths.

The background of this mosaic is a fascinating scene. It shows a group of buildings of the Roman period, red-tiled and entirely characteristic of the Fourth Century. Probably because I had recently been reading an account of Constantine's first basilica of the Holy Sepulchre in Jerusalem, it occurred to me that this scene might be a contemporary picture of that church and Golgotha; and, the more closely I looked at this mosaic, the more certain I felt that I was right. The mound which rises behind the figure of Christ, with the richly jewelled cross on the summit, seemed to bear a striking resemblance to Golgotha as it was in Constantine's time. The clearest contemporary account of Golgotha is that by the nun Etheria, whose travels in Sinai I have mentioned. She was in Jerusalem probably between 380 and 460 A.D. and says that Constantine's architects left Golgotha as an abrupt, detached rock standing in the open air in the midst of a beautiful cloister. The rock had been richly decorated with mosaic, and on top was a tall cross covered with jewels and gilding. After the pilgrims had prayed beside the tomb of Christ, it was the custom for them to be conducted to the Cross by the Bishop. Here, standing in the open air round the foot of Golgotha, they sang many kyrie eleisons while the Bishop's throne was moved round the rock.

My delight at having perceived what I felt was the artist's intention was increased some months later when I discovered that two authorities whose opinion is worth more than mine have already offered this interpretation: D. Ainaloff, the Russian writer, and Mr. George Jeffreys, in his book on the Church of the Holy Sepulchre. If this interpretation is correct, how enormously it adds to the interest of this mosaic, which is thus a contemporary picture, executed perhaps by an eye-witness, or prepared under the supervision of an eye-witness, of the first Church of the Holy Sepulchre, built by Constantine the Great in 336 A.D.

The Sacristan of St. Pudenziana showed me a portion of the
nave which has been taken up to expose the red bricks of a
Roman building. The remains of a house of the First Century
lie under the church, at a depth of about twenty to thirty feet,
and an ancient tradition declares this to be the house of Corne-
lius Pudens, one of the first members of the Apostolic Church.
Here, it is believed, St. Peter lived, preached, baptized, and
celebrated the Holy Mysteries. As I looked down into these
ruins, I tried to imagine the time when the light of day shone
into its atrium, and when, behind closed doors and with the
faithful around him, St. Peter asked for a table to be brought
for the mystery of the Last Supper.

During all the misfortunes of the early Church an extraordinary sanctity surrounded the House of Pudens. A table was
kept there for three and a half centuries on which it was claimed
St. Peter had celebrated the Holy Eucharist. When St. John
Lateran became the Cathedral Church of Rome early in the
Fourth Century, this table was taken from St. Pudenziana to
the new church; and there it has remained encased in the high
altar. So precious was the association of the table in the minds
of the Christians of the Fourth Century, that one plank of it
was allowed to be retained in its original home; and this is to
be seen to-day, built into the altar at St. Pudenziana. Cardinal
Wiseman, who was titular cardinal of this church, wished to
test the truth of the tradition that the plank at St. Pudenziana
and the table encased in the altar of St. John Lateran were of
the same wood. He had both scientifically examined, and the
report was that the wood is identical.

Standing in the House of Pudens, I remembered St. Paul's
words in the *Second Epistle to Timothy*, probably written in
Rome shortly before the Apostle's death. In this he sends greetings to Timothy from "Pudens, and Linus, and Claudia." That
Linus was the St. Linus who became St. Peter's successor as
head of the Church seems fairly certain, and that Pudens was

the Pudens of St. Pudenziana, or his son, seems also evident. But whether Pudens and Claudia were married, as so many people have liked to imagine, is open to doubt.

Many attractive theories linking these two with Britain have been built up on the strength of a Roman inscription found at Chichester, which is often said to contain the name of Pudens. Unfortunately a break occurs in the inscription at a critical point, leaving only the four last letters of a name, "ente," which might just as well terminate the name Clemente as Pudente. Therefore all these theories are merest supposition.

Still, as you descend into the excavated chambers beneath St. Pudenziana, your feet tread the pavements of First Century Rome; the walls that rise around may have sheltered the Apostles and their first followers; and you seem very near to the times when St. Paul wrote:

"Do thy diligence to come before winter. Eubulus greeteth thee, and Pudens, and Linus, and Claudia, and all the brethren. The Lord Jesus Christ be with thy spirit. Grace be with you. Amen."

8

The church which delights me more than any other in Rome is the church of St. Clement. It has belonged to the Irish Dominicans since 1623, and is the only church in Rome which has triumphantly survived the architectural reformation of the Renaissance.

This lovely building preserves intact all the characteristics of an early basilica. An atrium open to the sky, with a fountain in the centre and cloisters all round, leads to the main east entrance to the church, from whose doors you look westward towards the altar. It is a severe columned church of marble, with mosaics in the dome of the apse, a choir, or *schola cantorum*, marked off in the nave behind low marble walls and entered by a gate at the east end. Behind the altar is an apse with the episcopal throne in the centre of a semi-circular marble seat. As in St. Peter's, the celebrant at the Mass faces east and officiates with his face to the congregation, the altar between them.

There has always been a tradition that the Church of St. Clement was built on the site of the house of St. Clement, the disciple of St. Peter and third successor to the Papacy. As early as 385 A.D., St. Jerome mentions this church as a venerable building. Until the year 1857, it was believed that the present church was the one mentioned by St. Jerome. But the Prior, Father Mulooley, had for years suspected that earlier remains lay beneath it; he began to excavate and quickly saw that his supposition was correct.

For fifteen years Father Mulooley worked to bring this early church to light, and came upon an even greater discovery, which, however, he was never fated to see as we see it to-day, for he died in 1880. This was the actual house of St. Clement, upon which the first church had been built.

Steps lead down to this from the baptistry. I went with the usual crowd of tourists and pilgrims, in charge of a young Dominican who had a strong look of T. E. Lawrence about him. He spoke Italian, because most of us seemed to be Italians that day, but, when I got him alone, I spoke to him in English and he replied with a lovely brogue.

"Where do you come from?" I asked.

"County Cark," he said; and smiled with delight at the recollection of it.   .

He told me some interesting details of Father Mulooley's work. It seems that as soon as the First Century buildings were discovered, water began to fill them. Neither the method nor the money to drain them was discovered during Father Mulooley's lifetime, and it was not until 1912 that the work of draining the underground working was begun with the help of Cardinal O'Connell, Archbishop of Boston, who had been

made Cardinal Titular of St. Clement's. It was decided to dig
a brick tunnel to the church from the Colosseum, which is seven
hundred yards away. This was completed in 1914 and the
water now runs from St. Clement's to the Colosseum, where
it enters an ancient Roman drain that is still in working order
between that point and the Tiber.

"Ye'll excuse me a moment," said the Dominican; then turning to the crowd, he told them in Italian various things about
the place in which they were standing.

"Will I be saying it in English for any of ye?" he asked.
Someone said "Yes." Then, in his fine soft Irish voice, he said:

"Ye're standing now in the house where St. Clement lived
and where, maybe, he wrote his *Epistle to the Corinthians*.
Have ye all read that epistle? Take a look at the old walls.
The first Christians came here; the blessed saints and the holy
martyrs of the olden time. It's a wonderful thing I'm showing
ye. . . ."

And very earnestly he moved about, pointing out things here
and there, looking rather like a saint himself in the gloom of
that underground cavern, warning us to miss nothing because
we were in one of the most wonderful places in Rome.

9

I received a card of admission to St. Peter's for Easter Sunday, when one of the rarest and most complex ceremonies in
the world was to be conducted by the Pope: the creation of
three saints at a solemn Mass of Canonization. The saints who
were thus to be raised to the altars of the Church were St.
Andrea Bobola, St. John Leonardi, and St. Salvatore da Horta:
a Pole, an Italian, and a Spaniard.

The formal processes and the enquiries which take place
before the Pope consents to prepare a Bull of Canonization are
undoubtedly the most protracted of all human transactions. It

is the rarest possible event for a man to be made a saint during the life-time of anyone who knew him, even though the necessary procedure may have been begun shortly after his death. The courts of enquiry sit sometimes for centuries, examining the orthodoxy, the life, and the reputed miracles of the proposed saint, and it is no uncommon thing, after his qualifications have been discussed by successive popes and successive papal courts, for him to be denied the company of the elect.

It is first necessary for a proposed saint to become beatified. This also is a timeless and complex process. Having become beatified, he is granted the title of "Venerable" and achieves a local sanctity in the country or the religious order to which he belonged during his life. The next step rests with the proposed saint himself. He must perform at least two unquestionable miracles after beatification, by which God indicates that His servant is to join the saints of the Church. It is the task of a special court, known as the Congregation of Rites, to examine these alleged miracles with the utmost cynicism. The court is addressed by the Postulator of the Cause, who is rather like a defending counsel in a lawsuit, and he is opposed at every turn by the Promoter of the Faith, known as "the Devil's Advocate," whose task is to place every possible difficulty in the way. Should the claim survive the first meeting of this Court, which is held in private, a public meeting is called which is attended by all the Cardinals who are at that moment in Rome. The Pope attends in state. He is borne in, seated in the state litter, the *sedia gestatoria*, and vested in the *falda*, a white silk vestment which falls over his feet and is raised, as he walks, by two assistants; this garment is only worn by the Pope on occasions of great state. He wears also the amice, alb, girdle, a red stole and cope, and a gold mitre. Divine guidance is solemnly asked and a decree is published ordering public prayers. The third meeting is attended by all the Cardinals, Patriarchs, Archbishops, and Bishops in Rome, and also by every Bishop whose

Diocese is within a hundred miles of Rome. The Pope presides over this meeting, and, if a written vote results in favour of the canonization, His Holiness gives his consent and announces the date on which the ceremony will be held in the Vatican Basilica.

In the early morning I went through enormous crowds to St. Peter's. Every door of the church was besieged by men upon whose white shirt-fronts the morning sun shone strangely, and by women in black, with mantillas draped on their hair. Swiss Guards in padded doublets and steel breastplates, tall red plumes rising from their casques, stood on guard at the doors, while Papal chamberlains, in white ruff and black trunk-hose, examined the tickets. There was many a poignant and heated scene between these Elizabethans and those unhappy persons who had brought the wrong cards of admission, or who had forgotten them altogether. To return and find the right ones would have been useless. It would be impossible to get through the crowds, even if the doors of St. Peter's, which are always closed long before a Papal ceremony begins, had still been open.

One determined woman on the verge of hysterics flung herself picturesquely on the crossed halberds of two Swiss guards and tried to force her way in. It was a dramatic picture, but my appreciation was modified by sympathy for the woman, who had dressed with great care and had probably left her ticket behind from sheer nervous excitement. Nothing could be done; and the last I saw of this poor lady was a tragic figure in black escorted by two embarrassed but soothing chamberlains; as it disappeared round the corner of a baroque outbuilding, the group bore a remarkable resemblance to a scene from *Twelfth Night*.

When I entered the church, I became aware of an immense crowd which I could not see: the people filling the nave and transepts. They made a noise like bees about to swarm. This sound echoed all about the vast church in a constant, rhythmic buzz. Crimson and gold banners hung from the roof, long, narrow cloths that hid the pillars and gave an appearance of extraordinary richness to the church. There must have been hundreds and thousands of electric candles all over the building and outlining the dome.

Led by an official from whose velvet cape peeped the point of a rapier, I was taken to one of the most privileged places in St. Peter's: the small space in the apse, near the Papal throne, which is reserved for the royal family, the diplomatic corps, the Pope's relatives, and the Order of Malta. The excellence of my seat was bewildering, for to be privileged to see a Papal ceremony from such close quarters is not only a critical test of one's powers of observation, but of one's knowledge.

A few yards away, in the centre of the apse, a white throne stood beneath a cloth of state; it was approached by seven steps carpeted in red. Behind the throne rose that enthusiastic wave of baroque which terminates St. Peter's to the west: the Cathedra Petri of Bernini. Four immense figures in agitated draperies, St. Ambrose, St. Augustine, St. Athanasius, and St. Chrysostom, representing the Latin and the Greek Churches, stand at the corners of a weighty golden chair which is poised in mid air and escorted by two plump cupids, who hold the Papal tiara and the keys of St. Peter. Nothing could have formed a more remarkable contrast to this flamboyant throne than the simple white one below it on which the Pope was to sit.

Five hours passed imperceptibly. History was always crossing the blue carpet of the apse. Sometimes it would take the form of an officer of the Swiss Guard in Michelangelo's uniform, or a member of the Noble Guard in scarlet tunic, white buckskin breeches, and black thigh-boots, a cavalry corps that once escorted the Pope's carriage and guarded him on journeys. Although the Papal stables are now empty, these men still wear spurs. A man in a uniform that puzzled me appeared for a moment: a man in blue and orange, grasping a brass helmet. A chamberlain told me that he was one of the Pope's firemen, a corps first organized by Pius VII.

I saw a pathetic little comedy in the seats opposite, which were reserved for the cardinals. Two simple young village priests had somehow found their way, almost hand in hand, into this exalted part of the church. They grasped broad-brimmed black hats and their soutanes were made of black alpaca, or something that looked like it. They could hardly believe their good fortune to find themselves so near the throne of the Holy Father, and smiles of delight passed over their faces as deliberately, and with the casualness of complete innocence, they walked up the apse and carefully selected two of the best seats reserved for the Sacred College. At nearly every great ceremony which I have attended, something like this has happened. It is always the innocent who stray boldly into the seats of the mighty; but unfortunately they do not stay there very long.

It never for one moment dawned on these young men that they had done anything audacious. Their simple country faces glowed with pleasure as they sat there, and not one of the chamberlains noticed them as he passed to and fro with a wand, escorting the mighty to their places. A stately figure in red and ermine slowly walked over. One of the Cardinals had arrived. The expression on the faces of the young priests, as this Prince of the Church appeared, has been repeated many a time in pantomimes when a character becomes slowly aware of the ogre. They looked up, at first pleasantly, then doubtfully, and at last in panic. His Eminence leaned forward and, I am sure, broke it to them with kindness; for a pale smile answered him and, grasping their broad hats, they fled. I looked for them everywhere, but never saw them again. I like to think that someday one of them may have the right to sit there, even perhaps in the chair of St. Peter; for such things are not impossible.

Suddenly a silence spread over the church. The next instant

the whole building sprang into light. A sigh of astonishment passed in a long wave of sound through the building. The vast dome was now a colossal bowl of gold round which one could see the letters, glittering in fire: *Te es Petrus, et super hanc petramædificabo ecclesiam meam.* . . . From the direction of the nave sounded the tread of a slow procession. Monks in the brown, white, or black habits of their orders, each one holding a lighted candle, cross-bearers, and priests, could be seen diverging to left and right into the transepts. Painted banners of the new saints dipped over the heads of the crowd.

The space on each side of the Papal throne was now a court which lacked only its Sovereign. The College of Cardinals sat to left and right, and from the apse to the high altar, facing each other in two rows, sat the Archbishops, the Bishops, the Generals and Procurators of Religious Orders, and the mitred abbots, wearing white vestments and mitres of white linen or damask. From high above the entrance doors of St. Peter's sounded the stately music of the Papal March, played on mellow silver trumpets, and at the sound of it the whole church with its thousands of people broke into a roar of welcome; for the Pope was entering St. Peter's. The soft sound of the feet of priests was now succeeded by the deeper tread of marching men, in which I heard a faint background of spurs chinking and of arms. I could see nothing yet, for the view down the nave was cut off by the high altar and the great crowd of dignitaries around it, but I could tell where the Pope was by the sound of cheering which advanced with him. It came near and nearer, and then died away as the procession reached the high altar; and then I saw the Papal Court enter the apse. Lifted on the shoulders of men in suits of red damask, the Pope, startlingly white, was borne forward seated in the *sedia gestatoria*, every now and then lifting his hand to trace the sign of the Cross in the air. The *Sediari* walked with a gliding motion, so that the state palanquin passed smoothly on its way. Above the Pope was carried a white canopy upheld by poles which were borne by *Palafrenieri,* and behind them walked fan-bearers carrying long-hafted fans of peacocks' feathers. There were Swiss Guards, halberds, drawn swords, chamberlains, ushers and mace-bearers, all moving with slow, measured steps, and all part of a perfect historical group which culminated in the successor of St. Peter, seated in white, vested in the *falda* beneath a white cope, and with a mitre of gold brocade upon his head.

The bearers of the palanquin passed slowly to the throne and lowered the poles. The Pope took one step from the *sedia* to the white throne and turned to face the great church, where the thousands of still white candles blazed in arcs, clusters, and long glittering lines. Only on the high altar were the candles alive and moving in a current of air. Motionless behind the throne stood two officers of the Noble Guard, with drawn swords carried at the salute.

A Cardinal advanced to the throne, accompanied by the Master of Ceremonies and a Consistorial Advocate. The Advocate, kneeling, addressed the Pope in Latin:

"Most Holy Father, the Most Reverend Cardinal here present earnestly begs your Holiness to inscribe the Blessed Andrea Bobola, John Leonardi, and Salvatore da Horta in the catalogue of the saints of our Lord Jesus Christ, and to ordain that they be venerated as Saints by all the Christian faithful."

A secretary, standing on the steps of the throne, replied that his Holiness was much edified by the virtues of the Blessed, but, before making any decision, he exhorted all those present to assist him in imploring the intercession of the Heavenly Court. Whereupon the Cardinal and the Advocate withdrew to their places.

The Pope then knelt at a faldstool, while two cantors intoned the Litanies of the Saints, to which all the assembled dignitaries made the responses.

The Cardinal and the Advocate approached the throne a second time to make their request, and again the Pope ordered prayer. An attendant took the Pope's mitre, and his Holiness, his head covered with a white skull-cap, knelt at the faldstool and prayed while the *Miserere* was sung. Still on his knees, the Pope intoned the *Veni Creator Spiritus*, and then, rising, stood during the rest of the hymn. For a third time the Postulants approached the throne with their request, and this time the Pope replied that he would make the proclamation.

Wearing the mitre, and seated on the throne, the Pope then read the solemn declaration and named the date of the feast days of the new saints. The *Te Deum* was sung and the ceremony of Canonization was over. The Mass of Canonization was now ready to begin.

The Pope had given permission for Mass to be celebrated in St. Peter's by a Cardinal. I was too far from the altar to follow the intricate ritual, but now and again I could see the white figure of the Cardinal-Celebrant moving there, facing the east in the historical position of a Fourth Century priest, assisted by a Canon of the Lateran and with a deacon and a sub-deacon on the altar steps. Either the Cardinal or one of his assistants would walk from time to time towards the throne to receive the Pope's blessing. After the deacon had sung the Gospels, the book was brought solemnly in procession for the Pope to kiss. And it was at this point in the Mass that I was astonished to hear the sound of pigeons cooing in St. Peter's. At first I thought that in the silence which had now spread through the church I could hear the birds that fly about in the *piazza* outside; but this sound was too loud. There were pigeons, or doves, actually inside the church, and the mystery was soon revealed in the most beautiful ceremony I have ever seen. It was the Offertory.

The whole width of the apse was suddenly filled by a procession of monks, men in black court dress, and others, who advanced towards the Pope holding little baroque and Gothic cages made of silvered wood in which song-birds and ring-doves were chirping and cooing. Behind came men carrying silver and gold barrels of water and wine and a golden tray with loaves of bread on it. As they slowly advanced step by step towards the Pope, there was dead silence in the church save for the lovely cooing of the doves and the bright chirping of the little birds.

The men knelt at the foot of the throne, and as each one brought his offerings, the Pope leaned forward slightly and blessed it. The little birds did not know that they were in the presence of the Sovereign Pontiff and chirped brightly, putting their heads on one side and gazing up into the blaze of light in which he sat, and he solemnly moved his hand over them in the sign of the Cross. This ceremony was performed three times, once for each of the new saints, and it is a relic of days when the early Christians brought offerings of food, wine, and candles to church for the service of the altar or the upkeep of the clergy, and the aid of the poor. And whenever a new saint is created, these offerings are still given to the Pope; and I am sure that when St. Francis was made a saint all the small birds sang like a May morning as they were carried to St. Peter's chair.

The Mass proceeded, and at the moment of Consecration the Master of Ceremonies removed the white skull cap from the Pope's head and four chaplains knelt at the altar, holding lighted torches. All the silence in the church seemed to be gathered up and intensified round the altar as the Cardinal-Celebrant elevated the Host. But no bells rang, or are ever rung at this moment in the presence of the Pope. There was instead a ring of arms as the Swiss Guard knelt and as the Noble Guard and the other troops brought their swords down in salute; and from the gallery at the end of the church the silver trumpets played a slow and solemn anthem.

At the *Pax Domini* a Cardinal approached the altar and knelt side by side with the Cardinal-Celebrant, from whom he received the Kiss of Peace. He returned to the throne and gave the Pax to the Pope, who handed it on to his two assistant Cardinals, from whom it passed quickly in succession along the line of Cardinals, Archbishops, and Bishops; and watching this ancient ceremony in St. Peter's, and in the presence of the successor of St. Peter, I remembered the little bare-kneed acolytes in the Chaldean Church at Baghdad, who had run through the church in the early morning, touching the hands of the congregation.

Having finished the Mass, the Celebrant retired with his ministers. The men in red came to the throne with the *sedia gestatoria*, and once again the Pope passed whitely through the church, with his aged hand moving in blessing; and I went out into the sunlight to a great sound of bells.

10

I have always wished to see Ostia, but the chance did not come until I was on the point of leaving Rome. I drove out one lovely afternoon, for the ancient port of Rome is only fourteen miles to the south-west, and found myself in another Pompeii.

The Tiber now flows in a different bed so that Ostia is no longer the *ostium*, or mouth, of the river. Long low marshes and sand-hills stretch from the ruins to the distant sea, but as you wander about these marshes, it is possible to trace in the ground the shape of the harbours in which the Roman fleet once anchored.

The main street runs through the ruins for a great distance, paved with huge blocks of stone, and from it branch side streets which lead you to the private houses, baths, and blocks of tenement flats which have been lying for centuries beautifully ur Blessed Saviour. . . ."

he end of St. Jerome's journey was here at Ostia; the other
ethlehem.

he low land is wide and the sea is nowhere visible. In the
lays, however, waves pounded on the shores where sand
stretches for miles. Upon those shores, probably a full
ury before St. Augustine or St. Jerome were at Ostia, this
was chosen as the scene of that "little work of gold," the
vius of Minucius Felix, the first piece of Christian apolo-
s.

aree friends were spending a brief holiday by the sea, at
. "This is a delightful place," writes Minucius, "where I
d to find in sea-bathing an agreeable and beneficial treat-
from certain humours from which I suffered. Owing to
acation, legal work was slack and had made way for the
ge."

s friends were Octavius, a Christian, and Cæcilius, who
ot yet converted.

ie morning the three friends started to walk down to the
nd, on the way, Cæcilius saw a statue of Serapis and kissed
nd to it, which caused Octavius to say that he really could
ermit his dear friend to go about venerating stones and
in such darkness, especially on such a lovely day.

While Octavius was speaking we were half way between
and the sea, and were already nearing the open beach,
e the gentle waves, which laved the furthest stretch of
extended and as it were laid it out for a promenade. The
always restless, even when the winds are still, and al-
h it did not reach the shore in white, foaming waves, we
highly delighted to see it curling and winding round and
our feet, when we dipped them at the water's edge."

ey walked on together while Octavius told them about a
oyage he had recently made, and they stopped to watch
boys playing "ducks and drakes."

preserved under a covering of sand. Ostia should be entirely
comprehensible to this age, because it thought of nothing but
getting rich on trade, and evidence of this is everywhere visible.
It was, of course, the great granary of Rome. Here was stored
the corn which stopped the mouth of revolution, or failed to
stop it, as the case might be. The Egyptian corn-ships, which
were a State service, always came across from Alexandria and
anchored at Ostia, where the grain was stored until the capital
required it. You can see the remains of these granaries, and also
the barracks where the corps of firemen were quartered, an important department of Ostia's municipality.

Overlooking the theatre is a large open space, the Forum,
which is lined all the way round with the head-offices of the
shipping companies. It is an ancient Cockspur Street and, like
Cockspur Street, it indulged in decorative effects. Nearly every mosaic courtyard shows Neptune, dolphins, tridents, and
ships, and each office has a mosaic pavement on which are depicted corn-ships and such-like subjects, with a notice proclaiming that part of the world to which the company traded. These
are probably among the earliest examples of commercial ad-
vertisement.

It is difficult to imagine that Ostia was once the busiest and
most important seaport in the world. This now melancholy
ruin, deserted both by life and the sea, once fed the hungry
mouth of Rome, and most new things found their way to
the heart of the Empire along its paved main street. The Apostles and the Saints trod these stones in the early age of the
Church, and though we know from *Acts* that St. Paul was sent
to Rome overland from Puteoli, near Naples, it may well be
that St. Peter came first to Ostia. It is certain that other saints
and martyrs used this port in the course of their missionary lives.

Sitting in the theatre and gazing out over the forlorn marshes,
I remembered that it was in an inn at Ostia that St. Monica, the
mother of St. Augustine, died. The description of her death is

one of the most tender and beautiful passages in his *Confessions*. Mother and son were waiting at Ostia for a boat to Africa, and one day, hand in hand at the window of the house in which they were lodging, they gazed down into a little garden and talked together about eternal things in an exaltation of spirit. She said to him most lovingly that having seen him become a Christian at last, she felt there was no more delight in the world. Five days after she fell ill with a fever, and it was seen that she would die. St. Augustine knew how often she had expressed a wish to be buried near the body of her husband, and it pained him that she should die in Ostia, so far from her own home. Divining his thoughts, St. Monica told him to bury her anywhere, because, "Nothing," she said, "is far from God."

To read St. Augustine's description of his grief is again to enter one's own sorrow at the same parting in one's life, for never, I think, has a man's pain at the sudden ending of "that most sweet and dear custom of living with her"—as he put it —been more sharply and truly put into words. He tells us how he stood dry-eyed at her grave-side, unable to weep, and how, in order to drive sorrow away, he went to the baths; but "after I had bathed, I was the same man I was before; the bitterness of my sorrow could not be sweat out of my heart."

Then he pours out his heart in prayer, all the time thinking of her and begging God to be kind and merciful to her in the life to come.

As I sat overlooking this quiet place of broken walls and old roads, I thought how fifteen centuries ago this town must have gone about its busy work and its pleasure, watching ships coming in laden or setting off to the four corners of the Roman world; how the lights would have been lit at night and how people would have gone out to dinner, all unconscious that St. Monica had died, or that her son was suffering an immortal grief that would carry the name of Ostia with it onward into

the most distant future. And the very rui
sky, the ruins of the baths with their hot
their pretty floors, might be the buildings
tine tried to sweat the sorrow from his hea

Walking down to the harbour, where t
knee-high, I thought of another great nam
that of the fiery St. Jerome. Two years be
at Ostia, St. Jerome, smarting under the
picion with which the worldly-minded (
him, took ship at Ostia for Antioch. So
this very marsh where the weeds grow so
in which St. Jerome impetuously wrote
Ansella:

"I write this in haste, dear Lady A
spreads its sails. I write with sobs and t
to God to have been found worthy of t
Salute Paula and Eustochium, mine
world pleases or not, salute Albina, your
sister, Marcellina, Felicita: say to them
before the judgment seat of God, where
shall be revealed. Remember me, glori
and by your prayers appease the sea w

The ship spread its sails and took
Rome for ever. When you go into the
the Church of the Nativity in Bethlehe
you to a dark cave, half rock and hal
cell in which St. Jerome lived until th
tell you. "And here he wrote the Vul
ters and treatises."

He takes you on in the dark until y
sage leading to another cave: "Here
Paula, and St. Eustochium—the saint
who left a rich life in Rome to come

"This game is played as follows," say Minucius: "A shell, rounded and polished by the constant movements of the waves, is picked up from the beach and firmly grasped between the fingers on the flat side. The player then stoops, and, bending down, throws it as far as he can along the top of the water. The missile either skims the surface, or cutting through the crest of the waves darts along, springing in the air. The boy whose shell goes furthest, and oftenest jumps out of the water, claims the victory."

Only the unconverted Cæcilius takes no pleasure in the sight, but holds himself aloof rather sulkily, at last confessing that he deeply resents the fact that his friend Octavius should have made such a remark about his spiritual life. In the most friendly way the three men sit down on a rock jutting out into the sea and thrash out the question of Christianity versus paganism.

Their conversation is long and learned. Cæcilius defends the gods of Rome; Octavius expounds the faith of Christ. He admits that before he was converted he was more than a sceptic, and, as a lawyer, had probably tortured Christians who had confessed their faith, in the hope of making them recant. He proceeds to expound the Christian doctrines, and the end of the conversation is the conversion of Cæcilius.

"After this we retired, all three joyful and happy: Cæcilius because he believed, Octavius because he was victorious, and I myself because of the conversion of the one and the victory of the other."

I was happy to have ended my journey at Ostia among such memories as these. It pleased me to think that I had seen the Euphrates flowing southward through Mesopotamia, that I had seen the Nile carrying Egypt on its ancient banks, and that now, at last, I stood with my journey complete upon the place where the Tiber once brought ships to Ostia. I walked thoughtfully away through this old town, feeling the regret for something over and done, but hoping that a man may not have fared too badly if he returns from his travels with those words in his heart which were said in this town of Ostia so long ago: "Nothing is far from God."

THE END

BIBLIOGRAPHY

Attwater, Donald: *The Dissident Eastern Churches.* (The Bruce Publishing Co. 1937.)

Belgrave, C. Dalrymple: *Siwa.* (John Lane. 1923.)

Bevan, Edwyn: *A History of Egypt under the Ptolemaic Dynasty.* (Methuen. 1927.)

Breccia, E.: *Alexandrea ad Ægyptum.* (Bergamo. 1922.)

Brightman, F. E.: *Liturgies Eastern and Western.* (Clarendon Press. 1896.)

Browne, W. G.: *Travels in Africa.* (London. 1799.)

Budge, E. A. Wallis: *The Paradise of the Fathers.* (Chatto and Windus. 1908.)

Burckhardt, John Lewis: *Travels in Syria and the Holy Land.* (Murray. 1822.)

Bute, Marquis of: *The Coptic Morning Service.* (Cope and Fenwick. 1908.)

Butler, A. J.: *The Ancient Coptic Churches of Egypt.* (Clarendon Press. 1884.)

Cosson, A. de: *Mareotis.* (Country Life. 1935.)

Curzon, Robert: *Visits to Monasteries in the Levant.* (John Murray. 1851.)

Dalton, O. M.: *Byzantine Art and Archæology.* (Clarendon Press. 1911.)

Dobson, A. M. R.: *Mount Sinai.* (Methuen. 1925.)

Eckenstein, Lina: *A History of Sinai.* (S.P.C.K. 1921.)

Evetts, B. T. A.: *The Rites of the Coptic Church.* (Nutt. 1888.)

Fortescue, Adrian: *The Lesser Eastern Churches.* (The Catholic Truth Society. 1913.)

Fortescue, Adrian: *The Orthodox Eastern Church.* (Catholic Truth Society. 1916.)

Laborde, M. Leon de: *Journey through Arabia Petræa.* (Murray. 1838.)

442 BIBLIOGRAPHY

Lane-Poole, Stanley: *A History of Egypt in the Middle Ages.* (Methuen. 1936.)

Leeder, S. H.: *Modern Sons of the Pharaohs.* (Hodder and Stoughton.)

Mackean, W. H.: *Christian Monasticism in Egypt.* (S.P.C.K. 1920.)

Mattern, J.: *Les Villes Mortes de Haute Syria.* (Imprimerie Catholique, Beyrouth. 1933.)

Milne, J. G.: *A History of Egypt under Roman Rule.* (Methuen. 1924.)

O'Leary, de Lacy: *The Saints of Egypt.* (S.P.C.K. 1937.)

Palmer, E. H.: *The Desert of the Exodus.* (Deighton Bell. 1871.)

Pelly, Lewis: *The Miracle Play of Hasan and Husain.* (W. H. Allen. 1879.)

Pococke, Richard: *A Description of the East.* (London. 1743.)

Rabino, M. H. L.: *Le Monastère de Sainte-Catherine.* (Cairo. 1935.)

Rostovtzeff, M.: *A History of the Ancient World.* (Clarendon Press. 1936.)

Rostovtzeff, M.: *Caravan Cities.* (Clarendon Press. 1932.)

Salaville, Père Sévérien: *Eastern Liturgies.* (Sands. 1938.)

Scott-Moncrieff, P. D.: *Paganism and Christianity in Egypt.* (Cambridge University Press. 1913.)

Simaika, M. H.: *Guide Sommaire du Musée Copte.* (Cairo. 1937.)

Somers, Clarke: *Christian Antiquities in the Nile Valley.* (Clarendon Press. 1912.)

The Cambridge Ancient History.

Vansleb, F.: *The Present State of Egypt.* (London. 1678.)

Villard, U. Monneret de: *Les Couvents près de Sohâg.* (Milan. 1926.)

Wade, G. W.: *New Testament History.* (Methuen. 1932.)

Wade, G. W.: *Old Testament History.* (Methuen. 1934.)

Warren, F. E.: *The Liturgy and Ritual of the Celtic Church.* (Clarendon Press. 1881.)

White, Hugh G. Evelyn: *The Monasteries of the Wadi 'n Natrûn*. (New York. 1933.)

Woolley, C. Leonard: *Abraham*. (Faber and Faber. 1936.)

Woolley, C. Leonard: *Ur of the Chaldees*. (Benn. 1929.)

Woolley, C. Leonard, and T. E. Lawrence: *The Wilderness of Zin*. (Cape. 1936.)

INDEX